The Authentic Leader

T0309187

The Authentic Leader

Using the Meisner Technique for Embracing the Values of Truthful Leadership

Royce Sparks

Routledge
Taylor & Francis Group

A PRODUCTIVITY PRESS BOOK

First edition published in 2021
by Routledge/Productivity Press
52 Vanderbilt Avenue, 11th Floor New York, NY 10017
2 Park Square, Milton Park, Abingdon, Oxon OX14 4RN, UK

© 2021 Royce Sparks

Routledge/Productivity Press is an imprint of Taylor & Francis Group, an Informa business

No claim to original U.S. Government works

Printed on acid-free paper

ISBN: 978-0-367-90102-8 (Hardback)
ISBN: 978-1-003-02262-6 (eBook)

This book contains information obtained from authentic and highly regarded sources. Reasonable efforts have been made to publish reliable data and information, but the author and publisher cannot assume responsibility for the validity of all materials or the consequences of their use. The authors and publishers have attempted to trace the copyright holders of all material reproduced in this publication and apologize to copyright holders if permission to publish in this form has not been obtained. If any copyright material has not been acknowledged please write and let us know so we may rectify in any future reprint.

Except as permitted under U.S. Copyright Law, no part of this book may be reprinted, reproduced, transmitted, or utilized in any form by any electronic, mechanical, or other means, now known or hereafter invented, including photocopying, microfilming, and recording, or in any information storage or retrieval system, without written permission from the publishers.

For permission to photocopy or use material electronically from this work, please access www.copyright.com (www.copyright.com/) or contact the Copyright Clearance Center, Inc. (CCC), 222 Rosewood Drive, Danvers, MA 01923, 978–750–8400. CCC is a not-for-profit organization that provides licenses and registration for a variety of users. For organizations that have been granted a photocopy license by the CCC, a separate system of payment has been arranged.

Trademark notice: Product or corporate names may be trademarks or registered trademarks, and are used only for identification and explanation without intent to infringe.

Library of Congress Cataloging-in-Publication Data

Names: Sparks, Royce, author.
Title: The authentic leader : using the Meisner technique for embracing the values of genuine and effective leadership potential / Royce Sparks.
Description: New York, NY : Routledge, 2020. | Includes index.
Identifiers: LCCN 2020009825 (print) | LCCN 2020009826 (ebook) | ISBN 9780367900991 (paperback) | ISBN 9780367901028 (hardback) | ISBN 9781003022626 (ebook)
Subjects: LCSH: Leadership—Study and teaching. | Meisner, Sanford.
Classification: LCC HM1261 .S64 2020 (print) | LCC HM1261 (ebook) | DDC 303.3/4—dc23
LC record available at https://lccn.loc.gov/2020009825
LC ebook record available at https://lccn.loc.gov/2020009826

Visit the Taylor & Francis Web site at www.taylorandfrancis.com

CV 09 10 2020 1250

Contents

Acknowledgements

This book was a special effort of love. I intended to write it much earlier. A devastating illness and the consequences that followed delayed it. Through the support and kindness of some special people I have been able to find the strength to finish it.

First, I would like to thank my wonderful editor, Kristine. Your belief, positive kindness, and wisdom is worthy of the red-carpet gratitude. Thank you as well to the entire team at Routledge, who from the first to last moments made me feel supported and welcome. I could not have asked for a better experience. I would also like to thank Claire from Bloomsbury for all her help.

My knowledge and capabilities for these materials came from a few key sources who invested years and hundreds of hours of time and effort into me. To these two people I owe my immense gratitude: Scott Williams and Larry Silverberg. Your kindness and input into my development has been immense. You both gave me the confidence to take my own steps and find the unique ways to apply this wonderful technique to leadership. Further thanks goes to some additional incredible mentors: Marco and Eugene of UCL, Niki Flacks, Sarah Davey-Hull, and Tatsushige Udaka. At the origin of it all, I want to thank Paul and Joan, who with love pushed me to find my own way and not lose myself in the process.

Supportive friends and inspiring figures have done more with some kind words than can be said. Agnieszka, Al, Autumn, Barbara, Chris P., Gail, Geoff, George, Gina, Glen, Gordon and Olga, Hamira, Harry, Howard and Valerie, India and Roger, Jack, Jerry, Jules, Karl, Kathleen, Ken V., Kim, Kostas, Lacy, Laura W., Leslie and Ron, Lexi, Marta, Mo, Nickolas, Nigel, R. Adam, Robert, Ronan, Shizu, Steve, Tamaya, Taylan, Terence, Teresa and Gavin, Violette, W.J.J., Ysabel, as well as Clive, Gary, and the whole ITG family: Your warmth has carried me through the hard days and propelled me through the easy ones. I must also thank my wonderful doctors who restored my health enough to continue this journey.

Thank you to my beloved parents, whose continued belief and support in me has kept me strong.

Finally, I dedicate this to Sonia, who has taught me by example what it means to be a truly great leader and human being.

'My movement is a result of your movement.'
Bruce Lee

'An ounce of behaviour is worth a pound of words.'
Sanford Meisner

THE HEART OF LEADERSHIP

1

Chapter 1

Distilling the Wandering Mind

The Wisdom of Illness

The great martial arts legend Bruce Lee is known for his dynamic on-screen persona (most of the time blended with a fast-punching, albeit somewhat lacking, script and chest-hair ripping good ol' school special effects) alongside explicit displays of what can only be called his physical perfection. Biographers of Bruce, putting the quality of some of his films aside, looking through the persona he projected showed that behind the camera there was the recipe for a charismatic, powerful human being.

Bruce left the world too early, so it is hard to point out the subtle differences between his later body of work and his earlier projects. Those who are keen to look, though, will notice one curious indicator: there is something somewhat different about him on-screen in his later projects. Something more refined, deep, and magnetic. He lost the boyish roughness of his earlier works and seemed to adopt a more soulful, attuned presence. What changed? Not much has been released about his personal life. What is, or is not there, the estate guards tightly, but one bit of public information that points the way relates to a time when he was fighting not others but his own body, bound to his bed and almost constantly in excruciating pain. The last portion of Bruce's life was, in many ways, characterized by his mind's battle against a severely damaged body.

While lifting weights Bruce suffered a terrible injury that left his back, for lack of a better word, completely wrecked. Going from a weekly training regimen that would humble most Olympian athletes to forced bed rest was not only painful but also robbed Bruce of the core of who he felt he was and what he was doing with his life's work. Not only his career but his entire essence was suffering: without the ability to throw a punch, or share the wisdom of how to do so, there was no Bruce Lee. The once vibrant human being that entertained and inspired so many would now be not much more than a cripple, confined to using a walking stick.

Bruce did make a rather miraculous recovery of sorts, not remaining the weak man leaning over a cane for long. He rushed it, however, and ultimately began training again too early; his fight against the pain was severe and he suffered for it until his death. His determination, however, was more resigned than ever, refined in large part by his time spent in bed rest. Even while incapacitated, he found a way to be resilient, as during his months of bedridden agony he did not just lie there helpless: he began to read and write in a way that he had never before. His process and methods, once intangible, became more concrete. Floating ideas and theories were either cut or refined, melded, reworked, synthesised, and brought together to make ideas about his work and martial arts stronger, more cohesive. Thoughts and intuitions became concepts. Concepts were trimmed, and his depth of knowledge became married with his wisdom from tens of thousands of hours of experience. During this period he made few discoveries about specific techniques and steps but made many discoveries about the bones or the ideas underneath his work: he was now touching the essence of his short but filled life's meaning. He was creating a personal philosophy.

The result of this troubled time was a collection of writings called *The Tao of Jeet Kune Do*, which has become a classic staple amongst students of both the martial arts and business. Arguably, however, the inner result was far more significant to Bruce than the writings that manifested from it. When he returned to his work on camera, something had shifted inside of him, and it showed. Experience had given him ideas and wanderings, but the work he had done to distil his wandering mind had brought fruit. Engagement taught him, but pain and weakness tempered his determination. At the end of this process, there was a power and magnetism inside of him that had not been there before, something that transcended confidence and bravado and showed the heart of who he was.

Physically he was not the man he had been before. Though he had regained the outward appearance of physical perfection again, privately he suffered bouts of extended agony. But that was offset by the energy that now radiated from him, a transition that came too close to the end of his brief time here. Had he lived the long and fruitful life he deserved, this is the Bruce we would remember. His earlier days would have been celebrated for their origins, but they would pale in comparison to the new powerhouse of spirit and presence that had emerged from a personal darkness and radiated an unintentional, unconscious magnetism.

While I am no Bruce Lee (feel free to call my JKD instructor Clive to verify this and you will most likely hear the laugh of the day), I certainly have been an admirer of him and his few writings for many years. His depth of mind and applications are beyond my comprehension. Within his life, however, there is one great lesson that my life overlapped with as well, and that is life experience gained from immensely painful and debilitating illness. In my late twenties I was living in London and my career was taking off in so many ways. I had been teaching around the world and had just finished a workshop that had many incredible guest instructors, including world-renowned theatre company Complicite and legendary Oscar-nominee Terence Stamp. I had spent thousands of hours of my life devoted to the pursuit of truth through mainly one technique and approach (which you'll hear more about soon for your own interests in leadership) and now had people in different countries in Europe and North America asking to work with me. As well, I had begun my journey in executive and leadership research, having been one of the Masterclass lecturers at UCL on their MSc in Management. My interests focused on leaders becoming powerful and magnetic speakers.

My personal journey, I felt, was onto a running track, and after a great deal of planning I was ready for the next stage of my career. The centre of this new step was giving voice to a deep urge inside of me: I had all of these thoughts and concepts gaining momentum. Ideas I knew in my bones could help actors with their own personal journey towards greatness and success. My belief in them was genuine and passionate. After years of immersive work and experience, the most important thing to me was to try to put them down into some coherent format. It was time to write.

Little did I know, however, that life's chaos, alongside an unexpected sickness that I would spend the next two years of my life battling, were just around the corner.

Cliché as it might be, the phrase is genuinely true: I remember the day before everything went wrong so clearly. I had gone into Central London, where a branch of my gym was. I had a great workout, went to a Starbucks to work on some writing, and was making plans to reach out and meet with some people in the corporate sector who had offered to mentor me and give advice on the needs of emerging leaders. I went home to my wonderful partner. We made a quick run to Tesco for some delicious snacks and drinks and had a lovely evening of movies and cooking. It is a day that for me, in retrospect, has become so special because of its normalcy. A normalcy that I took for granted.

My partner left early the next morning. I woke up, alone, and almost immediately I noticed something unsettling: I could not get out of bed. I wanted to, I was ready to move, but it was as if every muscle in my body had become stone. I even wondered if this could be some form of waking sleep paralysis. When I finally managed to move I became overwhelmingly dizzy. It would rush in waves and my body felt continuously the vertigo one feels on a roller-coaster drop. I finally managed to put my legs on the floor: they felt like concrete. It took nearly five minutes to make it the few feet across the hallway into the bathroom, consciously dragging one leg and then the other. When I reached the sink, I could not lift my arms to brush my teeth. Everything felt like a battery had suddenly gone to zero. I managed somehow to get back to bed and stayed there until my partner returned.

The days, months, and years that followed would not be pleasant. Medical tests were slow going and for a long while my symptoms worsened: problems with walking, balance, memory. I had immense difficulty putting words together. Daily debilitating fatigue, dizziness, and shooting pains that would radiate and last for minutes or hours became my constant companion. I felt as a piece of furniture might if it suddenly became aware of the screws constantly twisting into its frame.

Writing and phone calls as well became nearly impossible. It once took me two weeks to complete a few simple sentences to a friend who had not heard from me in awhile. I lost touch with everybody, and without the support of my partner, life would have become unmanageable. Together we booked doctor appointments and hoped for quick answers. Reality, however, answered: nothing noticeable could be found on basic blood tests. The NHS moves very slowly if there is no clear urgency. After a year with no real answers, it was apparent that I had to return to the United States and seek better medical care there.

Working with five doctors in my home city as well as being a patient at the Mayo Clinic, I was put through the gamut I needed to be to find the answers. In just one year, between doctors' appointments, labs, tests, and consultations, my number of appointments peaked at over 80. The more specialised tests began to reveal the deeper problems in my body: unfortunately, one's late twenties are the perfect time for genetic disorders to arise, and mine has had vicious consequences on my body.

By the time answers came it had been two years without anything that could concretely diagnose or treat these problems. In that span the momentum of my growing career had collapsed in on itself, I had lost touch with almost all of my dear friends and colleagues. I felt as if I had been knocked to the bottom. But for all these setbacks, there now was hope again for a future. You cannot cure your own broken DNA, but you can sometimes treat the symptoms and manage it, and this is the path before me today. Things are not perfect. Treatments sometimes stop working unexpectedly, but after years of battle, my mind began to return in small, growing increments.

Those two years were spent in a kind of darkness and prison that I never knew could exist, one of the body's making when it loses its ability to function. Still, even in the worst times, I did what I could to fight. I could not write long-form anymore, and so I had to focus on being concise.

Every day I would write a few words. Over time, these ideas became distilled. Concepts would be challenged, thrown out and reaccepted, changed, cut, and combined. In bed for most of the day, alone, in the better moments I had time to examine my ideas from all sides.

Much of my career had been spent working with actors, and so I had originally intended to write an acting book. Surprisingly the concepts I became most preoccupied with quickly revealed they no longer related to acting. At their heart they began to focus on the essential dynamics within a human that can create movement in another person. Movement, I realised, was motivation, true motivation, where an impulse from another human being would translate into behaviour. The ability to create movement, I soon saw, is the underlying heart of leadership and its primary currency, power. Power is what great leaders spend and receive in the transactions of leadership. What I originally thought were distilled ideas for actors came full circle back to the early research I had been doing on leadership. There had been, right in front of me this entire time, a point of convergence.

As my treatments began and my health improved, so did the clarity of my ideas on the intersection of my thousands of hours of practical experience in the arts with their applications to leadership and business skills. Before long I had over a hundred pages of notes on leadership and almost none on acting. At that point the path was truly clear. I now felt once more the obligation to the voice inside of me: I needed to give these thoughts form. I needed to contribute something to the great and emerging leaders of today. My determination now tempered by the struggles against illness, I was armed with better ideas and resolve. It was time to write.

This book, in the same spirit that honours Bruce and other people who refuse to let physical challenges hinder them, is the fruit of my time spent with the wisdom of illness. Many of the ideas and theories about leadership that I discovered have been reworked and distilled into a series of concepts and exercises for unveiling and showing the greatness that people like Bruce were able to bring to their work. To be clear, I am not talking about the on-screen fast-punching, smooth-talking persona but rather the magnetic and genuine power he brought to his work towards the end of his life. This is the human greatness essential to powerful leadership, and it can be trained. For the leaders of today and tomorrow, these pages are an offering.

What a leader is, and is not, is something we will explore in this book. I will lay out my arguments and concepts of what makes for greatness in a leader. I will offer exercises and concepts for how to achieve this greatness in a practical way. Many of these ideas are unconventional and paradoxical. They go against the grain of normal coaching ideas and tips. This introduction, then, will give you a sense of some of the underlying bones of why I have chosen to buck the conventions in this field and offer what I believe to be a clearer path to achieving your leadership goals. I will explore many of these concepts in depth with examples in other chapters, but this introduction will outline some of the territory I see as relevant to you and your leadership needs.

Much, though certainly not all, of leadership training is about making the client feel better, and so built into it is a level of insincerity in the form of a glorified placebo. Though I certainly believe in respect and kindness towards others, I am not interested in conflating making you feel better with your being a better leader. Rather I want to get down into the bones of where great leaders emerge from and how that can flow from you. The first bit of paradoxical news I have for you is that the answers are much less complicated than you think. But be warned: simple does not mean easy. Skills often take time to learn, and the powerhouse tools offered in this training might be no exception.

If the previous sentence has put you off, then I would ask you to consider a truism of leadership and any other avenue of career fulfilment worth pursuing. Most people, regardless of their vocation or field, know their time is precious and so reasonably want quick fixes to their problems so as to get on with life. I too believe in the concept of minimum effort for maximum gain (a gem also personified by Bruce), but I cannot solve the time problem at the outset for you. The hard truth is your time will go by either way. You can fret over your time all you wish, but if you are unappealing or lacking in the qualities others treasure within a leader, then you will lose significantly more time trying to bring people over to your side. When considering how to spend your precious time if leadership is in the cards, you might as well invest it making your time seem more valuable in the eyes of others.

There is an ancient adage that you cannot make everyone happy all the time. There are, however, some general, or universal, principles for what makes great leadership. These concepts are often unconscious: most people cannot define them, but they can easily sense and intuit if you have them. That is what I mean by investing your time into making it seem more valuable in the eyes of others. You are not a slave to others, though you might feel like it now or have felt so at times, but to win the game you must have all the necessary pieces to do so, and that does involve to an extent taking your cues from, and responding to, the world around you. Your own genius is only half of the equation. Everything outside of you is the other, and I would argue more important, half.

The Placebo Effect (of) in Leadership Coaching

Everyone, it seems, is becoming an executive coach these days. Actors like to do it because it is easy and promises good money. You might not want to hear that many people who migrate from the arts into coaching think prioritising you is easy, but they do. If you've got one foot in the arts like I do you can recognise this in the recipe for most executive training syllabi: dig up some old voice and movement exercises from the 1970s. Talk about breath and posture. Use jargon like 'ensemble' and 'team building'. Add in some basic, short-form improvisation. Suddenly your high-profile executive coaching session looks strangely like a beginner's acting workshop.

I once was asked to design a syllabus for an executive coaching course based on some guidelines and materials from a couple of books that specialised in leadership development using performer training. It was a good experience, because I got to see what the experts were pushing from my own insider eyes. When I actually looked at these exercises, I felt like this was high school drama material packaged and translated to sound more far professional and meaningful than it was. I couldn't help but feeling on some level this was all looking a bit like needing careful medical attention and going to the snake-oil salesman because you can't tell the difference. For clarity I do not want to lump all coaches as charlatans, but continually my ethics metre pings when I read a pamphlet or watch videos of business coaching: large amounts of people are being taken advantage of with the smoke and mirrors that gulls many novice non-actors into complicated exercises and workshops that produce little to no clear result.

Again, it is worth repeating: there are a good number of intelligent business coaches out there. There are even more who don't use good exercises but deliver them in good faith, not knowing any better. My own experience, however, of talking with many coaches 'off the record' has left a bad taste in my mouth. I commonly hear in private conversations that they like the power that comes from associating with the top dogs in the business world. There is a sense of elite elevation that comes from knowing heads of companies and being on 'the ins' with name groups.

At the end of the day, whether in good or bad faith, strong or weak exercises, my personal experiences and research have led me to one general conclusion: in business coaching, there is an implicitly high level of bullshitting going on.

Take, for example, a classic staple of business training: the improvised scenario. In a coaching session you might be asked to improvise something relevant to your current needs. Maybe a negotiation or a confrontational interview. You could be asked to develop a scenario with challenges, obstacles, and to figure out both large and smaller solutions (sometimes called 'tactics') as you go along. Let's say at the end of this particular improvisation you receive feedback on how the exercise went and are told that you did extremely well – and you very well might have. The implicit claim, of course, is that excelling at the improvisation will directly translate to bettering your skills as a leader. To you, this reasonably *feels* right, because that kind of an exercise *is* challenging, as is your work in your own field. There is a correlation of experienced difficulty that creates an intuitive truth to what is being said about you being a better leader for having become a better improviser.

Until of course we acknowledge some other truisms: even for a seasoned actor, getting up and improvising in front of an audience is hard. The material is by its nature unknown. There is also the challenge of connecting conceptual plot points in a coherent way throughout, and of course add to it the fact that it is all being observed and happening in real time. The primary appeal of the television show *Whose Line is it Anyway?* is watching highly skilled improvisers, with decades of experience, grapple and struggle with on-the-spot creation. Improvisation is always, to some degree, going to be challenging: that is the point by design.

The first time you improvise, of course, is almost always harder than the second, especially if it is the same scenario. With tweaks or direction from the coach, when you run the improvisation a second time it most likely will feel easier, but not necessarily because you are better at improvisation – or, by proxy, leadership. This is because improvisation is full of what researchers call confounding variables, elements in a situation that skew and blind the results. Consider that you may feel more relaxed a second time around because you now understand the expectations of the coach. You might be more comfortable with the material: you've done it once and it didn't end in disaster, and even if it did, you survived. You may now feel more at home with the other members in the workshop. All of these factors and more can translate to the false assumptions that you are now better at improvisation and – because the implicit claim set up from the get-go is that improvisation makes you better in your own field – that you have improved your leadership skills. Now magnify the challenges of improvisation tenfold for a non-actor from the business sector. Is it any wonder that feeling great after an improvisation, a blend of writing and acting challenging even for seasoned pros, would make you feel like you accomplished something relevant that surely must make you better in your own field?

With no way to control for those confounders, the evidence is at best unclear. This is the core problem of most actor training and, in my view, leadership and business training that involves improvisation: there is a dangerous conflation that because doing an abstract exercise in one environment becomes easier, it means it will translate to better ease and ability outside of that environment for different needs. No coach I have ever met or read about, however, wants to acknowledge this, and so finding the line between a client feeling better in a class or exercise and knowing with assuredness that a reliable tool has been developed is perpetually murky. Similar problems can be identified, in my view, across nearly every approach, model, and tool in leadership training, even those that don't use improvisation.

In the midst of these challenges full blame does not fall entirely on coaches for the dilemma an aspiring leader finds themselves in when seeking clear, concise answers as to how they can develop their leadership skills. Clients at times do not make it easier on themselves. For example, an executive or manager might say, after an improvisation with a coach, that the next day they went into a negotiation and closed an important deal for their company. The natural correlation, however, is they assume they could not have done it without the class the previous day, or at the very least that it provided that needed boost. Maybe this is true: maybe the coaching session really did help. On the other hand, what that client does not consider is that their success might have been due to their newfound confidence and not actually anything from the session itself that was of value. I'm not undermining confidence, but it can be obtained across a wide variety of situations and so in this example the client's success was not dependent on anything special to the improvisation. If this type of entirely plausible situation occurs not rarely but often in the larger business training sector, it could very well be that most, if not all, the training offered in these regularly long and expensive coaching sessions is entirely irrelevant. Confidence, while a vital asset, is not nearly enough to propel you from success to success, especially in situations where reliable skills and strategies are needed.

Medical science and the field of psychology now acknowledge the power of the placebo effect, but I suspect we never hear about it in the coaching and training fields in either acting or leadership because that thought strikes terror into most teachers. After all, if their work turned out to be a placebo, what would they teach? The line between ethical obligations to the client and making a living is a fine one: we don't yet know how to identify placebos in these fields, and so we just won't talk about it. Clients actually end up believing that the intuitions and hunches of a coach, especially a seasoned professional, are good at sorting the many complex variables that determine a result. Research across many fields within the behavioural sciences, however, shows us that we are incredibly bad at using our intuitions and instincts when it comes to predicting and understanding complicated situations. The time of all clients is precious. It seems a shame a good portion of it might be being wasted on a coach's neuroses and ego.

Let's add up the following problems we have identified: wanting to keep the client happy rather than being honest with them, whether it is in good or bad faith; ignoring the possibilities for rival, or alternative, hypotheses accounting for the success of your training; and emphasising the value of instincts over data. What do you get? In my view, a recipe for a lot of spin and not of lot of forward movement. If you close the book after this paragraph and never look at it again here is my best essential piece of advice up front: when seeking a coach, look for one who is aware of these conflicts of interest and at least tries to know the line between when something is working and when it is not. Not every client needs training. A good coach will assess this, and if they believe you don't need it they will be honest about that. If, on the other hand, all you get are generalized answers about 'skill sharpening', 'keeping fresh', or some other vagueness with no clear end in sight to your training, then look elsewhere.

An Unexpected Lesson

While some of these ideas had gone around in my mind for quite some time, it was only when I began teaching at UCL that I started to give some of these concerns and intuitions about leadership clearer shape. I had been asked to be one of the masterclass lecturers on the MSc in Management, and the subject I proposed was on dynamic speaking for leadership skills. At the time I felt this was a vital and essential core component to leadership (since then it has been distilled into a deeper idea which we will explore in later chapters), one that many emerging leaders need in their arsenal to efficiently make use of, as well as to acquire, power. It wasn't the whole package, but at the time I believed it to be one of the primary structural supports of effective leadership.

The study of power has long been one of interest for me. Understanding and making use of power is integral to the leader's journey. When I say power I don't mean hooded figures seated around a long table in some basement, whispering apocalyptically, or a group of middle-aged men in business suits deciding which water reserve should the toxic waste be dumped in to save a buck (one of them of course has to be wearing sunglasses). Those iconic stereotypes reflect the unfortunate misuses of power that go on, but power itself is an entirely neutral dynamic. While not politically correct to say this, given that today it is popular to associate power only with its abuses, separating power from the action fuelled by it is essential to understand its function and how it can be attained, lost, or regained. This is what I had hoped to begin delving into with my UCL students. In reality, I was the one who was about to learn a very valuable lesson.

My education began with a surprise: with the exception to two, all of the students who signed up for my classes had none of the qualities of great leaders. I met a lot of people who had the stereotypical tough business guy attitude, and even more people flush with their own ego, as well as a few I am still convinced are extremely high-functioning psychopaths who could not wait to have a team under their sadistic, clawed thumb. Much of the atmosphere in those classes was so testosterone-charged with posturing that I remember humorously thinking to myself at one point, 'Ah! So this is why most business coaches tell me they spend a lot of their time kissing ass and not teaching anything of real value.'

You didn't need to be a rocket scientist to identify the first major concern: almost none of them had the charisma and draw that a great leader has. Ego-dripping personas put others off, and unfortunately they lacked professional standards, and perhaps the most surprising thing to me, they did not seem to know how to parse their bad ideas about leadership from the good ones. Though brilliantly intelligent they seemed to have very little capacity for honest self-reflection and assessment of their leadership qualities and whether or not they were growing or diminishing in their training. They could not see they were their own worst enemy.

To be entirely clear, I am not faulting UCL for my shock and surprise in this valuable wake-up call. I have no doubt they picked these students well. All of them were incredibly bright individuals, sharp as a razor I am sure in their own fields, and I was lucky enough to meet even two whom I felt were going to be knockout leaders. I certainly don't fault UCL for their selections. Besides, after years in the acting industry I know that sometimes an actor is cast who seems the perfect fit for a role until they end up being the nightmare casting decision to work with. It happens to us all, some people it seems are ninjas at conquering the interview only for the sole purpose of making everyone's life hell once they start on the job. After my classes finished, reflecting on the experience, I realised I couldn't even really fault the students – these were people from their late twenties all the way into their early forties who hadn't woken up yet. What can you do for somebody still asleep? Most had never considered that if your eyes are continuously shut to your own development then what chance have you really got?

The real-world lessons I gleaned from my experiences at UCL, equally enlightening and jarring for me, defined clearly the valuable distinctions between a leader and a manager. The majority of the students I met at UCL were not leaders – there's no other way I can say it. True to the title of their degree they were managers, and while both roles are vital to the success of a company or enterprise there is a succinct and often profound difference between the mindset of a leader and a manager. The mentality of a successful manager, I realised, is to behave like the top goldfish in its bowl. It oversees the resources currently available, keeps order, and makes decisions about distribution and redistribution, all while delineating the responsibilities for those tasks to other fish. Managers are vital and certainly benefit from leadership skills, in the same way that a leader benefits from having management skills, but a manager is not a leader. In this model, the mentality of a leader is the owner of the aquarium. They must see to it that all the fish have the resources they need to thrive in their environment. To ensure this, they must go and source those resources, sometimes across fields, as well as make structural decisions. Leaders must continuously be keeping an eye on both the minutiae of their creations as well as connecting with the world outside those places to source and build connections to support those creations. For a leader, there is a vast view at play. People with a manager's mindset build with what they are given. Leaders create those building blocks.

The essential difference between a manager and a leader is the scope of vision needed to excel, and in a leader a much broader one is required. It is a very specific mindset, as well as skillset, that can accomplish that. I mentioned that at UCL I did come across two students who understood that. They didn't understand because of my teaching or words, but because it was within them already. They were on a very different journey than the rest of their peers. So many of the people I worked with there wanted power, either because they felt they deserved it or because they had none: it was their end goal. The two gifted people I worked with *needed* power, because without it their visions could not be accomplished: they saw something larger, had an internal eye for manifest greatness, and recognised power as the vital and essential tool. For these two leaders, power was not the end goal but a tool to aid the voice inside of them calling for visions of greatness.

It may seem silly to talk about ideas like visions of greatness. They have a Churchillian tone that sounds almost archaic in our modern times. Some things do indeed change, but leaders always have and always will play with the bigger picture of their society and time. They don't have their eyes on small things – they see empires. And empire does not necessarily indicate objective size; so long as it fits their personal urge and vision, large or small, all that matters is it becomes an actualized end result that the leader puts their personal signature on.

The Unknown Path: The Values Not Often Shared

Developing the leader within you, I have learnt, is not about giving you handed-down skills or prescribed tools. There is no mould for you to fit in, and so training that insists on a mould misses the fundamental point. Despite this, many emerging leaders go to universities, take workshops or private sessions, and while they are told their individuality is important, the prescriptions for feedback are generalised and non-specific. There is a particularly dangerous concept in leadership training that I find especially counterproductive to the development of leadership skills precisely because, as many bad ideas do, at the outset it sounds like a great idea.

This noxious concept falls under the seemingly benign name of 'skills training', or 'skills development'. In these sessions, coupled with improvisation and team building exercises, you may be taught things like vocal exercises or the importance of focusing on breath to combat anxiety and keep a steady voice. You will learn how to stand in presentations, how to speak with your hands, plan your gestures, and keep your movements on point. With the help of a coach, you display the importance of posture and assertiveness that arises from it, keeping command of the room, planning your breathing points, not doing too much, not doing too little – and on and on.

The idea of skills training sounds like a sound idea at the start, until of course you consider that great leaders don't think about these things. Historical accounts reveal many things about great leaders, but they seem to miss the part where Caesar was constantly worried about his hands or how Susan B. Anthony could never go anywhere without her deep, diaphragmatic breath exercises or assertive posture work. Paradoxically for the pre-planning approach, it seems that the hands of great leaders take care of themselves. Even more dire for the voice and breath junkies, leaders don't seem to worry about their breathing. Unless of course I missed the part where Henry V couldn't finish his St. Crispin's day speech due to the sore throat he got from not properly warming up his voice (for the record, I realise it didn't happen as Shakespeare wrote it). It is almost as if all of these strange prescriptions that intuitively we know are not natural to the moment are nothing more than a cult of busywork.

What do I mean by 'natural to the moment'? Breath, for example, takes care of itself naturally. As do your hands and posture. The only time any of them becomes a problem is when you start to pay attention to them. Your shallow breathing and clammy cold hands only become an issue when they hit your conscious awareness and you go, 'Oh no! My hands are cold!' Does this ever help to reduce your anxiety? Of course not! Your attention, not the targets of your attention, is what creates the problems and interferes with your ability to take action. As Beckett wisely wrote, 'There's man for you, blaming on his boots the faults of his feet.'

Let's explore this example. Have you ever had the experience of walking down the street and something suddenly came directly at your face, perhaps a startled bird or a taut branch from a tree you were crossing under? Chances are you flinched, recoiled, duck-and-dived, and resumed your walk. All without any cognitive intervention. And guess what? Your heart rate might be elevated, but breathing was fine in those moments. Even in the face of stress, your body knows how to respond to a mortal danger simulation. I say simulation because, after all, it could have been an actual attack and not a tree branch. In that instance, your body's job and the functions associated with it, body movements, breath, alignment, was not to assess the scenario first but to *respond* to it, keeping you alive so as to make sense of it all later. But why does that happen? How can your body handle breathing, dynamic movement, what to do with your hands, all those important areas many skills coaches focus on, without a single ounce of your input or the wisdom of an expert standing by to give you feedback? For one simple reason.

Your attention was not on yourself.

Common-sense training in leadership is to put the role of correcting your problems onto yourself. Seems like good advice, right? After all, you are competent in your field, you've probably got visionary ideas and goals, so surely then you are the one to solve your own problems? Problems like why people might not take you as seriously as you wish them to, or why when you speak, negotiate, pitch, present, so on, you can sense their attention drifting away, that they aren't wrapped up as completely in your presence and magnetism as they should be. Just about any coach would agree: you are your own best solution. From there we have a clear path and with just a few mindful tweaks you will be on that path to success. Case closed. Stop reading now.

Except my noisy sceptical side, the one that seems to hate convenience, recognises something that throws a wrench into this solution: you, nobody else, created these problems in the first place. Certainly not intentionally but nonetheless the problems of you arise from you. That is the real-world challenge we have to tackle, and it's a complicated one, but the very first place of certainty we have to investigate is the possibility that more awareness and attention on yourself might not be the optimal solution. In fact, given that we've already started to see that when you put your attention on yourself it increases rather than decreases many of the stressors and anxieties that trip people up, why in the world is everyone suggesting that the very thing that created the problems for you in the first place is the same tool that can solve them? Isn't that a bit like thinking surely that gallon of gasoline will put that small fire out?

We have already used the examples of hands, posture, and breathing: the only time those things become a problem is when you increase your self-awareness, thereby magnifying the problems rather than diminishing them. Paradoxically, the less your attention is placed on yourself, as in the branch/bird scenario, the more easily your body takes care of itself. What if, then, the solution to training leadership is not to put more attention on yourself but to train so as to take it further away?

When I propose this, it scares most leaders. Understandably. Let's be honest: most leaders, yourself included I am sure, are control freaks. That is not only fine – in the right circumstances it is a good quality. I wouldn't take that away if I had the chance. It clearly follows, then, that releasing control, especially over yourself, feels like a recipe for disaster. When you speak, for example, or negotiate, you most likely sense yourself barely holding it together, constantly on the verge of spinning out of control. Experience in other domains of success has taught you that more, rather than less, control is needed. This may be true in many areas of your field, but when it comes to your abilities to successfully command the attention of others and motivate them to invest their energy into you – to gain the power essential for the success of your inspired vision – this may be a strategy that not only doesn't serve you but backfires completely.

This is what I mean by paradoxically. Specific prescriptions and prescriptive tools are a wonderful way to attempt to control the future. That is a sure-fire way to sabotage you, as especially when it comes to situations that require working off of other people, the future will always trip you up. That is not so good for you. For coaches, however, it ensures you will always encounter a real-world challenge to your supposedly strong tools. Which, if we're honest, equals repeat business. A savvy business coach can constantly find ways to rationalise why the problem isn't with their implicit – and by the way, impossible – recommendation for you to control the future but rather something *you* did. You were just too nervous. You didn't try hard enough. You did it, but not fully, or you didn't do it the right way. And on and on we go. All coaches, myself included, have fallen for this line of thinking at one point or another. Deeply attached to our ways and methods, we keep rationalising and yet still the future keeps surprising you. Your leadership skills don't improve in any meaningful way. All this does is keep both ill- and well-meaning coaches and leaders-in-training on a perpetual hamster wheel.

When it comes to training leadership in any meaningful way we have to acknowledge a sobering possibility: our model is not a strong one.

There will always be something that throws a curveball your way. Prescriptive tools for all scenarios will never hold up because it is too artificial a coating on the nuances and chaos of reality. Leaders create order, but they use chaos to do so. It is this real-world chaos we have to focus on. The only exercises, drills, or prescriptions of value to you as a leader are those that make you more, not less, malleable to chaos. Good leaders are able to absorb and thrive within it. That includes your own inner chaos. This leads me to suspect that those traits and qualities you see as problems within you are actually the building stones that can mould greatness.

Let's set a new course. Rather than try to artificially put a lid on your chaos, we should move towards it. It's there. It ain't going anywhere. Let's stop pretending you can overcome it. In the same vein, rather than try to get a handle on the terror that certain environments may pose for you (public speaking is, after all, statistically for most people a fear worse than that of death or dismemberment), we should move towards it. Rather than training you to dull the chaos within a situation and master all the variables, you should be training to lean into it, to wake yourself up to what is around you and what it is asking of you. To use it rather than trying to make yourself a shield against it.

This Book and Our Journey Together

Self-reflection after an event is a hallmark of greatness. Self-awareness during an event, however, all too often becomes a danger. The 'event' can be a meeting, day-to-day interactions with people of relevance, the pivotal negotiation of your life, an interview, a chat with the barista making your morning coffee, and so on. These examples span beyond the immediate scopes and confines of your specific field. What is the common denominator? All events relevant to great leadership involve an interpersonal component.

Whether you are new to a position of leadership or seasoned for decades, this work is designed to help you. You may be engaged in a start-up business, in an executive position at a high-profile company, a freelancer trying to build a portfolio, a manager of a specific project at an organisation, or the head of a nation: the training you will encounter in this book cuts across boundaries of career status, age, and the constraints of individual fields. It targets the heart of leadership itself and as such will meet you where your needs are rather than insisting you come to it. You will find the tools developed in the exercises you will engage in are not only entirely portable but incredibly effective in any interpersonal interaction.

Our journey together in these pages is the testing of a hypothesis that starts by going against the grain of common wisdom and even common sense: the less attention you put on yourself, the better your interpersonal interactions with others will become. The better your interpersonal interactions become, the better a leader you are. The better a leader, the more power you acquire to fulfil and achieve your visions. I don't need any faith or trust upfront. Just a willingness to try. Through specific exercises and concepts, I will give you what I believe to be compelling evidence for this argument. In practice you will discover first-hand that when you take the attention off yourself and put it onto the things in your environment you will become exciting and magnetic to watch.

Why exciting and magnetic? Paradoxically, the less you focus on yourself, the more inner qualities will begin emerging and that equals authenticity. In today's world of profiles, memes, and avatars, authenticity is a very rare and powerful sight to behold. People who are by nature rare and powerful are interesting. They are ones to be listened to, and somebody who is interested in you is the critical component to a successful leadership interaction. You can have the most brilliant ideas in the world, but without other people investing their passion and curiosity into you, executing them becomes well-nigh impossible. In your training, the truth of this paradox will become concrete for you: the more you take focus off of yourself, the bigger your presence becomes. Conversely, the inverse is also true: the more attention you direct towards yourself, the more it diminishes your presence.

I will be candid now about my intentions: this book is not designed to make you a lifelong student. The premise this training is based on is that, if you are not there yet, there will be a time when the skills essential to your leadership are as strong and developed as they can possibly be. When that happens this training will no longer be relevant, and it will only become so again if you ever need to refresh a particular skill or tool. Amongst business training there is far too much verbiage about your 'never stopping learning' that is used to justify cults of prolonged, never-ending expensive sessions and workshops. Good training is valuable and is worth the time you invest into it; the, sometimes addictive habit of training for the sake of it is deadly. Time for leaders is precious, and there is already so much of it wasted on bad ideas and inefficient training. This book, and the training within it, offers you an efficient and lasting solution to your problems. There are clear outcomes that translate to reality. There are myths about leadership and how to learn or train in it that are dispelled. There are clear descriptions of optimal ways of learning for your needs. This sets you on a path beyond the pages of this book: it gives you a sense of what leadership is and, most importantly, what it is not. It also empowers you with a standard of evidence that you can reasonably demand from other coaches and teachers.

The coaching industry is bigger than ever before. It is a business. Businesses, however, have to sustain themselves first, and that creates a conflict of interest that can have real-world consequences for the client. We won't go into much detail here, but I have no doubt that if research was done on the coaching field on subjects such as confirmation and selection bias, the placebo effect, and the prevalence of weak claims, most ideas within it would be revealed to be filled with problems. Clients deserve better evidence. This is a principle that applies to all coaches and trainers, myself included.

The task during the course of our time together is to break this process up into three parts. Part I of this book is called 'The Heart of Leadership'. Its focus is on defining leadership and the elements essential to it. Given that we are sailing against the common-sense wisdom of leadership training, it is good to make sure we are on the same page, especially when it comes to concepts like power and authenticity. I think at least some of the insights might surprise you or make you see this whole process called 'leadership' in a different light. The next two parts, respectively called 'Living Truthfully' and 'The Given Circumstances', focus on the practical training exercises for the ideas and principles defined in Part I. What these specific terms mean is something you will come to learn throughout the course of your training.

Each chapter after Part I corresponds to the exercises covered and explored in a single training session. The only exception, for reasons that will be covered later, is Chapter 3. Consequently you will find the exercises in this training are progressive. They start from an essential origin of power, which is what happens between two people in an interpersonal exchange, and from there building on that authentic exchange. Given this, I do not recommend jumping around chapters and doing exercises out of sequence, because each one carries within it a valuable concept that builds on previous ones to propel you one step closer to having the complete set of tools this training offers. Start from step one and progress from there consecutively.

I said in the beginning I cannot offer a quick fix, nor can I be specific about the time it might take for you to absorb these concepts. The journey of leadership is not prescriptive. It is individual. Some people will absorb certain concepts quicker than others. It is worth investing time into meaningful training, but having said that, with an eye for efficiency, you should begin seeing results even after the first few sessions. I keep using the word 'sessions' because you will find the practical work chapters in Parts II and III are structured like scripted, mock coaching sessions. In these chapters, when I refer to 'you', often I refer to the "you" who is present as a participant in these training sessions. You will also notice that sometimes I refer to you and others using the word 'client' to describe you while at other times 'student', but I don't mean this in a juvenile or novice sense. These are interchangeable terms that simply refer to people in the process of learning these skills for leadership purposes. In these mock classroom sessions, I will lay out examples of the exercises and training. I also recognise that some of you might already have a coach or trainer and may wish to ask them to incorporate these ideas. To support this journey and to help your coach, or any other educators interested in this material, the end of almost every chapter includes a brief section specifically for coaches and educators called 'Tips for You and Your Coach'. This section is considerably small, as the focus of this journey is on you, the client. For reference, however, you may on occasion want to look at the coaching tips yourself to ensure that your coach or trainer is keeping on track with the values and clarity of each exercise.

Before we move onto the practical training, we need to set some ground rules, to cleanly carve out the territory. Also, in the title of this book may be a strange name to you: Meisner. Who or what is that? I've already begun to lay out a few ideas related to Meisner, but a closer look will be helpful to create a foundation of how to see this training. Hopefully my comments on most leadership training and coaching have shown you that there is a huge lack of this clarity when it comes to training leaders. Transparent clarity is what we need to establish. I don't want us to get bogged down in semantics, but it helps us all to be on the same page. Before we begin training, then, let's take an in-depth look at you. By you I mean a leader with a vision. Whether fresh to your field or well established, let's get into the heart of what I see are your challenges. I also believe we can expand and perhaps constructively challenge some of your own thoughts and preconceptions about leadership. Once we have this strong foundation of mutual understanding, we can build all our training on it.

And where is the best place to begin when talking about leadership? With the mechanism at the heart of its engine room, as well as your own journey: power.

Chapter 2

The Three Pillars of Leadership: Vision, Power, and Technique

Who Needs Leadership Skills?

In this chapter I want to define our starting points as well as the territory we will be covering. If we are going to have a productive and honest discussion about your needs as a leader, it is vital for us to be confidently on the same page from the first moment (as you will discover soon, the first moment is the essential moment). To kick off this conversation, I want to start first with you: your goals, dreams, and ambitions.

This book is about leadership, specifically how to develop and hone your leadership skills so as to attain your aspirations. Leadership, however, is a charged and loaded word. Some of you might think that, from your understanding of the word 'leader', being a leader isn't exactly what you want to do. Maybe, for example, all you desire is to have a strong management position within a certain company. Perhaps your goal is to achieve that juicy promotion. Or maybe you want to have strong standing and recognition in your field even if you are not necessarily the face or leader of any one thing. Perhaps instead you want to make a difference in the world, see a change, but you don't wish to dominate or have your advocacy be all about you. We can expand even broader. Perhaps you just crave a certain career, one that means for you a life fulfilled. For most, those aspirations may be called life goals, career ambitions, markers of personal attainment, but they aren't leadership in the way most of us understand it. What if we look closer, however? Do all of these hypothetical ambitions fall under the umbrella of leadership?

Looking deeper, we can see that fulfilling all of these desires and ambitions reveals a fundamental unifying variable and core attribute that ties every one of these seemingly different goals and life pathways together. The unifying variable is, in a word, autonomy. The personal direction and forward momentum characteristic of autonomy is the essential ingredient needed to fulfil each of these dreams and goals: at its core, it implies ownership over one's life course. By itself, does autonomy imply a need for leadership skills? At the outset, it would seem not really, at least not in all of these cases.

An even closer look, however, reveals that independence brings us not to a final conclusion but an interesting paradoxical juncture. Autonomy's survival seems to be widely connected with dependence on and even cooperation from the outside world. Let's take an extreme example of autonomy: say your dream is to live alone in the Alaskan wilderness and never see civilisation again. Walden on steroids. Fulfilling this Schwarzenegger-meets-Thoreau vision will still require the cooperation of others. You will rely on the expertise of cartographers to find the optimal location. You will need resources and materials to build your cabin and most likely builders if you are not skilled enough to build it on your own. Red tape can't be fully escaped: the cabin will need to have several different kinds of permits. You'll still be a taxpayer and need to register an address. Even if you are capable of many of these things, eventually there will come a point where your expertise runs out and you will need other people to fulfil your ambitions. Yes, your vision and skill will be valuable: getting from A to B, knowing that it's done in the right way, and so on is still you. At the end of the day, however, it won't be enough. The fulfilment of even the most extreme independent goals requires a level of favourable interaction with the outside world. And this is a fairly simple example of moving to a remote location. When it comes to accomplishing something within a society, where there is a competitive marketplace of ideas, then the unique interplay between personal vision and cooperation does not decrease. It increases.

Let's ask it again: given this more real-world definition of autonomy we are exploring, where dependence and independence are intertwined variables, is there a need for leadership skills when it comes to fulfilling any autonomous ambition, goal, or dream? Absolutely.

In defining the parameters of leadership, it helps us to see that the core of all leaders is rooted in human impulses, desires, and visions that all circulate around personal ownership over one's life. Personal ownership, however, is not easy. If it was, everyone would do it. Fulfilling goals based on your vision for a life on your terms is even more challenging. Here, then, it helps for us to define what the desires of a leader are. To put it succinctly, a leader's successfully fulfilled dream or goal depends on personal vision triumphing over life's circumstances and challenges. That is to me what a leader wants: to see their vision, their dreams, manifest into reality. In spite of all the hardships and obstacles within it, as well as the seeming impossibility of odds, personal vision triumphs. That's not anyone's dream: it's a leader's dream.

Investigating the primal core of what drives a leader isn't the same as talking about specifically defined goals or visions. Those arise from innate desires, but they are not the desire itself. They are epiphenomena that arise from the deeper need inside you. Take for example the wish to see a positive change in the world. The desire itself is far deeper than choosing which clean water charity to support or what kind of organisation of your own you wish to found or be on the board of. These are choices arising from that which is deeper. While the manifestations are important, for our purposes here, they matter less than the fundamental need for the triumphing of one's vision over the challenges of life.

Your personal goals, then, depend on the same fundamental attribute as every great leader who has ever lived. You share that exact same primal origin of need for autonomy. You will note that many people are similar in this regard: nearly everyone has dreams and goals that need to be fulfilled against the current of reality. Few, however, ever accomplish this. Since we are beginning to see that leadership skills might involve the careful juggling of the interplay between personal vision and cooperation from the outside world, we are arriving at a simple but meaningful hypothesis: perhaps the better one's leadership skills are, the better one's chances for fulfilling their autonomous needs.

It may surprise you to consider that by virtue of being human and having lived on this planet for a time and reflected on what you want, you have already begun the fundamental process of becoming a great leader.

Via Negativa

In beginning to think of yourself as a leader, and as we move towards a good definition of what leadership is, it becomes helpful to start with what a leader is not. In dispelling these common generalised myths, we can begin to make the process of applying the label of 'leader' to yourself as something clear, personal, and shared by all great leaders throughout time. We are moving towards universal qualities.

A leader, then, is not somebody who:

■ Solely seeks conventional labels of leadership.
   Some people only aspire to a specific position or field that is deemed by *others* as 'leading', such as politics or upper management. These are leadership positions, but they are not the whole picture. Great leaders both build their empires from the ground up and enter into established positions and companies. Attaining a leadership position, however, does not make you a leader. Many examples abound of incompetent people who somehow found themselves in leadership positions and managed to display their lack of ability vividly, to the detriment of those around them.
■ Is power-driven or power-oriented.
   Great leaders recognise power as the essential tool that accomplishes their visions, but power is not the end in itself. Power-oriented people rarely emerge as leaders. If they do obtain leadership positions, they do not stay there for very long. Lacking greater vision and the ability to see beyond their own inner hunger, they soon fall to either circumstances or rightful leaders who use power rather than simply obsessing over it.
■ Gets a thrill from controlling others.
   Delegation of authority is vital, and so with it comes a level of supervision and management that is essential. Great leaders, however, do not get a thrill out of dominating others. Their pleasure comes from those under them working in harmony to fulfil the leader's vision. Good leadership also recognises that being a continuous tyrant means people are more apt to turn on you when they get a chance. People in management positions, for example, who are solely tyrannical and play power games, do not understand the balance of rewarding and punishing when necessary, making them inconsistent with their own responsibilities to others. These are sadists, not leaders. Deliberately making the lives of others around them hell is the low-hanging fruit of petty and sociopathic managers that leaders avoid and many of us, unfortunately, have had to put up with at one point or another.
■ Is in charge of a team or other people.
   This seems paradoxical, but it is an important distinction to make. The cooperation of other people is vital to the leader's success, as is enlisting help and rewarding in appropriate measures. Leaders, however, retain their leadership skills whether on their own or with others, at the top of the pack or for the time an entry-level worker. Even if you are not at the top you can still practice and develop your leadership qualities. This is perhaps one of the biggest

misunderstandings. The time to work on your leadership skills is not only when you are already in a leadership role. You work on leadership skills to attain those roles. Leadership skills are applied to others but are not dependent on others.

■ Is committed specifically to social change.

Virtue signalling and moralising are two of the classic weapons leaders use in political battles. This is true of any orientation on the spectrum: left, right, centre, etc. It can be easy, then, to conflate leadership and social justice as essential to one another. It is important to recognise that holding the moral high ground in the public eye means immense power and mobility for leaders. In politics, genuine social concern is often mixed with the desire for greater advancement. The social change component to leadership, demonstrated by politicians, larger companies, and even small grassroots organisations, is just as much about advancing oneself as it is seeing change in the world. Great leaders are committed to their own vision. Social change may or may not be a part of that. Though to some it seems politically incorrect to say, compromising your vision for the sake of appearing moral or concerned is an unwise move for a leader to make. It will only lead to distracted half-hearted measures and dampen your own vision. In fulfilling your dreams and greater desires you will do more for society than paying lip service to causes you may not believe in or feel passionate about. If social change is essential to your vision, that is a different matter. If it is not, let your advocacy and charitable work come from within your own successful contribution to the world.

■ Is incapable of working with others.

We may think of leaders as being the heads of state, corporations, large movements, in other words, the top authority for large numbers of people, but in truth, the job of a leader is a profoundly solitary one. History admires and remembers the trailblazers who defied conventions and community, even if the popular opinions of the present time shifted and turned on that individual. It is not uncommon for leaders to engage in profound solitude in the brief moments they might have free. Despite this truism about deep introspection and reflection, however, leaders do not exist within a vacuum. The power exchanges needed to accomplish your visions will be made between you and other people, not by yourself. Inward vision must be tempered by, and be flexible to, the outside world and circumstances. To have cultivated yourself internally but not have the skills necessary to enlist others to your vision is to only have half of the leadership skills. Fifty percent will never cut it long-term. Cultivating deep, meaningful professional relationships means loyalty and protection for you, even in the face of hard times and major mistakes. Conversely, a leader who is too self-oriented often finds themselves the centre of envy and hate. The second they have a chance to fall there will be everybody who can get in line holding their proverbial foot out to be tripped over. Leaders stay true to their vision but enlist the cooperation of the outside world to create and sustain it.

The humanistic roots of leadership, alongside our examination of what a leader is not, make the requirements for a great leader far more porous and malleable than you might have previously imagined. This results in a very open-ended image of a leader. Leaders can, for example, exist both in structured settings and impromptu daily interactions. They can thrive as the head of millions of people or when they have yet to find even a single person to aid them on their journey. Leaders work with others but wisely balance agreeableness with aggressive assertiveness and are sensitive to which is required in what moments. What you are seeing, I imagine, is that this makes both a leader and leadership incredibly hard to define. It seems broader, preconceived general notions of a leader weaken in the face of individualistic qualities and circumstances. Try to boil down all great leaders according to strict guidelines and you will watch your examples dissipate. As a consequence, training leadership becomes a challenge in itself. It seems we can't in good faith go about training you to be a successful leader until we are honest about what we mean when we use that term.

For now it seems like what we can agree on reliably from our investigations is that great leaders have an internal vision and possess the ability to enlist people to their cause. This is our meaningful starting point. It might sound simplistic but simplistic ground is solid. Solid ground is what reliable claims are built on. Starting in a clear way, you can begin to understand the necessary diagnostic tools for where you may be lacking in your leadership ability.

We have gone into at length what a leader is not. How about one quality of what a leader is?

All Leaders Are Aspiring Leaders

Great leaders recognise the ephemeral nature of time. The universe is in a constant state of flux, its properties constantly changing, evolving, disintegrating, and reintegrating into new forms. Likewise, people's temperaments are equally as changing. Human behaviour might have underlying universal qualities, but the social dynamics it exists in change frequently and rapidly. Smart leaders recognise their place within this dynamic system. Rather than fixed, they see their own personality as open and changeable and will go with what is needed, even if they feel unready for change.

To train leadership, then, the specific techniques and strategies needed must also be fluid and malleable to change. Your vision might stay constant, but at any time a strategy that has worked for decades may be overthrown due to new variables in a situation. Perhaps one of the most shocking examples is the rising trend in what I call social media determinism. It's a fancy name but nothing new: popular consensus is king on various digital platforms, and so social media movements for – or against – certain businesses and individuals can bring either transformative or devastating consequences. Those who adapt to these movements collectively fare much better than those who do not and are blindsided by them.

Fluidity is an insurance policy. You cannot be the master of the future, and so predicting it accurately lies beyond you. Wise leaders who learn this truism keep their eyes open. Perspective and hindsight, however, is not always easy. Retrospect in one's own situation and field is difficult. A trusted friend, ally, or advisor who is honest with you is a valuable asset, almost a luxury. In the event that is not available, then it is necessary to be as consciously keen as possible. The greatest fulfilment for you as a leader is to see your vision succeed; at the same time you must, however, contend with the ever-changing nature and chaos of time, trends, and popular opinions, all while working within the universal constants of human behaviour that seem to be found through all cultures and generations. It is a difficult path to balance. Smart leaders must be sensitive to both changes and new tools that can aid in their adaptation and survival.

If this is true, then by definition a leader's journey and development is never complete. Whether you are new or seasoned, you must give that idea of final arrival up immediately. There is no final state of finished mastery for a leader, just a continuation of awareness, reception, and learning until life ends for us. It is no surprise then that long-standing, established leaders throughout history found themselves most vulnerable when they became stagnant and detached. Lock down into only what has worked in the past and you will find yourself vulnerable to the changes of the future that you can no longer see barrelling towards you.

This is the human core of leadership, that the greater ambitions inside of you demand no less than for you to be regularly engaged within the world: one hand firmly on the established strategies, approaches, and means that you know from experience have worked, and the other grasping for new ideas and tools within the chaos of the present. All leaders who retain greatness, even on their last day on earth, are aspiring leaders.

Having said this, the ephemeral nature of the world, as well as social trends, are not the only challenge to a leader. Another more subtle reality exists that can undermine your ambitions and visions long before anything or anyone else does.

A Little of Nothing

Almost every leader, whether new or seasoned in their game, has arrived at their position not because of chance but because of merit, the foundations of which may be hard work, people skills, negotiation talent, and so on. There are rare exceptions. Some people are, as the phrase goes, thrust into greatness, into positions of leadership, but unless their innate skills and vision take over quickly, they soon find themselves brought to ruination. Poor leadership makes one the enemy of many people, the butt end of their dislike. These are the exceptions, however. Most leaders thrive because of who they are. The core of that person is an impulse of vision that exists as ambitious, externalised forward motion. That drive takes leaders above the cut of the average person who balances their domestic desires with their career ambitions. For a long time the esteemed writer Charles Bukowski would only allow himself .25 cents a day for food, enough to buy a PayDay bar, which became a powerful metaphor for him. Everything else would be spent on printing and mailing manuscripts. To him there was nothing else that mattered.

Leaders get this. They sacrifice. They lose on some fronts. They learn to treat time as finite and imbue it with a powerful meaning. Time is the key to achieving one's ends; the more of it leaders waste, the farther they see it drifting away, just as a lush, tropical island begins to lose shape and visibility when the sole survivor in the lifeboat gives up on paddling. For many leaders the drive is just as powerful as a life-and-death scenario: it is a hunger that grows, not diminishes, in the face of adversity and setback.

This dispels the popular myth that true leaders rise to where they are because they are driven by a hunger for money or power. It is true that for many leaders money is a key to the success of their vision, but arbitrary numbers are not what drives someone to work 80 hours a week. There is something deeper at play. You'd see it easily if you reversed the picture: if a great leader had to choose between their vision succeeding or loads of money, they'd choose the vision succeeding. Fulfilment and the desire to have the boxes checked for a life worth lived is a powerful motivator. The fulfilled life for a leader involves the triumphing of an inner vision, of what they see as their contribution of greatness to the world. In making that impulse real, a leader puts their signature on something that is now generating a place for itself in the world. Contrarian cynicism aside, generally a fulfilled vision makes all societies a better place.

The specifics of how vision manifests differ from leader to leader, but there are some general agreements. The primary one is that the odds of success do not fall into the 'easily done' margins. Oftentimes the greater the ambition, the farther at the end of the possibilities spectrum its manifestation: variables, probabilities, and chaos aplenty lie in one's way as pitfalls and traps. This is a point of communion between all leaders and your average person: many of us have seemingly impossible dreams. The difference, however, is in the trade-off. While it is true that we all have dreams, it is equally accurate to say most of us are terrified of discomfort and chaos. We choose to compromise and manage the plight of existence to the best of our abilities rather than fighting battles with odds greater than we believe we can overcome. Most of us with a little life experience don't scoff at this choice. Life is hard and filled with brutal surprises. We don't have to make it harder by pursuing silly pipe dreams. Besides, it doesn't have to be all or nothing: compromise is the essence of life. A little of something good is surely better than pursuing something great and never attaining it. Settling, many of us rationalise, can be enough.

A life of settling, however, is not consequence free – Thoreau described the psychology it produces as 'quiet desperation.' For driven leaders, the life of comfortable compromise, of quiet misery, is the most suboptimal strategy on offer, a viscous poison that almost always ensures an unfulfilled life. I have seen this many times in the performance industry, perhaps more times than members of other business sectors have seen it in their own fields. Using my own experiences in the entertainment field, I want to take you through a couple of examples of certain mentalities I have witnessed many times that destroy great actors and, in extrapolating these examples, to show how the same patterns of behaviour can be the undoing of great leaders. At times I'll bring the examples back to leadership, but for the next few pages, go through these examples with me and see if you recognise any of these traits in yourself or others you know.

What Actors Teach Us about Leadership

Actors provide an excellent case study for the strengths and weaknesses of leaders. Actors are essentially their own start-ups attempting to rise and thrive at the top in a highly competitive pool, with exceedingly few resources. In the performance industry, the risk is high but so is the reward. Working actors have to find ways to eke out small amounts of highly disposable income, often due not to lifestyle but the costs of living in major hubs of the industry. They have to work enough hours to support themselves in cities like Los Angeles, New York, and London, often at minimum wage. To complicate things further, they need to work jobs that allow them to have the time to pursue and develop what is essentially a full-time entrepreneurial start-up. Even with an agent, most actors still often have to source their own work and both make professional contacts and nurture them in ways that will pay off down the road. Being a professional actor is, as all start-ups are, gruelling, and the odds of failure are high.

Failure is a fascinating word. Its many implications reveal much about the different types of performers out there in the acting industry. To some actors, 'failure' means financial failure, with Dostoyevskian images of being penniless, destitute, or declaring bankruptcy, all in the name of pursuing an unlikely career in an uncertain field. Understandably, many people are not comfortable with this image. To them, the stark ideas of being on welfare and financial ruination are so vivid that the very thought carries within it the implicit notion that failure is inevitable and the pursuit of a self-sustaining career pointless.

To actors with this mentality, money is a dominating factor in their world view, as is the decision-making that stems from it. When they inevitably hit the moment when things financially become tight, the panic button goes off. To offset the near-debilitating anxiety of being destitute down to the bone, these people will take jobs that pay (sometimes well) above minimum wage. The trade-off? These jobs demand more time. The order-and-stability craving actor now receives set schedules, a profound relief for the struggling freelancer who fears for money constantly. In taking this fruit, however, they set the trap for themselves and make the devil's bargain which ignores the reality of the field they want to succeed in. For example, many times actors are called in to audition at the last minute. I have several times gotten a call or email at midnight asking me to be on location an hour away from my place at 6:00 a.m. That is the nature of this beast: meaningful things happen and oftentimes they happen on a last-minute basis.

The working actor who becomes a routine-seeker now lacks this essential flexibility. They quickly learn it won't be long before they strain the goodwill of the company they work for with continuous last-minute requests for shift replacements or backing out of a meeting an hour before it starts so they can get on a plane for an audition. Having pushed the good graces of their employers by trying to have it both ways, they come to the inevitable impasse: make a choice, their rationalisations tell them, compromise a little, or it's back to the firing line of poverty for you. The passive poison of compromise slackens their ambition inch by inch each day. They begin to pass on auditions, don't look as aggressively, or stop searching altogether. Ambitions die a slow death. Before long they consider themselves a failed actor.

The passivity, however, doesn't stay quiet long. Eventually their ambitious nature sounds the alarm, telling them they are getting far off course. Rather than take the cue from their inner vision instead, they curiously accept their position. They commit to this entirely self-created reality, further rationalising it as fate deeming their lot in life. 'Oh well,' they go, 'it wasn't really for me. It's my fault that I failed.' They exit the field entirely, continue on career paths that no longer fulfil or even remotely adhere to those inner visions of leadership, doing their absolute best to dull themselves entirely to their screaming intuitions.

The most curious part? Many of these people in their forties and fifties will join amateur drama clubs and theatre groups when they have better financial security, often once children are grown up and they no longer have to crunch at the full-time job. They return to at least a shadow of the path they walked away from. That forward, ambitious voice that called for greatness all those years ago has still not gone out. Despite their best efforts, they have not been able to beat the better part of themselves to death.

To condemn this at the outset would be to ignore the hardships and toll on health that financial failure takes. Leaders, like actors, often engage in risky entrepreneurial ventures. Despite careful planning and calculation, even the best entrepreneurial endeavours are, in essence, experiments to be tested in the real world, a place of unknown variables fraught with chaos. Sometimes things that should work perfectly fail hardest, while at other times what should never succeed takes off like lightning. No matter how carefully researchers in even the hardest sciences design experiments, there is always room for unforeseen error. Answers to questions can sometimes be unconventional and surprising. Throwing large amounts of money behind experiments that fail can be devastating and sometimes the perceived 'clear' message is that one is not cut out to be a success in their chosen field.

The essential idea, however, that must be remembered is that financial failure is not necessarily a reflection on a leader's qualities. They impact it, but they are dependent variables. The fluid nature of money and social trends shows that failures provide opportunity for rebound. Falling to the bottom is hell. Climbing out is not a quick process. In my own field, successful actors are successful leaders because they have achieved the fulfilment of merging their inner vision and ambitions with an external reality. Financial success was rarely a reliable metric in this process. Actors who are today wealthy had to battle through dire financial hardships: Al Pacino was homeless and slept on the stage of the Actor's Studio. On winning his first Oscar, Russell Crowe was still hundreds of thousands of dollars in debt from borrowing and scraping by for all those years before then. Dustin Hoffman, who lived and slept on the floor of his friend Gene Hackman's apartment next to a noisy refrigerator, once said that even if he had never had financial success he would still be doing community theatre in whatever small city he was living in. Hoffman, like many other great actors and leaders alike, refused to cease finding a way to fuel that fire within himself. Financial failure and the risk of it would not silence the leader's ambition inside of him.

When at the bottom, rather than try to convince themselves that they have been living a silly fantasy and it is time to grow up, leaders still bounce back. Nobody is comfortable with the idea of financial disaster and its profound, sometimes dire, consequences. Money-based failures, however, are largely fluid. Deficits can turn into profits again. The mentality of failure is far more dangerous than the failure itself. The great leader keeps going and in so doing inspires others to climb out of hell. Is it any wonder that the world finds the actors I have listed as examples of great leadership and so incredibly watchable?

The Perils of World View

Another type of actor who is an excellent model for the dangerous patterns of behaviour leaders must be aware of within themselves is the iconic stereotypical actor: the one who hungers for fame. Trace this hunger back, however, and you'll often discover some interesting psychological roots. Perhaps this actor came from a difficult background where escapism into fantasy became an outlet of healing and hope, just like Marlon Brando or Ian McKellen have spoken of in interviews. Maybe they were creative dreamers nurtured by their parents and schooling to develop their vision into something they believed must be shared with the world. Or, different entirely, they were socially awkward and learned to be expressive through performance, the joy and pleasure it brought others becoming a feedback loop for them.

The reasons vary, but a common thread ties them together. This is an actor with a world view dependent not on financial success but rather one intimately tied to fulfilment and emotional well-being through the approval of others. Push the red carpet, dazzling lights, limo rides, and big bucks aside: what matters is the millions of people cheering for this actor. Validation is a delicious narcotic for their wounded souls, and these actors dream to be the big fish. Why? To make it to the top is ultimate recognition. They have suffered, in their personal lives, and their careers – the bright lights and golden statues – symbolise a soul-filling validation of previously unrecognised talents and titanic struggles. The world judges them and, offering them the richest praise imaginable, it says: 'You did well. It was not all for naught.'

The majority of the actors I have met fall into this category. At their core is a potent dream tied in with their emotional wellness. There is deep passion and drive. It seems as if they are always performing, always fighting to be the life of the party. When they receive a role or an accolade it is not satisfying – it is *nourishing*. They see a career as fulfilling both the role of social ambition and emotional nurturer. You will find this actor in classes, networking events, going to as many auditions as possible, and at home practising constantly.

While the drive is commendable, do you read some of the above lines and think this is a recipe for disaster? Fulfilment is one thing, but intertwining one's emotional well-being and therapeutic needs with career advancement? If you share this same edging-towards-the-cliff-edge concern that I have about these people, you wouldn't be wrong.

The problems begin with the issue of delayed feedback. People who make accomplishment and mental health dependent variables find time is their worst enemy. There is almost always a delay between our output and the fruits that come from it. For those of us with a healthy understanding that accomplishment is often a thankless process until far down the road, this painful truth becomes bearable to accept. For this type of actor, however, it creates a cognitive dissonance where fulfilment is always perpetually just outside their grasp. 'Why haven't I made it?' they think, 'I work so hard and it never pays off. I give and I give but I never get. Surely the problem is me.' Discouragement can be a spur to ambition for some but for others with this world view, it becomes a powerful halting force.

Hopefully you can see that this is not just a problem unique to actors: it applies to anyone with irrational expectations for their ambitions, especially leaders with a currently unfulfilled vision. The challenge for people with this worldview is oftentimes it is an entirely unconscious process. Most of the time they aren't aware of the mounting pressures their own standards have created. Their feedback loop of effort-to-reward ratios is broken. Validation is a rare commodity, and when these people get some, it hits like a junkie's high. Moments of recognition and approval literally make life worthwhile for these people. People in normal, routine-based careers with moderate levels of stress and risk will never understand this. For leaders in high-risk, high-reward professions, of which there are many, the addictive risk of the high that comes from the prospect of global recognition and power is an entirely unforgettable drive – and a dangerous trap as well.

For our actor friends with this mentality, they encounter the same harsh reality that any leader venturing into their own start-up does: success is fluid, and financial reserves are not unlimited. Fewer professions exemplify this better than acting. It is entirely common for cream-of-the-crop talented actors to go literally years before making that one essential connection or getting their 'big break'. Ruby Rose, now an A-list star, went for two years without work until the opportunity to act in *Orange is the New Black* came her way. The brutality of the waiting game, which is reflective of success in many fields, can break those with even the toughest of nerves. But for those with the winning-is-fulfilment mindset, which is filled with the cognitive dissonance that comes from not understanding the time commitment and scale of effort-to-reward, the realities of these hardships take a critical toll.

In the face of these discouraging conditions, many actors commit a fundamental error in their reasoning that further exacerbates their anxiety around the situation. Good acting is largely done through intuition and feeling in the moment. Good leadership, as you will see, is also the same. Waiting does not feel good. Effort without recognition even worse. As a result, a dangerous intuitive conflation is made: waiting becomes equated with stagnation. This perceived rotting away of one's time and potential goes into the broken feedback loop and is filtered through the irrational distorted view of reality. As a result, one's inner computing machine prints out this conclusion: the message you are receiving from the world is that you are failing. You are waiting. Therefore you must on some level be doing something wrong.

If you had to boil down the trigger for this entire set of cognitive distortions, you'd come to a simple but likely culprit: for these people silence is the real danger. Not literal silence, obviously, but the silence that comes from waiting without answers. For actors, it begins with applying for dozens of castings and not hearing a word back. Silence. Suddenly, an email arrives at midnight saying, 'We would love to see you read for this part. The audition is at 7:00 a.m., please let us know as soon as you can if you can come in.' Let's say it is a good role, making the answer a resounding yes. The actor then rearranges their entire schedule, cancels a shift (knowing somewhere down the road they will have to make up those missed hours to cover rent and pay bills), books travel, and if needed, accommodations, both often for a much higher price than if they had some advanced warning. They arrive at the audition looking polished, do their best, and then wait for weeks only to hear – nothing. More silence. Disheartening? Of course, even for the best of us. A sacrifice on your end has not been met with either acceptance or rejection. It is treated with indifference. Ouch.

Not all leaders venture into their own start-ups, but almost all are in the process of being their only advocate to push themselves through an important door, secure a key deal, or make an important contact. Actors are, for better or worse, an excellent case study for the problems in thinking and fear that arise in the face of silence. Most of the time, regardless of the field, it seems as if the universe couldn't care less. Hundreds of emails and letters are written to various individuals who might open a door. More often than not, not even an acknowledgement or a polite rejection. Everything goes into the vacuum with nothing coming out. To many, it seems the message is blaring and obvious: your time is not valuable.

Since leaders are intelligent people, they tend to think on things. Potent, long stretches of silence, like winds across barren desert sands, lead any intelligent thinker to try to make sense of it. The fact that our hearts and souls are invested in our success and the fulfilment of our ambitions does not help: it complicates our ability to see soberly through the constant mirage of indifference. It is easy to intellectually recognise unpredictability in another field, to go, 'Yes, yes, success is fluid.' When you are the objective, the goal, there is no clear timescale. Many have succeeded as individuals before you, but none were you, and therefore the elements unique to your success, and the time they require to come to fruition, are entirely unknown variables.

It is easy to come to the logical conclusion that, when no problems can be easily identified, we must be the problem. Actors are experts at it. They tell themselves, 'Well, I've got the vision for success. I've had work in the past. I know I can move forward but I'm not. Therefore, the only thing that can be possibly getting in my way is me. That's it! I'm not doing enough! Problem solved.'

There is a temptation in seeking easy answers, reducing thousands of complex dynamics and variables out of your control to something within it. And in every delusion is some grain of truth. Sometimes we do not do enough for our careers. For people as driven and ambitious as most leaders are, however, the better likelihood is that you are grasping for straws of meaning as the fear of time slipping through your fingers takes greater hold. I see it in actors all the time: it is easier to blame themselves than accepting the silence from the audition, or the industry itself, as a necessary evil nearly all self-made successes go through. Counterfeit self-help gurus say, 'Gee, why make yourself a target?' The answer is glaringly simple: at least then you have a target.

Recognising the indifference you receive from your own efforts as having no inherent meaning is hard. Endurance is a lonely road that can take years to cross. The expanded example of the irrational thinking actors can land themselves in that leads to inevitable self-defeat is a good lesson for those entrepreneurs and leaders working day and night but seemingly seeing no results yet. You may not see yourself as an entertainer or actor, but you share a common risk with them as well as common ground in the frustration of seeking greatness in a world that seems to remain painfully indifferent at times. Surviving in the face of adversity is easier because it gives you constant spur and motivation; it is surviving in the face of nothing that can lead you to make error-filled calculations and grave summaries for your visions and success based on them.

The final conclusion to be gleaned from our failed-dream actor case study is what decisions based on error-filled calculations manifest as. When an actor finally falls prey to the false intuitive conclusion that they are not doing enough, the restlessness and anxiety such a conclusion produces soon leads them to desperately take any work they can. Rather than wait for the good thing, they convince themselves that any acting work, even if it's not what they know is best for them, has to be in some abstract sense good for their career. They might say when accepting pointless or menial jobs that they were asking for too much in the first place. Notice here I am not talking about jobs to provide a monetary foundation – these are decisions oriented towards a career path that at least have the shell of advancement even though they are hollow inside. The irony is these actors break their backs working low-paying unfulfilling jobs and out of despair end up taking equally low-paying unfulfilling jobs within their own field that don't get them any closer to their vision just to offset this growing dread.

We all have what I believe to be an inner bullshit detector. Sometimes it is very good at screaming at you when you are making a false move. It is no wonder actors like this often end up bitter and dissatisfied. The cognitive dissonance must be enormous. What is worse, unlike the financial fear actors, these actors often take forever to exit the industry, if they do at all. In the interim, they take or create jobs for themselves as casting directors, agents, teachers, and with their soured cynicism make life hell for everyone else doing their best to endure in the industry. The level of their misery must be tantamount to constantly dying of thirst while planted right next to the full glass, expiring because you have convinced yourself that the drink is simply not for you.

These plagues of mind are universal and have consequences for leaders across the board. Those who are particularly gifted, competent, or talented are not immune. I have seen the irrational world view destroy truly great and competent artists. I remember once I was fortunate enough to coach an actor who I greatly admired. It is no understatement when I say she had every component needed to be successful in the industry: passion, fire, emotional availability, and openness. She is also immensely beautiful, keenly aware, and intelligent. Every fundamental concept essential to the great actor was there. Our time, I felt, need not be spent focusing on basic training but subtle refinement and honing of ability.

The coaching session was to take place at the flat of a mutual friend who had a very large and spacious living room. Perfect for text work and some basic movement. We quickly sat down, she on the couch and I on a chair across from her, just to have a quick check-in. I asked her how things were and if there was anything specific she wanted to work on or was concerned about in her career. This is where things began to get strange.

'To be honest,' she said, 'I'm not doing enough for my career. I'm lazy.'

'All right, we can work on that,' I said. 'How about you tell me what an average week for you looks like?'

'Well,' she said, 'I'm working two jobs, about forty hours a week, to make ends meet. I get to auditions regularly, and I make sure and practice texts and monologues twice a day. But I'm not really getting anywhere. I'm also emailing and reaching out to people to set up scene practice sessions or film things for my online exposure. I'm also trying to build bridges with some theatre professionals and companies, so I'll email about five to ten people a day.'

Imagine me sitting there hearing this. She is saying this in good faith. Having known her for several years, I know her to be honest. I do a quick double take and look down at my notes. 'Lazy' she said? I check and yes, she really did say that.

'So . . . how long have you held up this routine?' I asked, trying to figure out how to tell a person working probably about 70 hours a week on her career how she's not being lazy.

'The past six months.' she replied.

My last ace-in-the-hole is out the window. I bite the tip of my pen and deliver the honest truth.

'I have to be honest,' I said, 'I don't see how that's lazy.'

And then it came, the voice of that unrealistic feedback loop:

'But I'm not getting anywhere.' she said.

So here it was. Right in her face. The silence from her field. A necessary reality for every successful actor now internalised and festering. Of course, with no answers she picked the easy target and made herself the problem. In doing so she wrongly assessed the industry, created a problem where there was none, and the only solution after a while would be self-defeat. She had declared a war on her internal visions for success and greatness. I am not going to lie: for me, as a coach, I don't want to cause more pain to a student. That is not coddling, it just means I don't want to be cruel. When it came to enabling her patterns of poisonous self-defeat, however, there was no compassionate outcome. Either I had to pay lip service to the delusions and make her life worse in the long term or strike a deal-breaker that would frame me as her enemy.

'Please tell me, because I am so depressed over it. What can I do more of?' she asked.

'I think you might be doing too much,' I said. 'In our industry, it is a marathon. Not a sprint. Burning yourself out has consequences. You're losing sleep and that will deteriorate your physical and mental well-being. When you overrun and overwork yourself, it puts people off. You seem exhausted. When you are this deeply stressed, your emotional availability is severely compromised. All of your main skill sets, including your mind and ability to strategise for your career, are weakened and begins to think poorly.'

'No, no, I'm not doing enough.'

'I hear what you're saying, but there is such a thing as doing too much. I think your biggest problem is you've convinced yourself you're not enough, and you're the problem itself. Sometimes that's true for other actors. It isn't in your case. You don't need more hard work. Instead, focus on the inessentials taking the form of hard work and robbing you of quality of life. The core of success in our field is endurance. Every day you tell yourself you are lazy and not doing enough, despite all this evidence to the contrary, you are destroying the only thing that will carry you through.'

Honesty has a price. My comment didn't land well, and it was our last session together. As a coach, it is still a moment in my career I have not fully reconciled yet. In thinking on it, I still ask myself if I did the right thing. I told the truth, as kindly but honestly as I could, but truth is a slippery slope when you know someone will hear something else. I know that soon after that session she hit a period of time where she became depressed and withdrew from the industry entirely. She is, to my knowledge, back on the scene, but only a little, working with small companies and not fully going back into the work like the career warrior I know she was. Leaders, take her example: even with a vision for success and all the necessary ingredients to achieve it, if you have a world view that is inherently against you, even the greats burn out.

A Challenging Balance

To bring these examples from acting directly into leadership, I'll start by saying that, on reflection, what I have learned from teaching and coaching is that you can teach tools, skills, and techniques. What you cannot do, unfortunately, is break people out of their own toxic world views that can erode even the most gifted leaders. It is discouraging on some level but it is also reasonable. Coaches are not trained psychologists. The line between coaching and therapy should wisely be left as wide as humanly possible. At the same time, if we completely ignore the impact that perspective and expectations can have on the development of ambitions and leadership ability, we run the risk of prescribing exercises that might harm the individual. Some people need to work harder. Some need to work smarter. Others simply need to work less. Effort and focus are finite resources so while the idea of giving 100% to everything you do is admirable in theory, in practice it quickly burns you out before you can get much done. Giving 100% to the right things is what matters. If you give it to everything, then you will stretch yourself too thin and end up giving 100% to nothing.

Leaders, then, must work to ensure their appraisal of their own unique situation is in line with reality. On one hand, if you ignore the problems you create and refuse to take responsibility, disaster will wait around every corner. Furthermore, you will never be able to fully understand what went wrong and so you will repeat those mistakes every time in the future. Conversely, if you place too much emphasis on yourself, your situation, and perceived shortcomings, you become blind to the variables in your environment that can be maximised. Sun Tsu phrased this in another way, 'When you neither know heaven or yourself, you will succumb in every battle.'

The great actor I worked with, the promise of success written all over her, could not see clearly. Consequently, long before the industry would have been done with her, she was done with herself. It largely comes down to world view. I have a background in psychology studies, but I am not a trained psychologist, and so I avoid using therapeutic tools to correct world view problems. I do believe, however, in using some of the tools and exercises from my professional career that I know address this issue indirectly, as appropriate and when needed, of course. A coach cannot ethically say they are doing everything they can for a student when we do nothing to help with obviously delusional thinking patterns.

This is driven by personal and philosophical convictions. I believe that great leaders are needed in the world right now, more than ever. When I meet a great leader who I believe is their own biggest obstacle, then addressing that candidly is an obligation not only to them but the many people they will better by seeing their visions and ambitions realised. Coaches are not therapists, nor should we pretend to be, but we have to address someone's views about the world and themselves if it is obviously holding them back. That is why built into this training is the development of a reliable bullshit radar for yourself that will help you appraise both yourself and situations reasonably and with some accuracy.

Napoleon Bonaparte is known for his successes in leadership. Fewer recorded leaders can be said to have had such spur to their ambition. What is less known, however, are his rebound successes – when he triumphed where so many 'dreaming' leaders have failed. Towards the end of his life, his career shattered from constant failures and the financial pressures he had put on France, Napoleon was marooned on an island off the coast of northern Italy, away from the country of France he so clearly saw as the helm of his internal vision, the place where he would leave his signature of greatness. The people could not bring themselves to kill him, but the thought of him even being around was dangerous, given how influential his abilities were.

At this point, Napoleon had already had the success of being emperor but with it now being taken away he decided, in pure Napoleonic fashion, one turn as emperor was not enough. Surrounded by the silence of isolation, as well as the perceived failures of his past, he made a clear decision: the answer was not to settle, consider himself finished, or to perceive himself even as the problem. It was not a question of *if* he would be emperor again: he *would* be. Through clever, brilliant, and utterly ingenious means, he managed to get off the island, returned to France, and reclimbed the political scene for a second, albeit shorter term, as emperor.

So many aspiring leaders take silence and failure as feedback from the world that they are the problem. While the strategies and tactics to achieving your vision that you implement might have to change based on the level of response received, it is equally valuable to understand that fundamentally you are not the problem. In identifying habits that hold you back, you might be the problem for a time, but that is different. The habit of self-defeatism and doubt is what I am referring to now. There is zero service to a leader in making themselves the perpetual enemy. It is much better to err on the side of hubris than underconfidence, although ideally the best balance is in the centre. Silence across time is the inevitable consequences of a self-made path. This is not to say never self-reflect; on the contrary, self-reflection will be one of your strongest allies. It is self-condemnation that seals the lid on the coffin.

It is important to consider this because often I see leaders perpetually concerned about their own inherent worth, to the point of paralysis. 'Am I a good leader or am I not, am I cut out to do this?' they continuously ask. You're going to very rarely hear me say this, but I'll say it here: that's a terrible question! Your job, the task of a leader, is to fulfil your inner vision to the best as can be done in this world. It is true that Napoleon was not a good leader towards the end of his life. His arrogance and lack of willingness to change his strategies sunk him. That is beside the point. Let history be the judge of your worth as a leader. Within your perspective and world view you must make that vision come true and believe the world more likely than not will be better for it. Even if history deems you to have shortcomings, at least you will have contributed something to the human narrative rather than passively letting yourself become the stagnant peg that goes nowhere. If you spend your whole life questioning your worth you will have lived a life of questioning rather than doing. You have no chance of history appraising your worth if you do not make any contribution at all.

Bringing all these pieces together to understand what leadership is, what we have begun to see is that there are a couple of identifiable universal elements of successful leadership. All leaders have a vision that must be manifested in the world. Since the world is an amalgamation of change, all leaders must be able to observe and, if necessary, change their approach. There are also universal traps to leaders in every field. Starting with a case study from my experiences in the performing arts, we can see that, somewhat counterintuitively, the real risks are not external challenges but rather the internal ones. It may sound cheesy or like a cliché, but it is still a truism that a world view bent against oneself is the key ingredient to not being able to recognise and make use of valuable resources and allies. A world view optimised for success does not guarantee it, but it is safe to assume that, just as one optimised for success increases those chances dramatically, so does a self-destructive one maximise the chances for failure.

Now that we have looked deeply into the nature of vision, openness, and world view in relation to leadership, we now need to turn our sights to the external means of accomplishing a vision: that elusive, often misunderstood, and decried force known as power.

The Morals of Power and the Power of Morals

It's worth making our starting point very clear: power is not the same as leadership. People often wrongly conflate the two, but they are separate components. It would not even be accurate to call them dependent variables but rather variables that fluctuate alongside one another. Take the example of a person with zero leadership ability who has suddenly found themselves in a leadership position with too much power for them to handle. On very rare occasions they succeed but often end up doing considerable amounts of damage. Now take the opposite and consider someone with true leadership abilities. He or she is either at the starting or a low point in their career; they may have excellent leadership abilities but find themselves power-deficient or completely stripped of it.

Just as having power does not mean one is suitable for leadership, it is also true that when a leader loses power, or doesn't have any to begin with, it doesn't mean the end of their career. Consider our example of Napoleon who, marooned and stripped of power with a terrible reputation, went and found more power to further his visions and causes.

What we can see even from some basic examples is that of the two variables, leadership is the constant one. It can grow weaker or stronger, but it is a more manageable variable. Power is entirely fluid. It comes in times of certain defeat and just as readily departs in eras of certainty. Its presence does not necessarily signify progress, and its absence does not signify defeat for a leader. It can be managed and maintained but never fully controlled.

When looking at power, it is possible to distil the power leaders encounter into two broad categories: institutional and interpersonal. I would generally argue we are far better at recognising institutional power by its common, gross examples: armies, capital, social influence, status, ability to enforce policies, etc. There are, of course, more subtle examples of institutional power, but generally it is easier to recognise than the latter type of power. Interpersonal power is inherently harder to spot given it implies power dynamics happening between individuals rather than in contexts with clear labels. Of the two, institutional power seems more appealing to many; we will soon see, however, that it is through interpersonal power that the mechanism by which interests can advance is created, largely enforced, and maintained.

Before we go further into these two branches of power it becomes helpful here to engage and move past the moral arguments around power. History is filled with misuses of power – there is no denying that. For the purposes of leadership, however, it doesn't help us to talk about power in those terms. To be useful for you, power in relation to leadership has to be viewed as something more functional. Two helpful analogies give us reason to proceed without needing to constantly moralise about power or to be apologetic for talking about it.

The first analogy is to take the example of a vehicle in which we treat power as its fuel. A car is developed and created through the negotiations, knowledge, and skill sets of thousands of individuals. Decisions are made about the model, what to include (or, perhaps more importantly, what not to include). Some ideas advance, while others do not. The car is put forth into the marketplace in the hope that it will be successful. Litigation, profit, and safety concerns aside, why all the complex deliberation? To give the consumer the highest degree of agency with the car. When you get behind the wheel, if you feel empowered, energised, and enthused (the alliteration is wholly unintentional, but perhaps could provide a good slogan for a car company or model), you are more likely to buy. There is a powerful visceral metaphor when buying a car we love: this is the vehicle that gives us agency. We can drive to our meetings looking like lightning on wheels, we can take a road trip, help mom get around better, transport the family safely, etc. There is immense variability in the needs of the consumer. Across all this planning and self-identification, the fuel remains indifferent. The car itself runs on fuel, but from the consumer's point of view, the car was not built for the purpose of running on fuel. It was built to achieve human goals, fulfil needs, help us in reaching our destinations. Without a power source, however, a vehicle goes nowhere. In the same way, power is not your end goal as a leader, but it is the essential means by which you'll achieve that goal.

How power is acquired or implemented may be a moral consideration, but discussing its nature and reasons it is needed is certainly not. It is both an immediate and long-term means to achieve reaching your destination. Leaders should not make the mistake of assuming then that making the attainment of power a goal of yours is by some reason or means immoral. Every morally driven cause in society depends on the power it has to execute its vision. There is no social movement without power. Furthermore, there have been many morally driven causes that ended up doing great harm with their power. Nobody has a monopoly on what the moral compass of power must be applied towards. It could even be said that those who claim otherwise are making a power play through such arguments. Whether you want to use the word or not, to achieve your end goals you must gain power. Will you use it for good, ill, or in an entirely neutral manner? That has always been down to the level of the individual who wields power and the vision it implements. The greater lesson here is to be wary of the criticisms of power rather than the power itself.

Another way of understanding power and its essence is through the second analogy: the concept of money. People consider money to be the same as power, but this is also a false notion. Money falls under the umbrella of power, as do other assets valuable to a leader such as time, alliances, social recognition, clearly defined enemies (villains within a narrative are essential to the success of a hero's journey), and many other manifestations of different forms of power. It is a common phrase to hear – that there is such a thing as too much money or that people with lots of money are power-hungry – as if the neutral forces of power and monetary currency were to blame for the choices of certain individuals rather than the individuals themselves.

A great leader must recognise that this is wrongly conflating cause and effect. Great amounts of power and its subsidiaries will simply provide you with access. They cannot be a moral compass in themselves because, as an example, money cannot comment on action, it can only facilitate it. In the hands of the wrong individuals, access leads to disastrous consequences for both individuals and society. We can all think of examples of individuals who fit this bill. We also must remember the beneficial contribution of individuals with great power and resources. One such example is when John D. Rockefeller, alongside Theodore Roosevelt, made some of the most important betterments to the American quality of life for all people through a commitment to nature conservation. In doing so, they saved some of the most stunning swatches of the American landscape from development and over-industrialisation. Rockefeller, of course, is controversial, but consider that a single individual who does both immense good and perceived harm with the same tool points to the agency of the individual rather than the tool itself as a cause for concern.

Some might say that individuals with great power who do evil things have abused their power. Again this characterises power in the wrong way. If power inherently cannot be for evil, then it cannot be inherently for good no matter how many cautionary tales we wish to tell about it. A neutral force cannot be abused or corrupted to personal whims. It can only be used for the desires of the person in control of it, just as a car cannot be held morally responsible for a driver who purposefully careens into a crowd of innocent bystanders. If we as a society wish to have a better dialogue about this topic, then we have to shift our focus away from power itself and more to the choices of individuals and the access it provides them.

If you possess the idea that power can corrupt, you must let go of it. It is the inherent tendency towards corruption in many individuals who are given access by power, just as it is the inherent tendency towards the socially good intentions of others given access by the means power creates, that is the real moral concern.

Power Applied: Divisions of Leadership

I have already continuously referenced the idea of vision in relation to a leader. All leaders have a deep, innate vision that arises from within. This vision is not necessarily always clearly defined into a specific path or set of steps, so I will sometimes use the word 'impulse' synonymously with 'vision'. While clarifying your vision is important, as from that clarity will spring intentions, goals, and assessments, it is important to distinguish here that exploring the notion of your vision isn't the same as ambition. Ambition is a fire in the belly that manifests from something else, it is a powerful forward momentum generated by something even deeper and more potent. This is why when discussing the raw fuel that fires a leader's spirit the word 'impulse' is more appropriate. What this impulse feels like exactly cannot be described easily but can be understood as a sensation you recognise inside of you. You'll know it because this is nothing like your experience of more common impulses such as 'buy', 'love', 'eat', 'sex', and so on. It feels innately different. It is an impulse towards greatness. For you, as with many leaders over time, this impulse will take shape and form. It will manifest itself into specific projects, life goals, and aspirations. The key thing to remember is that even when it does become more concrete, it remains deeply connected to intrinsic meaning. Fulfilling a vision of greatness becomes part of what fulfils a leader's life.

Ignoring impulses and intuitive callings is characteristic of most people who seek financial stability or give in to a self-fulfilling prophecy about defeat, accepting they will never fulfil their vision. Defying odds and inner doubt while heeding and attempting to fulfil your vision, however, is the domain of leaders. Leaders recognise that having a vision, as well as making it clearer and more concrete to themselves, is half the battle. The other half is building it in a world filled with millions of ever-changing variables. To navigate these dynamics and see a vision made tangible and real, you as a leader will need certain skills to achieve the following four generally universal components of manifestation:

- Develop sustainable, meaningful relationships.
- Define yourself and your vision clearly, sometimes in relation to others and at other times in opposition to others.
- Acquire resources and capital that become self-generating to ensure the safety and continued success of your vision.
- Eventually acquire recognition in some greater areas of society that will ensure interest continues to remain in your vision.

Looking at the above components, it can be seen that half of the essential qualities of being a leader are heeding, and staying true to, the clarity of the internal voice of your vision and the targeted momentum that stems from it. The other half is the successful acquisition and management of power. When both of these are in equal balance, these are the materials for the ideal and successful leader to make tangible their visions.

In this model, power becomes the interaction between two or more forces in an exchange that is about advancing the interests of at least one of the involved parties. Forwarding one's interest can be done either directly or by proxy. Of these two, the latter is the more risky one. One example of 'by proxy' might be the building or strengthening of relationships whose future potential is vague, agreeing to help with a project that may not have a clear return, or by building one's status across many social and individual circles, a profile amplified by association rather than specific collaborations. The risk for you is that it can be easy to forget that such a strategy must be focused on building targeted, relevant status, as in gaining recognition in areas that will immediately or eventually advance your own vision. It might be true that all press is good press, but some press can be meaningless. Outcome is of utmost importance, even if it is a time-delayed one and thus while association can be important, directly advancing your power through specific and relevant relationships is what we will focus on.

The most vital power exchanges, especially in the beginning of a career or project, or during a time of necessary transition, are interpersonal ones. Even in the strongest companies with thousands of members, the micro-world of dynamics that fuel it are a continuous stream of interpersonal exchanges, all of which filter into the larger aims of the company's model. This illustrates that while there is value in 'by proxy' power exchanges, the careers of great leaders are, for the most part, built on thousands of examples of successful direct power exchanges between individuals.

Using our via negativa model that we applied earlier to a leader, the same measurement tool can be used as a lens to better understand power. What it reveals to us is that power is not:

- The end goal in itself for a leader.
  In the same way that in the wild a predator's camouflage is not the thing that kills its prey, so must the aspirations of every leader be attuned to the differences between power and its markings. Power is a means. Making it the end creates a vapid, ever-empty existence.
- Its markings or makings.
  Power is not money, a label, a class status, physical appearance, race, sex or anything otherwise impersonal. Those are markings of power, and they are useful for end goals. At times, it becomes necessary for leaders to shift the focus of their current efforts away from their end

goals to maintaining those markings. Regardless, the markings in themselves do not necessarily imply power. It is valuable for leaders to know this, because there are many growing capable leaders who lack the resources of money, status, support, or other obvious indicators of power. These are things power will obtain for you or bestow, but power itself has deeper roots. Take the example of somebody who aspires to create their own business, building it from the ground onwards and upwards, yet lacks the essential resources to do so. They have the dreams, but let's say they work in a Starbucks, seemingly unable to get ahead, knowing if that one break could just come they would use it without hesitation. Well, surprise – news comes that a distant relative is dividing their money before they die and bequeathing gifts. Huzzah, a check for a million dollars is soon mailed. The money is applied judiciously towards fulfilling that vision. Without that guiding vision, however, the money would not be enough. You could give lots of people enough capital to start a business and they won't have the first clue of what to do with it. The roots of power for leadership often begin long before the resources to implement it arrive.

■ In the beginning, at least, dependent on having an institution behind it.

Power is interpersonal at its core. As you become more skilled at successful interchanges that motivate others to do things for you, in effect power exchanges where one individual willingly gives you control over their finite time, even if it is just a small amount (five minutes is just as good a victory as 1,000 hours if the request is well used), you will amass greater and greater support for your vision. To ensure, however, that the vision is self-generating, most likely an institution eventually will either adopt it or be created to support your vision. No institution, however, will help you in the beginning if you lack the interpersonal skills necessary to gain power from individuals. The key to success in leadership is to possess both power given by others, ideally willingly, as well as the intuitive skill set and knowledge for how to wield that power. Both are equally important. Institutional power can be built on that foundation. Consider the inverse. You can have all the institutional power you want but if you lack the qualities and vision of a strong leader, it will likely be far more finite and not lead to anything meaningful being accomplished except eventual collapse.

Eliminating certain misassumptions about power allows us to have a cleaner look at the actual dynamics of power exchanges and what differentiates successful ones from failed ones.

Natural Is NOT Necessarily Good, Good Is Not Necessarily Natural: the Dynamics of Interpersonal Power

Power over others is essentially motivation. Successful use of power is when motivating others to do something for you takes less effort than if you executed the action they are being asked to perform yourself. In this way, you are making the most of your time. Becoming aware, then, of the output versus input of your actions is very important. If you spend considerable time convincing somebody to do something that, had you just done it yourself would have been accomplished just as easily and would have spared you all the back and forth negotiation, then you are not using your power wisely and need to readjust your thinking about what you really want from that individual. Despite their good intentions, not all people who want to support and help you are competent. If you spend more time cultivating a working relationship than it will ever be worth, then without burning that bridge, lessening the frequency of contact and requests with that individual may be your best strategic move. This strategy can include reducing the time you spend helping them with their own projects. Caring for your time is not selfishness but one of the essential components of developing and sustaining a successful model of personal leadership that will nurture you and those working with you.

If you consider power a currency that is spent in interpersonal transactions, then you must also be aware of another challenging example. If you must engage with somebody in the hope that they will accomplish what you cannot, and that engagement takes more time than the task itself, then most likely you do not have enough power to spend in such a transaction. Your need for that person's help becomes a strong indicator that you are dealing with somebody with more power over you than you have over them, at least in that moment. There are many strategies available to you for reversing or changing that dynamic to make it more optimal for you, but what is important is that you see the fluid nature of power in play and how it is ambivalent to either party. Motivating somebody to do something for you with little effort and a large return is an example of your power investment paying off in dividends. Spending years on somebody valuable with no result until much later, yet yielding a grand return, is another example of a wisely calculated investment of your power. In the same vein, trying to deal with somebody whose help you need and the only response you are getting is that it feels like banging your head constantly against granite is a sure sign that the individual or organisation in that moment holds more power than you do and does not deem you a wise investment of their own power.

In considering power as a necessary dynamic to fulfil your visions, it helps for you to also be aware of the human response to power. Just as constant exposure to heat produces sweat in a person, exposure to more and more power creates an organic response in people. This organic human response in the presence of power is the sensation we call desire.

That Which Moves

Desire is essentially synonymous with motivation. People are motivated to acquire what they desire and so desire produces movement. The reward-oriented neurotransmitter that leads to movement is dopamine. Its release feels both good and anxiety-inducing. With that excited feeling we literally move. Movement sounds like a simplistic thing to pay attention to, but especially later in this training, you will see that the act of physically moving due to an impulse is quite profound. Consider that motivations without movement are only surface impulses. They are not the genuine kind of motivation that leaders are after. Items of desire, be they physical or abstract, living or preserved, material or immaterial, often have power over people, especially if the acquisition of those items is beyond that individual's grasp. Leaders are aware of this reality when it comes to other people and must make it a part of their knowledge and strategic planning.

Working with desire in a power exchange is often more complex than simply giving somebody what they want. The power of a leader is constantly in flux with the desires of those around them. Successful leaders merge the two: people must believe that performing actions for you, essentially acting on their motivation to physically help you, is in harmony with their own desires. This can be done through two means: through convincing, which is often a harder endeavour, or through finding those people who are naturally inclined to the nature of your project or you as a person. Finding these people, however, is a rarity, and finding those people whose skills and competency that match your needs is even more rare, and so it often falls down to strategies based on a combination of these two methods.

To give some concrete examples, a leader who gives flexible hours, for example, will attract people whose other desires depend on a more fluid, possibly chaotic schedule; having this freedom, they are naturally more motivated to work for that leader. By proxy, the leader has gained far more power than expended because they have created a deep and powerful link: the desires of others are now tied to the success of your ambitions. In the same vein, a strict, ordered schedule will attract people whose desires meld with a more structured environment. Perhaps they are happiest when given tasks in an eight-hour time frame and rewarded intermittently with measured recognition, or they might be looking for a steady job to help pay for their interests and hobbies outside of work. Either way, there is no such thing as the mindless worker. A keen leader needs to know what these other, deeper interests are. You don't need to be a mind reader to accomplish this. Often people will give clear indicators, along with that individual's competency and performance, as to whether or not they are suitable to aid in that leader achieving their visions. The observational skills for relevant signals you develop in this training will aid you immensely in this area. The forms of analysis we introduce towards the end of the training will also assist you in observing signals.

The lesson of desire is a profound and ominous one: so long as people see you, and see their working towards your vision as the fulfilment of their desires, they will be deeply loyal to you. Step in the way of that desire, however, and it may cost you valuable relationships, workers, and allies. A good portion of these calculation errors circulate around money. Do not make the mistake of thinking that desire and money are the same thing. Money may have a larger or smaller role in the fulfilment of an individual's desires, depending on the person and circumstance, but some people, especially the keen, truly talented, and bright, desire more. Money, then, is not the only thing that will attract those gifted people who will propel you forward; you cannot think that the promise of riches or writing a check is enough. There are many other people who can do that, and so loyalty based on these promises is fickle: if money is all you offer, as soon as a better paycheck comes, or the same pay for fewer hours, your gifted allies will go elsewhere.

Uncovering the psychology of desires in each individual you deem valuable to your own vision is finding the key to making that individual loyal and motivated. You do not have to give them everything they desire; on the contrary, that would be highly unproductive, as fewer things produce a greater surge of dopamine than the idea of 'maybe'. They simply have to consciously feel like working with you and for you, and they must recognise that working towards your goals is tied in with what they want. People naturally move towards fulfilment and agency. Gain a group, however large or small, of people who feel fulfilled by working with you, and you will see your power increase exponentially. There is nothing more profound or essential to any enterprise than a believer. Belief is based entirely on the prospect of deeper desires being met. Why else would people to go a religious service once a week for which they are not only not being paid but often give money for the service? Why else would people save for months to go to a special concert, or event, sacrificing dozens if not hundreds of hours to pay for those few hours? It can't be frivolity or naïveté in either of these examples; nor are they not unrelated. These are the markers of deeper psychological meaning for those individuals. If it seemed less relevant to you before, start considering the benefits of never underestimating the power of knowing and becoming a part of the desires of others.

Within this set of dynamics, individual temperament is a vital component. Leaders who ignore this variable risk misreading what talented individuals need in order to stay invested in you. Leaders, for example, who exercise too much control in their behaviour or actions over the wrong individuals will find themselves working harder to motivate those people. They will be expending more power than what they gain trying to be the leader of the pack. In the same vein, some people like to be bested or dominated. They enjoy being constantly reminded of who is in power because they also know they have a place in a hierarchy. That reassurance within itself carries value. Give these individuals too much freedom, or possibly be too accommodating to them, and they will start to become anxious and worried, accusing you of not caring or insincerity. They might start to believe you have given up on them, that the love isn't tough enough. It's not my cup of tea, but that's the point – when others are of value to you, find what *they* want in their cup. If the cost to you is worth it, keep it topped up.

Leaders who find the right strategy for how to meet the individual desires of people they work with will be using power wisely and finding themselves gaining more power as a result. Leaders who poorly calculate, or plainly ignore, the most optimal ways to treat individuals based on their preferences will find that those unmet desires now command more power in the workforce than the leader. People fixate on a person who gives them what they want. They also do the same to a person who denies them. Power will drain from the leader. A lack of well-delineated authority and strong centralised power in a work environment almost always makes it toxic and unsustainable. We like to think the best environments are democratic, but there is a subtle distinction between actually democratic environments and ones that feel democratic. We feel most confident being in a democracy where we know our ideas can be heard and where there is a central power that can right the balance if it tips and that doesn't interfere much otherwise. On the other hand, I suggest that if we are all actually equally in charge, it quickly becomes like a balancing act on one legged chairs and is a sub-optimal way to manage any group.

In summarising this section, we can see that, for you as a leader, the foundations of interpersonal power exchanges between individuals are simple: first, get to know those you wish to work with and wish to endeavor to achieve your vision. This first step could be called observation. Second, harmonise your requests of them with their desires to the best of your abilities. This we can label response. If you are successful, they will be motivated intrinsically, and intrinsically motivated individuals will go above and beyond with their knowledge, skills, and passion for their leader. If you try to enlist others without taking their nature into account, you will find your power needs at war with the tensions of unmet desires and ambitions. This makes it a much more tedious and longer process for you, wasting valuable power when it could have been saved all along. People don't stop being people simply because we wish it to be so. Self-interest almost always wins or at least wins with greater results when it does. That includes the self-interest of those around you, even at your expense. Knowing how to read meaningful indicators of relevant behaviour and circumstances with high-level observational abilities, and how to respond to them authentically will be a vital tool to implementing this strategy and is a core component of what you will focus on honing in this training.

Identity and Institution: Power by Association

Before we begin putting many of these concepts into practice, we should look at a type of power that I have deliberately not paid much attention to up until now: power granted by institution. Given that interpersonal power is of far more value to you than institutional power, your time in training will focus around that form of power. For clarity, I am not saying institutional power is of no value at all; on the contrary, it can be of immense value to your leadership needs. It is, however, a complicated double-edged sword. It is worth a few paragraphs here to analyse institutional power and why, in my view, it is a less valuable pursuit than power of an interpersonal nature. Institutional power is largely power by association, and it would be unwise to discount it, so we will also look at some general principles you need to be aware of when gaining power by association.

Perhaps one of the most potent, and easily understood, forms of institutional power is the power gleaned from identity movements. The twentieth- and twenty-first centuries can be largely characterised by a rise in identity power movements. While identity politics, and the institutions that spring from them, might seem to be a hot-button issue of contemporary debate, these movements are older than recorded history. Identity is hardwired into the human genome and multiple fascinating studies in perceptual studies and even endocrine-behavioural research support this. The earliest recorded history shows that group survival and reproduction within groups was the primary value for early peoples. There's a fairly simple reason for this: every group takes on patterns of established norms for its success in the environment in which they find themselves living. Some are universal, while others become unique to that group in those circumstances. When survival is a concern, it is easier to attempt to thrive within groups rather than across groups. Humans are generally bad at surviving harsh conditions on their own for long periods and pre-agricultural life was anything but not harsh. Association by group and the need for group power is one of the oldest, not newest, components of the primate experience.

This, however, is only half the story. At the same time, in humans especially, individual innovation has always been a valuable contributor to group success. We are not collective-minded but find ourselves falling into specialities that all feed back into the group, which rewards us in turn if our skills are deemed valuable. What you see then is cooperation and care between members of the same group developed alongside the need to think and problem solve as individuals. Humans are a wonderfully complex mess in this way. It is why the smartest leaders and companies take into account both the larger aims of the collective and the nuances of the individuals who make it up. People are a blend of social, group-dependent primates and surviving individualists.

The human experience is to be constantly in flux between choosing the interests of others or the interests of oneself. Think of some of our favourite films or TV shows involving the concept of survival: the protagonist is a lone hero who proves his or her competence by making a series of individualist survival decisions. After a period of time, however, what happens? The protagonist ends up joining a group. Either they make it better or conflict arises because of their maverick, unconventional style. Some of the tension we find most compelling in drama is the tension between the individual and the community they are a part of. This is not just by happenstance: it strikes at the chord we all must grapple with in our day-to-day living.

Given this inherent individualistic component, it is not surprising to see people throughout history transitioning into other groups when they deemed it was necessary to their survival or that of their offspring, current or prospective. The idea of group transference is well documented across primates, not just humans. This shows that humans have an incredible ability to move across groups, but once in a group that offers safety and the ability to gain power, they become attached and devoted to that group. You can see this in people who are radically extreme in one group and leave it for a polar opposite ideology. What they don't lose, however, is their extreme fervency. People become protective of their group. They become skilled at defining enemies and threats to the collective. It is no surprise that enemies usually come in the form of another group of people. Differentiations based on identity are potent and, more often than not, lead to tragic and violent outcomes.

Both sides of the political scene today are in a flurry over identity politics, and this tension has certainly trickled down into many fields. This shows us, then, that there is a lot of power in identity movements in the form of institutionally granted power. An institution may be either an actual organisation or the power of association with a popular trend. Depending on your visions, this kind of power may seem extremely valuable or problematic. Navigating this milieu, a smart leader first recognises that the push-and pull between favouring identity as part of a group versus individual agency is hardwired into the human experience. It is an emotionally charged topic, especially today, but it's old news. This doesn't necessarily make it easier on you. You are dealing, after all, with primal elements of human hardwiring regarding safety and enemy-defining.

Just as discussing the morality of power doesn't help you as an individual leader who will have to use your own agency to make moral decisions regarding the use of power, discussing the morality of identity movements is of no use. Some identity movements do good things for society, while others create the most unspeakable atrocities. Regardless, the power given to individuals from identity movements moves in trends. Today the dominant presence of social media and its inconceivable access to immense numbers of people can magnify this delineation of power so much more. As a leader looking to gain power, where you fall in the spectrum of the current popular identity trends will determine what sources of immediate, easy power might be available to you. If a group you can identify or claim association with is gaining momentum, then there is power on offer. You won't be a fool to take advantage of it, but neither are you being foolish to tread carefully. Institutional power, no matter how benevolent it may appear, often comes with hidden costs.

The first challenge you would want to analyse is what to do when social power due to an identity is on offer to you. Do you use your identity to gain such power, as a part of your leadership profile? What if you want the power but are hesitant to commit to the dogmatism or rhetoric around the cause? There is an honest truism when attempting to glean power from institutional association or membership and that is you don't necessarily have to believe in the rhetoric to reap the rewards. You just might have to convince others that you do. When the trend fades, as they all do, you no longer need to make the rhetoric a part of your verbiage in your exchanges with certain like-minded individuals.

Before some jump the gun and accuse me of advocating dishonesty, I think there is a reasonable middle ground for this argument. Obviously it is better and easier to believe in the tenets and underpinnings of a movement you are a part of. It is far more challenging to authentically and publicly support ideas while being a sceptic or contrarian at heart. It is really about balancing two dynamics: people need to believe in a group, and so more belief rather than less reassures them of their safety in the world. People also need to take care of themselves as individuals. Gaining power is a smarter way to ensure long-term survival than having no power, especially for one with leadership aspirations. Sometimes this involves being a part of a group temporarily while making plans to set off on your own course eventually.

To be clear, I am not encouraging you to be a wolf in sheep's clothing, but if there is some easily accessible social power available to you that deep down you doubt, remember that keeping a degree's distance can have its advantages. If a group or movement is easily accessible and simply by nature of your political leanings, physical characteristics, philosophy, personal preferences, so on, it can gain you power to achieve your personal vision, by all means make use of those resources. They are easily available to you for a reason and therefore meant to be utilised. Likewise, when the trend fades you won't be penalised for having made use of it, which is different than the scenario we are about to explore.

That second scenario you want to ask about is the flip side. What do you do if you're the odd one out? Social movements, especially about identity, thrive on defined enemies. Let's say you're on the antagonistic end of the current largest social movements, and your views or physical characteristics are deemed detrimental to social health. What do you do then? Oftentimes contra-movements will spring up in response to current identity movements. When people feel attacked they tend to bond together based on the traits they are being attacked on. These group bondings can turn into grassroots movements of their own. There is still some, albeit much less, identity power on offer through associations with these groups or organisations. Do you take those resources then?

There may be exceptions, but the short answer I would recommend is no. If you're seen as the enemy of a powerful social group, this may be the time to go under the radar. Unless you firmly believe in them, in which case you aspire to be a leader within them, joining contra-identity movements runs the risk of tarnishing your reputation in the present and future and makes you an easily identifiable target. You don't have a powerful institution to protect you. It is better, then, to seek like-minded individuals and build powerful interpersonal relationships. This is what you could call guerrilla identity power. Even between individuals there are fewer things more potent than the shared experience of feeling oppressed. If in the popular social scene you find yourself unfavoured on the basis of identity, you can still use this to your advantage in smaller, interpersonal power exchanges that will add up to meaningful relationships and powerful allies. When the heat dies down, or you have amassed enough power to weather it, you will find yourself ready to move with a strong base of support.

This might also sound like capitulation, and to an extent it is. You have to decide what is more valuable to you rather than what anyone else insists must be valuable. If you are a leader, and have a personal vision that must be made real, and find yourself unfortunately having immovable unfavoured traits in the current social trends, then sometimes adaptation and guerrilla tactics are your best allies. It comes down to your discretion and trusting your instincts over and above all.

This kind of dilemma brings us to the real questions and pitfalls with institutional power or power by association. Do you go with the group and gain great power, or if on the outs, do you gain power under the radar until circumstances change and you have enough power to move forward? It will depend entirely on the times you live in. The overall important thing to note about identity power is that it is easy power that is entirely circumstantial. It is, in terms of effort expended to attain it, a cheaper resource, and cheap resources come with a few drawbacks. First, it is highly transitory: rapid power gained from making use of institutional power is circumstantial and ebbs and fades, sometimes rather quickly. In today's times, we see this when seemingly overnight organisations grow to be extremely powerful on the basis of representing a critically important identity or movement. They stay extremely powerful until the social conversation shifts to another group or situation. Though they remain active, funding and attention to these organisations gradually or severely lessens, and so the loudness of their media voice diminishes. Part of this is the reality that people on social media heed the call of the newest trend or cause, and thus the topic of yesterday weakens and diminishes based on the hot new topic of today. To many of these social influencers, if you reminded them of the old cause, they would think, 'Oh yeah! It feels like one day we just stopped talking about it! Whatever happened to [insert world's most important problem of last week here]?'

Again, my intention is not to make light of the important problems society is trying to tackle but to make you aware of the quicksand dynamics that are a part of them. Enter too late into an identity power scene and you won't reap any fruits. Likewise, gain great amounts of power and don't use it to build stronger, less fickle forms of power, such as relationships or cross-group alliances, and you too will find yourself faded out and struggling to be relevant. This might sound pessimistic or cynical, but it is instead observing natural dynamics without the moralising. Both good and evil come from identity power movements, and all movements ebb and flow. The constant is the power that drives both. What is the good and evil of today is a conversation for another day. The power is what is relevant to you. Long-term, sustainable power is what is most relevant. It is very challenging, if not impossible at times, to get this from popular social movements and institutions. Institutional power is by nature a risk-reward: sometimes high rewards but always with long-term risk.

The larger take-home is that power gained from identity movements or institutions in general needs to be replaced with stronger forms of power that become self-sustaining. When the movement fades or the institution weakens, you already need to be engaged with new projects and cooperative endeavours closer to your individual visions. Another, albeit smaller, consequence is that institutional power, particularly the kind predicated on social combat, might make you a great deal of enemies. Enemies in your journey as a leader are not in themselves a bad thing, but they must be carefully managed. Make too many too early and you will find yourself having to expend a great deal of power on damage control and preserving previously strong alliances and relationships, making (probably fewer) newer ones in place of the ones that disintegrate due to external pressure from your enemies. The short-term power you gained up front might end up setting you back for a longer period of time, costing you precious resources and blocking opportunities for advancing your vision. Leaders making use of the power of social movements need to be extremely careful about this and take care to prevent it from hindering them in the future. Most people get the luxury of not needing to think about the long term, but the long term is the primary concern for you. Diversify your power as quickly as you can so you can survive when the tide goes out and all the others who took the easy meal and did not think about its future consequences are washed away.

Forward Motion

What we have gone through are many elements of three components of leadership: vision, technique, and power. Underpinning all of them are philosophical standpoints supported by what I think are good examples and evidence. Leadership involves your internal vision being made specific, the successful acquisition and management of power to implement it, and the ability to endure while it takes shape and form. Agree or disagree, or reserve your opinions for now, either is fine – what is important is that we are both now aware of the foundations I am basing the training on. What's that, training? Yes! It is time to begin making many of these abstract ideas, as well as ones to be introduced down the road, concrete.

Now that we have looked deeply into the interpersonal dynamics of power, it is time to begin the journey that gives you the necessary leadership skills to profit successfully from many power exchanges between people. Wherever you are in your leadership journey, these drills will make you better at whatever you're doing. That may sound counterintuitive, but very quickly you'll see the applicability across bodies of experience and wherever you are in a hierarchy, if in one at all. Instilling in you a charisma and magnetism that many might not have noticed in you before, as well as making you a razor-sharp observer of other people, is one rather immediate benefit. You will become more exciting to watch. People who are exciting are already worth paying more attention to. Later in the journey the rewards become deeper and richer.

My goal with this work is to aid you with strong tools to help you become the leader you envision for yourself. No one path offers the complete package, and I do not claim it here, but these are strong concepts that I believe will put you far down the road for the time you spend on them. They don't take years to show rewards. The benefits come quickly, and the time you keep putting into them multiplies them in dividends. You will also develop a solid internal monitor for when you have had enough training and when a tune-up is needed. Self-reliance based on personal experience is one of the more powerful tools you gain from this training.

The exercises and the skills instilled run deep. Though the structure of the exercises will be similar, the feedback in this training is as well highly individualized, and you will see this reflected in future chapters. As a result, be prepared when you engage in it yourself to encounter your own personal obstacles to leadership. We won't be taking the psychologist's standpoint and investigating your past and childhood for where these barriers come from, but instead we will be looking at how you can identify them in the present and manage them and then move beyond them. As I have said, this is not a self-help book. It is a book on leadership and a reliable method for training it.

The starting point in this training begins with a concept that forms the entire backbone of everything worth doing in your life: investment.

LIVING TRUTHFULLY

Chapter 3

Investing: The Beginnings of Everything

A Complex Puzzle

Before we begin the training, it is worthwhile to say a few things about the exercises in this book and some of the requirements around them. Structuring the exercises is vital to the learning, and so I will be providing this type of input throughout the book. Since this chapter is where I would begin a class, workshop, or coaching session, here is an excellent place to set some basic parameters to help give you a sense of how to encounter these exercises on the page, as well as what to expect from the training itself.

You may have noticed that I haven't yet said much about the origins of the exercises I teach. For context and clarity, we will go into it here a bit, but I won't spend too much time on it. The reason for this is that these exercises are modified for the purposes of training leadership skills. They originate in a technique created for performers called the Meisner Technique. The Meisner Technique, pioneered by Sanford Meisner in the mid-twentieth century, boasts an impressive clientele of some of the world's most renowned actors. Personally I have thousands of hours of training in it as an actor; I learned under two of the world's leading Meisner experts, did my master's thesis on it, and have experience teaching it around the world and across many cultures and countries. An extensive area of my research in the technique has been using it specifically for business and leadership training. The technique forms the core of my broader research interests and frames the values that I think are most crucial for professional actors and, in your case, leadership.

That said, there are a fair amount of experts in this technique. When I was living in London, one of the more common jokes I used to hear was, 'You could throw a brick in this town and you'll hit a Meisner teacher.' Unfortunately, we now have to add in a variable that complicates things quite a bit: most of the varying approaches to the Meisner Technique do not agree with one another. There may be some basic, shared fundamentals, but when it comes to the nuances, where it really counts, about how the concepts should be executed beyond a certain level of proficiency, the differences and the problems that stem from them start and only continue to magnify.

I bring this up because if you find you like this work, discovering in practice its relevance to your leadership journey, the temptation may be to go and take a class in the Meisner Technique. I can't discourage you, but I can say from my experience that studying with one expert who produces stunning results and then going to the class of another who gets equally good results will baffle you: the exercises share some basic concepts, but they are largely different. The feedback is structured differently. There is barely a common thread connecting them. The 'why' and reasons behind this are a dense set of weeds that we do not need to get into for one simple reason: you're not an actor, so reconciling the differences between Meisner authorities is not relevant to your journey, work, or process. From my own deep understanding of the work, I have extracted some concepts in the training and modified them so that they may be more applicable to you as a member of a field in the business world. You are not an actor, and you have different needs.

For this reason, I caution you about going to find a Meisner coach, class, or teacher to develop your leadership skills. This is not a pitch to work only with me – quite the contrary. I want you to get different bodies of exposure, but there is a difference between challenging yourself in the right way with conflicting views versus encountering total confusion. If you like this work and want to study it elsewhere, go for it – but understand you might have a relevant, excellent experience and you might not. The difference can be vast. You will be most likely working with a class designed for the needs of actors. They cross over sometimes onto the needs of leaders, but they will not be focused solely on leadership development. Words will be different, exercises will change, and rhetoric and theory may be contradictory. For just about every Meisner teacher out there, there are that many different ways to teach the subtler elements of the technique.

While for actors this can be enriching and valuable, for non-actors looking to gain the practical benefits of this training for their own field, this variability can become confusing and not a helpful use of time. You will find yourself having to reconcile the arguments about a technique to make sense of them rather than just using its core principles for your own needs. Even more problematic, the Meisner teachers are not all created equal, and so the quality of teaching vastly differs. This can translate into poor pedagogy (the *how* something is taught), convoluted instructions, and feedback that throws an individual off their course and costs them valuable time. I'm going to be blatantly honest: among most Meisner teachers, there is a culture of being a huge asshole to your students. It is bothersome, unnecessary, and for a non-actor provides just one more variable that can interfere with your learning.

Recognising these problems I have done my best to attempt to solve them. I do not want to be the only authority who can create and structure these exercises and experiences for you. These exercises can be used successfully with some guidance. What do you do, after all, if you already have a coach you trust and want to incorporate some of this work? They might be brilliant but not versed in it. I want to help that scenario, so for coaches, in all chapters with specific exercises I will provide a section (normally at the end) for feedback and guidance on how to successfully ensure your clients are getting the most out of these exercises. Reading these short sections, titled 'Tips for You and Your Coach', will also give you, the student (I again humbly recognise your expertise and use the word 'student' in the honourable sense of the word: as a learner of a specific skill set to aid your expertise, not detract from it), a sense of what to look for in a coach using this technique. This work is powerful, and I want to help both coaches and their clients use it for their needs. I am not the only expert on this, and I make mistakes too. For coaches who want to use this work, I have done my best to include tips and ideas for how to make the most of these valuable exercises for leadership.

The Law of Three People

Now we have to talk about the major hiccup of this training. Think you can just do one-on-one time with a coach and learn how to be a better leader? Not using this work, and I would argue you can't in general. This advice eschews much of the business and leadership coaching 'wisdom' out there, but I stand by it. Leadership, with its unique focus on power dynamics between individuals, is interpersonal. With rare exception, the majority of leadership training cannot be done alone. In addition to you, there needs to be two other people present at all times: one person to give the feedback (usually your coach) and at least one other to work with you. Contrary to some 'wisdom' among Meisner people, these exercises, even in their modified and adapted form for non-actors, should not be done alone between two people without a witness to moderate. Every successful coaching session in this work involves at least (ideally more) two people to work and one person to coach. Three minimum, not two.

I agree with what you probably just thought: this complicates things. There are, however, some vital reasons for this law of three people. First, the success of these exercises comes from immersion, from doing things in an organic, experiential way that does not allow you any time during the exercises to assess and analyse. This means that if you are doing this work well, you will find it very hard to remember clearly your own experience in a detached, clinical way. This is because being absorbed in the work between you and another person, you will be far more likely to recall what the other person did than what you did. For reasons you will see soon, this is not only normal but indicates you are working on leadership skills in a healthy, strong way.

The drawback is, having no frame of mind or reference for how the exercise went, you will be a poor judge of both your own work as well as your partner's, especially when it comes to the areas that need improvement. Another great theatre practitioner, Jerzy Grotowoski, put it this way: 'You cannot be inside of an experience and outside of it at the same time.' In fewer areas of learning will this hold more true than here. If it helps, consider that your daily, personal experiences confirm this: you cannot be deeply engrossed in an activity and in your head appraising it at the same time. You might be able to go back and forth, but you cannot do both at the same time. In an immersive experience the 'feelings' you have at the end of the work between you and your partner might not reflect accurately the objective nature of how the exercise went. Attempting to do both at once is an unnecessary (and impossible) burden placed on you, and we need to alleviate that.

The very simple solution, then, is to have somebody on the outside, a competent witness, who can give you and your partner feedback on what happened in the exercises. This removes the unnecessary pressure created by asking you to throw yourself into something and then reflect correctly on its success. Many coaches, however, believe they can take on both the role of coach and training partner. Their mentality is that they can work with you in any partner-related exercises and give you feedback on your performance at the end. It is true that technically they can accomplish this, but the seeming convenience betrays a major trade-off. That tradeoff is that a coach cannot be assessing you in an exercise and also be fully immersed in the exercise with you. There are some Meisner teachers who disagree with this and love to work with their students in exercises, appraising the quality of their work at the end. We are going to revisit this situation shortly, but for now I highly caution you about working with any Meisner teachers or coaches in general who claim this is a smart way to success. Almost always the weak results in their clients reflect this basic error in thinking.

The second reason we must respect the law of three people takes us back to the idea of a partner, who as you will discover is a crucial element to your training. If this is the case, however, it brings up a genuine issue for some of you reading this book. Leadership coaches that I have spoken to often tell me that executives, as well as other people in leadership positions, have a hard time working with other people. They prefer the safety of a one-on-one experience. I recognise the problem but have bad news: anyone who tells you that meaningful, interpersonal leadership training can be accomplished by yourself is more likely appeasing your ego than being forthright. Many coaches are afraid to offend those who are paying them. Deep-down they know that it makes a world of difference to have another human being present in the room but will say that the same amount of progress can be made with just you and the coach. In any exercise involving interaction, they end up spending part of their time being a student with you and part of the time being a coach, thereby wasting a sizeable portion of the coaching session on misguided politeness.

As we hinted at earlier, in any kind of deep, meaningful training of leadership through inter-personal interactions, if the coach works with you in an exercise as your training partner, then they are just as clueless as you will be about how it went. On the other hand, if they are only half-working with you (spending the other half of the time in their head trying to assess the progress of the exercise), then you won't be getting the full benefit of an authentic human experience. Rather than being fully absorbed in the exercises with another person, and having it reciprocated, there will be an imbalance, and so the learning and educational value of the exercise itself will be greatly diminished or lost. It is an impossible double sword to fix.

I cited Grotowski due to his elegant wording of the phrase but there are also decades of research in perceptual psychology to back these claims up. You cannot be inside of an experience fully and outside at the same time. Anything else is half-doing and, as my Meisner teacher Larry once brilliantly said, 'If you are half-doing anything, you are not really doing anything at all.' Though well meaning, any coach who thinks they can do otherwise by being the training partner in sessions with you sets themselves and their clients up for failure. Either they lose an objective eye or they don't give their client the full experience. Three is not better than two for leadership or business training in general. It is essential.

The Power of Observation

The case for working with a partner goes beyond the inadequacies of the coach in the learning context. It has to do with the heart of what you are working on in itself. As we have explored earlier, leadership at its core is a series of successful interpersonal power exchanges. Build enough of these in an intelligent way towards a vision and you maximise your chances of being a successful leader. Interpersonal exchanges are experiential, dynamic, and chaotic things, filled with all the variables that emerge from the spontaneity of human contact. Even if you are working on something that is seemingly solitary, such as presentation skills, the audience will be throwing at you real-time variables to juggle. Changes in mood, tone, and so on. You might not be talking with them in conversation but you can still feel them and intuit the emotional temperature in the room.

Even if it is just you and a camera, there is still something experiential, and with the right mindset, interpersonal to work off of. Every exercise of value to a leader, then, with very rare exception, happens in concert with another human being. In the same way that three people is a minimum, four is better. To push my own envelope further, yes, I recommend that the best leadership training takes place in concentrated, small-group settings. Why? Because now you can sit at times and observe two other people in the same exercise receiving feedback on their process. You might not believe it yet, but I guarantee the problems they encounter will be eerily close to yours. This is not a kumbaya, 'Oh we're all in this together, let's hold hands' sort of message. Since everyone will be working on the same material group work gives you an opportunity to see essentially an extension of yourself in the training grappling with the same ideas and challenges but with the benefit of having the outside lens.

This osmosis effect, of watching and quickly adapting by learning from other people's errors, is one that is built into our genome and evolutionary success. It is a potent biological hack that has immense benefits. In every workshop I have taught, wherever in the world I was, the same phenomenon occurs: I will introduce an exercise at the beginning of the class. Pairs will then work on them and struggle. Questions will arise, feedback will be personally tailored to their individual challenges, and so on. All good so far. During this time, the people who hang back to go later, engaged in the watching of others at work, won't think any of this will apply to them. When we hit the second half of the class, however, something impressive happens. The latter students who haven't worked yet get up to do so and make none of the mistakes their colleagues made in the beginning of the class. By proxy, they seem to enter into the exercise at a more advanced level.

What's going on here? Do the best always save themselves for last? Not really. They still make plenty of errors, but they are more advanced than their earlier peers. By observing and learning they have bypassed some of the obstacles encountered by others in the beginning and are reaping the fruits. Minimum effort, maximum gain. Never underestimate the power of observation in the development of your own individual leadership process. Remember, before you arrived in the training session you already knew this: observing deeply has helped you gain insights and vision into your own field, leading to novel intuitions that you believe in and wish to see made into reality or further developed. You cannot apply that same depth of vision to yourself while you work, but watching other people do this work is just as good. Leadership is solitary but paradox is where this training lies. To train your individual qualities even better watch others doing the same thing you will be asked to do. Up to a large point, the more the merrier.

Solving the Challenge

I've set up an unfair framework for you. I've written now of all these leadership coaches who say that many CEOs, executives, managers, and so on don't want to work with others. In their well-meaning efforts to solve this issue, the coach makes themselves both the objective eye and subjective partner. It is a bad idea, but with largely kind intentions. Do I sympathise, however? Of course not. In my hubris, I say, 'Bah! This is ego coddling to the highest degree.' There is a reasonable element of truth within this. Some people do want to take a seemingly easier road, bypassing work with other human beings, and often they either gain nothing for their time or worse – develop bad habits that will have to be unlearned at a later time.

Yet for others these are not concerns without merit. Status and hierarchy in some companies means a great deal. People in higher positions are right to have concerns about exposing their flaws and weaknesses in front of others who follow their lead. Will it make them seem weak or reduce their authority? Despite the politically correct stance that you are allowed to be human, have flaws, be vulnerable, and so on, we can't dismiss at the outset that sometimes these are legitimate concerns. Though not always, interpersonal equalizing can lead to greater problems, disrupting leadership and making leaders seem weaker in the eyes of employees and colleagues. Just as dangerous is working with people from other companies or other branches. We want to say, 'Oh, can't everyone just get along?' Sometimes yes. But sometimes no. And this is arguably when a leader needs the most help.

There is another problematic component to the problem of a leader working with colleagues. If death by competition is a concern for a leader when working with others, the same can be said of death by altruism. Some of these exercises at times get confrontational. A leader who is concerned about the well-being of his colleagues might find it difficult to take attention off of them and their perceived discomfort. In the process, the leader does not focus on their own learning as an equal member in the process. Different cause but same problem: working with others you know, or have ties to, can hold back your leadership development.

Regardless of where the problem originates on these concerns, I have a simple position: while the skills of leadership are something I can help in developing, implementation of those skills is up to the individual leader and their intuitions. If somebody tells me that working in a certain way might jeopardize the stability of a group or organisation, then I would be a fool to dismiss the inner voice of a leader as merely giving in to resistance or overreacting. The coach's job then is not to criticise or insist they are right and the client wrong. A valid point has been made. Supporting and nurturing intuition is a very important part of the process in this work.

At the end of the day, however, we still need to solve the problem. How do we get the best of both worlds for you, to have you working on developing your leadership skills with others in an environment that does not jeopardise the stability of your current situation and meets your needs? While other coaches might have their own solution, I will offer the one I use when I coach: I bring in one or two actors. I don't invite my client to my acting classes if I am teaching them, as protecting anonymity might be another important part of that client's conditions. Instead, I bring the actor or actors to them. That way you can work on the exercises free of pressure and with skilled and talented people who can support taking you farther and deeper in the exercises. The benefit of working with professional actors on a modified acting technique is that often they will adapt sooner, enabling you to learn faster, than if you were working with non-actors. Watching two actors work, you will also see better examples and manifestations of the applications of this work for powerful leadership skills.

The environment this creates is a type of incubator where you can engage fully, leaving your concerns at the door, and obtain a better sense of your own progress. To me it is more optimal than working with non-actors, but the most important thing is that the necessary conditions for your learning and thriving on your current journey of leadership are being met. You can even have the actors sign non-disclosure agreements so everyone is discrete in the event anonymity if part of your learning conditions. That's it. Problem solved. For me, I have a list of quality actors to choose from who I know will bring out the best in a client without pressure or judgement. Working with these people on your leadership is a roller coaster of thrills and joy. I also tend to bring new actors every time so there is constant variety. It is one thing to test your skills on the same person, but it is another entirely to know you work solidly with different individuals and temperaments. For coaches it is quite easy if you live in a larger city to find actors versed in Meisner. Finding skilled ones is important, ones who are also flexible to these interpretations of the work, and it is far from impossible to do so.

The essential conclusion is if you think these exercises and concepts might be of value, then there is a way to make them work properly. Don't short-change yourself or try to shortcut the conditions of getting the training into your bones. It won't work. You have successfully applied strong strategies of advancement to your field. Applying them to yourself and your learning is equally valuable to your continued development in gaining power as a strong and able leader.

Let's start the work. For the rest of the book, I'm going to cast you as a client in a session. Sometimes I will script you as doing an exercise in the workshop, sometimes I will talk directly to 'you' the reader, and at others to hypothetical members to the class. Others? Yes. I write as if you are part of a group all engaged in training leadership. At the end of each chapter you will find a summary of the essential points of the session before the 'Tips for You and Your Coach' section that you can show the person who is coaching you. This is a deep, rich, and powerful journey. Let's begin.

Exercise: Investing in the Reality of Doing

I will now ask you to do something seemingly simple and easy. Grab a piece of paper as well as a pen. Find a place to sit rather comfortably so you aren't distracted by your physical circumstances. Set the paper and pen down. Get cosy. And listen. That's it: just listen. Do that for about 30 seconds to a minute. Now, on your piece of paper, write down all the things you heard. Yes, what you heard. No trick questions. No deep, creative, or clever answers needed. Leave your inner Hemingway at the door. Stupidly simple is not only good. It's great.

Here are a few examples of what I mean by stupidly simple:

A car going by
My own stomach rumbling
My knees cracking
The coffee machine
A bird outside my window
The air-conditioner
The sound of the light bulb
See? Simple. Write down as many as you can comfortably remember.

Now, looking at your piece of paper, I am going to ask you another question. You don't need to write down the answer. Just think about it. Here we go:

When you were doing this now, were you leading? Not leading as in leading the exercise, you obviously weren't, but in the moments when you were just listening, were you being what we could call a leader?

No, most people in the class respond, what a stupid question! After all, you weren't leading the exercise, therefore you weren't engaging in anything related to the art of leadership. Furthermore, there were no intentions on your part. No exchanges, interactions, etc. You had no plans, no objectives, and so without any conscious directing, input, or planning from you there is no way you were engaged in the art of leadership just now. The general group answer is a rebuking 'No': when you were sitting there in that moment, just listening to the sounds of your surroundings, you were doing nothing related to the art of leadership.

But hang on. A smaller minority senses a trap, and now they've got some questions and suspicions. Just because you weren't asked to lead the exercise does not mean you could not be working on some leadership skills. Leaders, after all, can be students when necessary, and so possibly you were working on your leadership in a different way by being a student. Not the strongest argument, for sure. But also consider you were present for the entirety, or at least part of, the exercise. Surely being present is an important aspect of leadership. You were also deeply listening and observing. For the contrarians, what's the evidence you were present and listening? You listed the things you heard. So now we've identified an interesting possibility, which is that even when you are just sitting and listening, you may be doing something that is quite commonly agreed is a valuable part of leadership.

Now the discussion is rolling. It can't just end at some abstract philosophical statement of being and being 'present'. There's something deeper here, and we revisit our initial disqualifying assumptions, such as the one that you did not have any intentions. That doesn't hold up so well any more. After all, in some contexts leadership doesn't depend on intentions or having a plan. Sometimes the greatest acts of leadership are spontaneous and in the moment. Other instances of leadership might involve allowing others to come to great conclusions under you, which is leading indirectly, and so your direct input is not always required as a leader. Just because you were sitting there being present doesn't mean you weren't working on another core aspect of leadership, which is being open. Great leadership does not always have to be dependent on your planning or giving commands; it can be greatly affected by your openness to a situation. Now just as most began to argue 'no' on reasonable grounds, the smaller minority starts to argue 'yes' on equally reasonable grounds. Through a simple act of mindful sitting you are working on presence, listening, and openness. These are powerful tools in leadership.

What this simple exercise shows us is that we often take the complexities of leadership for granted. True, leadership is a difficult undertaking. But even the most complex manifestations have simple roots. Here, our seemingly complex relationship to something like leadership is challenged by even a simple act of listening. It shows us that even basic actions cannot be carefully slotted into what does and does not constitute leadership, implying that even the best leadership might be a collection of simple components that interact dynamically rather than some complicated mystery.

The punchline often disappoints everyone: both sides of the debate are correct. No, it wasn't the whole package of leadership. We all know that. For our purposes, however, yes, you were being a leader, even when you were seemingly doing nothing but listening. Now, to be certain, you weren't doing the entire thing, but it's day one and step one. What you were doing, however, is engaging with what is at the heart of great leadership, and that is a very good step one. In acting, we call this 'investing in the reality of doing'. What we mean by this is that when you were listening you weren't pretending to listen (if you did, you played a clever mind game but missed the entire value of the exercise), nor were you indicating listening through gesture or mimicry. You were simply listening, and the hypothesis goes, had a camera been on you, capturing you listening, or had you been in a live setting with an audience, you would have looked remarkably like you were listening. This may sound simple, but there is an incredibly potent concept at work here.

Investing in the reality of doing carries within it a level of authenticity. By investing fully in the task of listening you were able to bring 100% of your authenticity to what you were doing. How do you know that? Because you wrote things down. It may be a silly metric, but it's a good one. Authenticity is a loaded word, abused often among self-help gurus and coaches, usually with the implication of pushing you towards the attainment of some meditative, mystical state of being. That is not where we are going. Contrary to those hollow claims, we have already started to introduce the idea of authenticity as something incredibly simple, easily attained, and grounded in measurable experience. Sitting in a chair and writing down sounds you hear might appear strange, and that's fair enough, but the authenticity that it provides a glimpse of is a quality in a great leader that few can turn their nose up at. For a leader, having the reputation of being authentic carries with it a great deal of power. Our starting point is not with your leadership as some false persona, or something to be crafted, but instead as something that builds on the richness of your human experience without pretence.

If you go back to all those infamous 'skills building' sessions with other coaches, the emphasis being on your crafting a perfect, polished, and entirely inauthentic version of yourself, this approach marks a huge departure from that model. Consider, after all, that in most presentation and negotiation training, leaders are often taught how to stand, move, gesture with their hands, project their voice, time facial expressions as well as jokes, intonate, and so on. These are all incredibly effective ways of robbing you of your authenticity, making you into a cardboard cut out of a human being. The specifics of why this is the case is something we will get into in later chapters, but for our purposes here, all of these prescriptions for how to behave become a metaphorical giant paintbrush that coats all of your human dynamics into a narrow representation of you. You'll gain confidence, but the trade-off is massive and not worth the small boost of feeling better.

Anyone can offer a prescriptive formula for how to have better leadership skills. The argument is that by following the formula you will slot yourself into an acceptable way of being, implying there is a standard way a leader behaves and expresses themselves. We are going to defy that conventional, deeply held wisdom and start instead with your authentic self. We are going to base this decision on the argument that leaders are dynamic individuals whose humanity, both enlightened and flawed, makes them incredibly magnetic. There are many examples from history to back this up, which we will explore in the future. Sitting in a chair and listening is no big deal, but when we say start your work as a leader with investing in the reality of doing, of really giving your time and attention to something, we are already starting to coax out the fundamental qualities in you that make you exciting and powerful to watch.

The Trouble With Counting Bricks

Let's build on this some more. You won't need your pen and paper for it, so you can put those aside. Choose a simple task and do it. Avoid anything complicated or cerebral like writing something densely creative or thinking about a complex problem. Just something simple and physical. The classic example in the acting world is counting bricks, so if you have some nearby then pick a wall, or section of wall, and count the bricks. That's all you have to do. Just count. If there aren't many count them all, and if there are a great deal stop after a few minutes. All you are being asked to do is invest in the reality of doing by counting bricks.

In a group session, people do these one by one with the rest of the group witnessing. Some people at this point try to get clever, shortcutting the counting by multiplying or making groups. Let's say one of the classmates tasked with counting bricks does this very thing. He notices the bricks are aligned in rows of ten and he counts the top bricks and comes up with 60. See how quickly his thinking tries to get in and help? And it would be a great strategy if that was the task, but it wasn't. This person was not asked to multiply bricks, just to count them. Instead of going one by one, he implemented a strategy to shortcut the process. Why might someone try to make something so simple more complicated? There are two possible reasons.

The first is that this student might think I, the coach, am withholding some information. This is a trick, he thinks, and he wants to get a jump-start on me before I pull the rug out from under his feet. It's inaccurate but fair enough. Unfortunately, this is learnt behaviour. Most teaching and coaching is done by withholding information. You are asked to do something, you do it, and what do you know, the coach surprises you with that 'one thing' you did not consider or think about. It is a silly and cheap trick to establish hierarchy, but it does have one benefit for the insecure coach: a little humiliation is excellent for crowd control and asserting dominance.

You will find that a common theme throughout this book will be exposing the habits of the bad teacher or coach. Consider it a type of self-defence training to save you time and money that may be wasted on charisma or posturing masking incompetence. Pedagogies (styles of teaching) of bad behaviour and chest pounding waste time, and they don't perform better than ones where the tone of the room is honest but comfortable. Horror stories of previous clients, however, compel me to declare it: there is zero benefit to working with someone who uses bad behaviour, bullying, or humiliation as part of the coaching process. Yes, it is immoral, but it also doesn't work. In fact, it tends to make more trouble. Coaches may get an immediate result from the student, but down the road the student becomes more resistant to the constant berating. The dose then has to be increased, and the cycle continues.

I have also met students who like this style and insist they aren't learning from me until I best them or beat them down, accusing me of coddling and handling them with kid gloves unless I behave in a way that in any other context would merit accurate and fair accusations of being a real asshole. So let me be clear. The optimal tone of the room is one of honesty but also a constantly controlled comfortable emotional temperature. Don't spend time, effort, or energy with a chest-beating coach, and if you are a student who insists I perform like a gorilla on a bad day for your neurotic relationship to learning, find a different coach. Back to our original question – that is reason one why some people have trouble just counting the bricks.

Once we remove the issues of a teaching style, the second reason, far more relevant to the leader's process, arises. Let's go back to our brave classmate who chose to multiply instead of just counting. I suspect, if you really delve into the root of his reasoning, the core of it has to do with boredom. Boredom? Yes, not his, of course, but rather a concern with boring the audience. We know it's an exercise, but let's be honest: who really wants to watch someone count bricks? To that student I might say they are right. What happens, after all, when the audience gets bored? That is when the deeper motives start to be revealed with a little gentle prodding. The 'concern' for boring your audience is not an altruistic effort for us but rather a response to the pressure that comes from being scrutinized and observed by others. Consider that in our mock class we have changed the dynamic. No longer do you have the safety in numbers that comes with a group activity like with the first exercise. Now it is just you out there being asked to be authentic while being scrutinized by a group of strangers. Even a task as simple as counting bricks can bring up a strategic response to solve the pressures of being the target of observation.

Counting bricks. Another stupidly simple exercise. And yet it has exposed something everyone in the room can relate to: it is one thing to have charged ideas, concepts, and impassioned visions running through your head. You tell yourself, 'Yes, it is time to go and win the audience!' You swallow fear, cross your personal Rubicon into our field of vision, and suddenly you feel it: you are now being observed and watched. The room is quiet. The visceral truth begins to sink in: fewer people are under more scrutiny than leaders. Tension floods in as your adrenals and hypothalamus get busy sending out the danger signals. Your nervous system responses are now overriding your genius intentions. In psychology, this is called the Hawthorne effect, where being observed can derail even the best of your intentions. This is why in your training we are starting simple. If even a rudimentary task like counting bricks can bring out irrational, shortcutting defensive strategies, I don't think we're going to fare much better starting with more complex tasks like speeches or negotiating.

If you think about the implication of this, you'll find that reality has just created a giant pain in your ass. We began our session with this brilliant idea proclaiming great leadership begins, at its core, with investing in the reality of doing. Forget all the phony stuff, I claimed, and be you. Be authentic and messy and human and we will love it. Don't bother with personas or crafting falsities. Let's start with authenticity. We go into the very first basic exercise and suddenly, as with all great ideas, reality throws a wrench in the path.

I write this somewhat tongue-in-cheek, but the pressures from others is no joke. It brings up a massive fear response that can override a lot of important cognitive processes. If we don't face it head-on, or if we pretend it isn't there, we are setting you up for failure. Most people, if the statistics are accurate, would rather jump out of an airplane, run through a blazing fire, and be bitten by a venomous snake than speak in front of other people. It is a deathly terrifying concept, and from even the first session we need to begin working on how you can successfully invest in the reality of doing in front of others, and from there how to build onto that more complex tasks, all without compromising your authenticity. We need a solution to the audience and we need it fast.

Several options present themselves. First, we'll look to several conventional approaches to coaching and mindfulness training. Let's see what they've come up with. Both involve the same underlying concept: pressure from the audience can be solved by your conscious means. The claims state that these conscious means, when trained properly, can be so powerful that no matter how great the pressure from the audience, or the nervousness it produces, we can stay mindful, present, and calm. Breath and vocal work is a very important aspect of this type of training. Knowing how to use your diaphragm prevents the tightening that occurs in an anxiety response. As well, the open diaphragm allows your voice to generally be much more powerful and have more presence, which will boost your confidence. If these approaches have their way, your ideal look as a leader then is a calm, rational, and mindful type of presence, ready to coolly handle any challenge thrown your way while still keeping the occasional humorous moment. Congratulations, you are a living TED talk.

While it sounds impressive, a few flaws begin to present themselves when you start following the logic. I've got no personal gripes about mindfulness. I've been a practitioner for more than a decade and consider myself blessed to have worked with some of the great teachers in it around the globe. But would I say it is an optimal strategy for handling the pressures of observation? Absolutely not. Your brain is clever. It is sensitive to threat responses. A bit of neurology shows that there is an interplay between two parts of the brain, the hypothalamus and amygdala, in distress signals and threat detection. A consequence of severe anxiety is suppression of your prefrontal cortex, responsible for rational decision-making. Take the scenario in which you've just detected a threat response. You check in and breathe through it. You feel further tightening. What have you just done? You have just sent the signal back that yes, there is a valid threat response. The body responds by releasing more glucocorticoids, stress hormones, into your blood. In that same situation the next time you try to use your calm, rational, process it's going to make it harder, agitating your nervous system more.

As you are continuing to sing namaste to your navel, you'll notice your tension and physiological responses continue to increase. Putting more attention on yourself in the midst of a danger response only reinforces to the primal parts of your mind that there is a reason the environment is producing this response. Your body isn't stupid. Your sudden switch into deep, diaphragmatic and entirely abnormal breathing (compared to how you normally breathe) can become a cue for your threat response to increase, not decrease. It senses there is a reason you are desperately trying to remain calm.

You can see a similar reversal when it comes to the idea of 'warming up', which in this approach involves doing lots of breathing and vocal exercises before you go in front of an audience. Results in training sessions can be impressive: after about 30 or 40 minutes, when you have had a chance to get comfortable with the group you are working with and can relax more naturally, you will find yourself as resonant as John Gielgud and able to do entire paragraphs on a single breath. You learn how to condense these results into a shorter, pre-event warmup.

Outside of the sessions, reality reveals something different entirely. Now able to leap the vocal equivalent of tall buildings, you warm up, go straight in front of an audience, and promptly your body will forget most, if not all, of what you did in your warm-up just minutes before. Your tension comes right back. Your voice returns to a tight, higher register. Why? Your body is very smart at being incredibly specific about context. In a context with a threat response your body is going to instantly adapt. This is unconscious: you don't get to tell your adrenals when to pump cortisol into your blood or command your hippocampus at will in the face of a perceived life-threatening situation. Before context hits our awareness our body has already sprung into action and that's the point. I cannot tell you how many times I have seen this happen to hundreds of actors, who sometimes spend hours warming up and then stand there with a deer-in-the-headlights look, wondering why all their pre-show yoga frog poses and recitations of *Charge of the Light Brigade* did nothing as soon as they walked onto the stage or the director called 'Action!'.

A personal experience of mine illustrates this quite well. I was living in Tokyo, in a quaint part of the city called Saitama. Saitama was then, and I am sure still is, a lovely set of quiet suburbs, filled with peaceful streets, spacious schools, stunning architecture and old houses. Even at one in the morning I could walk from Nishi-Kawaguchi station all the way through it and arrive at my apartment complex feeling completely safe. Until one night, just before midnight. I was on the way home from a hot yoga class, as relaxed as could be. About 200 yards from my apartment, for no clear reason, suddenly my hair literally stood on end. I felt a gripping worry in my stomach and without even realising it my hands had begun to open and come near the lapels of my coat, ready to call on my mediocre martial arts training and to strike and fight violently for my survival. Against what, though? It was a primal response I had absolutely no reason for, and for the life of me I had no idea where it was coming from, especially given these kind of hyper-defensive responses are totally uncharacteristic of me. Until I looked to my right and saw the two men approaching me. I could not make out their faces but as soon as I made eye contact they stopped and so did I. We hung in a suspended silence for a few moments before I began to walk forward, keeping eye contact all the while. I watched them with my reflexes keyed up, hungrily looking for the slightest movement. I could feel the same watchfulness reciprocated from them. They did not speak or follow, and I never saw them again.

That's the reality of biology we try so hard to deny. It's the reality we have to deal with. We are programmed to sense danger and we're reasonably good at it. At the end of the day I'll never know. Perhaps there was no danger. Perhaps it was my aggressive response to them that put those two on the same guard. Or maybe there really was a threat of mortal danger. Even you as a reader have probably just done it. The moment you read the line about the two men your brain put the pieces together and went, 'Of course, totally reasonable now.' But we'll never know. Right or wrong, my body was not going to take chances. By the time my mind had caught up with the situation I was already preparing not for an argument, or pushing some drunk guy out of my way with mild force, but for real, primal violence.

As I said, totally atypical, this reaction is one of only a few that has ever occurred in my life. For the hundreds of times I had made that walk to the thinking part of my brain it was always the same environment to me. That experience, however, drove it home: other sensory drives were far more sensitive and attuned to the environment, with an eloquent and razor-sharp precision my intentions could never hope to have. In less than a second all my loose, easy-going feelings were replaced by an existential threat response, all before I was even aware of it. That's two hours of well-received hot yoga that did not even last three seconds in that environment. We cannot underestimate the power of context.

So we have established that your body is much smarter than you are at perceiving threats. Barring of course overactive drives, such as those in people with anxiety disorders, this unconscious radar is generally a good thing. Unfortunately for your leadership training, your threat detection system also perceives the audience as criteria requiring an immediate threat response and acts accordingly. You can do all the warm-ups you want, but most likely they will go out the window the second an audience is in front of you. Your booming Gielgud voice will suddenly be cracking in the top of your throat and your open, loose diaphragm will be vacuum-tight in your body's attempt to keep everything as constricted as possible, protecting your organs for the inevitable ensuing fight and possible goring from the non-existent infuriated charging buffalo. When considering mindfulness, putting your attention on those sensations will only strengthen them. Any relaxation you do gain will only be after a while, when you have reduced your stress response naturally through time exposure, but this process is also largely unconscious. Everything will have been a bunch of ritual that wasn't needed at all, and none of it will solve the problem of the audience.

Perhaps there are some exceptions to this. For example, there are people who have natural protective mechanisms against threat response. These might be individuals with more resistant nervous systems, or damage to their hypothalamic or amygdalic responses, or whose adrenal glands naturally produce fewer stress hormones. There are often consequences to these traits, and one thing is certain: you can't re-hardwire massive amounts of biology like this through training. You can, however, reconfigure certain things, and this is where we get the more than 10,000 hours of meditators who can reduce their heart rate through conscious intervention. There is still a bottleneck to this, but more importantly: are you going to do 10,000 hours of meditation to get this effect? If you won't, fear not, this book is still for you.

If we depart from mindfulness, we're still left with basic questions related to the process. Take the oft-prescribed remembering to breathe recommendation, for example. It sounds reasonable. We know that if we don't breathe we generally get stressed, so common sense would imply it only follows to remember to breathe while in the middle of a huge stress response. It seems, however, that there are some issues even with this idea. One of the last things to develop in babies is the prefrontal cortex, the voice in your head that can say with Neil deGrasse Tyson gravitas, 'Remember. Breathe.' By all reasoning, babies don't know how to consciously breathe. And many babies, even in non-stressful situations, are programmed to scream and wail in existential terror because their hardwiring has been created through generations of natural selection that metaphorically says, 'No nutrition or contact: no life. Scream to get what you want when you need something.' This is not to say that constant stress exposure doesn't damage infant health, it certainly does, but the point here is in the midst of extreme stress or their worst screaming fits, babies don't forget to breathe. As we get more developed, and we hope smarter, are you telling me we suddenly lose that capacity?

Well, let's test it and see if you did lose it in adulthood. You'll recall a few chapters ago I gave an example of walking and suddenly having a bird or branch fly in front of your face. You execute a complex series of avoidance manoeuvres without thinking about it and resume your walk. Your heart might be racing, but are you on the verge of collapsing from not having breathed? It seems despite all the complex claims and theories, you know how to breathe. In emergency situations your body knows what to do, including keeping you alive through oxygen intake needed for immediate glucose metabolism. That brings up a question for us when it comes to your leadership training: if you leave your breath alone will it take care of itself? We will have to wait for future exercises and training to get this answer in practice, but I'll give you the punchline here: yes.

Rival Solutions

We've done a good job of identifying the problem of the audience. We've also done a generalised sweep of some of the larger 'tried and true' solutions that more conventional approaches to leadership coaching offer. We can be snarky all day, but we still haven't actually come up with a solution to the challenge of the audience and the pressures they put on you. Since some of the conventional coaching wisdom isn't holding up too well let's turn to the field I am familiar with and see if actors have some helpful angles on the problem. After all, actors make their bread performing under the pressures of audience observation.

Not to pick on my fellow actors too much, but there are a lot of profoundly stupid ideas about how to solve the problem of audience-generated pressures. I won't go into them here – that's how confident I am that they don't apply to leaders, let alone the actors who devoutly believe in them. But there are a couple theories within the field worth investigating that can yield some potential solutions. Remember that our goal is to give you a strategy to deal with the audience in a way that facilitates the rich, individual authenticity good leadership is build on.

Without being too crass, here's the first solution I've come across in the acting world: fuck 'em. Just pretend the audience isn't there. You can accomplish this easily by envisioning an imaginary wall between you and your audience. On the wall you can mentally project various items, people and images that you speak to and imagine are there. This, the argument goes, will mimic the relaxed, uninhibited success you get when you rehearse speeches and presentations alone, since the audience will in one respect no longer be there. With their presence all but diminished or entirely eliminated through your cognitive gymnastics, you will find your anxiety retreating and your ability to be authentic returning.

At the outset it isn't an unreasonable argument: it is pressure from the audiences that robs you of your naturalness, and since we know people have an incredible ability to use imagination, employing this strategy to diminish the presence of the audience should see increases in authentic behaviour. This is called the fourth-wall technique and is the big fish of most acting approaches to dealing with this issue. It has a history of being vetted: many great actors across generations and mediums use it, genuinely believing it enables them to be successful. Long history and a big clientele list: you can't get more legitimate than that.

Since, however, history shows most sounds-good-at-the-time ideas are wrong, this is no exception. If using a mindfulness model is a standard-size bad idea, the fourth wall's scale equivalent is not the Titanic but the iceberg it struck. It is profoundly suboptimal and is often what lands a lot of trained actors in courses that don't utilise it or teach alternatives like the Meisner Technique. One positive word for the mindfulness approach is it at least is rooted in reality and acceptance. The fourth-wall approach, however, is about denying reality. If you couldn't fool your brain with trying to change its view of reality by working with it consciously then this really won't fly. Here's a simple question to get this conversation started: has a thought ever come into your head that you tried to not think about it? I'll use Daniel Dennett's brilliant example: try not to think of pink elephants. You hear it and find yourself already doing it. Damn. Well, try harder not to do it. Just keep trying and eventually you will reduce something that exists to a negative void.

You'll find the more you reinforce a negative concept (negative referring to something not there) the more it becomes there because you have chosen to make it an object of focus in the first place. Through constantly reinforcing the idea that something is not there, you begin to put the idea in place that it is there. If you're prone to being spooked or startled, the next time you're alone in a house and you hear something slightly strange, just try telling yourself: 'There's nothing there. There's nothing there.' See how well that works for your anxiety. A denial-based approach to reality is the best, most sure-fire way to kill the authenticity of a leader. It asks that you ignore so much about what is really going on with you, as well as the feelings you are getting from an audience. That connection to the audience is a valuable thing and losing it comes at a cost. Rewind that feeling of pressure that creates anxiety. At the core of it is a unique empathic response. You can *feel* an audience, you can feel being watched and studied. That is the reality you are living in: you are connected before you are aware of it. That is the one you have to work with.

Performing mental gymnastics ('don't worry', I am sure some fourth-wall naturalism experts will assure you, 'it gets easier with time' – yeah, right) to the level of denying a huge stimulus is an excellent way to send this message implicitly to your audience: 'I am not listening to you. You are not a part of this experience. The subtle cues and rhythms unique to your energy at this moment are not important. You might as well not even be here.' That's definitely not the smartest habit for a leader to adopt. We all know everyone likes to feel excluded from something they are meant to be a part of.

By your sending that message, it further alienates and irritates your audience. Sooner, rather than later, you are going to start feeling their resentment. At that point there will most likely not be anything you can do to bring them back to your side in the time you have remaining. Leadership, whether it is between you and one individual or you and 10,000 is a relational exchange. Do not begin putting up fourth walls and denying reality. It will not work and will cost you dearly. More importantly, keep an eye out for the subtle habits in yourself and the advice of other coaches who encourage this approach.

Does that mean our actors have failed us? No, and in fact, I believe they still have the answer. There is another school of thought on this issue that can aid the needs of leaders to be authentic while being observed. It is elegantly captured in a phrase that comes from the big fish in the actor training world, Konstantin Stanislavski. Sanford Meisner imported it directly into his work. The concept is called 'public solitude'. True to its name, it simply means to be alone in public. I'll give you an example of how this differs from the fourth wall: say you are driving and are stopped in traffic at a red light. You look over and see a woman (or man, let's not be too picky) putting on make-up. They know that they are surrounded by cars. Some cars might even contain people who are staring. In the mind of the make-up applier, those people exist but are simply not part of the experience of putting on the make-up. If the person applying the make-up happened to look to the side and saw someone attractive smile at them, they might smile back and then just as easily go back to their task of putting on make-up. At no point have they denied the existence of anybody or pretended they were not there (the fourth wall approach), they have simply not made anyone else a relevant part of their experience (public solitude).

Public solitude, then, implies a fluid, sliding-scale relationship between you and the audience. You are not alone, nor do you need to pretend to be. The audience is there, but they are simply not a part of what you are doing. You can feel them, however: their emotional temperature, the pressure they create, and the anxiety they produce. And guess what? You can take that on board. No need to run from it, and you can get on with what you are doing. To what extent you choose to include the audience or not will depend on the circumstances you are in and the necessary variables. The fourth wall approach closes down your range of experience. Public solitude opens it up. Working in this way, we accomplish two vital things: we give you the most freedom when it comes to dealing with the audience, at times allowing them to be a part of your experience, while at others not worrying about them. Second, we do not try to fix your feelings of pressure or anxiety. They come from the audience, who you are already tethered to. They are a part of your authentic experience. Our path ahead is to say, rather than transform or deny those paralyzing anxieties or fears, we want to train you in a way that you can use them as dynamic, powerful energy.

Public solitude is a healthy concept for a leader. It enables you to engage and invest deeply in whatever you are doing and not allow the audience to interfere with your leadership. They are now assimilated into your experience, and as such are no longer a problem. That clean integration will automatically reduce pressure on you since it will diminish both the irrational expectations on yourself and your over-appraisal of the audience's role. Rather than what you do being for them, they are simply a part your experience, to greater or lesser degrees depending on when you need them to be. In this way, the audience does not compromise your authenticity but rather is a natural element of your authentic expression. Do you see why, even from the first session with solitary exercises such as counting bricks, it is important to have other people present observing you to create those conditions necessary for you to deal with one of the biggest perceived challenges to most leaders' careers and to begin neutralising and integrating it? This is a massive benefit you will never get in just one-on-one coaching and supports our law of three people concept.

Now that we have introduced two concepts in theory, investing in the reality of doing and public solitude, and touched on them very briefly in practice, it is time to being training them much more in depth so that they will become a part of you as naturally as all that breathing you no longer have to worry about. This is the authentic foundation that you can hone your leadership technique on.

Summary

Great leadership is not rooted in a persona or character for you to play, a distorted version of yourself, but in you expressing your authenticity in whatever it is that you do. The heart of this is known as investing in the reality of doing, of giving yourself fully over and completely investing your attention in what is asked of you in the moment, neither pretending nor indicating. While it is easy to invest in the reality of doing when in a group or alone, i.e. unobserved, it becomes immensely challenging for most when observation by an audience, however great or small, is introduced. The audience for most people creates the deathly fears of public speaking; for a leader, however, audience observation extends even to how people watch you in interpersonal exchanges without a formal audience-speaker setting.

While there are several strategies for solving the 'problem of the audience' the most optimal is a concept known as public solitude, where the audience can at times be a part of your experience while at other moments they are not relevant to it. This fluid relationship reduces anxiety and pressure on leaders and is the healthiest approach to balancing authentic expression in front of others and, when necessary, including them. Both concepts are attainable and can be trained in the development of one's leadership technique.

Tips for You and Your Coach

The purpose of the first exercise is to simply generate a necessary and vital conversation about investing in the reality of doing, as well as to highlight that there is a power in starting with authenticity rooted in reality rather than persona or pretence. While every exercise we do seems simple, there is a deeper, often profound, idea underneath it that articulates and later solves the problem of the leader. In this case, the problem being voiced is answering questions such as what is the best place to work from? What is the foundation to base one's leadership on in order to gain power more efficiently in interpersonal exchanges, whether between one or many people?

The second exercise is a natural evolution of the first. Watch and look for signs of performance pressure. These could include, if counting bricks is the task assigned, indicators of counting (such as obvious nods or finger pointing done for our benefit), mathematical strategies such as multiplying, nervous laughter, and so on. All of these are indicators of the fear of boredom. Don't be afraid to ask if the volunteer could feel us watching them and if that might have impacted how they performed. Some students try to save face, acting like it is no big deal, but their body language might tell a different story. Be honest and direct, but remember some people are sincere and honest when they say that the pressure from the audience did not bother them or impede their task. In this case, bring up the idea of audience pressure as something most people go through. You will be surprised that some students at this point open up a bit and admit they were in fact feeling pressure from the audience. Regardless, even if the volunteer did not feel it, nearly everyone in the room can relate to these ideas. If you introduce the concept of public solitude and why it is a more optimal strategy than other approaches, such as mindfulness or the fourth wall, you will find the learning value of this exercise won't be wasted on the volunteer even if they did not feel audience pressure.

Throughout the rest of this book each chapter correlates to a single training or coaching session. The only exception is that normally the material and exercises in this chapter comprise the first half of a session. It can be the entire first session depending on group size and time allotted, but I recommend making it the first half with the material from Chapter 4 taking up the remainder of the time. This is because this chapter is much more cerebral and discussion-oriented than the rest of the work. This is a good thing. It breaks people out of the mould of waiting to engage until their own standards are met and gives them a dog in a fight they want to be vocal about.

Almost everybody has dealt with problems of being authentic in front of an audience, and almost all leaders who have done so are aware of how these challenges can compromise leadership abilities. This strikes right at the core of most people's problems. I have never seen lack of debate and conversation as an issue, and I don't think it will become one for you. Remind people, however, that this conversation is part of the structure of the lesson, and that the concepts of investing in the reality of doing and public solitude don't exist just as cerebral dogma. They are practical components that will be trained using practical exercises. They are not gospel that must be unquestioningly accepted but hypotheses to be tested.

The final tip in giving feedback on this portion, and the rest of the work, is that belief is never a requirement. As a coach, you can articulate your foundations and still support clients using this material even if they disagree with you. Who cares if they buy the theory so long as the material helps them? Managing disagreement is how you keep people in charge of their own process, so they always feel like they have ownership over their work. If people disagree, you can ask them to just try the approach and then they can decide whether or not it fits with their process. You are providing learning, not a belief system. Let your ideas and theories lead people to the best understanding of the material you can provide; share your conclusions, but at the end of the day let them own the ones that work for them. Ownership, you will find, is at the heart of what this work demands of you to instil in your clients.

Chapter 4

The River Between Two People

Creating Context

Thus far we have introduced several concepts unique to the leadership process. We began from the premise that if you track the course of great leaders throughout history, the successful ones never became a fixed point and remained ever evolving. This would imply that all great leaders are aspiring leaders. A technique for training leadership then, in theory, should be formed of concepts that can be applied to anyone at any stage in their career process. Since leadership is both a general state and target-specific, the concepts should be equally applicable to already well-established projects and endeavours and those green in their development. This flexibility across these areas becomes the testing ground that all concepts introduced in this training must survive on to be of value to you as a leader.

We have also introduced the notion that, at its core, leadership depends on power. The foundations of all power in leadership can be broken up into two domains: interpersonal and institutional. The relevant one we concern ourselves with is power derived from the interpersonal exchanges between you and another person. These add up into a potent force over time, are generally more reliable than institutionally granted power, and have the potential to lead you further to other facets of power, including resources and social recognition. When it comes to a skill worth developing as a leader, people are a first and utmost priority. More relevant than just people, however, are people with meaningfully invested attention. Rather than have 100 people generally interested in you, or you in relation to a social trend, as a smart leader you would rather take ten people devoted to the success of your vision. This was eloquently summarized in a quote by American Vietnam War General William Westmoreland. When asked about how he felt the North Vietnamese, fiercely devoted to their leader and his ideals, fared in combat, his simple answer was: 'I'd give anything to have 200 of them under my command.'

While power might be on the outs today, trendy and fashionable to criticise, powerful figures always have and always will captivate our imagination. Dynamic individuals who have a magnetism and charisma that doesn't seem forced, or part of an inauthentic persona, are people we want to associate with. They have a natural passion and warmth that emanates from them. Or they might be contentious, fiery, and intimidating. Either way, though we cannot put our finger on why, something about their path appeals to our own desires. We see in them the formula of success we want to be a part of. This brings us to an object of our training. It is essential that this electric power be a part of any leader who wishes to enlist the support of others to see their own personal vision fulfilled. In testing our ideas about leadership, we must also include this magnetism as an essential component.

In my field of acting, desperation is perhaps the most common ingredient to being a working actor. There are, however, a rare few who don't seem to have the weight of despair but a different quality entirely. Encountering such a rarity can change one's life. One of my earliest memories in the professional world is of seeing an actor do incredible work on stage. Meeting him afterwards, he had such a relaxed power radiating from him. He had that unique recipe for success, and when I spoke with him there was something about him that made me naturally want to be a part of his projects and to help him if I could. Perhaps without realising it he had qualities of great leadership. I wanted to be a part of his journey because I intuitively felt those clear markers of leadership from him. This was not a conscious decision from me. It was a pull that began before it hit my awareness.

Now here's the sad news. I cannot tell you what happened in the two years that we did not see each other, but I can say that when I saw him again something drastic had changed. He had begun to produce his own works in order to give himself more roles. While that may be controversial to some, I have no problem with that. Something, however, had shifted. His energy and interactions with people seemed more grasping. Needy and desperate almost. Something had gnawed at him and he had listened to it. Now the charismatic, radiant leader was replaced by a walking-talking sales pitch. Every time I now spoke to him I felt a hustling pressure, a forward energy too aggressive for what was being sent across by the people interacting with him, myself included. Once a compelling presence, now he repelled me, and I saw him do the same to others. After every chance meeting and run-in, I always felt covered in a kind of slime, as if he had not really spoken with me but used me as yet another soapbox to push his ideas and his needs. It also bled over into his acting. I saw less humanity and more caricature in his work. It has been over a decade and nothing has changed with him: he is still trying to hustle out of desperation, still trying to be the king of 'branding and pitching', and I am sure that for as many people as he enlists to help him, he pushes 100 away. I can write about it now, but in the beginning this repulsion was not conscious either; rather than the initial pulling-towards feeling, this organically became a pushing-away from sensation.

Cases like his are not unique. We have already examined the prudence of cautioning against desperation as well as the urge to do nothing but push your needs onto others. In the context of this session, the relevant thing is desperation destroys the authentic exchange between two human beings that gives leaders so much power. Great leaders, whether they are icons of compassion or prickly types, seem to have that magical ability: they can say nothing about themselves and somehow make you more interested and curious about what they do (and being a part of it) than if they had yammered for hours on and on about themselves. But what is going on? This points to something critical. If leaders do not draw in people on the content of words about what they are doing, there must be something preverbal that captures the wonder of people and creates that unconscious pull. This is what I mean by magnetism: before even seeking the interest of others, great leaders seem to have already found it.

On a brief side note, it is worth mentioning that while a good thing overall, drawing people to you has a small double edge. There are some people whose competencies, ethical deficiencies, and lack of loyalty you will not want anywhere near your work. If there is one person the desperate actor mentioned earlier would probably be a shark in the water for today, it would be someone with the charisma and power of an actual leader. You can't prevent those people from finding you; my general advice then, is to keep them far away from your own pursuits. The flattering attention will be detrimental in the long term. There will be those individuals, however, who will be valuable in supporting your leadership visions, whose willing investment of power into you will help forward you in the right ways. For them there will need to be something about you that draws them in even before you speak.

This brings us to where we are in the training. We have already introduced as our starting point the concept of investing in the reality of doing, the deeper idea behind it beginning from a place not of persona or spin but rather something human and relatable: individual authenticity. Already we are putting forth a testable hypothesis to increase a leader's power: if you fully invest your attention in something, not half-doing it, then for others observing you in full immersion with a lack of absent-mindedness, you become far more exciting than somebody who is just phoning it in.

We also introduced the tool of public solitude, the notion being that this is the most optimal way to manage balancing your authenticity with the pressures from other people observing you. Public solitude is a sliding-scale relationship where sometimes people are a part of your full investment in what you are doing and sometimes they are not. The percentage depends entirely on the situation and your needs in that context. We are going to begin today and onwards testing the idea that this, rather than fourth-walls or other avoidance strategies, is the premium solution for how a leader both deals with the pressures that emerge from being observed and uses them to full advantage.

The Human Target

Starting from today we are going to test these values and theories in a much more relevant way, asking what happens when you take this concept of authentically investing and apply it to an interpersonal interaction not with an object or yourself but another human being.' We all intuitively know it is possible to fully give your attention to another human being. We rarely ask, however, what's the big deal about that? Rather than getting on my soapbox about the loss of connection between humans today in the digital age, let's look at the current state of social interactions as an environmental shift that gives you a strong piece of information. Many prominent social and behavioural theorists recognise that as a species we are struggling to deal with the sudden and rapid influx of impersonal communication and social media technology that has, in many ways, changed the rules of cultural exchange. Despite the naysayers, I believe we will get a handle on these issues in the future, but for now there seems to be a legitimate stunting of interpersonal communication skills that is hitting younger generations harder than older ones. Rather than this being bad news, could this be an advantage for emerging leaders today?

In a world of likes, stories, double-taps, hearts, pins, pings, and all other social media jargon, it seems that what has become a rare commodity is attention. We hear about this across multiple domains. In marketing today there is a hyper-obsession with how to catch people's fleeting attention within a second or less. Relationship psychologists are also concerned with the lack of prolonged attention exchanges between partners. It seems that in this kind of an environment a leader who is able to pay attention and, more to the point, give somebody their full attention has a powerful and potent tool in their arsenal. To really see, recognise and be with another human being who lives in the same starved-for-meaningful-attention society you do is incredibly exciting for them. This is one of the best ways to gain power without much effort and only a little training.

Public solitude complements this notion perfectly. When you are investing your attention in somebody, rather than being constantly distracted by the compulsion to check your phone or divide your attention, you create the feeling that you two are the only people in the room, even if there are hundreds surrounding you. Down the road we will focus on expanding this model to include other people as well as tasks, but for now this is a profound idea to start exploring. If you have been filmed before you know there is a difference of intensity between the wider shots and your close-up. Most of us are treated, and treat other people, with wide or long-distance shots, either too afraid or uninterested to make closeness a priority.

In the close-up, however, you will find an immediate intense connection that gives you access to a person that most people ignore. Remember how we said it is important to appeal to the desires of others? Most people desperately want to be seen. Most of us feel like we are drowning in seas of indifference. Rather than complaining about this, a smart leader asks how to use this. Our current age acts as a kind of social alchemy, turning the silver-value of contact into gold. Invest fully in another human being, make them the full attention of your public solitude so long as it is appropriate (again, that differentiation comes later in the training), and you will see immediate openness and access. This already is a sign of being given power.

Now, it is time to test our theories and in doing begin to train these concepts and values deeply into you.

Exercise: You–You Repetition

This exercise begins with two chairs facing one another. Your coach and anyone else in the room should be seated in a position where they can see the two chairs easily. This is an exercise between two people where the rest of the members of the session will observe the partners at work. I'm going to make you one of the participants in the exercise. You'll sit in one of the chairs, and your partner for the exercise will do the same. This means you two are facing one another. A general rule for starting in the beginning is your knees should not be touching your partner's but there should be no more than a few inches between the two of you. What we are after is sort of a dynamic: the two of you are not touching but are in 'each other's space'.

What follows is the first hypothetical coaching scenario I have alluded to in previous chapters. These are distilled from lots of hours teaching this work. It doesn't mean this session always goes this way, but rather this is a generalisation of what normally comes up. Treat this as more like reading a novel or transcript. I want to give you, as close as I can, a first-hand experiential taste of what comes up in these sessions, and that's why I will often make use of this tool in future chapters. We did this a little in the previous chapter, but now we are moving forward with you as a scripted character in these sessions. Rather than trying to gleam how-to steps, look for what comes up in these exercises and how it does or does not fit into our values of leadership. This will start to give you a clear sense of the skills they introduce and develop where it counts: not in theory but in practice.

In the beginning, who begins the exercise is determined by the coach. You'll see why later, but this keeps things simple in the right way. In this scenario, with me as the coach, I'll ask you to begin the exercise. Here is what I am going to ask you to do:

> 'Look at your partner and notice something about him. What you notice has to be a fact. It cannot be an opinion, a question, or a speculation. Just a simple, basic, fact. You are going to say what you see. How about we try a test run of what that looks like?'

I ask you to go first. With brave courage you look at your partner and you say: 'Brown hair.'

'Pretty good. But let's make it specific to your partner. How about 'you have brown hair.' Try a new observation like this and see how it feels.'

You look again at your partner. 'You're wearing glasses.' you say.

'Excellent!' I happily say. That may worry you slightly. Has this guy lost his mind? Before we answer that question, here are a few more hypothetical examples of what a good starting observation to this exercise looks like:

You are wearing jeans.
You've got earrings on.
Your hair is parted.
You're wearing sandals.
You've got blue on.

I continue by saying that now we seem to have a good grip on the starting point of the exercise. Now comes the next part: 'After you notice something about your partner and say it, your partner is going to repeat word for word what you say to them. Then you are going to repeat back, word for word, what you hear them say to you. Then they are going to repeat back, word for word, what they hear you say to them. And so on, until I stop the exercise.'

Now with stares of utter confusion across the room, implying that finally the cheese has slid off the cracker for me, you bravely begin the exercise.

You: 'You're wearing boots.'
Partner: 'You're wearing boots.'
You: 'You're wearing boots.'
Partner: 'You're wearing boots.'
You: 'You're wearing boots.'
Partner: 'You're wearing boots.'

About two or three repeats in, you can't help but crack up. This has got to be a joke. I let the exercise go on for about a minute before stopping you two. The looks around the room say I have some major explaining to do.

I first start by asking a question for both the partners and the group. 'What are the instructions of the exercise?'

Invariably I almost always get the same reply: 'Repeat the same thing over and over again.'

This is good for me to hear. It tells me that there is a difference between the message sent and the message received, a truism of all human communication. Because, actually, that's not what I said. What I said was that when we get into the exercise you are not repeating by-rote, but rather repeating the phrase you hear the other person say to you. It's a subtle but profound distinction. Does this mean the words stay the same? For the most part. But let's look at what happens every now and then. I'll use the example above. Let's say you and your partner are going on and, we all know by now, he's wearing boots. But at one point, this happens:

You: 'You're wearing boots.'
Partner: 'You're wearing boots.'

You: 'You're wearing boots.'
Partner: 'You're wearing [unexpectedly coughs] gloots.'

This is interesting. Intellectually you know what the phrase is supposed to be. You only heard the world 'gloots' because your partner's unexpected cough changed the word. If the instructions were to repeat by-rote this would just be a technical error, noise in the signal, and you could go back to repeating the same phrase. But the instructions are to repeat not a universal phrase but rather what you hear is being said. In the moment your partner coughs, you heard 'gloots'. Do you violate the instructions and repeat what you didn't hear or follow them and repeat what you did hear? Here's your answer:

You: 'You're wearing boots.'
Partner: 'You're wearing [unexpectedly coughs] gloots.'
You: 'You're wearing gloots.'
Partner: 'You're wearing gloots.'

Now, here's the thing, since message sending is important: at this point some people hear me say this and think that word games or changing the text is the way to win the exercise. This is wrong on many levels that we will get into later and is not what I am saying. For now the simple reason that will suffice is you don't yet understand the exercise and so your attempts to get a head start on it will often make you more miserable and deprive you of the values of the work. Take it step by step.

So, if repeating the same phrase by-rote isn't where the value of this exercise lies, this implies that what is important is a degree of listening. Perhaps more profound, if we say that missing a chance to repeat a natural hiccup in the text (again, not an intentional change in the words but a completely random one) is losing out on a golden opportunity, it implies that the words are of less value in the exercise than something else. What might that be?

You and your partner now do another exercise. Your partner begins this time. The "call" (the observation you or your partner make to begin an exercise) is 'You're wearing a black shirt.'

Partner: You're wearing a black shirt.
You: You're wearing a black shirt.
Partner: You're wearing a black shirt.
You: You're wearing a black shirt.
Etc. (implies the exercise keeps going on in this way)

There aren't any noticeable changes in the text. I let it run on for longer than the first. There are many moments of clear discomfort. Awkwardness, uncertainty, some nervous laughter, and a general tone of, 'What is going on here?' After about two or three minutes, I stop the exercise and we have a check in about your experiences.

If it feels like you are starting to have more questions than answers, this is normal. The first and second times you do a repetition exercise will feel awkward and you most likely won't get the point. That's okay. This is true of many skills. You don't master much on the first or second go-round. It is good to acknowledge that and move past it: this feels damn weird. What feels weird, however? Let's say I ask you both a question:

'Was it dull?' I ask.
'Not really,' one of you says. 'But it was weird. It just felt awkward.'

I agree with this. The entire exercise this time around seemed awkward. There was palpable tension in it, which at times would be relieved by nervous laughter. But we can establish something else.

'Did it feel deeper, even a little?' I ask.

'Yes.' is almost always the response. It wasn't life-changing, but qualitatively this exercise felt, in just a few small incremental ways, slightly deeper. Something did arise between you and your partner and it has to do with the tension. Your experiences in the exercise and us observing confirmed the tension was not fake: it was entirely real and authentic. So this begets the question we will begin to answer here: how is this going to make you a better leader? We will need more examples to start getting there for sure, but already something is being teased at. Repetition as an exercise is showing itself to be simple but deep. Obtuse but not easy.

Another exercise between you both. This time you begin with a new observation. At one point you exhale in frustration and your partner begins laughing uncontrollably. The result is contagious, and for a good few seconds you both are infecting one another with laughter at the absurdity of the situation. It is real, rich laughter. To the two of you it feels like an expression of the ridiculous, an admission of how absurd this all is. It looks similar to us, but it is also entirely authentic. It is a moment too good not to capture in feedback.

We quickly finish the exercise and I check in with you about it. We have begun to identify a common trend across three different sets of behaviours: in the first exercise, the complete awkwardness. In the second, the awkwardness and noticeable tension. In the third, an explosion of uncontrollable laughter. What is the common denominator? All three of these things happened independent of the words. Since from the first exercise onwards we already introduced the idea that the words matter less than something else, bowing to a deeper value. Your experience confirms this. No matter how many times you repeat 'You're wearing jeans' with your best intention, after a while it turns to word mush. The simple structure of repetition then seems to act more like a conduit.

Notice that all three of these behaviours were entirely authentic since there was no fakery or intentional manipulation from either end. Notice as well that there was no person who clearly began them, rather they seemed to emerge in an organic flow. Neither of you planned those responses to one another. Neither of you planned to generate perfectly authentic awkwardness or to lose it laughing as the weight of such a seemingly stupid situation bore down upon you. They were rich, deep spontaneous expressions that arose regardless of the content of your words. While they emerged from you they weren't created by you being inventive or deliberate. It is clear that if there is a conduit of repetition, it is a back and forth between your partner. You may also notice that, when those behaviours arose, the words took on the quality of the connection between you two. When the moment was awkward, the text was filled with it. When the laughter came, the text took on the quality of madness. You didn't plan to infuse the words with such authenticity. It seemed to happen naturally.

We can extend this phenomenon beyond just these three small exercises. If there is frustration, the text will come out sounding frustrated. If there is laughter, the text will take on that quality. The same is true of other experiences. This is the first deep lesson repetition can teach you: the words between you and another human being are for the most part only surface elements of a much greater experience. A brief caveat is that sometimes words do matter and we will accommodate that in later exercises, but for the most part they don't. The richness is what is happening between you and another regardless of the words. We call this the subtext, the human life beneath the text. My Meisner teacher Scott always used to say, paraphrasing Meisner himself, the words are like a canoe on the river: the river determines what happens to the canoe, not the other way around. Text floats on the connection between you and your partner. The more you explore that the more you will see that the interpersonal element which engages you with another is often not what is said but the life underneath the words.

Words and language are a functional necessity in life, especially for a leader. You will have to use words to convince others to support you. At the same time we place far too much emphasis on the content itself and not what is underneath it. We know that a person can be magnetic even if they are speaking in a language we do not understand. Consider also a hypothetical conversation between you and another person. You are discussing the weather but underneath your words is a charged subtext: it could be joy, rage, flirtation, and so on. Leaders are taught to use their words. This is important, but it is not leadership. In placing too much emphasis on yourself you forget that even when the words are entirely meaningless there is a whole stream of connection and inter-action that gives you much deeper access to the relevant parts of another human being. Likewise, you could be the equivalent of a modern Shakespeare and no one will care if you are not engaging.

Most importantly, repetition shows us this connection is on offer from moment 1. The broader concept we are beginning to see is that we are all pushing a social persona, littered with seemingly relevant goals and pursuits, but all of these surface goals come from our humanistic needs and desires. Even in smaller examples such as a bit of tension or awkward laughter, this exercise shows you it is possible to cut out the middle person of language and get into the meat of what happens between two people when the veneers and conventions of society begin to be peeled back. You don't need a degree in psychology to do it either. But you do need something else.

Before we get to what that is, this brings us back to a comment I made a while earlier: don't play word games in repetition. It is a temptation that comes from a half-reasonable place: if the text doesn't matter and what matters is my connection to my partner, then I'll just play with the text to get more out of my partner. Isn't that better? From this well-meaning gesture, combined with inevitable human temptation for competition, I see all sorts of inventive things coming up early in the training. Spontaneously created agendas to be silly, improvising, one-upping, all types of clever games to juice the exercise. This happens early in the training and stops almost just as quickly. Why? Not because I become a tyrant about rules. The simple answer is it drives itself into extinction. The driving force behind that is dissatisfaction.

As you continue to do these repetitions with your partner and watch others, when game play-ing and trying to 'win' comes up, you will always notice afterwards the feeling is one of shallow accomplishment. You drove the exercise, you thumped your chest, you ascended the mountain, and you viscerally feel as if you didn't budge an inch in terms of the experiential power on offer in the exercise. The exercise now somehow feels hollow. What's the difference? In the first few ones the spontaneous and authentic behaviours that came out of you weren't your own creation. They were generated by you being connected with, and observing, your partner. The more closely you are with them in the exercise the more you will feel surprised by what seems to arise natu-rally: laughter, joy, as well as darker things like annoyance and irritation. You aren't the common denominator in your experience: your partner is.

Game playing in this training is often defensive behaviour. It is normal in the beginning for the real stuff that comes out of you seemingly uncensored to set off the alarm bells. You quickly begin to feel that when you connect with your partner there can be other things on offer. Not just happy times but also aggression, attraction, things we don't know what to do with in relation to both this training and leadership. Some of that is generated by the context of the classroom: boundaries that haven't been made clear by me yet in the training. Much more potent, however, is these experiences won't feel like self-created emotions. They are more real, feel more raw and, as a result, unpredictable. This is all normal in this work. It is day one. So the best advice for day one is drop the game playing, and we will deal with the relevant questions when they arise.

All of this is inching us towards another deep value. The first value: the words are just a conduit for the connection between you and your partner. Now we are asking that if playing games or being creative isn't the real value, what is? The audience answers the question: as you continue to do these repetition exercises something unique happens for us watching you. It can best be summarized as the more you release control in the exercise to your partner the more exciting you become to watch. Don't believe me? Watch your colleagues work well in an exercise. It seems that, if winning is defined by besting the other person, the more you lose the more you win.

Sorry to be crass, but that is an utterly paradoxical mindfuck for many of us. Giving up power to gain more – are you kidding me? Let's ask a follow-up question: could it be that your desire to control and manipulate the exercise, as is the case when participants make games out of it, is draining more power than it is returning? Perhaps this is a case of effort expended in the wrong way. We know that without going to utterly authoritarian measures you can't control another human being well. Perhaps by allowing yourself to be malleable, then, to the chaotic variables of another person you are now expending less and gaining more. Is it possible that by putting more responsibility on the other person, rather than yourself, you can get better returns on power exchanges between you and another individual?

The responsibility that I am talking about, to be clear, is one that is unique to the exchange between you and an individual. We have already introduced the idea, and seen mini examples from the first three hypothetical exercises in practice, the possibility that the more you release control and let the other person determine your behaviour, the more power it gives you. Putting the responsibility for the exercise on the other person, then, does not give you a passive role but rather frees you up to have a very active one, and this is what becomes exciting to watch. Because you have now put the responsibility of the exercise on the other person, your behaviour is determined by what that other person will do, not what you want them to do. As Bruce Lee wrote in *The Tao of Jeet Kune Do*, 'My movement is a result of your movement.'

There is a grain of hard reality at work here. You are neither prophet nor mind reader, and so both the future and the other person is well outside your cognitive mastery. When you accept and work with the fact that you do not know what another person is going to do, you realise you no longer know what you are going to do. This makes you incredibly exciting to watch. Arguably, if your repetition partner does the same to you, if they put all the responsibility for their behaviours onto you, now we have the recipe for a very exciting, spontaneous and interesting exchange.

The reason for this sudden amping of interest has to do with what we see as audience members. Consider that as observers we are trained and primed to take our cues from the object of our attention. If that object is a person, then in that moment they have become the leader of our attention, setting the tone and conditions for the event we are witnessing. Even when eavesdropping on a conversation between two people, we allow ourselves to be led by the speakers, taking our cues for important tones, signals, body language, and so on, from them, rather than our own expectations. Even better, part of what makes this kind of voyeurism exciting is when our expectations are dashed, rather than met. 'I thought I knew where it was going but I had no idea she was going to say *that*!' That is the psychology of an audience most forget: we want to be led. We are going to look to you for what in the experience is relevant and, most importantly, what is not.

You might be starting to see now why I harp continuously on about the dangers of pre-rehearsed behaviours in presentations, negotiations, speeches, meetings, and so on. Knowing your content is one thing. Knowing how you are going to deliver it, with all your gestures, breathing points, and so on robotically planned is an excellent way to send the signal to the audience that you are not really present with us. To you it feels like you are delivering something you spent hours polishing, but that is actually the problem: most people who prepare in this way become dangerously disconnected from the energy and presence of the audience, a variable that cannot be prepared in advance and must be intuited in the moment. As a result, the overly pre-rehearsed leader unconsciously (or consciously if you are using a fourth-wall technique to cope with audience-induced anxiety) ignores the individual cues and stimuli coming from each moment. From our perspective in the audience we see you not really connected. Looking to you for the answers we come away with this message: 'This speaker knows exactly what they are going to do. They aren't even really present. There's no risk, no unpredictability. We don't need to really pay attention to them. They aren't here, so why should we be?' You cannot forget that audiences are extremely smart and get bored easily.

Following this logic, it is only when you don't know what you are going to do next that the audience doesn't. This makes your leadership immensely attuned to the present moment. It is important not to conflate this with being unprepared. You might know what you are going to say, but how you do it, the way it comes out, and if even all of it will be relevant, is determined by the thing outside of you: the audience. This principle can be applied successfully to one-on-one exchanges all the way up to your addressing tens of thousands. Its core value is what we are beginning to train in this first exercise: take the responsibility for what happens off of your shoulders and put it on the other person. Let go of the desire to have an agenda, control the event, or to win. Instead, being now richly connected to what the exchange with that person demands of you, you will become unpredictable in an exciting way. This is much better for an audience. People might know what you are going to say, or they might not, but they will now get the subtle message: this person is richly connected and living moment-by-moment, so I need to pay attention.

The secret ingredient comes down to engagement. When you are deeply engaged you become engaging to watch. We are already saying invest fully in the other person. Make them the object of your public solitude, and put the responsibility for the success or failure of the exercise on their shoulders. You won't lose ground or power; paradoxically, you will gain it, as you will be sharply catching every moment of their behaviour and responding to it. And when they are doing it to you, you are facing a worthy opponent in training. Looking down the road, this makes exchanges with people outside of the training, less technically able to engage in such a detailed way, a much easier thing to handle.

Here then is the core value of this work, the Meisner principles, and the exercises modified to suit the needs of you, the leader. I first heard it from my original Meisner teacher Scott and have since heard it echoed in many other classes elsewhere. It is the heart of the training: what happens to you does not depend on you, but on what the other person is doing to you. 'Person' eventually will be magnified to 'situation', but that will be a subtle modification to this larger truth. For most leaders in training, this is a terrifying concept. They think I am advocating for them to have no control and to give up all their power, and the irrational fear beneath is summarized along these lines: if you do things this way, you will always be a victim to the situation rather than the commander of it. Victory, however, as I will spend the entirety of the book trying to make a case for, does not come from entering with a fully formed plan and *insisting* that it work, especially to the exclusion of all variables. That is a very bad strategy. Victory comes from entering with some semblance of a plan, some structure, and then letting the moment and the situation determine its relevance. Most importantly, this approach gives you the ability to adapt. This strategy does demand that you give up control, because to gain control you need to work with the situation without imposing on it. Developing within yourself the value of putting the responsibility on the other person is how you will see more clearly and gain more power from an interaction without working so hard for it.

Let Me Get That for You

Thus far we have seen some hypothetical repetition exercise examples before exploring some of the deeper concepts around them. This gives you a sense of the form and the reasoning behind this seemingly strange exercise. Off the page, however, don't be surprised if three repetitions will not be enough for you to actually experience and develop these values in practice. As you continue to do more repetition drills where the text has no meaning and the entirety of what happens to you depends not on your wishes, desires, plans, or agendas, but rather on what the other person is doing to you, and by proxy what they are making you do, you will begin to realise something: repetition exercises go into strange territory quickly. Because both you and your partner have the instruction to put the responsibility on each other, there are no clear boundaries. Naturally, questions of what is permissible in exercises soon arises. It usually first comes in micro-moments or exchanges; for a few moments you might become irritated or frustrated by something your partner is doing. The irritation comes from your being present with them, so technically it is fair-won, but is it okay to express that? I mean, sure, when it is laughter and playfulness, the exercises are fine, but what happens when they veer into darker territories, such as the first glimpses of anger, intimacy, hurt, and so on? This also raises, even early on, questions about the relevance of this training for leadership. Let's get into that a little and see if we can field an answer or the start of one.

It is worth explicitly stating again that this is not a self-help or self-therapy book in disguise – I can promise you that. This is a book on leadership and testing certain hypotheses for how to train it. The best leadership, as we have discussed, is the kind that gains the qualitatively best power with the least quantitatively expended effort. We say that this often comes from interpersonal exchanges, and such success is based on authenticity. Authenticity makes you exciting and engaging to watch and interact with. Engagement with people in an authentic way is immensely powerful and will bring you a great deal of power without much, if any, effort. As we are discovering, however, authenticity runs into another problem soon enough in our work: through training the combined skills of public solitude and investing in the reality of doing may solve the issue of the audience, but now we are already running up against a new, even larger threat to your leadership technique. In one way or another it will comprise the majority of your frustrations and grievances throughout this entire training. This particular gauntlet has to do with social conventions, what you believe you are and are not allowed to express as a leader and, perhaps more to the point, a person in a specific culture with rules. We are, essentially, running up against politeness.

Let me get a head start on some concerns: I know that there will be restrictions on your authentic expression in meetings, negotiations, presentations, speeches, or any other tangible interpersonal elements of your field I have not named. What I would like you to consider is that there is a difference between training your authenticity versus my insisting I know the limits of how it must be expressed in your field. While there might be some basic agreements, the specific nuances of the limits of certain types of behaviour do vary greatly from individual to individual, and I would even suggest field to field. Rather than make a moral case about what should and should not be allowed, I am going to let you determine those restrictions for your field after the training. You understand best what behaviours will and will not contribute to your success in your field. But that said, you are not on your own: down the road we will see that there is a way to stay authentic even if you cannot express something in a certain way. It is possible to filter authenticity without compromising it. To get that, however, you need to have a comfortable range of vast authentic expression. You can't limit what is already severely restricted. As I said, my goal is to help, not to expect you to bend to my view of what a leader should be. Having said that, however,

I am also interested in making sure that your ability to express your authenticity attains that vast and unhindered quality.

One easy example to make this all more concrete is anger. We all know that it is a foolish move on the part of a leader to express anger and aggression regularly. Very quickly people soon retract the amount of power they give you due to your perceived emotional instability. Smart leaders know, however, that there is sometimes nothing more powerful than a well-timed outburst. This sudden explosive flash must be fully genuine or you will come off as histrionic, insincere, manipulative, or unable to commit. The important variable in both of these situations is the external circumstance that tells you how to express your authenticity. That is what we are working on. When you are in the chairs with your partner, the important habit to train is to express the authentic responses that arise from clearly observing your partner. That is the habit that can be built on. You cannot build authenticity on a self-censoring technique.

Politeness, then, is a social agreement that does not have a role in our training. It is a coating on all behaviours that deters authenticity. It is not polite to express anger, or intimacy, or joy, or pain. We don't want to impose our 'extreme emotions' on other people, and this is why in training a leader, politeness is toxic poison to their development and must be removed. The Meisner Technique offers the most eloquent phrasing of it: fuck polite.

To be overtly clear, fuck polite *does not* mean go in to an exercise and be rude and aggressive with your partner as a default; that would be an agenda being imposed on the interactions between you both. It would be in violation of the idea that you let them determine what happens to you. Rather it means that in being fully engaged with your partner, you don't deny certain observations for fear of them being impolite. Since you are not trying to make things happen in the exercise, feelings and behaviours will arise seemingly on impulse from these observations. Fuck polite is expressing those impulses without fear of the consequence. If you do so, there will most likely be a powerful response from your partner. What that response is you don't know, and that is what makes repetition so exciting. To be extra clear, however, outside of the exercises, towards one another in sessions, and when necessary in daily interactions, it is good to be able to retain our ability to be polite. Fuck polite is a metric first to be applied within exercises, and then later as a potent tool in your leadership arsenal once you have the complete set of skills this training provides, but never a tool to suddenly be adopted 24/7.

Introducing 'fuck polite' into this work means we absolutely must delve into the mechanics of repetition in order to see how this exercise works under the hood. There is a very important reason for this. Repetition as a training device depends on a 50–50 balance. Fifty percent of your time is spent in deep observation and engagement with the other person, your partner, while the other 50% is spent responding authentically to what that person is doing. This observe-and-respond rule is what keeps repetition safe and on point. As a result, a repetition exercise can go to intense places, and both parties come out better for it as leaders because of the 50–50 balance. We have to ask, however, what happens when the 50–50 dynamic is tipped out of balance?

When the balance is tipped too far in favour of observation, the exercise loses its dynamic power. It seems to dry up. This is because both you and your partner enter into a kind-of observational staring contest with one another. Unlike the following example, while this type of situation does lose the value of the training at its core it does not present any issue of urgent concern and is easily corrected. Imbalance on the other side, however, is a different matter entirely. When repetition is tipped too far in favour of responding, it is a big warning sign. Such a dynamic means one or each of you is just responding and not really seeing the other person. When this happens, the exercise becomes solely about one person bringing in their agenda for dominating the exercise without observing clearly what their behaviour is doing to the other person. This results in them relentlessly pushing and provoking their partner. This is the same partner who has been given the explicit instruction to express any impulses that arise due to your behaviour regardless of how impolite they are. Sacrificing the 50–50 balance of observe and respond in favour of the intention to stir the pot not violates the core values of the technique, thereby losing any real leadership value, but can you see how this type of situation can escalate and quickly become physically unsafe for both participants?

The core of such a situation arising depends on a fundamental misunderstanding. Unfortunately, some people might think that when I am asking them to adopt the mentality of 'fuck polite' it means I want them to go into the exercise and aggressively provoke their partner. This scenario loses all the values of the technique. It happens rarely but it does happen. In times like these, it is best to stop the exercise and get both participants back on track. There's no more benefit when this occurs, and safety concerns that never arise otherwise pop up. As I said, this type of occurrence is a very rare phenomena. After years of training thousands of people, it has only been an issue for me three or four times, but it is the only time a repetition exercise can become physically unsafe. One of the reasons it has been so rare, I believe, is because of an in-depth examination of the mechanics of repetition with people early on in the training, just like the one we are having now. Repetition's components may be simple but they can be easily taken for granted, especially when a concept such as casting politeness aside is introduced. Fuck polite in a 50–50 balance of observe and respond is a gold mine for training leadership. Without the equal balance of observe and respond, however, it loses any real relevance to our journey.

This is a good place to introduce our definition of leadership in this training. Conveniently it is plucked directly from the verbiage of the Meisner Technique, as it crosses over perfectly. Successful leadership, according to the principles we are training in you, is living truthfully under a given set of circumstances. This perfect phrase encompasses fully what great leaders do – they go into a set of circumstances and live truthfully by observing and responding authentically. The course of this training will be dedicated to your understanding viscerally, rather than just theoretically, what that means and feels like. For now, however, let's look at a few elements of this definition to get this conversation started.

The first question that often arises with this phrase is what is actually meant by the word 'truthfully'? You'll recall earlier in the session we established that at this stage the content of an observation is not too important, even going so far as to say it can be a lie half the time with no value lost to the learning process. Truthfully, then, cannot refer to literal truthfulness. Truthfully for our purposes means more in the sense of behaviour that is truthful. We can identify this behaviour by the interaction of two components, which is the process of a leader responding authentically to a clearly observed situation and the behaviour of the people within it. Fuck polite also filters into that as it allows you to make truthful observations without the pressures of societal conditioning. Building on the model for truthfulness, the given circumstances filter your behaviour while preserving its authenticity. How they do that you don't know yet, since we haven't gotten there, but that is one of the larger goals with this work. This equal emphasis on both truthful behaviour and the given circumstances is how you will train to do expansive, deep things in the exercises and then know with assuredness these tools will enable you to still behave 'appropriately' outside of this training. Half of the equation in leadership is living truthfully, and the other half is connecting that truthfulness directly with the situation you find yourself in. One cannot exist without the other.

As I said, this is bigger-picture stuff, and you certainly aren't expected to fully understand it, let alone do it, on day one. Repetition, what you are starting now, is the process of training a leader to live truthfully. This is very important for any future questions: repetition does not – I repeat does not – encompass the given circumstances. There are a few basic conditions imposed on the exercise to give it structure, but these are not the same sophisticated given circumstances leaders have to deal with. Don't worry about the given circumstances for now. We will cover them thoroughly in later chapters and training sessions, and you will know when we get there. For today and the near future, the core aim of this work is training yourself to live truthfully with another person. The more you do this in repetition, the more you develop the concepts we have introduced: investing fully and deeply in what you are doing; determining a target of public solitude; and observing fully and responding authentically to what you are seeing without the pressure of social conventions, politeness, and other cultural inhibitions.

This is how you develop that magnetic, charismatic presence without creating a false persona or overemphasising gestures to the point that you look like a bad mime. Gestures are fine, objectively there is nothing wrong with them, and I am not saying you can't use them ever again (we've got this covered much later in the training), but they are not the place to start. At best they are given circumstances to be brought into your process much later. In the same vein pre-planning and diligently rehearsing your behaviours, from inflections to posture and winking, has nothing to do with authenticity and by virtue with living truthfully. If you've done public speaking or leadership training elsewhere, you may have found the opposite to be the starting point. It is insane to me that we try to start people with preconceived prescriptions rather than beginning with working on and developing what makes a person exciting in the first place, which is their ability to make us engage hungrily by observing their own spontaneous, authentic engagement with another human being.

Gesture and posture training to a leader is similar to what make-up and costumes are to actors: you can put on as much as you want, but no matter how many putty noses you have plastered onto a person, if they cannot live truthfully, all the make-up, funny accents, and strange walks in the world can't save them. If you can't live truthfully as a leader, then it doesn't matter how 'polished' you are or how perfectly timed and executed your mannerisms, lines, and gestures. You will be lacking that human dynamism that will make people want to pay attention to you.

These paradoxical concepts introduced here are not new but have been around for thousands of years in more esoteric schools of thought, including combat strategies: give up power to gain it. Release control and you flow in total accordance with the situation and so will respond in the best possible way to it. Training, however, must drill this habit into you beyond cerebral concepts and must dispel any mysticism or vagueness. By engaging in a seemingly simple exercise where the words turn to mush without the distraction of dialogue and conversation, thereby quickly becoming meaningless, we can introduce and explore the deep possibilities of human connection. For leaders who need power from other people, there is no more profound place to meet a person than where they are at their most authentic and open, demanding the same from you.

Now that we have spent some time training in you–you repetition and begun to open the door on what it means to live truthfully (eventually living truthfully under a given set of circumstances), concepts we will continue to revisit, it is time to reintroduce an essential component that anchors this work, moving it continuously from abstraction towards applicability: point of view.

Summary

The essence of great leadership begins not with persona or false crafting but rather with an enhancement of one's authentic qualities. This authenticity, especially when combined with invested engagement in another person, becomes an immensely unique and powerful experience that will gain you valuable power. Training this skill set, then, becomes the core aim of the leader's development. We call this living truthfully: a process of engaging fully with another person through deep observation and responding authentically without self-censoring. Living truthfully forms the first half of our definition of leadership which is also the same definition of acting that Meisner gave, although we are using it for our own purposes: living truthfully under a given set of circumstances.

The drill known simply as repetition, which begins with a simple phrase that generally does not change (although as we have seen, it could if circumstances in the moment created a change), is the training process for the leadership skills that fall under the umbrella of living truthfully. It will remain a core element of our work, even when the idea of given circumstances are introduced at a later point. Very quickly, living truthfully brings up the question of politeness in this training. While politeness is an excellent quality to have outside of training within the process of living truthfully, it becomes a hindrance, as it denies you the ability to give yourself permission to express yourself authentically.

Our response then is to say 'fuck polite', which does not mean be rude or intentionally antagonistic but to not deny yourself permission to express the impulses generated by observing your partner, no matter how taboo they might seem. This is not only possible but advisable due to the inherent 50–50 balance of observe-and-respond within repetition which keeps the exercise safe.

This expansion of one's range of authenticity through training is a potent tool that will make your leadership skills adaptable to many situations. How we filter those authentic expressions through the unique given circumstances you will encounter in a situation is a topic we will build on in later exercises. For now get comfortable with the idea of engagement and giving up the need to control or dominate a situation as a key strategy to gain, rather than lose, power.

Tips for You and Your Coach

Before I go into my advice in support your work as a coach I just want to clarify the format and structure of these chapters from your point of view. Generally in these chapters I will begin with describing a few hypothetical exercises. This is to give you and your clients a basic sense of form and perhaps more importantly a sense of what the form is not. From there, however, I tend to delve more deeply into the concepts surrounding the training. This is not how I structure a class, as you will see here and elsewhere. The exercises are simple and much more easily understood in practice than in writing. As such, there is only so much value in hypothetical exercises on the page. In a practical situation you will have to disseminate a lot of conceptual information in this work. It is best to do this in between lots of practical work rather than saving it all for a giant discussion the end.

As a coach taking clients through repetition, it is important to understand the core component of repetition that differentiates it from many other types of exercises, wherever they may be imported from. Breathing exercises, for example, are concrete and specific, and there is a measurable before and after component based on physical grounds to test the efficacy of a breathing exercise. Even imagination-based (such as guided visualisation and meditation sessions) and improvisational exercises to an extent, so long as a perceived result emerges after employing them, are grounded in a concrete, albeit somewhat flexible and fluid, set of rules.

Repetition is not like this. It is inherently abstract. If you try to treat it otherwise, as many Meisner teachers in the acting field do, you will find yourself locked in your inability to express clearly the dynamics of living truthfully and how your students can build upon them. This is because trying to apply canned phrases and specific examples at timed intervals will only lose the authenticity of what happened in favour of what, in your mind, should have happened. Teaching repetition is more about engaging with what you see and leading the unique exercises to similar conclusions, rather than every class being moulded into an artificial set of phrasings and wordplay. It is worth stating again: repetition is an entirely abstract exercise. It is a vehicle for your own individual preferences for what you wish to see leaders develop. It requires a coach because it needs an outsider's point of view to guide the journey that you deem necessary for your clients to take. Your own perception and ability to articulate the values of great leadership through it are key to its success.

Since repetition is abstract, being attuned to feedback in the moment takes precedent, and as such there is no specific order to introduce the ideas in this chapter or when to stop an exercise. In general, however, my teaching tends to follow these patterns – but experiment and see what works for you:

- In the beginning, a repetition exercise should last 2–5 minutes; usually within that time I will see the next relevant point for discussion to emerge. Later on, exercises can go up to ten minutes if something is happening that is important and needs to take on a long form. Generally in the early-stages the points of relevant feedback happen within 2–5 minutes, but again, stay open and flexible with respect to what your intuitions are telling you in the moment.
- It is very easy to overload people's minds in this work. The exercises themselves are already full-on and strange. Given that, I tend to give one piece of feedback or concept in between each exercise. One piece is enough to start digesting and to let it sink in. The larger block of ideas I covered at the end of this chapter really would be broken up in between many repetition exercises.
- I almost always give a pair of participants two rounds of repetition, sometimes three, if I feel it will be of value to them, before rotating one or both out to give them a break. Understand that even though the exercises themselves are only 2–5 minutes long, the feedback might take four or five minutes to articulate. With two exercises, you could be veering on 20 minutes of total time per pair. Your client will need a break after that to let things sink in and not be overwhelmed, as well as to observe others grappling with the same exercise and their own unique challenges. A client being overwhelmed is a problem in this work as it usually results in some kind of a shutdown and temporary block. You don't need to coddle your clients, but be sensitive to when they seem to be approaching their mental and experiential threshold. Attention is a finite resource, and that doesn't change just because you are in a training session.
- Going off the previous point, stressing the value of observation is vital. Sometimes clients will become discouraged when they realise they are only getting what they feel is a smaller portion of class time for themselves rather than the entire time of session. They are discounting or forgetting about the immense importance and need for observation of others in this work. This is not just lip service: as proof, watch the last pair to work and I promise you will see organic improvements that the first or second pairs did not have. You will be able to replicate the finding across every single class. The challenges do not disappear for later pairs, but they become more nuanced, subtle, and complex. This is entirely due to learning from observation.
- In the exercises, you will see your client sometimes sitting on the impulses brought up by their partner; you don't want to push them to act on them but rather make them aware of what they did not express and remind them that they, too, are allowed to say 'fuck polite'

and train their truthfulness. Be immensely clear with yourself about the boundaries of exercises and how far things can go before the learning value is lost. It won't be an issue too much here, but down the road this inner radar will be critical for you to maximize learning and minimize inessential places to go in exercises. If you ever feel unsure about an exercise, stop it and give your clients a chance to reset. It is better to err on caution's side if you are still finding your feet as a coach in this work.

■ Have your priorities in order: is it more important that the client get the concept first or work on the impulses they did not act on? There's no clear answer. It depends. This will depend on the room, the first pair and their temperaments, as well as other unique variables neither you nor I will not be able to predict here. Keep attuned to both possibilities and trust your instincts.

■ While word games and playing around in the exercises will happen they are often wastes of time. The point of repetition is to live truthfully, that is, to express authentic impulses generated by clearly observing another person. Games and one-upping are just agendas that will prevent the dynamic back and forth of repetition that gives it the depth and the learning value. Point out when people do it and remind them there are better options available in the exercise. If you get a client who, despite all your efforts, is posturing or refusing to budge, consider using another approach than Meisner to teach them and make your own life easier. There is a difference between clients who need time and patience to learn and ones who are a deliberate pain in your ass, especially with this work.

■ If it looks like one or both members of the exercises have gone lifeless or are blocked, but they are still carrying out the technique of the exercise, then it just means they are observing well but not responding. Repetition can only exist in a 50–50 balance of observe and respond and when those scales become tipped too far in favour of observation, then the authentic impulses are not being expressed and the exercise will become dull and flat. This can be addressed in feedback after the exercise finishes. Likewise, if the balance tips too far in the other direction, then it means one of the two members is only responding and no longer actually seeing their partner. Their impulses are no longer coming from their partner. If this happens, then stop the exercise quickly and point this out as this is the only time when exercises can become dangerous to the safety of students. It is very rare but develop and keep an eye out for it; the balance of the exercise must always be honoured.

■ For now, if a change in the text organically happens, let it ride; if students, however, begin to make changes in the text, stop the exercise and bring them back to repeating what they hear the other person say and not what they want the text to be. Sometimes in the beginning people confuse a genuine impulse from the other person that changes the text organically with an impulse from themselves that has nothing to do with their partner. Repetition is not a dialogue exercise. The meaninglessness of the words has immense value and should be relished.

Chapter 5

The I in You

Beyond the Shallow Rim

If you are like me, and you space out your training sessions in accordance with these chapters, one session for each chapter (with the exception of investing in the reality of doing from Chapter 3, a concept that works either as a stand-alone session or as a springboard for diving into the repetition exercises), then what you will see is that a lot happened in the previous session. Through a seemingly simple exercise, with just a few ground rules, where two people worked facing each other, one introducing a phrase and then the pair repeating back and forth what they heard each other say, we began a deep exploration into the concept of living truthfully. This included exploring the value of language in relation to authentic human communication, as well as the notion of training and developing within your leadership a rich capacity for truthful observations and responses. We also began to touch on the issue of politeness and how it can be a barrier to your ability to express yourself authentically. The exercise known as repetition in acting is used to train truthfulness in an actor, as well as handle the challenges of politeness and societal conditioning, and is the core drill of the Meisner Technique. It will become one of your staple training exercises as well. Rest assured, however, that we are going to continue to build on it, and in just a few chapters it will look nothing like what it does to you now. What we are doing at this point may seem like a simplistic exercise but gradually we are going to build it into a powerhouse technique for honing your leadership abilities.

This concept of living truthfully, synonymous with fully authentic observation and expression, is entirely portable into any field where leadership is required. The question I would ask when hearing this, however, is so what? Lots of ideas are portable across domains, especially bad ones. Why am I arguing that this concept of living truthfully (eventually living truthfully under a given set of circumstances) valued so highly in the performing arts industry is not only a strong tool for a leader – even in fields which have no relation to the entertainment industry – but an optimal one to adopt? We can begin to explore this extremely important question with something we briefly touched on in the previous chapter. In our via negativa spirit it has to do with what truthfulness is not.

Take, for example, a repetition exercise between you and your partner that looks like this:

You: You're wearing glasses.
Partner: You're wearing glasses.

You: You're wearing glasses.
Partner: You're wearing glasses.
Etc.

Let's say that both you and your partner are wearing glasses. Going by that one observation it would be easy to assume that training living truthfully is about you putting value in literal truth, in this case, the truthfulness of the observation itself. There's some reasonableness to this. If, for example, you had observed that your partner was wearing glasses when he or she wasn't, then that would be a creative writing exercise that didn't come from your partner. It would violate our core value that what happens to you does not depend on your agendas or intentions but rather what your partner is going to make you do. Though I say 'core value', by the way, this is still very much a hypothesis that we will be testing throughout this training, but let's stay with this concept first. For now it seems that truthfulness in your observations is important, but is that the whole picture of living truthfully?

The answer is not by a long shot.

Let's take a far more common occurrence seen in repetition. Your partner is wearing glasses. You are not. You say 'You're wearing glasses', and your partner repeats it. Unless the phrase spontaneously changes, which is astronomically rare at this stage, 50% of the time the text will now be a lie. If your partner gets a bit of dust in their eye, takes their glasses off, and continues the exercise while trying to clear it (a set of behaviours fine with me so long as someone isn't in any visible discomfort or pain) the text will now be a lie 100% of the time. Is this a problem? More importantly, is there still value in the exercise for your leadership skills? The answer would be yes: you can still observe and respond authentically to another person even if the content of your words, the text, is not literally true.

For leaders this is an incredibly important point. From the outset we are prioritising truthfulness and authenticity but not truthfulness in the literal content of what you say. Rather we are concerned with what is underneath the words. This hearkens back to our canoe on the river metaphor that Meisner and many Meisner teachers use. In the metaphor, the current of the river, that interconnected dynamic underneath the language, drives the exercise. The value of the exercise, then, is not determined by the content of the words but the extent to which you let the experience underneath the language take you somewhere. You can probably see why this is not a far-fetched concept in acting. Actors almost never have direct experience with the lives of their characters and so, when they speak their character's words, are almost constantly lying. Is this even an issue for an audience? Of course not. What is of value to us is that actors are being authentic. It has been replicated so many times across great performances that there is ample evidence it is entirely possible to live truthfully without respect to the content of what is being said. Leadership training, like actor training, does not equate its emphasis on expressing oneself with authenticity with literal truthfulness. It is not only possible to lie and be truthful: it is at the centre of this work.

To avoid the hounding of moralising, let me be clear: I do not at the outset condone leaders lying nor am I encouraging you as a leader to lie. To be perfectly honest, however, those are moral boundaries that every individual must draw, and so it would be arrogant and foolhardy of me to try to impose those kinds of restrictions at the outset. Even worse, to you it would be irrelevant. My personal bent leans heavily towards being honest whenever possible, but this is about training leadership, not morality policing. You will find, when carefully considered, that there are many occasions when leaders, especially those involved in constant negotiations, must be very careful of what they reveal, when they reveal it, and how much is revealed at any given time. These are selective disclosures based on calculations aimed at achieving the fulfilment of that leader's vision.

As I have said before, in my view the fulfilment of a leadership-driven vision is almost always of beneficial health to the individual and society. Leaders must factor means and ends as part of an equation towards seeing their visions come to life. That's not being immoral. It's reality.

The nurturing and optimisation of success of vision is what good leadership training aims towards. All leadership training must, regardless of who dislikes or is upset by this notion, take into account this reality: leaders might only be able to disseminate partial information in a given exchange, but they still must be able to be entirely authentic when doing this. This training supports that necessity by making living truthfully more about interpersonal observations and responses rather than textual honesty.

Living truthfully under the given circumstances, which is the core definition of the Meisner Technique as well as our definition for successful leadership, targets this need, I believe, in a way no other approach to training leaders I have seen or read about does. I have been critical of other means of developing leadership skills and for good reason in my view, though there are some that have their merits. I see this approach as being the cleanest and most efficient way to give a leader what they need, which is the ability to live truthfully, i.e. observe clearly and respond authentically, under a variety of conditions, pressures, and demands. The more truthful a leader can be under whatever circumstances they need to succeed in, the more power they will gain from other individuals who will recognise this authenticity, as well as adaptability, and take that as a marker of value. People place their trust in what is valuable and are motivated to work for it. That is the essence of acquired interpersonal power. An optimal tool for leadership, then, aims at acquiring interpersonal power while being able to handle as many unique variables as possible in the process.

Training a leader using this technique demonstrates that in conversation, the text does not always have to have meaning. This is a known inherent value that can be seen in most dimensions of leadership. Negotiations that include small talk, for example, might already begin far before the relevant language content comes into play. Beneath the words is an entire subtext of gestures, tones, inflections, and physical actions, of careful observations and subtle expressions. Presentations are another good example: given the short attention span of people, rarely is your being listened to dependent the literal content of your presentation. Unless people are forced to listen to you – and even if they are, they might become unavoidably bored – how successful your delivery is does not depend on how polished or structured your words are. Don't get me wrong, crafting a good speech or presentation is valuable, but it is a writing skill, not a presenting one. Successfully presenting either lives or dies based on how attuned you are to the energy and interactions of your observers in the moment. Don't believe me? As a learning experience, go and do a couple of acting auditions. While auditioning, try to ignore dealing with the energy in the room as well as the impact it is having on you. It will only override you. In each of these examples, whether it is negotiation, presentations, or even auditions, subtext, that which is underneath the words, determines what you do and how you respond. How well you work, or do not work, with reality and its many variables will determine how well you come across to an audience.

Becoming a careful and keen observer of these subtextual cues is of utmost value to a leader. What to do with them then becomes your next issue. As we will see later, however, attempting to decipher all of them with equal attention will not only set you up for disaster, as human behaviour is often too complex to accurately interpret a significant portion of the time, but it also pulls you from the direct, momentary nature of the interaction. Trying to become a master of subtext by cerebral interpretation, as repetition shows you early on, will quickly make you a master of nothing because you will be constantly in your head and having no time to respond to what the other person is doing. It is akin to blocking in the martial arts: unless you proactively strike, you will always be on the defensive, a victim to your opponent's continuous moves. This leaves you stuck while they have the ability to adapt their strategy freely. Your priorities and values are all in the wrong place.

The better and wiser option, then, is in the response: to respond with truthful impulses to what is presented before you. The more we train this value in repetition even more interesting questions will arise. Truthfulness, after all, as we have seen is not about niceness or politeness. Remember our motto a good leader must live by? That's right: fuck polite. Now again to repeat, that doesn't mean be rude or ignore the customs of the people in front of you. As you will see later, those polite behaviours can still become a part of living truthfully under your given circumstances. One of the questions fuck polite begins to beget at this stage is what do we do when things like aggression, irritation, or downright rudeness come up in the exercises? We'll get into this in this very chapter, as at its core this is an equivalency problem that we must deal with: the more powerful your observational skills become, the deeper, and sometimes bigger, the impulses will be that are generated by them. Do you express those impulses or do you not? Are there limits to authenticity's value? By virtue of these questions beginning to arise, this session progresses into deeper waters than the previous ones have.

One of the functions of good leadership training is to not only make you ask questions of yourself but to ensure they are the right questions. Training you in an exercise where the words have no inherent meaning but bringing you directly into contact with the meaning that comes from observing your partner in a rich way already brings up important questions. That we take it even further and suggest that not only do you want to observe deeply but respond authentically has brought us to even more profound questions, not just about leadership in general but you specifically as a leader and your own boundaries. You won't answer these questions in this session. Most likely you'll have to see the training through to the end to discover your own answers and limits. Still, we won't shy away from these questions and will explore them as deeply and thoroughly as possible. This is, after all, a journey into the heart of what it means to be a great leader. That's worth taking some time to consider.

Point of View

The average person's existential experience, especially the younger they are, is spent living in a largely isolated, self-oriented bubble. Learning how to work with another person in the way demanded by the Meisner Technique gives you a leg up. Having someone fully put their attention on you is deeply provocative, powerful, and seductive, something we are not used to even in our personal lives. This full attention is the root of the power of eye contact, but we have extended one step further: if eye contact is powerful, then eye contact with deep authenticity is utterly engrossing. This brings us to the next step for you to take in this training.

Developing a leader with the exercise of you-you repetition confers major advantages. If we just stopped here, however, we would leave you with a large gap, a major flaw in your training. The gap can be best summarised this way: while not often, sometimes the content of speech, the words and text, do have meaning. Meaning in this sense means beyond just literal or perfunctory meaning: this is the meaning that has personal value. Sometimes the words themselves are more important than the behaviours producing, and existing around, them. Arguably, when they do have such meaning is the time you want to be able to spot them the most.

I'll give you an example from my personal life. As you read in Chapter 1, for the past two years I have spent a lot of time in doctors' offices and, though less than before, I still do. Almost all of those appointments begin with a greeting: 'Good morning' or 'How's it going?' Most of the time it is absolutely meaningless, a cordial lubricant for further conversation. This is the function of text in most situations and pairs perfectly with the values we are exploring in repetition. There have, however, been some exceptions:

> 'We got your test results back and … well, I've got some news.'

Each time I heard that, I can promise you the text would have far more meaning in the next few moments than all the empty salutations that came before. The meaning of that sentence was far more potent for me than any of the previous words heard. This shows that, though rare, there are times when the literal value of words carries exceptional value. We need to build into your leadership training a way that can facilitate both possibilities: for authentic exchanges to occur regardless of the language, flowing on that river of subtextual interconnectedness between you and your partner, while at other times achieving the same level of high-quality interpersonal interactions when the content of language becomes the prime object of value and importance to the exclusion of everything else happening in the moment. Here's how we are going to do that.

Exercise: You–I Repetition

Let's start another repetition just like the one we worked on before. You and your partner are the guinea pigs, as usual. The basic ground rules are the same: you are going to look at your partner and notice something about them. What you notice has to be a fact. Not a concern, question, opinion, speculation, or anything else. A simple fact. You will say what you see. Nothing new, so far. Let's do one to get us warmed up. I'll ask you to begin. Let's say in this hypothetical scenario your partner has had a bad hair day and is wearing a cap in the exercise.

You: You're wearing a hat.
Partner: You're wearing a hat.
You: You're wearing a hat.
Partner: You're wearing a hat.
Etc.

Now that we are remembering our feet in the exercise and ready for work I give you a break. And a new instruction. I let you know a modification is now going to be made to the repetition exercise. You are going to begin the next exercise with a simple observation of your partner just like before. That is the first important thing to note: nothing will change on the end of the observer, the person who begins the exercise. The modification occurs solely with the person repeating the initial observation, in this case your partner. Beforehand your partner would repeat word for word what they heard you say. Now they will repeat back word for word what they heard you say but *from their own point-of-view*.

This is where I normally get an eye glaze. What did he just say? It's actually quite simple. For a demonstration, I ask you to make the same call you used before.

You begin: 'You're wearing a hat.'

Beforehand, your partner would have repeated: 'You're wearing a hat,' provided that is what they heard.

Now, however, the exercise will look something like this:

You: You're wearing a hat.
Partner: I'm wearing a hat.

You: You're wearing a hat.
Partner: I'm wearing a hat.
Etc.

All that changes is your partner now repeats from their perspective. You'll do the same if you're the one repeating the initial observation. Let's see an example of that where this time your partner begins:

Partner: You have blond hair.
You: I have blond hair.
Partner: You have blond hair.
You: I have blond hair.
Etc.

Just to remind you, the 'Etc.' implies that I let the exercises run on for a bit beyond the written example, and this one here is no exception. Repetition exercises in the early stages often go for 2–5 minutes, and later in the training may go for even longer. When you and your partner finish this round, we have a break and talk about the experience. I ask the group if they notice a difference in the quality of the work between you and your partner. Almost always everyone nods. I now ask you both if it felt different. Normally I get a 'yes.' What isn't clear immediately is 'why' it feels different, so let's rewind one degree and ask 'how' did it feel different? Again, just for clarity, these answers are not the responses I expect clients to say. On the rare occasion that I do get a 'no' when I ask participants if it feels different, the conversation progresses just as well. Those are rarer examples, however, so I don't include them here, since I want to represent the most commonly encountered experiences in this training.

Back to our question of how it felt different, the answer is almost always the same: the exercise feels more personal. You may not be able to put your finger yet on why but it feels qualitatively deeper. Words such as 'real,' 'connected,' and 'intimate' have come up, all circling around the same feeling of somehow being more richly tethered to each another. Looking at this in technical terms, we can arrive at the 'why' then. Go back to the idea of the text as a canoe on the river of interconnectedness between you and your partner. In this new incarnation of repetition, at times the text floats on top of the observing and responding going on underneath the words. Now, however, at times the text can have more meaning. Suddenly it feels more personal. Why? The answer is simple. In order to facilitate text being able to have meaning in the moment, we have introduced a key ingredient of human connection: point of view.

Allowing for point of view to be a part of the experience expands possibilities within the work. There is a degree of *ownership* introduced, a concept we will revisit often throughout this work. In this instance, instead of both of you owning the observation equally now your partner owns their end by repeating 'I'. In addition, unless there is a change such as your partner taking their hat off when they started the exercise with one on, the text is no longer a lie. That, however, does not mean it will always have meaning. To explore this further let's do another exercise, this time with you beginning.

You: You coughed.
Partner: I coughed.
You: You coughed.
Partner: I coughed.
Etc.

It's a spirited exercise. During it you both fall into the trap of playing word games with the text. You inflect the phrase in novel ways, posture at one another, make faces, almost a pantomime. It is clear that this comes not from the behaviours coming from one another but from your mutually shared desire to play with the phrase itself. My excitement at point of view now seems to have turned on us, as it appears more like an invitation to forget the values of repetition and create an improvisation. When we finish, I point out all the gallant verbal jousting, asking if, qualitatively, the experience this time around was more or less rewarding than the first two exercises when you weren't playing word games but just letting the moments come from one another, responding organically rather than concerning yourself with what you wanted to do with the text. More or less rewarding? Their answer 100% of the time? Less.

This directly exposes the core of the issue. Allowing text to have meaning in the moment doesn't mean it always will. How relevant its content is in the moment will vary from moment to moment. We are not determining outcomes but broadening possibilities. At the same time, the core value of the work still has not changed: what happens to you still does not depend on you but rather on what the other person is doing to you. The same goes for them and so we are left with the question at the heart of the exercise: now that the text is far more specific in that one of you takes ownership of the observation by using the word 'I', when does point of view have more or less meaning in the moment? What determines when a phrase will have more or less relevance to the moment? The answer is in the question: the moment itself. That is the spontaneous nature of responding truthfully to what you are given rather than trying to control and dominate the event as you wish it to happen.

Seem vague and slippery? Yes, and it's only going to get worse from here. To be clear, however, this is still a concrete answer. The moment determining the validity of something is not a matter of faith or believing me on principle; rather, it is a question of your sensitivity to subtle changes within a dynamic. You'll feel it first-hand in the exercise: the more you try to control the event, the more hollow it will feel. There's an even worse reality you'll quickly figure out when you are observing others do the work.

Let's say if you and your partner are working and you decide to make a meal out of the text, a phrase from acting that describes word games, of the nature seen in this last exercise. What happens if your partner doesn't take the bait? Rather than engaging in some game of textual one-upping, they just continue to observe you and respond truthfully to your antics. From our perspective in the audience it is the game player who begins to look very quickly less authentic, more plastic. Conversely your histrionics will cause your partner to seem more alive, dynamic, and beautifully effortless. In trying to dominate the event you hand victory over to the other person.

You can see this value play out in leadership when one person is too busy posturing and the other is simply flowing off of what they do. The solution this training offers? I'll say it again: avoid word games. Do less. Surrender control to your partner and watch your magnetism increase. If your partner doesn't do the same back they lose all hope of holding their ground and you will show a level of non-intentional presence that will easily dominate in the eyes of any observers. This meaty paradox that produces results was best summarised in a phrase my Meisner teacher Scott would always tell us: 'You will win this by losing.'

The value then of this session to your leadership is in your beginning to train instilling within yourself the concept that even with a point of view, where your words can have the possibility of strong meaning in the moment if the moment determines it is needed, you can still make your responses fully dependent and connected to the other person and their environment. Words do not always need to be meaningless; they can have immense meaning and still retain the core values of this work. If that is the case, then every response you have will be truthful if you follow that rule. That places a potent and powerful tool in your arsenal. Now, however, let's talk about some other important essentials.

Daring Pandora's Box

Let's say you and your partner take a break. Other people in the class do you–I repetitions. Normally by the time I teach this it is the second session and we have broken the ice a little as a group. We are also beginning to be more willing to try the concept of 'fuck polite' and, as such, some interesting things begin to arise in the exercises. Partners more freely display taboo behaviours like annoyance, flirting, aggression, joy, sorrow, and so on. Their responses start to show deeper, richer hues of emotions and behaviours that are often seen as 'grey area' in society. This can alarm some people. I know I *said* 'fuck polite' and live truthfully but now the waters really are getting qualitatively deeper. The accomplishments of the previous session are not the end point for this training, and they won't end here. Experiences will continue to become deeper and more powerful with each session. It may not be clear on the page but you'll find it is a pretty powerful experience when you observe and respond truthfully and spontaneously. As we go on we will continue to revisit the question of boundaries and permissible behaviours, not to retread the same ground but to look closer as newer, deeper expressions of authenticity with more subtlety and nuance arise. This work is personal. It brings up a real question: when you brush up against the walls of your comfort zone what do we do with that?

Authenticity seems to be prized in leadership. When you hear most people talk about an authentic leader their descriptions of that person may be: relaxed, at ease, warm and open, agreeable but aggressive. Basically that human TED Talk. As you are quickly seeing and experiencing, however, real authenticity is not some enlightened one-note quality but something more primal and animal, nuanced and complex. We grew up as a species responding to a cruel environment and taking care of each other. Sometimes the lines between those two realities become incredibly blurred. Co-habitation is an experiment we are still testing. We don't like to admit this, however, and so ignore that our responses to the outside world haven't stopped being so complex just because a few comfortable generations have gone by. Through repetition and fuck polite we seem to have a doorway opening to the real thing. Are we really walking the walk when we say these authentic expressions are allowed in, of all things, leadership training, or are we slowly opening a Pandora's box where all that awaits is disaster and regret?

There is a simple answer and an expanded one. I'll give you both. The simple answer is that, according to our ground rules, so long as your responses come from the other person they are truthful. Truthful responses are fair game in the training especially since we have placed a premium on truthfulness as a key ingredient of being authentic. Since authenticity is a magnet for power, then training yourself to act on a truthful response, rather than inhibit one, is the better general strategy to adopt. Acting on truthful impulses is an essential component of the success of this work being applicable to your leadership development. If it came from the other person and not an idea or agenda of your own, then express it. If you wish to have a response based on some clever idea of yours, then instead of acting on it, redirect your attention to your partner. Not sure yet of what exactly an impulse from you versus another person actually feels like? That's fine. You aren't expected to know the difference yet on day two or three. Understanding that distinction as a matter of learnt intuition is also part of your growth in this work.

This leads us to the expanded answer, a deeper exploration into this question that has profound implications on what leadership means for you. In using this training to develop your leadership abilities you can and should allow yourself to go farther beyond the limits than you ever thought possible or permissible. If examined closely enough, I would argue that the majority of conventional leadership training is about training you to be polite and appropriate, thereby denying a wide range of your authenticity. This means that many people who feel like confident leaders have glaring weaknesses in their abilities. Just by virtue of this training not being bridled by the conventions of appropriate and polite behaviour we are creating a distinct advantage for you. It's not just about giving you more options, though. The conventional habit of pre-emptively reigning in your authenticity feels more comfortable. It feels better to minimise our own chaos and uncertainty, which is an example of where we mistake what feels good for what is actually good for us. Self-censoring will gain you far less power and advancement if authenticity is what really matters to others.

Just to be clear, this training is not aimed at turning you into a callous, rude, uncensored authoritarian monster. What you will find is it makes you more flexible, equally comfortable with the more confrontational dark sides of you as well as the warmer ones. The key ingredient you don't have yet is the given circumstances part of the equation. Down the road when we get to it, you will see it shows you the way to get the best of both worlds, to at times be warm and genial, while at others unleashing less conventional and polite authentic responses and to know when which is needed. Currently in these exercises you have no given circumstances. They haven't come up and are not a big deal right now. If you wanted to be hyper-specific you could say you have the given circumstances of a student in a class, but if you really work through this, we come back to the same conclusion: you currently have no actual given circumstances of relevance to your leadership ambitions.

For now, you'll have to wait for me to answer the question of how given circumstances are the meditator between training a wide range of authentic responses, some of which might not seem applicable or appropriate, and how to import that authenticity into specific circumstances and scenarios. We aren't worried about the given circumstances work because we are after something else right now. What we are after is to understand what your default mode in this should work be.

Default mode? Yes. Consider the inherent Pandora's box we have hinted at with authenticity, far more messy and chaotic than many of us are comfortable with. Fuck polite pulls the curtain back and shows us the box and begins to pry its cautionary lid open. We are arriving at an impasse which will determine the course of this training and how much value it is to you. Either we keep saying your authentic responses are permissible or we hem them in now. Is your default mode as a leader one of real, chaotic authenticity or of self-censoring? My answer is that your default mode should be truthfulness. It gives you a level of depth and flexibility to adapt to any given circumstances you might encounter. Authenticity is less comfortable. No one wants to break the social conventions and seem more human. Leaders, however, aren't made because of their adherence to norms or blending in. As the bigger impulses start to bubble up, so long as they are truthful go ahead. Act on them.

Though we aren't worrying about given circumstances yet, it can be said here that you will find, if you adopt truthful responses as your default mode, that the given circumstances of a situation do not become an imposition on authentic behaviour. Instead, they become a filter for it. Let's take a good example that a number of clients get worried about early in this work: aggression. You'll find there are times when aggression is not the prime strategy to adopt in an interpersonal interaction, and its use may prove costly to your needs with that individual. Other people, however, won't respect you unless they see a display of aggression. In these interactions, aggression is a vital tool for a leader. What's the difference? The circumstances. In some given circumstances, one set of truthful behaviours are needed while in others a different set is required. In the latter example, however, are a series of behaviours we may have been tempted to dismiss outright as having no relevance solely because of our discomfort with the response itself.

This principle extends to all types of authentic responses in the taboo or grey area at best. It is not that they are always inappropriate; they just become less relevant in certain situations. Later in this training you will experience first-hand how the given circumstances filter your truthful impulses in an extremely powerful way. For now, creating a foundation of authenticity and truthfulness from which to work is the ideal strategy. Yes, things get messier in a very human way, but it's worth it. Consider the inverse, where you are continuously censoring and judging certain responses of yours as inappropriate. Eventually you create blanket categories of acceptable and unacceptable. This will only limit you. Look at our above example of aggression. One challenge I have seen female clients from certain cultures run into is overestimation, by telling themselves to never respond aggressively and that it will never be needed. If you are a leader, I guarantee you there will be times when some form of aggression will be essential to your vision's survival. On a side note, I have run into the opposite problem mostly with male students who think that testosterone-charged headbutting is a sure-fire way to successful leadership.

The conclusion in either case is that inflexible blanket strategies for the future fail often enough to be a major hindrance. Intuition is a valuable guide, but it performs poorly when adopting strategies for the future. Your intuitive calculations about how to restrict your authenticity will only give you less access to certain responses when they are needed, severely weakening and disadvantaging you as a leader.

The Value of Dosed Chaos

The concept of dosed chaos is worth introducing here and is an extremely valuable one to consider in relation to your leadership development. All this idealist talk about expanding, rather than restricting, authenticity has one caveat. Rarely is developing your authenticity a comfortable process. It is exhilarating at times, but comfort rarely comes with overcoming one's limitations. Given that this is a personal process, it makes sense that every student has their own specific limit. That limit is the line where things go from intense learning to intensity without learning value.

I'll give you an example that comes up not for many but for some. At this point in the work, touch tends to start arising organically in the exercises. I'm not talking about anything dramatic, either, just normal physical contact: a hand on an arm or a small hug. Even small moments of human contact in this work can be immensely powerful because they rise from the organic spontaneous nature of the moment. In the past, some of my oldest clients, however, have not wished to be touched. Why? A simple but vital reason: they have arthritis, their health may not be good, they are sensitive to contact, etc. Other older clients are fine with it, but this is a clear example of someone's personal line in this work. The solution to this example isn't difficult either. When they get up to work, those who don't wish to be touched simply say, 'I'd like not to be touched, please.' Completely reasonable and so long as the rest of the moments between people are truthful, there can still be immense value in these exercises with healthy restrictions and boundaries.

Other people do not wished to be touched not for health but for personal reasons. A hand on an arm or a playful shove may be too much. These are personal comfort zones based on past history or other reasons. The beauty of this work is no one, myself included, needs to know the reasons. We just need to know the boundary. If someone says, 'I'd like not to be touched, please', then that is fine. There are still lots of valuable things to be gained from these exercises. Having said that, if there's no reason my advice is don't impose restrictions. Our aim is to reduce the self-censoring tendencies within you, not define ones where there weren't any before. Even small moments of meaningful physical contact are profound, especially when the exchanges get this authentic. As a coach, however, this is the important thing I will keep emphasising with clients: having limits is perfectly fine. Honouring those limits is part of my job. All that is asked of you is to make people aware of them when you discover them for yourself so everyone can support your learning in this process.

I say 'discover' because touch is a fairly obvious example, and restrictions on it are simple. Emotional boundaries are harder. Unfortunately, there is no way to pre-empt the emotional temperature of this work. Consider the scenario where you say, 'I don't want the exercise to get angry, or intimate.' This puts you at a complete disadvantage, as the entire exercise will be spent with both you and your partner self-censoring and monitoring, resulting in almost no meaningful time with one another.

The optimal strategy then is not to try to pre-emptively safeguard your emotional safety. Dive in and see what happens. If you sit on truthful responses, then that is the teaching material for you. If you find yourself ending up in emotional waters that are too much, just say, 'I'd like to stop the exercise.' I may check in to make sure you are all right, but you won't need to give any justification or reason. The learning is not hampered by taking a break. For context here, these are incredibly rare occasions, not the norm. In my whole career I have only seen an exercise stopped twice because it became too much. Both of those instances were met with support from me, as no learning value had been lost. If it's too much, it is better to stop before passing your threshold than to force yourself past it and later convince yourself the training is not for you because it is too intense. The work is deep but gradual; it builds up to a range of authentic expression that matches your needs. Doing damage control is much harder.

The idea of boundaries becomes more subtle and nuanced as this training progresses. It may surprise you that for most people, boundaries never become a halting issue to their development in this technique because it is exciting and rewarding to widen your threshold for authentic experiences. Part of what allows you to venture to your own personal limits regarding what you will and will not permit yourself to express is you know that both you and your partner always have the right to set boundaries or stop an exercise if either of you feel too uncomfortable. It is not up to me to judge what determines the limits of a person's learning – that is entirely in their own hands. Why do I say this? To caution you to be intensely wary of a sizeable number of Meisner teachers out there who do not feel that way. It is in the culture of the training itself for teachers to continually wish to push students beyond their limits. If you are pushed too far and shut down, according to them, it becomes your fault and inability to handle it. Clearly, so say the wise ones, you need a thicker skin. This is nonsense. It's ritualistic hazing, and it doesn't do anything for the actors who go through it, and it certainly won't aid your leadership skills.

As an aspiring leader you must know, or at least discover and then vocalise, your limits to the coach so they will know when to rein things in if ever necessary. Repetition is an exercise that trains authenticity. Authenticity is a primal experience we are not always used to. It is far better to communicate what you are and are not comfortable with earlier on rather than braving through it, which I have seen cause some people to shut down emotionally. This isn't coddling you: we are talking about inefficient, wasted time. Classical conditioning shows us that if you encounter a stimuli that is highly distressing, you will develop avoidance habits. Those habits weren't there before. The time it takes for us to get past a habit of avoidance in this work loses a great deal of time for your development. It is far better to be overt about boundaries in the exercise and then move or alter them later as you see fit.

At this point, some of you may be wondering, 'What the hell is he talking about? What goes on in these classes?!' At this stage, not much. Down the road, things don't suddenly erupt into the worst-case scenario either. We are having the conversation now so you can have a sense that the depth on offer in this work is vast, and you have only just scratched the surface of it. If you are using these exercises in a class, you might be thinking, 'But nothing intense has happened yet, are we doing something wrong?' Of course not. Each exercise is different and each one has its own unique characteristics. As a coach, I don't have expectations on these sorts of outcomes. In the beginning, I mostly look for the technical structure of the exercise. I have a clear understanding of this, but the rest, the good stuff between you and your partner, is in the hands of the future. What happens from moment to moment is, to me, like everyone else, a mystery until it arrives. These exercises are filled with possibilities. The waters run very deep.

False Positives in Training

We've covered the importance of not pushing yourself too far too fast. There is, however, an equally important concept around the boundaries conversation, one that directly relates to technique and training. It is a principle that almost every Meisner teacher violates to the detriment of their students. This, however, is not just an error confined to this approach. Beyond the Meisner Technique, just about every leadership or business coach crosses this boundary. The reason it is worth talking about is twofold: one, you'll be able to recognise it if you study this technique with another teacher and can avoid taking the bait. Two, and most importantly, this problem does not need to come from a teacher, as you can create it just as easily for yourself. Let's examine what exactly this issue so you won't set yourself back in your leadership development by falling into this trap.

What is this universal woe I keep alluding to? It's best introduced in this simple way: if you have worked with leadership coaches before, you may notice that many like to push their clients towards a result. It can be a large or small result, but it relates to some learning experience offered within the material being covered. The pushing doesn't have to be a major event, either; oftentimes it looks like gently nudging students farther than they knew they could go. Overt phrases like 'Keep going' or 'I think you could go a little farther' capture it, but this is also done in so many subtle hues and variations. The benefit to you, the leader, seems huge: with a little help from the coach, the client experiences a breakthrough moment in their development. A discovery is made. You save yourself time and get the benefit of advancing further than you would have on your own. Everyone wins.

Except that's not really what happens. It's why I don't push students. It's poison to a leader.

From a coach's perspective in training leadership, the feedback I give is critical. The nature of the feedback itself is even more vital. Is this about a leader's development or is it about making them *feel* as if they've developed? You can feel like you've made progress and not gone forward at all, so which is it? This is not an easy one to answer. To start, everyone progresses at different rates in their leadership journey. Inevitably, at some point, everyone plateaus and the plateau is self-reflective. You find yourself encountering a facet of your personality (a habit, principle, or belief might be an example) that begins to continuously get in your way. The idea of some quick fix that solves all your problems in a single session is a myth. In reality, self-rooted challenges to leadership can take weeks or even months to address. Within that truism is a bitter honesty for both coach and client: it is hard to keep coming back if all that happens is you circle around a breakthrough for months on end with no clear outcome in sight. After all, it's in the language: you don't know when you'll break through the plateau. It will suddenly happen. Tipping points are a powerful thing in learning but profoundly unpredictable.

This situation can create reasonable frustration. You feel as if you aren't getting anywhere but could if you just had a little help. Your coach doesn't want to see you suffer but also reasonably is concerned about retaining you as a client. To offset both your frustration and the concerns a coach has for their place in your development, a big, red juicy apple of temptation easily arises: a little nudging and pushing from the coach can help the client get there faster. You really like this because it keeps you confident that you are making progress and I, the coach, am relieved by it because there is an ends-justify-the-means thinking I have bought into about my student: 'Well, I've nudged him this time but down the road he'll go longer and longer without needing my support' or 'She just needed a push, it probably won't happen again' Or even more broadly, 'What's the problem? They still made the discovery!'

In the Meisner world, I see this all the time in repetition; there are fewer better case studies for this temptation to arise. Let's take a hypothetical example. You and your partner are doing a repetition exercise. A moment arises between you and your partner that we could describe as quietly gentle. It's not huge, there's no giant behaviour, but it's a warm intimacy that, even though quantitatively small, is qualitatively extremely powerful. Let's say this is a minor boundary area for you, that for whatever reason this kind of contact is a little too much for you. Because it's not a huge boundary, rather than stop the exercise you choose to shy away from your partner, staying inside the experience but avoiding this series of moments until the exercise goes to ground you are more comfortable with. It's not an optimal strategy, but it's not a terrible one either.

Let's say, however, you've been working with me as your coach for a while now. Let's also say this isn't the first time you've run away from this kind of interaction. I intuitively know once you get past this hurdle there will be some incredible discoveries waiting for you on the other side. I'm tired of your indecisiveness and impatient to see you get to those discoveries. The next time you begin to shy away from your partner, I call out, in the middle of the exercise, 'Stop running away! Stay with your partner! Don't be afraid!' You comply and what do you know? You make the breakthrough. It feels great, you finally didn't run away! You feel as if you've really expanded your range and scope of authenticity in this discovery. It feels intense to go there, but you now also see it feels great.

This is not an abnormal type of situation at all in this kind of training; it goes on all the time. And in this scenario you really have made the breakthrough. It did happen. You crossed a boundary in a healthy way. And guess what? Now, as a consequence of what I have done, you own zero percent of that discovery.

An essential core concept in training leadership is the idea of ownership. Every leader must think of the tools they are acquiring in terms of ownership: will these translate outside of a classroom or coaching session? Can I take them into any context they are suited for? Ownership equates to portability. If you don't own all of the progress and discoveries made in training, you will be lacking the essential key of ownership and therefore portability.

So let's go back to our moment in this session. You feel yourself on the edge of new territory in your range of truthful responses. You have sat on these impulses long enough: to hell with it, you say, and you make the plunge. Who owns the discovery? You! No one made you go there. You went there of your own accord, and part of what made you go there was your being sick of your own avoidance habit. There is a structured, intensely personal learning process happening here. You are teaching yourself in an experiential way to adopt a more optimal strategy by expressing the authenticity you have been denying for so long.

Except that is not what happened. What happened is that I saw you teetering on that edge and decided to give you a helpful nudge. I saw you sitting on the impulses and I pushed you towards a discovery. Who owns the discovery? Not you. You didn't go there yourself. It was entirely dependent on me. The evidence? Had I not pushed you, you would not have gone there. How is that going to be portable for you? 'But it felt good!' some might protest. Of course it did, you didn't have to do any learning! In effect, what happened is I structured a challenging scenario and solved it for you. It is of real value to you to become acutely aware of how the teacher gives feedback if you actually wish to have ownership over the material you learn rather than simply feel better about yourself. It is worth trading the time to circle around the impulse long enough for you to get sick of it rather than my taking your learning into my hands, giving you a bump over the hurdle, and thereby increasing dependence on me.

Where this is taking us is into some of the psychology behind the learning of leadership ability. The conventional push-and-nudge coaching is an example of classical conditioning at work. In classical conditioning, if you want to program a response, you introduce an intermediate stimulus that eventually triggers the response. The response we want is for you to express your truthful impulses so long as they arise from the other person. If the stimulus that triggers the breakthrough is me, my voice, my motivation, my intervention, then the second you leave the classroom and find yourself inhibiting an authentic response you're going to be up the creek because you no longer have your stimulus. Every time as a coach I intervene and motivate a client to perform a certain behaviour in the hopes of making a discovery, I am conditioning myself as the stimulus for learning. This is a disaster for training leaders.

There is an alternative stimulus in this work that is far healthier but less pleasant. You will quickly learn from the inside that, as these exercises deepen, sitting on an impulse does not feel good. If you are in a rich interaction with someone and a truthful impulse arises but you sit on it, for fear of being rude or impolite, that action will plant a feeling of discomfort inside you. It physically does not feel good in an exercise about expressing authenticity to be the designated self-censoring driver. Every time you sit on that impulse in future repetitions, that frustration will continue to build. Eventually, in classical terms, this will drive you to seek an alternative behaviour, called avoidance. What is the best solution for avoiding habitually inhibiting yourself? You got it: expression. Creating avoidance strategies of this kind involve a rich learning process that over time leads you to have a way of working that is entirely portable and not dependent on a coach. You eventually learn from the inside it feels better to express your authenticity and is far more gratifying than having someone push you to do it. Ownership, you teach yourself, is the best reward for overcoming your challenges.

Feedback before or after the exercises is fine. A coach intervening during an exercise is not a good idea. There are exceptions, but they are extremely rare. A good coach will intervene maybe one in 50 times, and I only give this possibility because some unaccounted for rare variable may arise that must be addressed in the moment. As a good rule of thumb, if a coach keeps intervening in a repetition exercise as it is happening, guiding you and directing you, then find a new coach.

How a Leader Learns Best

The psychology of learning is a deep and fascinating topic. Since you are sincere about honing and developing your leadership skills, then exploring it further is a worthwhile endeavour, especially early in the training when you are still not only learning the content of the training but the environment around it. Such a discussion also helps you better understand yourself in this process. Let's look at the concept of feedback after the exercises have finished. Feedback is either the art of good teaching or the downfall of poor instructors. You don't even need to examine the coaches themselves – clients often reflect the quality of feedback they have received in their development. Successful feedback, I argue, follows the way of Lao Tsu's *Tao Te Ching*: it is structured in a way that makes all of the participants feel as if they came to the conclusions themselves. This is targeted indirect feedback. The result is that the client owns the discoveries made in the process. Direct feedback, on the other hand, often robs the student of the discovery. It allows the coach to take ownership of the problems in the client's process rather than allowing the clients themselves to come into close proximity with the problem and then decide whether or not to take action.

Let me give an example that illustrates the two. I mentioned earlier that when I work with some female students, particularly from certain cultures, aggression is a major problem for them. They have been taught to be always smiling, elegant, polite, seductive, or any other social constraint you want to name they might have been force-fed, but it all equates to the same problem: in their work in repetition exercises their learned habits stunt their ability to express aggression or anger when the moment calls for it. This is not a virtue for them at all. This is a whole range of authentic expression being denied through learnt behaviour. Those roots take a strong hold and overcoming them usually causes great suffering.

From my experience, if I can name a general struggle when I work with these clients, it is in trying to make the case that there is a role for aggression in their leadership. Intuition and the given circumstances will determine when to have a response different than aggression, but when it is needed, to not have access to these responses robs them of one of the key elements of leadership that goes back to Machiavelli and Sun Tsu: successful leaders must balance kindness with their ability to express their power through anger, rage, and severity. To be clear this is not to be confused with people in upper-management positions who are chronically short-tempered. When this type of sudden outburst is called for is determined by the moment and situation, the given circumstances. A leader attuned to the people around them will find this measure is rarely called for, but when it is required there cannot be room for hesitation or trying to muster the courage to express it.

When I encounter a censoring habit in a student that stunts aggression, I've got a choice as a coach for how to work with it. The first option is addressing it directly. I could say, 'You're not getting angry when you should. You're holding yourself back. Show some rage!' It's specific and to the point, but it doesn't really help the deeper problem. The reason for this begins with the value I place on not interrupting exercises, because I don't want to become a stimulus in conditioning new learnt habits. As a result, I give feedback at the end of an exercise. When a student hears direct feedback like the above, they engage in a problem-solving strategy for the future. You can't repeat the past but maybe you can fix it in the next exercise. Ergo, the newly learnt strategy from that feedback goes like this: anger and aggression are a problem for me. In the next exercise I'll get angry and that will solve the problem.

That strategy undermines everything in this work. All of the values are lost. Goodbye 50–50 balance of observe and respond, farewell living truthfully, no more what happens to you does not depend on you. Everything we have built is thrown out the window, so long, Marianne, you get the idea. Now you have taken complete responsibility of the exercise. All that is now being taken into the work is an agenda that will be imposed on, rather than taken from, your partner. You'll learn something, all right, but it won't be anything that helps you as a leader. Direct feedback in training leaders almost never works.

The implication for you is that you may have convinced yourself that you learn best through being pushed and given blunt, direct feedback. Maybe that's going to work in some domains, but if you bring that habit into your leadership training you are just going to deny any actually meaningful learning, creating far more challenges than are good. You may learn to identify problems that aren't really there and become dependent on another pushing you to obtain results. I'll give you a sad but true example that illustrates it.

One of the best actors I ever had the pleasure to train was one whom I taught in a workshop in Berlin. She had every gift and talent imaginable to work with and had career success painted all over her. At the same time, however, she didn't have the confidence in repetition exercises that reflected her actual abilities. I also sensed within her a growing frustration about my feedback. Finally, it all came out one afternoon: some coach, a long time ago, had told her she was emotionally blocked. The key to identifying the emotional block was that whenever she was nervous, she would 'run away' by laughing. Her frustration stemmed from her perception of my either not seeing it or commenting on it.

This caught me off guard, to say the least. The idea of being emotionally blocked, in the way I often hear it used, is an emotional defence mechanism that's a modified hand-me-down from Freud. There are certainly some people who learn how to inhibit certain emotional responses, but this is much more specific than the idea of a general block on one's ability to live truthfully. Nervous laughter can be a completely truthful response, therefore, it can be valid. Her coach had set up an impossible situation: how was she to know then when nervous laughter was genuine and when it was 'fake'? If she didn't know, how was I supposed to? Over years of repeated self-reinforcement she had developed an ingrained irrational belief about this issue. In my view, it completely offset her confidence in her work. This is an actor any common-sense person could see having an A-list career, and they're worried about laughing when they're nervous because some idiot made a blanket statement that is impossible to tell when it is right or wrong?

This is the danger of trying to be an authoritarian coach. People will remember what you tell them. It is also the danger of liking authoritarian 'brutal honesty' coaches. You end up overcompensating and overestimating the actual size of the problem. Or you'll just engage in unsolvable, non-existent challenges. That's because direct feedback, especially in this work, often gets translated into universal rules by the mind of the person hearing it. That mind also looks for evidence, as it is human nature to try to get clever at finding reinforcing examples. Sometimes you can find evidence for truisms that make no sense at all. In psychology this is called an illusory correlation, establishing a pattern where there is none in reality. This is a clear example where direct feedback, in my view, damaged the career and abilities of one of the most gifted people I've met, and it completely put us at an impasse for the majority of our time working together.

Acknowledging there is a delicate balance with feedback, however, doesn't mean I've solved it for us. Let's head back to my example of helping someone field their inhibitions about expressing aggression. We've already seen that a direct approach won't work, at least in the way we want it to. Is there an indirect route available? Indirect feedback is highly dependent on the individual. If we return to the example of a culturally learnt behaviour becoming a hinderance to an individual's learning, in my experience some people cannot or will not discuss their cultural background. If that their preference, it's fine, I won't use it in feedback. It may surprise you to know, however, that I've encountered an ample amount of people who are not only very open about the challenges their societal and cultural upbringing has created for them personally but also recognise it as a challenge to their leadership development. Let's say I am speaking with someone who falls into the latter category. If I know something about the values of that culture, we will talk a bit about them, and I'll ask questions. If I don't they'll fill me in and I will listen carefully. What we're both looking for in these questions is the cultural value that is getting in the way of their expressing themselves. We might discover, for example, the societal value that to be seen as large and imposing (personality-wise) is akin to social rudeness. The prescriptive treatment then, the norm, is to teach people from childhood on to shrink down. Now we've found a habit that is valuable within that society but runs counter to moments in leadership where aggression is needed. What happens if in feedback I let that client know that they don't need to shrink down in this work, that it isn't necessary?

You can see that through this way of working into a challenge, instead of asking them to express a specific behaviour in the future, the message is more malleable and personally specific. They haven't been told what to do prescriptively. What they now know is in this training environment they are not only allowed but encouraged to have the thing that they've been denying themselves for years: permission. If in the next exercise aggression rises organically, they might feel more confident about acting on it, but also there will be a spillover into other areas. By focusing on the macro rather than getting hung up on micro-issues, they've heard they don't need to make themselves small. What if other things arise that are also in off-limits territory? Now they might be willing to reconsider and take a risk, acting on the impulse they would otherwise sit on. Indirect, sometimes metaphorical feedback seems abstract, and it is, but when phrased correctly almost instantly it is made concrete by the individual and applied to their needs. Overtly direct feedback risks the bigger picture especially if I misinterpreted something about that student's behaviour in the exercise, which can happen to anybody teaching this work. Indirect feedback targets the big picture of that person and is, paradoxically, far more specific to their learning and needs.

To make this concept slightly more concrete, in feedback to you I won't talk about what went right or wrong in an exercise. That is a silly metric to use in the repetition drill, not only for its over-simplicity but also its missing the greater point. Yes, there are technically stronger or weaker repetition exercises, and so one could say that technically stronger ones are right while weaker ones are wrong, but as you will see later, this is a very poor tactic to take as sometimes 'breaking the rules' of the exercise leads to the most profound learning moments in leadership training. In a technique focused around dealing with what 'is' the inherent experience in an exercise is neither right or wrong. Either you observe clearly and respond truthfully, in which case I will reinforce that and encourage you to continue to build on that success, or you will encounter your own obstacles to responding truthfully, and I will do my best to lay out the territory of how you can improve. No right or wrong: just dealing with what is rather than what you want or expect. As my Meisner teacher Scott brilliantly says, 'Live in the "is" world, not the "should" world'.

Examining the types of feedback essential for success in training leaders, as well as the psychology of learning for certain people, may challenge you and your own preferences for how you learn. You may have a certain view regarding what a coach is and is not, and therefore an implicit expectation for how you will be spoken to. Depending on your expectations, this may pose as many challenges to your leadership training as the material itself. I am often told in the beginning by suspicious students that I am being too nice, that because I haven't berated them or pulled the rug out from under them surely I am being insincere. Or worse, if I am not borderline verbally abusing them, that I don't care about them. I know. As George Carlin wisely observed: 'People are fucking goofy.'

In terms of feedback here I often also encounter a gender split, although not as polarised as my example of aggression. For the most part, however, the men I work with prefer a noisy gym trainer approach: they want someone who will posture more than they do and push them further and harder. They have convinced themselves that a coach who is strict with them really means business. The reward centres in the brain light up at the phrase 'no bullshit'. To them the perception of niceness is a cover for insincerity. They want the straight talk. They don't want me to coddle them. In my experience, when I look closely, what I see is these are often the people with the most fragile egos. They rail against the notion while secretly begging to be babied.

I bring this up because there is a substantial minority of students I have worked with, both in the leadership and acting fields, who like this dominance ritual. The implications for this are not passive; your expectations on others have a very active impact when it comes to your leadership development. When I coach, I don't think about being nice. I am just not in the business of being an asshole on principle. There is actually a specific educational reason for this rather than a moral one. When I get a student who really presses me on the matter about why I am not pushing them further or why I am not being hard on them, I let them know, as gently as I can, that they can't fool me. What I see is someone hypersensitive to non-aggressive behaviour with a compulsive need to have a place in a dominance hierarchy. This seeming desire to 'work hard' or 'extra hard' and 'be pushed' is actually laziness and fear disguised as worth ethic. There is also a pernicious self-narrative that has been bought into. Think of it this way. If you need somebody to constantly push you, then what does that say about you? Obviously that you can't do it yourself and are clearly deficient.

More often than not this belief that one needs to be pushed becomes a destructive self-fulfilling prophecy. If you feel you perform best when pushed, you are convincing yourself of the narrative that this is the way to maximize results. Any technique based on pushing you, however, makes you dependent on another person. At the top, where leaders usually are, on your own, nobody will be there to push you. If you can't be able to tighten your bootstraps in a class or coaching session you paid for, then you certainly won't be able to do it when you are fighting for the very survival of your vision. This is an expectation on the world that is going to continuously erode you. No one else can push you to the ownership you need on this path.

If I have described you, then we need to find a solution to this dynamic. I don't want you to work hard, insisting on my driving you like a donkey down the Grand Canyon. You are not a donkey, you are a leader. I want leaders to work smart, to see that the exercise of repetition is a simple, albeit not always easy, pathway into efficiently addressing and solving the problems surrounding leadership skills. The path ahead of you is more simple than my posturing or making grand gestures: I simply say what went well and then lay out the territory for your next step. The values of this training leave it to a leader to make the leap when ready, to own their discoveries or conversely, to decide when not to act on the demands of the moment and for us to deal with that choice in feedback. Either way, however, you must make that decision for yourself. Regardless of whether they label themselves as Meisner or something entirely different any coach who tries to push you or make you work harder is in my view sabotaging your ability to own your technique. To the extent you've convinced yourself that this is the way you learn best, there is a sore wake-up call ahead of you when the moment you need to take your technique into your own hands, regardless of who you learnt it from, arrives and you find yourself unable to replicate the successes of your training. For the chest-thumpers out there, that's the 'straight talk' for you.

The Pivoting Moment

There is one final component to training leadership using this work that is valuable to understand and may appear, depending on how you prefer to learn, profoundly paradoxical. We've examined the ways a coach or teacher can interfere with your ability to own your discoveries. We've also talked a bit about how your own expectations as a client can swim back to bite you. We also began to introduce some possibilities that will have to be tested in practice for how you can solve the problem of sitting on truthful, authentic impulses. This latter question is of vital importance for you in this work. Let's expand on these possibilities further.

Let's say you are working with a partner in a repetition and the impulse arises to touch their hand. You hold back on it because for you this is territory far too intimate to be appropriate even in an exercise. In feedback we talk about it indirectly and on consideration you think: 'You know,

I've been too cautious. Next time, if the impulse comes up, I'll act on it. I won't force it but if it comes up organically I'll go for it.' All good so far.

By true chance in the next exercise, that same impulse arises. You feel it…and then are stuck in your head. Again. 'Should I? Shouldn't I? I mean I said I would but this feels slightly different…maybe it wouldn't be appropriate this time.' On and on your inner monologue goes. In real time the moment has passed already but your mind just won't let it go. Eventually you decide: to hell with it! And so you do it: you touch your partner's hand. The world doesn't end and the exercise continues to no great disaster or demise. You finish the exercise. You congratulate yourself: not a single impulse sat on. You've made the breakthrough and you own that discovery. Right?

Unfortunately, not quite. I'll grant that you came close, closer than you ever had, but you missed the mark in a subtle way. Consider what is true and of value: it is true that you did not force anything initially and so the impulse that arose was from observation of your partner. That made it entirely true to the demands of the moment. That would have been the moment to respond. That was not the moment you did. Instead the nature of the exercise shifted: you became trapped in your own mind, your attention swirling entirely around itself. This didn't go on forever – in real time it was perhaps just a few moments where your attention wavered from your partner and onto yourself. In those moments, however, you lost your ability to observe your partner, instead paying attention to your own sensations and thoughts about the dilemma of acting on a difficult impulse. Obsessing over the missed opportunity you opted for the bold move and acted on it anyway. You didn't respond truthfully to a moment: you responded in a new moment as you believe you should have to one already long gone in the past. You were attempting to resurrect a missed opportunity rather than deal with what was happening in the present and the consequences that arose from the action you did take rather than the one you wish you had.

At this point what is entirely clear that you were not responding to your partner but rather to yourself. The response might still be truthful to the new moment, but with your attention trapped on yourself, you wouldn't know either way. Had you put your attention back on your partner, it would have been clear whether that impulse was still in line with the demands of the moment. Maybe it still would have been true to the moment, but maybe a different authentic response would be in line with the moment. In pushing yourself, you overcame the illusion of a boundary but not the boundary itself. You can't go back and correct the past. The moment came and went and you have to deal with that reality, not the reality you wished had happened. The strategy you went with is the one that feels half-right, which is to impose an agenda to recreate the correct moment, the one in which you act on the impulse you should have. Your response then was not truthful according to the values of this work. It did not come from your partner and therefore was not authentic according to the 50–50 balance of observe and respond. You let the monster go but fought its shadow. You confused the map with the territory.

It's a fine line between generating inauthentic behaviours and taking the plunge, and this issue will arise more and more for you as you progress in this work. The solution I can begin to propose is that not acting on a truthful impulse in repetition will become an unpleasant feeling all on its own. It will nag at you during the exercise and sometimes long afterwards. In the early days of my training there were many nights I would ride the tube or bus home regretfully mulling over individual moments in exercises where I did not act on my impulses. 'What did I have to lose? What was I so afraid of?' I would ask myself. The specific impulses were unique to my own individual challenges but variations of the same core issue exist in all students. For some, like me, it takes time. Others get and act on the message much sooner. The growth in this work is personal and not time-bound, for better or worse.

The practice of training truthfulness within yourself finds everybody confronting viscerally their own forbidden territory created by years of individual and social conditioning. Forbidden territory (what some people in Meisner refer to as 'border territory'), however, is not black-and-white but rather a very grey, murky continuum. Certain impulses for you might be easier to act on sooner than others, and this will be true of your partners in the exercises. We are all working on our own individual steps. This is not meant to be a new-age sound bite but rather a simple truism of the process of training leadership qualities. We don't have a choice. Leadership is uniquely individual and so the challenges to your own will be individual. These exercises are unique in that they draw out your own individual challenges, and that is what makes them profoundly organic and relevant across ages, genders, cultures, and career status.

Everyone comes into the room with the material they signed up to work on, whether they are conscious of what it is or not. As a result, the training only draws out what was already there. When one of those challenges appears, it can be tempting to seize it head on, to push yourself into a discovery or finally get over a hurdle. The chance to act on an impulse, however, is momentary: it arises, and either you plunge without thought or it is gone. And what is in its place when it passes? A new moment that demands you attention. The solution we will test in practice in future sessions is this: rather than attempting to correct the past, work within the present reality. This is not just a concept but an entirely trainable skill set. Another brilliant truism from my Meisner teacher Scott: 'Rather than doing the right thing, do the thing right now.'

Summary

Living truthfully under a given set of circumstances is the most powerful approach a leader can have in their work. Though I use this particular verbiage to describe this unifying characteristic amongst great leaders this trait existed long before Meisner coined the phrase. By its nature, living truthfully under a given set of circumstances is the surest approach to acquire the most power and its usefulness is entirely portable across numerous strategies, fields, and contexts. Training it, however, is a slippery process, which is why in the past this capacity for authentic observation and response has been thought by some to be the mysterious domain of only a blessed few. Part of this challenge lies in the nature of truthfulness itself: to be truthful does not mean to be literally truthful, i.e. to say accurate or genuine things. While the hyper-polite nature of our times would conflate those two, in reality truthfulness goes deeper than the content of our words. It is a mechanism by which any words can be said with authenticity even if their literal truth value is deficient or partial. What we gather from this is, for many of us, in most conversations the majority of time, the words themselves do not hold real value. Rather they float on top and act as a kind of access point or portal for a meaningful exchange; this was the crux of the material covered in the previous chapter.

Building on those ideas in this chapter, we have to recognise that sometimes text does indeed have meaning in the moment and even can be the primary object of meaning over everything else. It is important for leaders to understand that what determines this meaning is not their intentions, will, or attempts to force something organic out of a moment. This is a fool's errand which will lead you to be clouded about what the demands of the moment really are. The demands of the moment are, as they always have been, what will determine when or if text will have meaning in the moment. In the Meisner Technique we facilitate this possibility by introducing the concept of point of view. It is trained through a simple modification of our staple repetition exercise.

Digging deep into the nature of training leadership within oneself is not just a process of the coach disseminating knowledge or handing down wisdom from above. It is, in fact, the opposite:

a bottom-up process that begins with investigating the mechanics of successful learning itself. For a leader to flourish, they must understand their own learning process. This does not mean delving into decades of psychoanalytic cause-and-effect patterns from childhood onwards; rather it simply means that the leader understands what types of feedback are optimal for their own development. Through this inquiry they also recognise the tendencies and desires in themselves that might run counter to their own learning, such as the desire to be continuously pushed towards a result rather than having the courage to go towards that result of your own volition and willingness to surrender to the moment.

If a leader understands the nuances of their personal foundations, and the dynamics that optimise its success, then they will always have a strong base to keep developing from. Understanding the qualities of what makes up good learning and valuable feedback is a powerful component to being able to discern for yourself which coach or training model will fit your actual needs.

Tips for You and Your Coach

Since this chapter turned a portion of its attention to feedback and its nature, I won't spend as much time here on it, but for coaches it is worth pointing out that there are overlaps in this training between the concepts of training and the learning process. It is valuable to have these conversations with your clients at times as they continually frame the reference points of the learning. Rather than my telling you how to implement them, however, I would much rather you take the concepts and notions discussed in this chapter and harmonise them with your own unique voice in your teaching or coaching process. To support you, I will give two suggestions here.

The first is that attention is very important in this work, both yours and the client's. As you get more adept at teaching this material you will find yourself able to more clearly see where a client's attention is. This enables you to track the moments when it goes from their partner and back onto themselves. Your goal as a teacher is to keep your student's attention off of themselves and on their partner. The more you do this the more you will facilitate their development and training of living truthfully in this work. One helpful metaphor that my Meisner teacher Scott would use is that of the attention ball: ask the student to imagine that there is an imaginary string connecting his or her forehead to their partner's. On the string rests a ball which is called the attention ball. The goal of your student is to shoot the attention ball all the way over to their partner and ensure it has been successfully received. The same direction applies for the other student in the exercise. The attention must always be on one another in a very clear way and images such as the attention ball are an effective way in the beginning stages to facilitate that. You may not need it, but for students who have trouble focusing it can be a helpful teaching device.

Second, from the first moment of repetition, where the attention is on each other, truthful impulses are there, and they will begin popping up like uncontrolled hiccups. For students new to this work, this is an intense sensation. It is unnatural for us to be so deeply seen by another person, in this case our partner in the exercise. The feeling of uncensored impulses arising organically can be for some, many perhaps, an alarming experience. We are equally not used to releasing this kind of control. Most of the early exercises in this training will become exercises in clients attempting to sit on their impulses, particularly the bigger ones. This is not the end of the world, in that the process has already begun to take hold: in having to sit continuously on their impulses this means the students are aware of them. They now know they have truthful impulses that they don't want to let out and are being awakened experientially to what self-censoring feels like. As they continue the work they will begin to ease up on their grip. In developing the confidence in themselves and their technique they will act on more impulses over time and do not need to be pushed then towards a result. This is an entire discovery process that happens simply by virtue of them being inside of the experience.

In feedback, try to isolate the essential impulse the student is sitting on, whether it was anger, intimacy, joy, so on, and make that the object of your feedback. Making a laundry list of all the impulses a student did not act on will become easily overwhelming and misses the point of this work: repetition is about expanding the territory of truthfulness as demanded by the moment, not pushing yourself towards some final outcome. People are intelligent about their own experiences. Help someone become more at ease with just one inhibited impulse, and they will apply the concept to other impulses they do not act on. As a teacher, remember that fewer things for a student are less satisfying than sitting on truthful impulses. They will feel their conditioning and background holding them back. Oftentimes you won't need to even mention it. Simply feed this intrinsic hunger they have to broaden their scope of authenticity and they will of their own volition.

In terms of feedback, it might be worth mentioning what to do if you are still encountering word games or clients trying to 'do something' with the words at this stage in the training. It helps to recognise that habitual game-playing, which is different than the impulse to play, is another strategy of the client's desire to assert control over an exercise. Sitting on impulses carries the benefit of feeling unsatisfying and is self-teaching; game playing and trying to make something out of the text, on the other hand, doesn't seem to have the same weight to it, so not all students over time learn to avoid it without some input. It is worth addressing in feedback if you see a lot of game playing happening in the exercises. This can be done quite simply through comparative questioning such as asking 'what felt more organic, the word games or the rest of the exercise?' Almost always the response is the rest of the exercise.

Games are just clients' ways of finding safe territory, but it is usually a conspiracy of compliance between them and their partner. Just give them a gentle nudge out of that habit and let them get back into the deeper waters of living truthfully. When they are insecure, people will do everything they can to not go into the deeper possibilities on offer in repetition. This is almost always due to their fear of the unknown. As with most things, exposure and experience is the best teacher. It is excellent for them to see not only that they will survive truly surrendering their responses to another person but they will thrive when doing so.

An aside comes up as a final note, as this will become more clearly explained in later chapters, but it is worth introducing here. Resist, should it come up, any temptation to demonstrate a successful exercise for your clients. Never, ever think it is a good idea for you to do a repetition exercise to demonstrate how it should be done. Those are strong words from me. Consider how many times I have been blatantly prescriptive with you. Which is none. I've got to make an exception here: do not do it. Never do a repetition exercise with your student or almost any other exercise in this work for that matter. There are only two exceptions which will be explicitly clarified later on. Otherwise you will make your life far harder than you ever expected and violate so many ethical boundaries in the process. As I said, this is an aside, but it is worth stating early. As the old saying goes, 'An ounce of prevention is worth a pound of cure.' This is an ounce that will make everyone's life, your own included, easier in this work.

Chapter 6

Catching the Floating Moment

Shoes over Soul Searching

Now that you have begun to attain some depth in your training of living truthfully – giving you an idea from the inside of what kind of authentic expressions and experiences we are after as well as the mechanism by which it can be achieved consistently every time – it is time to now sharpen your living truthfully technique so that the depth of results you achieve will be magnified and reliably deeper each time you work. By doing this we target one of the primary objectives in training your leadership skills, which is expanding your range of authentic responses so that no impulse, however large or forbidden, will ever catch you off guard. This will become a topic of much greater exploration in latter chapters, but it is worth introducing it here. Eventually, when the moment demands a response from you, whatever its nature or emotional hue, you will be able to handle it without premeditation or the danger of becoming trapped within your own head. That doesn't mean you will always act on the impulse, but it does mean it won't overwhelm you when it arises in moments of extreme pressure or exceptionally demanding circumstances.

Living truthfully, however, does not depend solely on your own intentions. It is admirable to want to be a truthful leader, but to actually do so depends on a profound degree of accuracy. Consider for a moment why certain calls are not encouraged in repetition. Simple observations of fact are okay, but speculations, opinions, questions, and concerns will be immediately called out by me with the sole purpose of discouraging you from doing it. Why, what's my problem? After all, that seems counterintuitive. Why is it more profound and valuable to simply say your partner is wearing shoes rather than attempting to speculate on the depths of their inner state such as observing, 'You are nervous.' Or even better, we could ask a provocative question, such as, 'Why are you looking at me angrily?' (this is a tame provocative question compared to some of the ones you'll hear in conventional Meisner training). The flip side is also possible, which is to voice an organic concern: 'You're making me worried.'

Those are qualitatively juicy observations. They also come from your point of view, which I encouraged you to allow back into repetition drills under certain conditions we've covered in the previous chapter. But let's get to the biggest, most relevant point: all of those observations are about your partner. Isn't this a technique about observing your partner deeply and responding truthfully to what you observe? Surely calls like the ones above fit within the values of this work since both your observations and truthful responses will still be based on your partner. Let's also face it: these are rich calls on offer, way more exciting than the simple and banal observations you've been making thus far. Seemingly to the detriment to the work, I've cut out a huge spectrum of worthwhile possibilities. Surely those types of calls will take you further than something as bland as 'you're wearing shoes.'

As usual there is both a short answer and an expanded one. Both are worth your time. Here's the short one: No. Just to reiterate that: No. No. No. If you find yourself having to choose between a profound commentary on your partner's emotional life or saying 'you're wearing shoes,' you'll get more mileage out of the shoes every time. That's the short answer. If it has left you wondering 'why', then it's worth going into the larger conversation around the reasoning behind why this is the case. As it happens it's the entire subject of today's material.

Intuitively, most of us would consider emotive calls (observations of the speculative and opinion type) as better than simple factual observations. Why? To start, it seems we are beginning to circulate around the concept that it is possible for there to be observations of higher value than others. But what's our metric? Since this work is rooted not in pretending or inauthenticity, then it seems the higher value observations for our purposes are those that are the most accurate to the moment. Not all moments are the same, however; there will be different things of value in each moment. The moment in which you suddenly notice you partner's beautiful earrings may soon change its value if they accidentally sneeze all over you in the next moment. Any call, then, that better captures the nuances and specifics of the moment with accuracy is of higher value than a call that does not capture those dynamics as cleanly. If we boiled that down into a word it would be *specificity*.

Specificity is the metric by which observations can be judged and still retain the core values of the work. As a tool it gives us a way of parsing quality among accuracy without tempting you to go for more creative or complicated observations. Let's take an example. You and your partner are doing a repetition. It goes like this:

You: You're wearing a red shirt.
Partner: I'm wearing a red shirt.
You: You're wearing a red shirt.
Partner: I'm wearing a red shirt.
Etc.

As far as technical structure goes, this is strong.. But why? After all, you could have simply said, 'Red' and it would have been just as accurate. Or 'That's red.' But it's not as good as *'you're* wearing a red shirt.' That call is far more valuable because it is more specific to the nuances of the moment. What is red? Something being worn, in this case a shirt. Who is wearing it? Your partner. Those other possible calls do not capture the specifics as cleanly as 'you're wearing a red shirt.' By our metric of specificity this is a great observation to make since it is specific to the most relevant thing in the moment, which is your partner. This falls in line neatly with one of Meisner's favourite phrases of choice: 'Be specific.'

This is where we are at now in the training. We have established a structure of simple yet clean calls based on accuracy and some specificity. We are also recognising, however, that the observations on offer to you might be limited in how specific they can be to the moment. This means that to progress further in today's session we have to ask and answer some important questions. Questions like, why can't we use those juicy, sexy emotive calls and speculations, which feel qualitatively better? Is there a way to still create some kind of qualitative structure based on our metric of specificity that honours the other values we are building on?

This latter question is the thorn in the side. Keep in mind our agreement from day one: we have to always honour the foundations we are building on. If we introduce new ideas or theories that compromise your authenticity, then we're changing the rules entirely. A value on day one needs to be perfectly interchangeable with a value on day 100, even if the technical appearance has changed. Values that are lost or no longer applicable stop being portable within the training and as a result are impossible to take outside of it. Authenticity is powerful but easily compromised in any training program. It is so much easier to impose structures and rules that make things cleaner but render them inauthentic. At times it may seem as if we are splitting hairs over nuance, but it is worth it to be always clear about what we are and not doing. The devil never exists in big general agreements. Especially for leaders the details matter.

Today's session also has one additional perk: it will solve one of the greatest problems that has plagued actors, speakers, and leaders alike throughout all of history. Prepare to say goodbye to one of the most elusive and biggest mysteries in this field once and for all.

Exercise: The Three Moment Exercise

The exercise I am going to introduce now is called the *three moment exercise*. There are many incarnations of it. While it is not worth getting into the weeds of the different versions here, for clarity I will be recommending and prescribing the version I learnt from my London teacher and mentor, Scott Williams. The value of telling you this is that I have seen immense varieties of using this exercise across Meisner teachers. If you take a Meisner class to expand on your leadership development and find this exercise is wildly different than my approach, consider yourself forewarned.

One of the reasons it can be so different is that it addresses a variety of needs for actors. Though, as we have explored, there is some overlap with your needs, the needs of actors, as far as training goes, differ in some fundamental ways from the needs of leaders in training. Obviously, I teach the version of this exercise that I believe is best, but I have selected this version specifically because of its immensely optimal applications to your leadership development.

The three moment exercise starts just like a repetition exercise. You and your partner are going to sit across from each other in the chairs as before. Nothing new there. You'll start in the same way that you would a repetition with a simple observation of fact. Example:

You: You've got brown hair.
Partner: I've got brown hair.

Here, however, is where things take the primary, major turn. In a repetition you two would just keep going until I stopped you. Not so in this exercise. Since you began the exercise in this example this new and next step now falls to you. After the first cycle you won't continue repeating. Instead, you are going to make a new observation of your partner and then that is the end of the exercise. Yes, to say it explicitly: this exercise is far shorter than repetition. This will become more clear as we explain what's going on with this new observation.

Let's go back to our example. For clarity let's name the observation and repetition slightly differently. We'll label them according to the moments in time in which they occurred. Now they will look like this:

Moment 1: You've got brown hair.
Moment 2: I've got brown hair.

Suppose that during moment 2, as you watch your partner repeating, she bites her lip. Let's say in Moment 3 you say what you saw in Moment 2.

Moment 1: You've got brown hair.
Moment 2: I've got brown hair. (Partner bites lip)
Moment 3: You bit your lip.

And that is it. That is the end of the exercise. Your partner won't repeat the new call, it is done. We'll do more than one obviously but this is the three moment exercise in itself. The architecture of it can be cleanly broken up into three moments:

Moment 1: You make an observation.
Moment 2: Your partner repeats it.
Moment 3: You say what you saw in moment 2.
End of exercise.

Since we are doing more than one exercise we take a nice long pause to reset. This is a new pace and rhythm, and I want us to get comfortable with it. Given that you began before, I ask your partner to start the new three moment exercise. It goes like this:

Partner: You're wearing jeans.
You: I'm wearing jeans. (you smile)
Partner: You smiled.
End of exercise.

We take another pause, a span of time we call a reset. This is to prevent rushing. There are no points for speed in this exercise. It is worth taking our time. Continuing on, it might look like this. Your partner began the last one, so you begin the new one:

You: You're wearing lipstick.
Partner: I'm wearing lipstick.
You: You raised your eyebrows.
        (Long reset)
Partner: You've got tattoos.
You: I've got tattoos.
Partner: You wiggled your nose.
        (Long reset)
You: Your shirt is dark.
Partner: My shirt is dark.
You: You moved your hands.
Etc.

Though the pace is wildly different from repetition, you'll notice there is a common thread: once we get the pauses down, finding our feet with this new staccato rhythm, you two will continue on until I let you know when to finish, going through an extended series of three moment exercises with each other.

From the examples just presented you have some excellent demonstrations of the three moment exercise. There's nothing more to it. That's it in its entirety. If you are as confused as I was when I first saw and did it as to how this is even remotely valuable to you, don't worry, you're in the right place.

The first place to find our way into both the exercise and its values is by breaking down the moments themselves using the examples just presented. For moment 1, notice the first call stays simple and factual, as it always has. The repeat in moment 2 follows the familiar structure of repetition where the other person repeats the observation from their point of view. For moment 3, using our examples just presented, the new observation also stays profoundly simple. No opinions, no speculations, and no questions. In effect, it has the same clean quality as the first moment. The primary difference is that this new observation made is directly connected to what was observed in the second moment.

Let's talk about the reasons for why this structure is valuable. The first reason you may not glean from reading on the page, so you'll have to take my word for it until you jump in the exercise yourself: the three moment exercise seems simple, and it is. For most people, however, once they actually try it, they find the intensity level goes through the roof. They are not used to both scrutinising someone and themselves being seen in such a sharp, rich manner. Perhaps the language I just used is the best indicator: we are used to people *looking* at us regularly, but rarely are we used to being *seen*. Now your partner is really seeing you, and you are being asked to do the same. Sticking with simple calls helps you get through the tunnel vision created by the intensity of the exercise in its early stages.

A second, far deeper reason for the structure emerges here, revealing the key reason why certain calls, like opinions, for example, are not encouraged. Let's take a new example where you and your partner are working together. During moment 2, I will again put into parenthesis something that your partner does in response to your observation in moment 1.

You: You've got a hole in your jeans.
Partner: I've got a hole in my jeans. (goes red in the face)
You: You liked that.

At this point, I'd stop the exercise and I would ask your partner, 'Did you actually like that?' They may say no, but they also might say yes. After all, humans are reasonably decent at inferring emotional states and your call may have been accurate. There is, however, a notably large chance that other answers will arise. 'No,' your partner might say, 'I didn't like that. It made me nervous' or 'It made me angry' or some other alternative answer entirely, revealing that your observation got it wrong. Let's say for our purposes your partner does respond that they did not like that. Consider the implication of this. Let's say it was not a three moment exercise and was instead the observation you used in a repetition exercise:

You: You liked that.
Partner: I liked that.
You: You liked that.
Partner: I liked that.
Etc.

In this exercise, you would have begun basing your responses on an incorrect observation. As we have said, sometimes text has meaning while at others it does not. The text having meaning in this exercise would be based on its inaccuracy. Likewise, with such a provocative call there is a good chance you and your partner would start responding more to the truth value of the call rather than what either of you were doing. You might start to get fuelled up by the call while your partner would end up in their head going, 'But that's not true! I didn't like it.' Since the interaction starts from a place with a lack of clarity, a reasonable amount time spent in what could be truthful responses runs the risk of not being in relation to one other at all but rather your opinions about each other.

Now, yes, some of you could argue that these people should get over it. You're mad because the call is inaccurate? Use that! Put your attention back on each other and let the exercise go on. But why the wasted effort and energy? Why the risk of not seeing clearly? It doesn't lead to anything deeper or more efficient. Furthermore, by its very nature, an opinion is not generated by your partner. It is generated by your *appraisal* of them. Even though we form these conclusions relatively quickly, there is a greater cognitive effort needed to compare the behaviour of your partner against other examples from your past to reach conclusions about their emotional state. You will find in repetition you don't have time to think, so you'll make these judgements quickly and without consideration. Hasty judgements about another person run into greater margins of error and are the source of much misery in communication in everyday relationships. Extended considerations in a drill that emphasises observing and responding impulsively are irrelevant. Importing either habit into your leadership training doesn't help. What you end up with when you try to make opinionated guesses are a lot of responses based on an appraisal of your partner rather than something more objectively true. Very little about your observation and the responses that follow from it will be in line with the core values of this work.

I've used the example of a repetition exercise to illustrate these problems because it is longer than the three moment exercise, so the increasing magnitude of the error can be seen better. The same problems, however, equally apply to the three moment exercise. Returning to our hypothetical example, let's say the exercise between you and your partner went this way instead:

You: You've got a hole in your jeans.
Partner: I've got a hole in my jeans. (goes red in the face)
You: Your face turned red.

Let's say I stop the exercise here and question your partner. 'Did your face turn red?' Your partner may not know, but it's a pretty obvious one to answer. It can be argued that while humans have the same capacity for identical biochemical reactions some people's complexions don't present a blush, but if this was the case a different behaviour would be observed. When examining the observation of involuntary redness in the face I guess in some rare hypothetical context this could be wrong due to a lighting problem, but we really are splitting hairs at that point. It is far more in line with reality to assume that the majority of the time, no matter how many times I stop the exercise and ask if it is true, that call will be true every time. If your partner's face went red, it went red, simple as that. The success ratio of that call will be consistently markedly higher than 'You liked that.' Whether your partner is aware of it happening or not doesn't matter. We don't always know what happens in an intense moment, but that's the value of it: the redness in the face implies a powerful change in the body that is far more easily observed than trying to guess the inner emotional state behind it. That the call of redness is qualitatively just as good, more so for its reliability, but it is also as provoking. Pointing out changes in one's facial colour is immensely provocative. The observation is true. It is also a great example of fuck polite.

We started the chapter with a problem to solve, phrased in the question about why we are excluding all the juicy, provocative calls on offer and sticking with boring facts. It is a valid question, but now you can see it is harder to answer than just saying, 'Well, let's make all the opinionated calls we want. So long as we believe it's true that's enough.' Not at all. Your belief in something being true does not make it true, and opinion calls don't provide the return of accuracy within your observations. You end up creating so much noise in the communication process that you lose the values of the work. We've also debunked the idea that opinionated calls have validity because they are still about your partner. Opinion calls are not about your partner: they are your attempts to appraise them. This is why I said if I had the choice between the most insightful, compelling guess of emotional inner life observation versus the most boring call of 'you're wearing shoes,' you'll get more mileage out of the shoes.

The last leg that emotive calls try to stand on is the provocation argument. The claim goes that you can provoke your partner and get a deeper response out of them. As we've already touched on a bit, what the redness in the face example shows us is that it is possible to have our cake and eat it too. A observation like that doesn't need help from your interpretative powers. It is provocative enough. It also stays in line with the values of taking the burden of responsibility off of you and putting it onto your partner, because it requires zero interpretation and forces them to deal with it. To make such a powerful observation it only asks that you say what you see. It also facilitates your partner doing the same thing to you. As far as fuck polite goes, it is a juggernaut of a call. Sure, someone can provoke you by trying to get a rise out of you, it can happen, but you'll quickly learn that it's a game and stop falling into the trap. It loses the surprise element. Ever been told by someone, however, you were blushing or flushed? It feels like a spotlight is being shone on your inner emotional private life. It is an involuntary and entirely authentic response and will get you every time someone calls it. Such a clear and precise observation often brings up huge responses all around. All of that is fair game in this work because it came from the reality of the moment and not your opinion of it.

Opinions can be, and are often, wrong. There is research that shows that even people with expert training do not become much better at interpreting emotions over time. Their capacity bottlenecks. You are not a mind reader. To the extent that you try to be, you are going to lose the values of this work. Better, as Epictetus advised, to leave the gifts of the gods to the gods and rather focus on your human abilities. You might not know what is going on in someone's head, but you can certainly observe what it is doing to them on the outside. That's the difference between getting better at guessing versus getting better at observing. Your partner is always going to be far more exciting than your opinion of them. People, for better or worse, will never cease to surprise us.

This is bringing us to an exciting implication that the three moment exercise offers you. Using the examples just presented, do you sense any difference between the observations made in moment 1 and the observations made in moment 3? Most students agree that there is actually a rich, qualitative difference between the first and third moments in a three moment exercise. But why? Both calls are accurate, specific, and simple facts. What is it about that observation in the third moment that seems more exciting? There are two answers, and I'll tease the first one here: it feels exciting and good to finally solve one of the biggest problems you will ever face in your leadership journey.

The Moment in Isolation

Ever heard the phrase, 'Be in the moment?' I certainly did. All the time. When I was first starting as an actor and long before I came to my Meisner training, this was the most common criticism I received: 'You need to be more in the moment.' Exploring it further, I identified a possible culprit for my out-of-the-moment woes: I was too much in my head. If you hear a pair of phrases long enough you begin to take them as gospel and that's what I did. These two phrases actually drove me quite mad, as each time I would attempt to address them it seemed as if there was no concrete way to really solve these challenges. I knew there was a problem. So did my instructors, the same ones who were using these phrases. Yet when pressed, none of them seemed to be able to give me a clear, technical, and simple way to fix the issue of being in my head, a problem that was preventing me from being in the moment.

These weren't philosophical musings. They were specific problems interfering with my job prospects, and so investigating them became of utmost importance. It began with the idea of being in the moment. The moment is a time-bound phenomenon, so I wondered whether one can ever be outside of the moment. You could argue it philosophically, but I was looking for a concrete solution. What would it even look like if you weren't in the moment, as in not time-bound? You simply wouldn't be there. This brought me to an even more confusing possibility, related to the problem of being in my head. If you can't ever not be in the moment, then even if you are stuck in your head you're still in the moment. You're just inside your head in the moment. Furthermore, the head is the seat of consciousness and conscious experience. It's where your decisions are made but also where sensory information is processed. We talk about feeling with the gut and all that, but those signals are rooted in brain communication. Looking at an end goal, how could I not be in my head but still execute actions in the moment?

Looking deeply into these two concepts of being in the moment and trapped in your head brought up an old truism. If it smells like garbage, it probably is garbage, and these phrases are, for the most part, garbage. Without hyper-specific definitions, which most people who use them can't provide, they mean absolutely nothing. It's why I rarely use them in my own work with clients. The jargon about being in the moment, as if you could be outside of time, or not being in your head, as if you can step outside of conscious experience, are vapid and largely meaningless. They are what Daniel Dennett might call a 'deepity': a simplistic phrase that is made to sound far deeper than it is by the brain's desire to seek meaning and ascribe value to even meaningless things.

Of course you can never be in anything but in the moment. You are a temporally bound person, and so to prescribe to someone 'be in the moment' or even better 'be more in the moment' simply reflects the inability of the coach to accurately express what they perceive is the problem their student is grappling with. It further extends to the warning against 'being in your head'. Where else are you going to be? Your conscious perception of the world is inside your head. There is no getting around that. Your observations come into your head and are neurally processed in such a way that you can verbalise them and then respond truthfully. Thank goodness you are in your head. You couldn't observe and respond if you weren't!

Here some colleagues of mine will shake their head and say I am getting caught up on the semantics, that we all 'really know' what we are talking about when we say 'stay out of your head' and 'be in the moment'. But this I will argue is the real problem: we actually don't know what we are talking about. We can't appeal to common sense and intuitions and pretend we will all come up with the same mutual conclusions. I may intuitively think one way about something while you believe something entirely different. Without clear, concrete understandings and agreements between us, we are doomed to large amounts of error and misunderstanding in our communication about these vital concepts which then spill over into our ability to provide clean technical solutions. The abstract impressionistic nature of those phrases will mean something slightly different to each individual. We are not doing any good by being participants in a conspiracy of unspoken agreement where we are using the same general phrases that may mean entirely different things. Prescriptions based on intuitive claims are a foolhardy endeavour. This is a technique about clarity. Vapid, empty phrases have no place in a leadership technique that values efficiency.

If 'in the moment' can mean anything, then to quote a brilliant old friend of mine, it actually means nothing. Unfortunately that doesn't mean there isn't a problem. There is *something* going on with a leader when they are told they are stuck in their head and not really in the moment. Even if those phrases don't mean anything, they still point to a problem of real value: something is still going on that is interfering with your ability to be authentic in front of others, even if the verbiage used to describe it is nonsensical. What's more, neither of those phrases is going to go away from the common language, so for us to forbid ever using them or your considering them is not helpful either. Instead, what we can do is to solidify the meaning of being in the moment as it relates to leadership. We can't solve it for other areas, but we can at least solve it for your needs. In making it more specific, we can actually begin to understand the real problem at the core of those phrases. The way we make them more specific is by injecting our values into the phrases. Let's start with 'being in the moment.' What if being in the moment had something to do with your partner, as well as our values of living truthfully?

It seems that if we start to think about being in the moment this way, we also solve the equally facile concept of being versus not being in your head. The problem isn't about being anywhere. It's about attention and relevance. When you put your attention on your partner, you open the channel for your responses to be determined by their actions. 'Being in the moment' starts to really mean putting your attention on your partner, the most relevant variable in the exchange. That as well gives us an inverse metric: as far as our work is concerned, when you are not 'in the moment' it's because your attention was not on your partner but rather on something less relevant. No one goes through the temporal Stargate; you're just paying attention to the wrong thing.

If we start to reframe these concepts according to the needs of leaders, then they become trainable.

You can train yourself to be in the moment by paying attention to relevant variables. We can examine how well you did this by isolating specific moments and evaluating them for the quality of attention you gave to your partner. And this is exactly what we are doing in moment two of the three moment exercise.

In moment two, when your partner speaks, followed by moment three where you say what you saw, we know four things for certain:

One. A moment of relevance has occurred.
Two. This moment can be captured with a verbal observation.
Three. An observation is made about what happened during moment two.
Four. As a result, presuming the call is accurate, that observation has assuredly captured that moment.

The debate about it might be the quality of nuance and observation, but your attention was on the relevant variable: your partner. These facts tell us we are training you to be in the moment by concrete technical design. According to our definitions and values, only by being in the moment could you have observed what your partner did. Your third moment call is your way of cleanly carving out that moment in time and identifying it. Consider the huge weight off your shoulders: you are now training, in a technical, non-abstract way, to isolate the unit of the moment. No more mystery, no more spooky language about the concept. As that value is ingrained with more practice, 'being in the moment', and its equally evil partner 'in your head', will never be a problem for you again. If in the rare event you find it is, your attention becoming habitually distracted by irrelevant things, you have now a clear, concrete, and specific exercise for solving it again.

The problem of being in the moment and not becoming trapped in your head, especially when communicating or speaking, is huge. It is almost tempting to believe there could not be a solution so simple, but there is. It is the clean and clear efficiency of the Meisner Technique that makes it such a valuable tool for training leadership. The three moment exercise alone is worth the price of admission for the problems it solves. True, we could have used repetition as a means of addressing these challenges, but it is more difficult. Repetition finds its rhythm as a constant flow, and that makes extracting these values from repetition sometimes more challenging for most individuals. For one, there is so much happening at once and over an extended amount of time. The three moment exercise, with its brief, staccato nature, slows everything down and exposes its values clearly and demonstrates the power of both reducing the moment down to its technical components as well as the power of accuracy to the moment you are isolating.

Accuracy, and more concretely, specificity, is now how the qualitative value of each moment will be determined. This brings us to an even more powerful possibility for how you can get better observational calls without losing the core values of living truthfully in the moment, the moment that is now a non-mysterious, hyper-clear unit of technical relevance.

A Hierarchy of Specificity

Let's go back to our earlier hypothetical three moment exercise of choice:

You: You've got a hole in your jeans.
Partner: I've got a hole in my jeans.
You: Your face turned red.

We've agreed that there is a qualitative difference between the first and third calls. Our first reason for this is due to the fact that the third call is isolating a highly specific moment in time. The jeans will in all likelihood stay constant throughout the exercise, but that redness in the face is by nature momentary. This seems like only part of the story, however. Both holes in jeans and redness in the face are good calls. Both are provocative and great examples of "fuck polite" but there's a noticeable quality in difference between them that transcends the time-bound aspect. Most of us would agree that in most circumstances observing someone's facial expressions are of far more value than noticing something about their clothes, but why?

Using our example, let's give a name to the kind of call that is happening in moment 1. We can call this a *basic call*. Basic calls are just what they sound to be: clean statements of fact that don't muddle accuracy with opinions, assessments, questions, and so on. We love basic calls in this work. We began our journey with them. They are, and will forever remain, a technically strong call. Just to solidify the concept here are some other examples of basic calls:

You've got a hole in your jeans.
You have blond hair.
You're wearing a ring.
Your nails are green.
You have a gap in your teeth.
Your eyes are blue.

As a few of these examples illustrate, basic calls can be provocative and punchy in themselves. That said this isn't really the goal of a basic call. Simply put, its main function is to root you in the reality of being with your partner and your attention being on them. Though observances of fact are good and have merit, the likelihood is that they won't change throughout the course of the exercise. Look at the examples above. If we used them in repetitions, it is possible that some of those might change in the duration of a three- or four-minute exercise, but not likely. Despite all of the things that might happen across a set of moments in an exercise, the observation itself is likely to remain static and unchanging.

This brings up the idea we are now working on of the moment as a unit. Being in the moment, we have agreed, is deeply tied to the values of this work if we make it about specifically observing your partner and being accurate to them. If we follow this logic we can say that observing specific things about what your partner is *doing* are more specific to the moment and its temporary nature. As we have said, specificity is where the value of observations can be measured. That would imply that there is an entire set of calls on offer to you that are of much higher value than basic calls. Take a look at these examples:

> Your face turned red.
> You're smiling.
> You raised your eyebrows.
> You wiggled your fingers.
> You shifted.
> You coughed.
> You moved from side to side.

Notice anything unique about these calls compared to the examples of the basic call? If we could group all of these calls under one large bracket, they would fall under the label of 'behaviour'. Given that, it becomes my pleasure, then, to introduce you to the *behavioural call*. In this work, we love behaviour. It's one of the best crossovers between the roots and origins of the Meisner Technique and the version we are working with today. My Meisner teacher Scott would always tell us that behaviour is the currency we spend and receive in performance. The exact same concept can be applied to leadership. Behaviour is of premium value to you and this work, as well. Meisner himself had an equally great, slightly tongue-in-cheek, phrase: 'An ounce of behaviour is worth a pound of words.'

Let's not take it for granted, though. Let's look closely to just what makes behaviour so compelling. Look at the first and third moments in our hypothetical three moment exercise from earlier. For convenience I've labelled the moments for reference:

(Moment 1) You: You've got a hole in your jeans.
(Moment 2) Partner: I've got a hole in my jeans.
(Moment 3) You: Your face turned red.

You can now see that moment 1 is a basic call while moment 3 is a behavioural call. As we have discussed, while it is true in some vague, hypothetical way that in the span of two moments your partner may not have a hole in their jeans anymore (don't ask me how, I probably don't want to know), the likelihood is that the hole will be there for the duration of the exercise. How about redness in the face? That certainly seems far more transitory, and the likelihood falls on the opposite end: it is extremely unlikely that it will be there for the entire exercise. In an exercise designed to isolate the unit of the moment, and where specificity to that individual moment is how we determine a stronger or weaker call, then behaviour is almost always of much higher value than a basic call. Behaviour is, by its very nature, momentary. To be specific about your partner's behaviour is, generally, far more accurate to the moment than making observations about their clothing or cosmetic features. This shift in what you prioritise in your observations develops your skills with razor-sharp precision. It also keeps you fully in line with all the values we have laid down so far.

There are, of course, exceptions to every rule. There may be times when a basic call is of far more value than a behavioural one, but it will be rare. The flip side, however, is that the basic call is always the best one to make if you get trapped in trying to find the right word to describe your partner's behaviour or how to phrase your observation. In these cases 'you're wearing a shirt' is just as strong and keeps your attention on the right variable.

At the end of the day, these are exceptions. Almost always behavioural calls are qualitatively better than basic calls and have higher value. This introduces the idea of ranking and hierarchy. In my Meisner training, this was called the 'hierarchy of observations' and it is what we are going to spend the rest of the chapter exploring. Especially since we won't just stop at identifying behavioural calls. There are categories of observations on offer to you whose value runs even deeper.

Thinking of the applications of this differentiation between observations in practical terms, using just basic and behavioural calls alone as primary objects of attention will gain you far more ground in an interpersonal exchange outside of training. As far as the quality of your observations are concerned, when compared to anyone busily attempting to guess the emotional state of another person or some similar mind reading game, you will be almost at a continuous advantage because you'll be constantly rooted in reality. At the same time, we can't just throw out the imperfect opinion call yet. We would be pretending to say it has no benefit. Consider that a well-aimed opinion observation, especially if accurate, can capture the inner state of another person. If you say, 'You're pissed off.' and you've nailed it, then that is far better than letting the other person know they raised their eyebrows. Nailed it, however, is where the grey area appears.

As we've shown, the reason the opinion call falls short compared to behaviour is the wide margin of possible error. Opinions are often wrong, incorrect, or malformed. Our experiences in life teach us this regularly. Also, they are often made with too broad a brushstroke, regularly failing to capture the specific nuances of an emotion. Anger, for example, takes so many hues and shades that to simply summarise it in a blanket term actually loses much of the specificity of how that anger is manifesting in a specific moment. It feels specific, but actually, if you say to your partner 'You're angry,' you've really only made a generalisation of their experience of anger. Though it bears the same name rage that arises alongside pain feels experientially different than that same fury with glee. Your target of observation may not be angry in the specific way you infer, and so this mistake can bring more attention to the call itself, creating distance between you two. A behavioural call fixes this because the behaviour of anger is always specific to the moment it is appearing in. All that having been said, however, there still seem to be some tangible benefits to a well-placed opinion call. What we want to ask is can we get the best of both worlds? Can we get the power that comes from labelling a specific, deep inner state while reducing the massive margin of error and risk that comes from the guessing game of opinionated observations?

Let's go back to our example exercise between you and your partner. In the third moment, you observe their face has turned red. Redness in the face, however, wasn't the only call available. Just as easily you could have made a basic call. It wouldn't have been of as much value since it is less specific to the moment, but you could have done it and it still would have been technically sound. One example might be if your partner had raised their arm in moment 2 and you suddenly saw a vibrant tattoo on the inside of it you had not noticed before. That exercise could look, then, like this:

You: You've got a hole in your jeans.
Partner: I've got a hole in my jeans.
You: You've got a tattoo!

Totally fair game and a great call. Generally, however, the observation in moment 3 will be a behavioural call. As you become more comfortable in this exercise, and the intensity diminishes a bit (again, it is worth stating that on the outside, and certainly on paper, it seems a very bland exercise, but once you are in it the experiential intensity goes up quite a bit), you will start to notice not one but several behaviours happening at once. Let's take the example of your third moment observation of redness in the face. Is that all that happened in moment 2? Likely not. Let me introduce a few completely plausible behaviours that can occur simultaneously in moment 2:

You: You've got a hole in your jeans.
Partner: I've got a hole in my jeans. (blinks, moves mouth, nods head, goes red in the face, swallows)
You: Your face turned red.

If I pointed this out to you, reminding you that any one of those would be excellent calls of behaviour, and then asked why you chose the redness in the face you might say something like, 'It just stood out.' I completely agree. It was, in this example, far more profound than any of those other behaviours. Think of what redness in the face means? A lot of things: embarrassment, anger, irritation, arousal, fear, an allergy, stifling a cough or sneeze, about to laugh, repressing a yawn, about to cry, or many other things. Maybe it's not even rooted to the now. Maybe they suddenly were reminded of something that happened in childhood and are experiencing Freudian guilt. Or maybe they need to pee and they can't hold it any longer. We have no idea, but what we do know is that the redness in the face tells us something specific about what is going on inside of that person in the moment, and it does so far better than any of those other behaviours they were displaying. The implies a next possible step in our hierarchy.

Redness in the face, over all else, points to the concept of a specific type of observation, what we can label the *essential call of behaviour.* The word 'essential' gives it away: this is observing and naming the behaviour that indicates the essential experience your partner is undergoing in that moment. It does not tell you exactly what is going on inside of them but catches a very exact marker that something profound is happening.

Essential calls are extremely powerful. Think back to if someone ever told you that you were blushing, or fidgeting, or sweating? My god, the response when someone has caught you with your emotions on your sleeve. Entire disciplines are devoted to cultivating the infamous 'poker face', designed entirely to eradicate any essential behaviours that might reveal such information. By removing the pressure on you to interpret and encouraging you to simply observe, we keep the essential call in line with the values of this work. By not interpreting, we reduce risk and maximise specificity to the moment. As far as fuck polite goes, call someone on an essential behaviour, or have it done to you, and see just how provocative an experience you'll create. The essential call gives us far more punch and provocation than any opinionated call can hope to get, all the while losing no accuracy to the moment.

The value of the essential call of behaviour to leaders is immense. First, fewer things will make you personally feel more exposed than when someone truly calls one of your essential behaviours in a given moment. Facial expressions such as blushing, or being flushed, provide wonderful examples of this, but they go beyond the face as we will see soon. Having one of your essential behaviours observed feels like being hit with a perfect bullseye arrow. How is this a good thing for you? Let's take the concept of vaccination or, perhaps more accurately, repeat exposure. Napoleon would stare into a mirror for hours to perfect his piercing gaze, and the rumour goes that, when he looked at you, he really looked *into* you. There was no way to hide.

The result was people became transfixed, sometimes unable to speak or do much of anything under the intensity of it.

If we break this phenomena down, what we see, in addition to probably a well-crafted expression, is the development of hyper-observational abilities. The more you climb the rungs of leadership and grow in your field, the more likely it is you might encounter someone with this gift of calculated, intense vision. The poker or stoic face may be the traditional buffer against this, but in actuality this is not your wisest strategy, in that it already reveals information about you rather than showing pure neutrality. A poker face, for example, tells me that the person who has cultivated it is doing damage control to hide their breaking point. When they do break, the walls will really come down. People with exceptionally good poker faces don't do very well in the grey area. They have forced themselves to define their behaviour in terms of black or white: tell or no tell. This habit of constant concealment is not free.

As a defence mechanism, cultivating an expressionless, granite exterior will only give someone like Napoleon, with his incredible eye for observing these micro tensions at work in you, a distinct advantage. He will know you are hiding a fuse, and now he can constantly observe you to see when he gets closer to or farther from lighting it. By confining yourself behaviourally to a single static point, someone fluid will be able to constantly work around and manipulate you.

The simple answer, then, is not to get caught up in this kind of a game in the first place. In this training, you repeatedly go through the experience of feeling exposed, knowing when you've been caught in a tell, but over time this stops triggering the anxiety response; repeat exposure, in fact, reduces it. After a while, when you meet someone with that razor-sharp vision, guess what? You'll recognise it as the same set of skills you were training with this entire time. And more to the point, they will see you have the same ability. You'll recognise what they are doing because it is exactly what is going to be done to you in the majority of this training: to really see someone and to know what their essential behaviours in any moment are.

The difference is that this observational precision, when you encounter it, won't stifle you but will bring up a fluid, truthful response instead. That response may be the granite stoicism, of course; we shouldn't deny any behaviour from the moment, but it may be something else. You'll find yourself still able to perform under this unique type of pressure and better. This is akin to, in combat, recognizing a tactic of the enemy as it happens and being able to manoeuvre accordingly, rather than simply becoming prey to it because you were too attached to your static plan.

The second and more obviously valuable aspect of adopting the essential call of behaviour into your leadership training is that it gives you an immensely powerful advantage in your ability to read other people. Have you ever been yourself, or witnessed someone, in a negotiation that became far too mired down because you were trying to read the other person, to really understand what you were seeing and interpret it? If you look at our values in this work, we can see that for anyone who falls into this trap their attention is on the wrong value. During a negotiation, in the moment between you and another person, you are not going to be the solution to your problem. If you were, you wouldn't be negotiating. The other person is the solution. They have something you want, so having the strong facility of putting your attention on them and working off of their behaviour is of premium value. You don't have time to keep exiting the moment between you and another to interpret or assess how it is going. Instead, now you will see a constant stream of behaviours and essential behaviours. These show you the minute changes in behaviour that determine your response. It is not mirroring so much as flowing. As Bruce Lee said, 'My movement is a result of your movement.' The value for your leadership of training the ability to catch a person's essential behaviours in the moment and to respond organically to them is hard to overstate.

The Power of Stillness

There's one additional benefit to the essential call of behaviour. It solves a grave problem that actors and leaders alike face. Consider that in this training, things feel good when you are working with people who are following the values of observe-and-respond. In the outside world, however, people often aren't that open. Usually when you talk to someone it feels like they're giving you nothing. You might not believe it but this happens a lot in the acting industry. Working with another actor is often a great exercise in getting nothing. I'll often hear about actors who go to their director and say, 'I absolutely cannot work with my scene partner. She's giving me zero, absolutely nothing. It's like trying to act to a brick wall.'

That is a notable problem for a profession where career success is based on relational authenticity. Actors are aware of this but consequently don't make life easier on themselves. Let's say I'm in this situation and need a solution. One option is that I can try to solve the problem myself. I say to my scene partner, 'Can you just give me something different? I'm having a hard time here.' For reasons you can probably imagine, this is most likely going to backfire on me further (actors generally resent anyone other than the director telling them what to do), but there is a broader problem circulating the situation: is my scene partner really the problem?

To answer my question let's start with looking closely at my problem. My problem actually isn't with my scene partner. Consider that I can envision a scenario where they do give me the right responses and are actually good to work with. This, in my mind, is a very real possibility and is what drives me to ask either the director or my partner to change things up. This means, then, that since fundamentally the person isn't the issue, the problem actually seems to have less to do with them and is more specific to what they are either doing or not doing. In other words, their behaviour. Their current behaviour is absent of anything of value to me. I am judging my partner's behaviour based on what I determine to be of value to me. When I don't get behaviour that I want, then I deem them the problem and base my problem-solving strategies on my expectations of them.

That's where this issue hides in a subtle pattern. You might think that for me to be able to form this opinion, my attention would have to be on my scene partner. In actuality it has been on myself for the majority of time, appraising the situation by qualitatively stepping in and out of the experience mentally as it is happening. You can confirm this quite easily by trying to analyse, moment for moment, a repetition exercise after coming out of one. You can't do it. So much time is spent on your partner and working with them in repetition you don't have time to decide in each moment what you like and don't like. In this scenario I'm not making my responses dependent on my partner: I'm making them dependent on what I want, or don't want, them to do. I've internalised the idea that if they can't perform according to my standards then I can't do my job. Extracting this conclusion reveals that I am doing is putting the responsibility of another human's behaviour, as well as the success of the entire event, entirely on myself. If I don't get what I want then I can't function and so, I tell myself, I better get something from my partner right now or we are all in real trouble.

Looking at the components of this situation, we can reliably conclude, is a blatantly terrible strategy. It's only going to set everyone, myself especially, up for a lot of grief. What if instead I give myself a proper Meisner slap across the face and put my attention fully back on my not-very-expressive scene partner? When I do so I notice something interesting. True, my partner is not moving much outwardly, but there is still a living human inside. Rather than an absence, I sense a presence: stillness. Now that is a behaviour I can respond to. I'm not only getting something – I'm getting a lot.

Consider, for a moment, the behaviour of stillness. If you do, you'll find it is immensely power-ful and provocative. It brings up so many things. Have you ever had an argument with a loved one in which your anger or hurt was met with complete stillness? It can be infuriating or signify one of the biggest betrayals. Stillness, however, also flourishes in other scenarios. Consider an example of extending yourself, opening your heart to someone who listened with compassion, even though physically all they did was remain still? Stillness is an exceptionally potent essential behaviour. I think it is its potential, not its un-impressiveness, that makes us respond so viscerally to it, mani-festing behaviours such as, 'My partner isn't doing anything!' Oh, but they are. They are giving you stillness. It's just that we have learned to be wary of stillness and are attempting to avoid it. To be clear your response of not liking it is just as valid. The problem comes when you try to develop a strategy to solve your authentic response rather than embracing it.

Our solution, then, is to redefine the parameters around stillness. Stillness is not the absence of a response. It is the presence of stillness. Its power runs deep, and if you put your attention on it and let it be part of your vocabulary of observations, it will bring a lot of responses out of you. It also solves the essential problem of dealing with less expressive or stone-faced types, summarized in this way: make stillness a part of your technique and you will never be without anything to truthfully respond to.

For the leader dealing with a stoic individual, this is an especially useful tactic. Rather than thinking another is not giving anything, it is much better to make their continuous stillness an object of response. They have chosen to make themselves a static point, you don't need to. This works in your advantage in even another way in that your continuously truthful responses will begin to rob a habitually poker-faced individual of seeming to be authentic. Observers will quickly see how you are fluid and adaptable while the other individual remains committed to a static choice, unable to yield or adapt. There you will be responding moment-by-moment to their still-ness, fully organic, and the stonewalling person will become prey to their own narrow habitual, self-imposed strategy. It will quickly reveal what is really happening: you are continuously work-ing off of them and they are not connecting to you. This won't give them status. It will make them appear unable to take action.

Recognising how this applies to leadership took zero effort for me, as I see this in acting all the time. There will be two actors working together. One is constantly connected and flowing off what is given to them. Their partner, on the other hand, has all their attention on their self-generated agenda and what they wish to happen. Stuck in perpetually trying to execute a concept, they are bulldozed by the truthful actor. One will seem continuously stuck, while the other creates moment-to-moment contrast without even working for it.

This brings us to the heart of Lao Tsu's concept of relative opposites and helps us find a practical way to work with it. When summarized, the concept states we only deem some things as tall due to the existence of short things. Beautiful exists because we can actively identify ugliness. Contrast is dependent on two established points within the human mind. This implies that there is a continuous relative experience at play between the hundreds of thousands of objects we perceive daily. Interactions between people are no exception. Put two poker-faced individuals across from one another and they will have to work incredibly hard to expose each other's weaknesses. It comes down to subtle moments that appear as a game of masterful behav-ioural chess. That, however, is not the only game in town. Why in the world would you want to play that game? Put a poker-faced individual across from somebody who is continuously responding truthfully to their mannerisms and you will, by default, create an organic contrast. You appear fluid, authentic, impulsive and dynamic, while the other individual appears stiff, inflexible, and unable to adapt.

This adaptability is especially valuable in the context of today. I have cautioned leaders to beware of the popular trends, but I also advise you to make use of them when the power is easy for the taking. Currently, the timely popularity amongst leaders is for transparency and openness. This gives you a default advantage. The irony is that the classical attempt at the offensive-defensiveness that is the stone face will allow you to continuously trap someone. This principle can be applied to presentations, speeches, meetings, and a variety of other situations leaders might find themselves in, but is especially valuable in interpersonal exchanges and negotiations where there is some risk. Akin to what we are talking about is Bruce Lee's water principle. It is nearly impossible to trap water due to its continuous dynamic motion and ability to meld perfectly to the momentum of the moment. Introducing stillness as an acceptable and valuable essential behaviour to respond to puts much of this dynamic into your hands.

A New Starting Point

Currently if we were to place our hierarchy of observations into a type of structure it would look something like Figure 6.1.

Before we move on, it is worth making one final note about the essential call of behaviour. You'll notice I haven't given many examples of it yet, unlike other calls. I'll list a few here, but these come with a vital cautionary note: essential behaviours are profoundly momentary. They are not like basic or behavioural calls which can be identified moment from moment. What may be an essential call in one moment might not be in the next; likewise, what might be a common behavioural call nine times out of ten can take on profound meaning in a single moment. Essential calls can take any shape or form. This makes them hard to identify on the page but identifying an essential behaviour takes zero effort in the training. They are not always on offer, but when they are, they

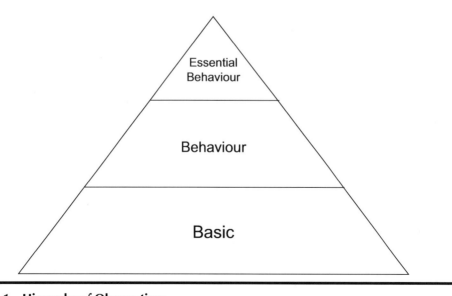

Figure 6.1 Hierarchy of Observations.

will be the loudest thing calling your attention in the moment. You won't need to work to see them or reach for them.

Having said that, examples of the essential call of behaviour can include:

You blushed.
You're still.
Your palms are wet.
You're sweating.
You licked your lips.
Your hands are shaking.
Your eyes are red.

This now begets the question, 'Is this where we stop?' Are these all the categories of observation of worth to training your observational powers as a leader? The answer is no. There are a few very special types of calls I will introduce you to here. Before we do that, however, let's revisit the three moment exercise and see if we can import some of the ideas in the earlier discussion into it and see how they may appear in practice.

Generally, up to this point, moment 1 has always been a basic call. As we've said, we like the basic call for its factual simplicity, but now we can ask, 'Is there a generally qualitatively better way to begin moment 1?' Essential behaviours won't always be there, but what about plain behavioural calls? Behaviour is of higher value than basic calls, given its momentary nature, and so we may want to ask, 'What if we move our general starting point from a basic to a behavioural call?' Let's see another set of hypothetical exercises between you and your partner where we compare the two starting points and see if we can discern the qualitative difference. We'll start the first exercise with a basic call and all of the ones after with a behavioural observation.

Partner: You're wearing a red sweater.
You: I'm wearing a red sweater.
Partner: You blinked.
      (Long reset)
You: You're looking at me.
Partner: I'm looking at you.
You: You smiled.
      (Long reset)
Partner: Your hands are shaking.
You: My hands are shaking.
Partner: You swallowed.
      (Long reset)
You: Your eyes are moving.
Partner: My eyes are moving.
You: You looked down.
      (Long reset)
Partner: You're touching your ring.
You: I'm touching my ring.
Partner: You blushed.
Etc.

Much better and technically sharper. There's nothing wrong with the basic call used in the first example, but since both types of calls are on offer, you can see how making behaviour the primary object of your attention boosts the quality of the exercise significantly because now it is attuned to the transient variables much more relevant to the interpersonal dynamics of the moment. Let's then move our goal post then and make behavioural calls our general starting point. We will still recognise that an essential behaviour or even basic call can dominate any moment, but if we start with behaviour as a default then technically speaking it sharpens the exercise immensely.

Both starting and concluding with behaviour automatically enhances the depth and enriches the value of the exercise for your observational technique. Within the examples just presented we can also see what most likely are some essential calls of behaviour. Just to drive it home, in any of these cases, a basic call would have been totally acceptable, since it is always the celebrated alternative to letting the attention come back onto yourself as you try to figure out how to put a certain observation into words. Even as you become better at naming behaviours, and this is especially true if English is not your first language, you always have the basic call to fall back on and you'll still get lots of mileage out of it.

Two Wild Cards

Taking our next steps, there are three more categories remaining within the hierarchy of observations. For this chapter, we will only look at the next two. The last one won't become relevant until we enter the territory of the given circumstances. For now, however, you will find these remaining two unique and controversial. I will lay out my best case for the circumstances under which they are not only exceptional but brilliant calls that outrank even the essential call of behaviour. I will also, however, be entirely clear about the many more circumstances under which they will undermine and detract from the values of this work. These are both unique types of observational tools for how to capture the reality in front of you, and your discretion will be essential in using them.

Looking at our current hierarchy of observations as it is now, we can call the first three categories of calls top-down. By this I mean we can introduce and assess the concepts of basic, behavioural and essential calls and then in a metaphorical sense 'hand them down' to your technique, going so far as to even say you can make the behavioural call a default observation unless the moment calls for something else. These next two calls are not like that. They play by very different rules. We can call them bottom-up. These calls arise in response to practical challenges you will run into while attempting to make observations. Rather than your becoming mired in your own thinking and losing the attention on your partner, they offer rich, helpful alternatives that sometimes make them even more true to a moment than even an essential call of behaviour.

I mentioned briefly that, in my experience, people with English as their second language will most likely struggle a little more with the three moment exercise, especially in the beginning stages. While this may be especially true of ESL learners, fundamentally it extends to everyone in the early stages of learning the three moment exercise. In the beginning, this is a powerful experience. It can be hard to find words to capture it. As the intensity of the exercises, as well as the bodies of the people in them, literally relaxes, more behaviours start to appear. The physical expressions of your partner start to increase in complexity. Whereas before, your partner may have only moved their hands slightly, now they are more confident and may use their arms. This is not an instruction so much as a natural outgrowth: people become more comfortable and confident with using their bodies to express an authentic response. It doesn't become acrobatics but rather starts to look more like normal human communication.

While this expansion of range is excellent in one sense, in that it shows the participants are becoming more at ease with a wider array of authentic responses, it poses a challenge for you when attempting to make an observation. As behaviours in these exercises become more complex, it becomes equally more complicated to accurately capture what your partner is doing in a simple call. Finding concise words (remember, no points awarded for long, complicated observations) will be a challenge. Very few people are walking dictionaries of precise labels and terms for behaviour. As the exercises progress, you may find it harder to actually find the call for what you are seeing without considerable effort. While this doesn't happen to everyone, this is an entirely normal experience for a good portion of students. If you find yourself stuck, this is the reality we have to find a strategy for. Rather than asking you to put your attention back onto yourself to find some clinically correct phrase for your partner's behaviour, losing precious moments of interpersonal connection between the two of you, it may be more helpful to use an *impressionistic call of behaviour.*

Here's a semi-hypothetical scenario based on an actual experience I witnessed in my own training. Let's say you are working with your partner and at one point they begin to erupt into uncontrollable giggles. This is more than just a laugh: their whole body is writhing side to side. Your observation could be that your partner is laughing, but you know this doesn't capture with any specificity all the nuances of that moment. The almost manic nature of their behaviour makes this far more than just a laugh. There's no easily available phrase for it. A made-up word suddenly pops into your head. You don't take the time to analyse it for appropriateness. You just go with it.

You: You nodded.
Partner: I nodded. (erupts into manic giggling)
You: You scwoogled!

Scwoogled? What the hell is that? I don't know. And neither do you. But let's say I stop the exercise and ask you, what gives with the made-up word? You say to me you didn't try to come up with a clever label for it, the word 'scwoogled' just popped up and it was the best way to say what you saw but couldn't capture into otherwise real words. It seems like this made-up word, then, rather than being a bid for your candidacy as the next Dr Seuss, was a strategy to solve the discrepancy of the richness of the moment versus your ability to accurately capture it. Instead of getting stuck in your head, searching for a more appropriate term, you made an impressionistic observation.

My response: Well done to you.

Impressionistic calls are, by nature, meaningless to everyone in the room, normally even to the person making them. They arise from spontaneity, a collection of sounds that captures a complicated behaviour. The impressionistic call's place in our hierarchy tells us something valuable about where we are in this training as well as its deeper values. The use of the impressionistic call is not part and parcel to all approaches to Meisner. There is a very well-known strand of this work that encourages participants to put their attention back on themselves in between observations and to carefully rack their brain for the most appropriate, best way to label their partners' behaviour. The argument is that this ensures a hyper-accurate observation, and it is worth sacrificing moments in the beginning to ensure your observations are pristinely and perfectly accurate. That's the claim. In reality, all this does is train the habit of micro-pausing between responses rather than actually eliminating that gap over time.

Our interests, however, are not in losing moments at the expense of text. Even from the first repetition session in Chapter 4 we established that text is of less value than the connection between you and your partner. If it comes down to a choice between investing in the reality of perfect calls versus being perfectly with your partner at the expense of language, then the latter is the one option that stays in line with the core principles of this work. Consider also that our exercises don't happen fast or slow; they take on the organic rhythm between you and your partner. Whether that looks fast or slow doesn't matter: what matters is each of those moments are richly filled with authentic interchanges. When an experience is happening moment-to-moment in such a way, you don't have time to put your attention back on yourself and think. It is better to use some meaningless articulations but keep the moment between you and your partner. The impressionistic call is a response to a real-life situation you encounter in this training. Made-up words sound silly, but their design is to keep you entirely within the values of this work.

Are impressionistic calls clean? No. They are very hard to judge for quality, and this is what makes them controversial in this work. They are not like basic, behavioural or essential calls, which can be judged top-down for quality. That is the wrong metric to apply to the impressionistic call. Do you remember in *Raiders of the Lost Ark* when there is a moment when Indiana Jones is confronted by an especially athletic and vigorous swordsman? The warrior swings his sword around for a good 15 or 20 seconds in a dazzling display of primal posturing combined with unquestionable skill with his blade. At the end of his war dance, the message is clear: there is no possible way Indiana Jones will survive this encounter. Remember Indie's response? He pulls his gun out, shoots the guy once, waits for his dead body to hit the ground, holsters it, and gets on with his day. Sometimes the 'appropriate' solution has to give way to the efficient one. Impressionistic calls are efficient solutions. They are an alternative to what otherwise would be a long, complicated observation to capture all the specifics of a moment. They are technically 'dirty', but they are true to the chaos of the moment.

Analysing the impressionistic call also reveals your growth in this work. If our exercises take the form of sterling technique, with perfectly phrased observations of behaviour, and lots of pauses to be mindful, wording our calls so elegantly, as I have seen in some approaches to this work, then we might look technically strong, but we are losing all the values of the moment and the relevance of text as a device. Language facilitates an interpersonal exchange that is impossible to get in any other form of training. The text is not the object but enables the object. One of the valuable lessons the impressionistic call imparts is that you might not always be able to make sense of what you see, but you can still respond to it, even if the words are vapid and meaningless. This doesn't mean you'll suddenly begin speaking gibberish at the office. What it does mean is that you won't be as fazed by extremely complex displays of behaviour and will be able to work off of them even if you can't easily even observe them.

The criticisms of the impressionistic call, however, are not entirely unfounded. If you try to make up a fake word for the sake of it – to sound clever, funny or creative – as far as technique goes, that is one of the weakest, and at this stage, pointless strategies you can adopt. If you love to be inventive, then the impressionistic call might create unwanted chaos for you as you might be tempted to seek safety in meaningless phrases. Under these circumstances, if the call is not spontaneous, or if it plays on habitual creative tendencies, it is not in line with the values of this work and shouldn't be used. It only has value under the rare circumstances when you see your partner do something, and the correct, or appropriate, naming of it would lead you into complicated mental gymnastics if you searched for the right term. If, when in this situation, alongside a long, complicated call there is a word on offer that captures their behaviour in the moment, regardless of whether it is made up or not, then be Indiana Jones. Just say it and get on with the exercise. Scwoogle away.

Thus far we have gone into the reasons why the impressionistic call, even though it may seem strange, under the right circumstances is far superior to any of our other calls. It is also superior to the ones we are trying to omit, such as the opinions, emotives, questions, and speculations, which all depend on cognitive processes of comparison and appraisal. Having said this, what you might be sensing is the caveat to all this, which is that impressionistic calls, as well as the one to follow, are exceptionally rare. If I see a lot of them in a single exercise, generally it indicates to me that one or both partners doesn't have their attention fully on each other and is attempting to seek safety in the slightly distracting nature of the call. On this basis you're doing nothing for your technique. Reaching for made-up words and phrases is as technically weak as trying to assign your partner's behaviour to a cohesive social category like the label of a specific emotion. On impulse, however, if there is no other way to say what you have seen than a made-up word, then the impressionistic call is a strong solution to the problem of being at a loss for words and not allowing that to trap your attention onto yourself.

Top of the Mountain (For Now)

This is it. The final and rarest call to complete our hierarchy of observations in your leadership training, for now at least. What we have seen thus far is that all of these tools solve your problems in unique ways when it comes to reading and labelling the behaviour of another human being. *What* to do with all of this information is something we have not begun deeply training yet, but this brings me back all the way to the starting point of this chapter. The depth of your leadership technique will be constrained by your abilities and powers of observation. This is the value of starting with observation. By making your ability to deeply see another person razor sharp, both in terms of accuracy and the time it takes you to spot the most relevant behaviour, it enables us to move forward and focus more intensely on the responses within you that those observations generate. Having a hierarchy of observations in your training is a gold standard by which your abilities can always be cleanly, reliably, and technically measured.

This last call solves a problem that continues to grow throughout this training, a problem we have already begun to identify with the impressionistic call. As you and your partners throughout this work grow more comfortable, the levels of physical expression are organically going to increase. You are both still in the chairs (for now), but within those parameters there will be more movement now, especially when the impulses from the exercises go into less polite territory. In those moments, as you are now more relaxed within this work and know that you really can respond authentically, you and your partner's bodies will begin to embody the exchange between you two, what we can call 'taking on the quality of the moment'. This is an entirely organic process that occurs without effort.

As an example, let's say you are working with your partner and you spot an essential behaviour. 'You're sweating,' you call. And this just lights the whole exercise up. Your partner goes red in the face, stomps his or her feet, waves their arms and screams their repeat in your face. There is a lot going on. As far as a call goes, how do you capture that? There aren't only behaviours on offer. There are at least four essential behaviours that just happened at all once. Essential behaviours don't really have qualitative value amongst themselves – one indicator of a person's inner state is as good as another – so what is the solution? Do you just list them all, making a laundry list that drones on? If you do that, you'll find you quickly lose the 50–50 balance with such an elaborate and long call. It does nothing for the exercise and is easy for you to trip over. So what's the solution?

There's no right or wrong answer. You could call any one of those behaviours, and it would be great, but you sense that by naming just one behaviour you miss a greater picture. Let's say in the moment no impressionistic call pops into your head, but instead an image suddenly does. Without intentionally generating it, you suddenly see King Kong, from the old black-and-white film, beating his chest and howling angrily. Are you just distracted? Should you push it aside and get back to the task of solving the problem before you? Or is the answer staring you right in the face?

Let's consider something. You didn't reach for this image. It arose spontaneously from your partner's behaviour. Of course, they aren't King Kong, but neither are they a 'scwoogle'. Since this isn't an attempt by you to creatively write an interpretation of the moment, maybe we shouldn't be so hasty to dismiss the image. What if the image itself could be a call? Let's be honest: for you, in that moment, it captures all four essential behaviours beautifully.

You make the call: 'You're King Kong.' Of course, being the pain that I am, I stop and ask, 'What gives?' You say you didn't try to be clever. You didn't even think much about it. In that moment, your partner was King Kong. Was this an okay observation to make?

It is not only okay – it is brilliant. It took the entire complex constellation of behaviour in front of you and integrated it into one concise, truthful observation. It came entirely from your partner. It arose spontaneously. Under these conditions, an observation of this nature scores a direct hit like no other can. This is the beauty of what we call *the metaphorical call of behaviour*.

The first point worthy of reiterating is from the section on the impressionistic calls. Metaphors, like impressionistic calls, are incredibly rare observations. Rather than being top-down, they are also bottom-up, an inevitable response to a moment rather than a concept to train yourself to look for. Most of your calls in this work are going to be good old behavioural and essential behaviour calls, with the support of basic calls if you ever need them, but on rare occasions the moment, not your creative instincts or desire to be clever, will demand a metaphor as the observation. The example above is one such moment.

You may be wondering about how to qualitatively judge a metaphor. In the example presented, if you were one of the people in the exercise, is your metaphor a good metaphor or a bad one? What if your partner was King Kong to you, but I disagree, perhaps preferring the subtle nuances to the gorilla found in Tim Curry's *Congo*? I'm being tongue-in-cheek here (especially about the film *Congo*); the only reasonable answer is that it doesn't matter what anyone else thinks of the metaphor. The same principle is equally true of an impressionistic observation. Both are solutions to an especially complex moment. If we start to debate the quality of the metaphor we are essentially introducing components of a writing exercise into this work. Those specific components would implicitly place the values, and pressures, of being creative onto you.

What I hope is starting to become more clear is that even at the level of the metaphor, there's nothing creative about this work. On the outside, in the audience, we might enjoy or hate your metaphor, but that is secondary. All that matters for training your observational skills is that a metaphor arises as a spontaneous observation of your partner's behaviour. Any qualitative discussions of these last two calls beyond some basic guidelines undermines the heart of this technique. What is vital is that in the moment you did not reach for it or attempt to be clever. It was there before you knew it.

Your partner responded and you saw, for that moment, they were King Kong. You said what was true in that moment. It is a given that what is true in one moment may not be true in the next. The metaphor scores a perfect hit not for objective truth but for your personal point of view integrating seamlessly with the spontaneousness of the moment and your partner's behaviour within it.

As I have hinted, the metaphor is controversial. Some find it unacceptable, and I'll grant it is at the extreme end of what are smart observations to use as training tools. Even some people who are willing to concede the value of the impressionistic call still have a difficult time accepting the metaphor. It lacks the punchy, clinical accuracy of an essential call or the obvious in-context need of nonsensical verbalisations the impressionistic call provides. To them it sounds so close to an opinion or speculation that it feels like an unnecessary hair split. They recognise the impressionistic call is a smart way to solve a problem in the moment. It allows us a way to make a useful observation when words fail. The metaphor pushes one step too far. It is literary in nature. There is nothing truthful about it.

On the nature of the metaphor, these criticisms are, up to a point, valid. There are certainly many opportunities for a metaphor to be misused or to create more confusion than help. That, however, is where there is value in considering context. Any call in this work can be misused. You could make a basic call that is blatantly untrue (saying your partner's hair is red when it is brown, for example) just to provoke a response. Potential problems with observations can run up and down the line and are not unique to the metaphor. If you have good technique, are making strong observations, and, on a rare occasion, a metaphor comes up, this has to be considered in a different context of potential than if you are abusing the metaphor call, making them regularly so as to sound clever or to deflect your partner.

If you want to never use a metaphor, your technique won't suffer for it. Having said that, based on my experiences and the experiences of thousands of people I have trained in this work I am going to make the sceptics a wager: a moment will come in your training when your partner does *Something*. Whether it is exploding into an array of behaviours, or projecting a canopy of subtle, minute ones, one thing is certain: it is going to be massive. In that moment an image will flash in your mind. My advice: break your own rule. The moment is smarter than any of us. Listen to what it demands. In allowing the metaphor to be a part of your observational spectrum you will find, I suspect, you concisely capture all the behaviour on offer and not lose a single one of our truthful values in the process.

The final note on the metaphor's value before we conclude the chapter may help drive it home. For a refresher, take a look at our current hierarchy of observations in Figure 6.2.

Look between impressionistic and metaphor. Notice something we are missing? Our linguistic fans may spot it. We haven't allowed any room for a *simile call of behaviour*. This is strange because, on the surface, it runs quite closely to the metaphor. After all, you could have just as easily said with one minor tweak, 'You look like King Kong' or 'You're like a gorilla.' You may begin to sense, however, this feels considerably technically weaker than 'You are King Kong.' Why? Similes, like opinions, imply a cognitive comparison process. It happens quickly, but it still involves one more additional step than is required. There is a qualitative difference between observing that something looks like another object versus declaring it is that object. One implies common traits across moments. The other implies an objective reality confined to one specific moment or series of specific moments.

Training you to see people in rare moments as assertive metaphors rather than cooperative similes may seem like splitting hairs. To highlight the value, however, let's go back to someone I continuously reference throughout this book: the incomparable Bruce Lee. One of Bruce's most well-known mottos was to advise students to 'hack away the inessentials.' When you are

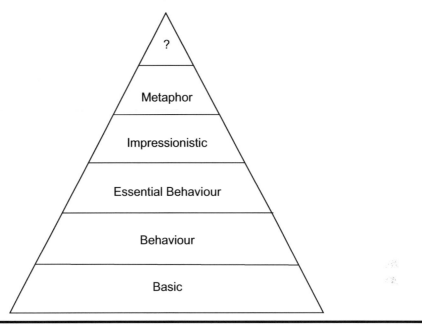

Figure 6.2   Hierarchy of Observations.

working with, and against the best, every micro advantage counts. Train for the situation when you encounter someone with years of honed skill and aptitude or an equally challenging situation. Suddenly even small imperfections in technique can make a difference between success and failure. The same is true of why we omit similes and opinions from your observational vocabulary. You need a reliable, efficient, and sharp power of observation when looking into another person. Some won't have a clue and will be easy to observe. You will also encounter people who can do the same to you, wherever they learned it from, being able to with fine-toothed accuracy catch all your behaviours and tells. Who do you want to train to be able to handle in your leadership journey?

For a simile to have value, it means you have to take the observation and process it according to your past experiences, searching for the most accurate comparison. It messily blends the moment that exists now with moments that no longer exist. When verbalising it we understand that in considering what something is similar to you have also, by proxy, compared it to what it is not similar to. It is true that thinking happens very fast, and so the difference in objective time on the page seems minuscule, but in practice you will notice that moments in this work are filled and rich. To miss time in a moment, or water down the accuracy of your observations even to a small degree, will slow you down in the future exercises we introduce. This work may sound very holistic and accommodating: take the burden off and put it on your partner. This is entirely true. At the same time, this work also has razor-sharp competitive edges buried within it. You are competing to make the best observations as the moment determines them. Don't be guided by your intellectual insistence but rather by your sensitivity to the other person in the moment. Similes have a very weak dynamic in the fine-tuned situations you are training for.

The Wiring Under Like King Kong

Examining the simile helps us articulate the values we are after in developing your observational powers, both within the training but also as portable technique. Comparing people and having opinions about them both share a commonality: as they are each 'seem' calls. In other words, abbreviated guesses. Let's look at our earlier example. You could have forgone the metaphorical call of King Kong and said to your partner, 'You're angry' or 'You're really pissed off.' Granted, in that moment, it probably would score a point for accuracy. Opinion calls, however, at their root are speculations. The translation of your observation, therefore, is at best, 'You seem angry.' That is the best you will ever get out of an observation of somebody based on your opinion of them. You're not in the mind of your partner. You can't do better. Furthermore if we take a look at one of my favourite fields, cognitive psychology, you'll see that to get either an opinion or simile call you're going to have be more in the past than in the present.

When you try to infer the inner emotional life of a person based on their behaviour, the information travels from your retinas to your brain where it is parsed for relevance. The brain is hyper-efficient, and so a need for a label is determined quickly. One theory of the consciousness-brain link is that the brain stores information in neural networks, called schemas. We'll have to abbreviate this a bit for our purposes, but think of schemas as boxes of data with a categorical label. For example the schema for 'ice cream flavours' may include chocolate, vanilla, pistachio, taro, whatever. The schema for 'desserts' however, includes all of those types of ice cream as well as cakes, cookies, pies, and so on. Schemas overlap and they are a handy way for your brain to quickly access, parse, and store relevant information.

When you observe another human being many schemas are activated but two stand out for our purposes. The first accesses and retrieves behaviour models. This helps you make sense of what you have seen and determine if any of the behaviours you are seeing now should be stored as memory. The second is the emotional labelling schema. These schematic processes consolidate different regions of the brain but we'll just focus on the schemas themselves for now rather than the physiology behind them. Schemas, a theoretical by-product of your brain's perceptual system, are a fantastic example of the truism that perception is both incredibly active and lazy at the same time. Our perceptual systems are constantly trying to build a stable model of reality. Though the models can be updated quickly unless a cue for new information storage is received the model remains relatively unchanging. This means the schema for emotional labelling is based on previous assessments of behaviour. It is a database built entirely out of quick judgements due to the trial and error of your past. The ability to 'know' another's emotions is learnt behaviour. You have learned through life experience what anger most likely looks like, the same with intimacy, with fear, and so on. There is a unique counter-theory to this from ethology that suggests some of these emotion recognition systems are in-built and so the learning comes from knowing how to execute them better and in which situations. Even within those rival arguments, however, learnt behaviour is still a vital component.

Whichever side of the debate sounds more plausible, the core problem remains the same: this database is far from accurate. The human capacity to read emotions varies from individual to individual. Your own experiences, when it comes to inferring emotional states, confirms this. You and I spend our lives going through life 'normally' but also being continuously surprised where it really matters. Anyone who has ever had a fight with a loved one over a misunderstanding where both parties had no idea why they were fighting but continued to do so understands the imperfect nature of humans attempting to interpret other humans. Observing an emotion, then, is not about subjective facts but an *attempt* at an objective fact. Your views about what is and is not anger don't exist within a vacuum, they come from somewhere. Observing to your repetition partner that they seem angry is your way of trying to interpret the moment based on the past rather than simply capturing it in the now.

This is why in your training I don't encourage you to try to interpret other people or to impose similes on them. 'Seems like you are' is sloppy technique and when it comes to observing people, you have to dispense with it. Whole strategies of leadership are devoted to trying to win the mind-game of knowing another human's thoughts. This training takes the opposite standpoint, where you train to stop worrying about their thoughts, recognising it for the fruitless chase that it is. Look instead at the behaviour. Behaviour is always going to be there. All this 'what does it mean?' matters a whole lot less for your leadership purposes than if you can observe it and respond to it authentically. The alternative, the perpetual guessing game, is weaker technique and weaker technique translates outside of training to less accuracy and specificity to the moment and the people within it. Ergo your authentic responses, the truthfulness you are working so hard to infuse your leadership skills with, will be compromised from the get-go.

A hierarchy of observations for leadership can best be summarized in this way: the authenticity required for leadership depends on the ability to see others clearly in a profound way. You develop this by saying what is explicitly in front of you without interpretation or hesitation. Basic calls are an excellent way to root you into reality while excluding your need to interpret it. Soon you will learn there is more richness beyond just basic calls and this realisation further develops your observational skills by shifting your priorities. Now if there's a behaviour, you'll spot and call it. It's more valuable to the moment. If there's an essential behaviour screaming out at you'll name it. If you find yourself at loss for words then in training freely let something fall out of your mouth and condition the habit that there will be times when you encounter extreme behaviour that defies verbalisation but can still be observed and responded to. The furthest extension of this is the metaphor. If you see something so profound there's an image attached to it then get comfortable with the image and use it. These are all forms of observation attuned to the reality of the most relevant variable, the other person, and fall perfectly in line with the values of our training. So scwoogle away. Call King Kong out. But for the sake of your leadership skills, the stopping of the compulsion to compare and interpret behaviour as it is happening will alone gain you immense mileage. That is not to say interpretation has no place. We will get to interpretation down the road. Way down. For now the primary objective in your training being expanding on is to stop thinking about what you've observed in the moment and just respond to it.

Now that you have begun training in the three moment exercise, widening your range of observations, deepening them in the process, it is time to make an adjustment to the exercise that will continue to strengthen your leadership technique and solve even more of the problems leaders encounter in their journey to attain power using their interpersonal skills. Brace yourself. The intensity is about to go through the roof.

Summary

Many leaders encounter the perils of 'not being in the moment' mostly because they become trapped 'in their head.' At least that is what they are told. These phrases are often used to denote a level of unmet quality and so have real pressures attached to them. Being stuck in your head, and not being in the moment, often equates to failure in presentations, meetings, and negotiations, where the humanistic abilities of the leader are at the forefront of relevance. Attempts to solve them, however, are vague and general, creating a falsely reverential and unclear understanding of what these problems really mean and how they can be solved clearly and technically. Meisner's three moment exercise introduces the notion of isolating the unit of the moment not in a general sense but in direct relation to the values of this work as it develops your leadership abilities. It accomplishes this firstly by your partner presenting to you a specific moment and you observing it in the next moment. Not all observations in this work, however, are equal. The stronger the technique of observing another person is, the deeper and more profound your responses to their behaviour will be. In this way, your authentic leadership abilities depend on your having an excellent degree of interpersonal observational skills. To the extent that you lack them, your leadership will be constrained by this limitation.

We have talked at length about the value of living truthfully for a leader. Truthfulness is a marker of authenticity people place value in, eventually investing their time and energy into giving you power. The ability to be truthful, however, depends entirely on the quality of your observations. The more clearly you can see deeply into another the more accurate your authentic responses will be. Rigorous technique that is entirely clear about what it includes and does not include in the observation of another human being is a key asset in training truthfulness in leaders. The three moment exercise takes the large problems of being in the moment, as well as being in your head, and solves them in a simple, technical way that makes them accessible to you every time. For a leader, this is an invaluable advantage to have: to not worry about the problem of being in the moment ever again. It also introduces you to a hierarchy of qualitative observations that enables you to dispense with inefficient forms of observation, such as opinionated or comparative observations, utilising instead the behaviours, both simple and complex, that keep you rooted to the reality of rich momentary interpersonal exchanges between you and another person. A leader who never misses a moment will never be without a moment in which to be authentic.

Tips for You and Your Coach

The three moment exercise is best utilised with practice, over and over until the staccato nature, which runs counter to the flowing rhythms of repetition, becomes ingrained into the participants. What you are after as a coach when it comes to the structure is called automaticity. This automaticity is very important because in the next chapter we are going to make a modification to the three moment exercise that dials the intensity up considerably. You want the structure to be deep in the bones of participants by the end of the session. If they get bored out of their skulls, no problem. They will thank you in the next session.

The pause in between the three moments is the vital key to automaticity and should often be stressed. If there is any hint of rushing slow your clients down. They will be glad you did when the next session rolls around. It is better to have a long, relaxing (or boring – either is just as good) pause in between the exercises rather than one that blurs the line between whose turn it is and where in the sequences participants are. In the next exercise, they will gallop, but in this version walking, and getting comfortable with walking, is of the highest value. Make that pause a central character in this session, keep it wide at all costs. You are working on developing a reliable base from which to expand considerably in the next session. Patience and perseverance is the key to this session that enables the absolutely chaotic free fall just around the corner.

Chapter 7

Moment by Moment

Leadership Across and Within

Every session we go deeper. Deeper into what it means to truly see another person and to respond authentically. This takes us further into the bones of leadership itself and has led to some interesting places. For one, we completely dispelled the myth that leadership, with particular respect to acquiring the power necessary to see your inner vision fulfilled, is inherently dependent on you. Rather only half of it is. That vital half we can define as 'observe.' Given that the most sustainable, meaningful power you will acquire comes from other people, whether it is through interpersonal one-on-one interactions or broader mediums such as presentations, meetings, speeches, negotiations, and even writing, it is no coincidence that the half of the leadership process that is entirely dependent on you nonetheless still has to do with things *outside of you.*

Even more paradoxically, there is a second vital half of leadership that is not dependent on you at all. That we can call 'respond.' Many of us want to believe our responses come from us. They may literally emerge from you, but they are not dependent on you or your intentions. This is a phenomenon studied across several strands of the social sciences and goes by names such as environmental determinism. While the environment is a valid component as far as leadership goes, the metaphorical environment that determines your responses is the other person. Eventually this concept of the other outside of you will be broadened to include other variables within your environment. Even when this occurs the deeper message is going to remain the same: your ability to lead and see results will be based on deeply observing and responding authentically to the world around you rather than denying it. This gives us two components to leadership: observe and respond. When coupled together meaningfully in our work, the phrase used to describe them is living truthfully.

Despite its good intentions, this set of ideas might seem to present a problem. Consider that great leaders gain power from others by having markers of interpersonal value. These are not physical so much as personal qualities that can excite and motivate people to place their time and energy into you as a leader. When you interact with another, they must see in you the potential fulfilment of their own ambitions and desires or an embodiment of values they aspire towards. There is a drawing-towards that implies a type of personal magnetism present in successful leadership.

The problem is that obviously not everyone has this quality. It is actually exceedingly rare. This parallels quite well with examples from history. It would appear that the greatest leaders have had both personalities and accomplished things that were larger than life. Caesar crossing the Rubicon in utter defiance. Josephine Bonaparte smashing bottles of musk upon her grand exit so that Napoleon and his new bride would always remember her scent whenever they walked through the imperial apartments. Cleopatra, immortalised through images and writing, with her asps. You may be a leader currently in training, but you are a leader nonetheless. Authenticity sounds great but how will you know if your personality is large and grand enough to inspire people to invest in you, allying themselves with your ambitions to see your visions materialise into existence? Is effective leadership trainable or does it come down to strokes of luck alongside some mysterious neural chemistry of certain individuals?

It is a worthwhile question to look deeply into. It would seem that most leaders feel the pressure of the concern that their personality is not enough. This goes beyond knowing certain limitations and flaws; rather, it is a habitual self-doubt that seems to be confirmed by comparing yourself to history. You know you are not Napoleon or Cleopatra. In your mind, your personality could never compare. If the concern is one of worthiness, then rather than do some generic self-help talk about self-acceptance, let's treat this as a valid question and see if the historical examples we presented earlier can provide some support. Examining them using the values of our work, we will be able to determine if these concerns are legitimate or if there is a bit of smoke and mirrors at work in the mysterious grandeur some leaders seem to posses

Let's look more closely at the historical examples just presented. All of those titanic gestures, and the personalities they flowed from, are wonderful examples of fuck polite. None of these individuals seemed to be as concerned with the veneers of politeness and social customs. Nor were they terrified of not constantly courting the favour of all people at all times. That gives us a starting glimmer of hope. Fuck polite is not a magical, ambiguous touch of luck, but a value we can target and technically train. A brief glance indicates that history seems to favour leaders who live by the rule of fuck polite. Authentically responding to others is fuck polite. Training it as a skill then aligns ideally with what time shows us people value in a leader across cultures and eras.

At the same time, however, we know this can't be the whole story. There seems to be an additional component needed. Remember that fuck polite does not mean go and be habitually rude. We can recall other examples of leaders who were constantly brutish and cruel, such as Caligula or Mussolini. These leaders are not remembered for the greatness of their personalities but rather the great deficits within them. The general consensus is to consider it best that they met their demise, some of us wishing it would have been much sooner. In one sense this complicates the issue around the value of fuck polite. What it also confirms for us is that there is a difference between fuck polite and being habitually impolite. Rudeness is not something off limits to leaders, but like all responses, it seems to require an element of timing. Consider that Patton, renowned for his ferocious hostility, has also been described as being incredibly personable at other times. Some disliked him, but many wished to be around him. He could rain fire down upon you at any moment if you set him off, but he could also be warm and inspiring. His real gift as a leader was his sensitivity to know which was needed in what situation.

It is incredibly rare, though not impossible, to climb the career ladder and continuously succeed by being a habitual monster. The great leaders of history seem to have been neither habitually rude nor habitually warm. Their individual personalities probably landed them more on one side than the other, but they displayed a facility for both qualities. But what does that leave us with? It implies that living truthfully is a vital element of leadership that creates a magnetism. It also reveals, however, that a sensitivity to the circumstances of any situation is of equal importance. Breaking social conventions is incredibly powerful. All the leaders discussed previously found themselves in situations where their responses unapologetically overrode the norms of the time they lived in. Examined in a vacuum, however, there is nothing supernatural about any of the actions of a great leader. Jilted lovers in fits of rage break things all the time. People with a maverick flair defy orders and commands, not always successfully. Others take their life into their own hands, sometimes ending it voluntarily as an ultimate political statement. What's the difference? What separates Churchill's acts of social defiance from Caligula's? Some would argue nothing, but many of us recognise a qualitative difference between their capabilities as leaders. One striking difference stands out for us: Churchill knew when the time was right to act. Caligula was profoundly insensitive to the given circumstances he found himself living in. One acted based on external cues, while the other was driven by internally generated ones.

Sensitivity is an interesting word to consider. The given circumstances of any time can be interpreted and analysed, but for a leader they have to be viscerally felt and intuited. How do you begin to train yourself to develop this sensitivity? Looking through the lens of our work, it begins as you are training the process of living truthfully. Learning first to take attention off yourself and to direct it onto something outside of you goes the distance in spades and expands your range of relevant variables considerably. An even better value was introduced in the previous session, and that is the idea of becoming attuned to the demands of the moment itself. It is through attunement to the moment and its perceived needs that the great actions of leaders resonate in a powerful way throughout history. The outcome is of less relevance. Sometimes they succeed, and sometimes they fail, but both of those are determined after the action is taken. You cannot have an outcome about an action if the action is never performed.

We can say, then, that developing an intuitive sensitivity to the moment greatly increases one's chances of success by reducing the failure that comes from being insensitive to the moment. We have not introduced the given circumstances yet, but already you are training to be able to import them into your leadership technique in a very real and visceral way. This would imply that at least some of the values of great leadership can be trainable and are a core element of this work. It also allows us to consider the many contexts in which living truthfully and fuck polite can be vital strategic tools for a leader to utilise.

Our examination of these nuances reveals that the most successful leaders across time are generally able to display high levels of authenticity. This includes at times being personal, empathetic, and sympathetic. It is both possible and likely that this flexibility across the spectrum of interpersonal responses is what creates a major component of the magnetism found in certain rare individuals. How they attained these skills will forever be a mystery. Most people don't keep detailed records of their education, be it formal or from experience. The beauty is that we can still look at the components and ask if those can be trained. The technique of living truthfully, with its emphasis on a 50–50 balance of observe and respond, alongside a sensitivity to the given circumstances you are in, provides you with the means to draw others in, inspiring them and whetting their curiosity. There is a tangible result from this which is literal proximity. We wish to be around those who inspire us.

Inspiration, however, is a tricky word. It has its own degrees of authenticity when it comes to others. Consider those annoying, constantly motivating positivity gurus who are always 'inspiring' others while seeming to retain none of their own human qualities. Their aggressive inspirations and attempts to motivate are entirely insincere. Our intuitions pick this up before we do consciously. They lack that genuine human dynamic; there is nothing messy or chaotic about them. They aren't 'real'. Their authenticity feels more like branding than honesty. We either know someone like this from our personal lives or social media, at the least. This to me describes the bulk of motivational speakers and self-help coaches. We may seek these people for a quick feel-good fix, but in times when we feel more low and are in genuine existential need, these are not the people we want to share our imperfections with. Nor are these the people you want to aspire to be, even if they do command followings and can continuously hustle new desperate followers to support them. You will notice everyone around them changes, yet they remain incapable of adapting. These are not the leadership values we are working towards when we use terms such as authenticity and inspiration.

One the other hand, authenticity that stems from living truthfully emerges from your human experience and is constantly adapting. It flows around another person like water. This is close to the concept of mirroring but is more refined. In good leadership, the equal emphasis is on your own authentic responses as well as observational abilities. People with this type of authenticity are the people who we seek out in both our best and worst times. We wish to feel close to them because they offer acceptance and unforced motivation. That is the essence of a leader who bypasses social convention with their authenticity. Before you ever need to try to tell them what is wrong you feel as if they are listening or speaking straight to your heart and concerns.

Though this may seem like some sort of argument for the value of social or personal compassion, making others feel this way is of immense advantage to you as a leader. People remain grateful to those who see them and invest their attention into them. Some people will never reciprocate, and these are the ones you will organically lose contact with. They are not honouring that 50–50 balance of successful communication. Most individuals you will find, however, remember the feeling of being deeply seen. When they hear you have a vision, as well as the ability to communicate it, you have a far greater likelihood of being selected for support than leaders who lack the personable traits and qualities that make others around them curious and willing to invest their attention in that individual. That is another example of how a leader makes use of fuck polite in an entirely unconventional and powerful way to inspire others organically.

Individuals who are less truthful in their responses tend to be seen as more reserved, inhibited, closed-off, and less prone to action. They are the antithesis of what, for many of us, makes an exciting leader. Today more than ever the trends towards popular leadership move in the direction of transparency and authenticity. We like to see our social icons not as deities on thrones but as both: rock stars who also take us behind the scenes into their daily lives and problems. We want both the magic and what is behind the curtain. The popularity and rise of YouTube and vlog star personalities cannot be underestimated. More and more people want authentic and close connections with their icons. This has been a part of popular culture for longer than we think. How often is it we find ourselves loving the bloopers of a film more than the movie itself? If social trends follow Darwinism, then truthfulness in leadership has always been more highly selected for. Social media and accessibility with just a click has put those selective pressures for leaders on steroids. This shows you that leaders do not need to be perfect products to succeed. Thankfully, the majority of business and leadership coaches, myself included, naively think we have the genius answer: just be authentic. All that people ask is for you to be you. Easy, right?

Not at all, as we keep learning in this training. Real authenticity sometimes honours while at other times breaks social boundaries. Social conventions are an essential component of a society's successful functioning. Most people can thrive, and even advance up to a point, using social norms. For leaders, however, there will be times when it is necessary to shake off those ingrained habits, and this may prove extremely challenging. Learning when to break, as well as honour, social norms in interpersonal exchanges is a topic we will continue to work with. Before we can work with it, however, we have to begin unpacking your unconscious, inbuilt socially polite habits. You cannot decide when to utilise something until you are aware of the thing itself and how it impacts your interactions with others.

Unpacking and redirecting habits is a matter of time and training. It starts with refocusing and getting the attention off of yourself and your self-censoring tendencies. Through experience you learn that to be open and let your responses be determined by an external stimuli – for now, your partner – is a matter of pure technical ability and not mystery. This begins the process of greater redirection, which is removing your isolated, disconnected intentions and desires as the core priority in your leadership. Yes, your inner vision is essential, but the vision alone is not enough. Consider that both brilliant and malformed ideas can gain support. The common denominator in both cases? People are the essential component to your long-term success. Given this, the ideal training for leadership begins with developing as wide a range of authentic responses to another person – and attunement to the moment – as you possibly can. In doing so, you will quickly begin to rub up against general social conventions as well as feel the friction from ones unique to your personality and background. You will find this training provides the forum and arena for you to face those inner obstacles head-on.

You don't have to be concerned that a radical change in the direction of this work is coming or that you are becoming somebody else. These strengthened habits move you further into, rather than away from, the uninhibited authenticity within you. You have already begun this process. Adopting fuck polite as a matter of technique starts to remove the strength of your ingrained habits by making you aware of them. This applies equally to your observational powers. It is rude to notice holes in jeans or people blushing but the only thing that determines the rudeness is the limitation of politeness. It is also rude to respond authentically to what you see; whether it is with aggression, joy, tenderness, or any other response, you will easily soon step outside of the generally accepted parameters for how to interact with another person. This is why, in training, you are deliberately asked to put aside polite conventions in favour of fully experiencing the authentic exchange.

Fuck polite worries people far more than it needs to. They think because they observe or respond truthfully in an exercise it will turn them into savage brutes outside of the exercises. Don't worry: your ability to be socially appropriate is not going anywhere. You have decades of experience with it. What you most likely don't have nearly as much experience with is being fully authentic in your observations and responses. You will never lose the ability to be polite when necessary. Great leaders never do. What we want, however, is for you to also have a wide range of access to truthfulness so that when those pivotal, career-defining moments come that ask you to defy the conventions and wisdom of the times, to cross your personal Rubicon, you can do so without hesitation. That won't make you Caesar or Josephine, but it will mark you as a great leader for the time you live in: making the unconventional, sometimes hard, decisions when the circumstances demanded it and having the ability to observe those dynamics and respond to them with uninhibited authenticity.

Which brings us to today's training. We are going to make a fundamental change to the three moment exercise, where you will discover very quickly that there is no time – absolutely no time – to be worried about politeness anymore.

Exercise: The Three Moment Exercise 2.0

In our previous session, we took the concepts of being 'in the moment' and 'in your head' and completely trashed them for the nonsensical phrases they are. We then repossessed them for our work, defining them not in vague, general prescriptive terms but in a technically simple way. By putting your attention on your partner and using your developing skills of observation to cleanly capture that person in a moment of time, you have a concrete metric to determine that you were in the moment and your attention not trapped on itself. It is beautifully simple and efficient process.

From there, we distilled a hierarchy of verbalised observations. For the specifics of each, as well as the reasons for why they rank in this order, you can reference the previous chapter. Figure 7.1, however, is our current hierarchy of observations as it will remain for a long while in this training.

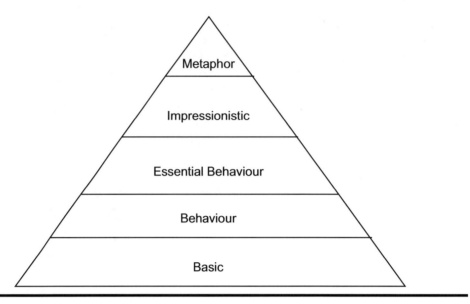

Figure 7.1   Hierarchy of Observations.

Our previous session's intensive and deep look into the nature of how to observe another human being will now begin to bear fruits as we make an adjustment to the three moment exercise that will significantly expand your range of truthful responses by utilising your now-honed depth of observational powers. To familiarise ourselves with our starting point, let's have you and your partner do just a few three moment exercises before we introduce the change.

You: You're still.
Partner: I'm still. (raises eyebrows)
You: You raised your eyebrows.
  (Long reset)
Partner: You wiggled your nose.
You: I wiggled my nose. (laughs)
Partner: You laughed.
  (Long reset)
You: You're biting your lip.
Partner: I'm biting my lip. (goes red in the face)
You: You blushed.
  (Long reset)
Partner: Your hands are shaking.
You: My hands are shaking. (smiles)
Partner: You smiled.
Etc.

Technically, this is a very strong exercise. The calls are clean, and the values are there, along with plenty of examples of both behavioural and essential calls. Also, equally important, notice that you and your partner are not rushing from exercise to exercise. The structure of the three moment exercise as it is now is you are both focusing on isolating a single moment (the second moment) for observation, and you each take a long pause in between exercises, what can be called a reset. This allows you to calmly and gradually get comfortable with isolating the unit of the moment in a clean and technical manner. Let's say, however, we just stopped here, not the training but the three moment exercise. What would we be left with? Something with promise but entirely abstract, a great and trainable concept with its actual applications to interpersonal interactions unclear.

Let's identify why this would be the case and then introduce a change that can continue to push this towards having more concrete relevance. The big hint comes in the structure. While some people imbue the number three with mystical relevance, it is hard to make the case for it in linguistics. Outside of training, in the glorious 'real world', people do not habitually speak in three isolated, clipped sentences, complete with long pauses in between to resettle. I'm not sure whether the world would be a better place or not if they did so – let's leave that one to the jury for now. Of course communication between people sometimes is staccato, but these are rarer circumstances. For most of us, more often than not, communication unfolds in a continuous flow so natural we are not even aware of it. This flow continues for as long as the interaction goes on, with the changing tempos and speeds ultimately being a continuous, largely unconscious, experience.

When we break apart the communications we take for granted, analysing them through this work, what we find is that human interactions are not just 'one moment'. Rather, what we see is a flow of moments. We have a phrase for this in acting: working *moment to moment*. To begin to make this training more applicable to 'real life' interactions, we need to introduce a modification to the three moment exercise that can accommodate flow and enables you to work moment-to-moment with your partner.

It is worth pointing out that this modification is a bit of a tightrope, as each development in your training demands that it fits perfectly with all the other values we have built in. It needs to be simple and technically clean and clear. No mystery. The interactions also need to allow for you to be able to observe and respond truthfully. How will that be accomplished? If we target the structure of the calls or changed the number of moments, we would destabilise too much. Three, after all, is profoundly easy to remember, and you did spend all that time learning the sequence in the previous session, as well as the kinds of observations to keep and stay away from. Altering either of these won't strengthen the exercise's quality. How about that reset, however? That long pause you and your partner take to resettle and encourage yourselves not to rush? It's been highly valuable up to this point, but maybe it has served more like training wheels rather than something essential to your technique.

Let's consider what the reset, or holiday, an endearing term my Meisner teacher Scott uses, means in the context of our training. We arbitrarily create the pause between exercises to emphasise the structure. This allows you to focus on the most relevant moment of observation which is what your partner is doing in moment 2. In reality, however, there is no pause, we have created it artificially so we have a conscious way of breaking apart this experience. In reality moments do not suddenly vanish until the next exchange begins. What actually happens when either you or your partner take that reset is that a series of moments go by until the new exercise begins. Consider all of the things that happen between the exercises that we have conveniently ignored up until now: the two of you may readjust, go quiet, be still – a whole series of transitory behaviours between the exercises that we have been pretending do not exist. Again, I want to emphasise this mutual conspiracy has been of value as it allowed you both to get the structure and primary value into your bones. We can't deny, however, that missed moments are all observational opportunities you are losing. To create a moment-to-moment experience, then, let's try eliminating the holiday and see what that does. This can be accomplished by making a very small, simple adjustment in the exercise.

Let's say you and your partner are working together. One thing worth noticing here is that I have numbered the moments, which will help in clarifying the new step in this exercise. This time your partner will begin first:

(Moment 1) Partner: Your eyes are watering.
(Moment 2) You: My eyes are watering.
(Moment 3) Partner: You shifted in your chair.

While your partner is making their third moment call, they are not just a neutral entity. During this moment they are also exhibiting behaviours. Let's say in this hypothetical exercise that what happens to your partner in the third moment is:

(Moment 1) Partner: Your eyes are watering.
(Moment 2) You: My eyes are watering.
(Moment 3) Partner: You shifted in your chair. (smiles and leans in while saying this)

That's two good behaviours right there. Depending on the moment, either might be an essential call. Why waste a good behaviour to have a holiday? What if, rather than a reset, that third moment from your partner will yield you the behaviours that become the material for your first moment observation in the next three moment exercise? Totally confused? Let's take the same example and break it down by moments:

Moment 1: Your eyes are watering.
Moment 2: My eyes are watering.
Moment 3: You shifted in your chair. (smiles and leans in while saying this)

Traditionally now there would be a long pause. In eliminating that your task is to start the new exercise by observing your partner as they speak in the third moment and then, when they have finished speaking, without pause make a call based on what you have observed as the new first moment. Let's see what that looks like.

(Moment 1) Partner: Your eyes are watering.
(Moment 2) You: My eyes are watering.
(Moment 3) Partner: You shifted in your chair. (smiles and leans in while saying this)
(Moment 1) You: You leaned in.

Your partner now will repeat what you've said and you'll make a new third moment observation, completing the pair of three moment exercises. Let's see what this looks like:

(Moment 1) Partner: Your eyes are watering.
(Moment 2) You: My eyes are watering.
(Moment 3) Partner: You shifted in your chair. (smiles and leans in while saying this)
(Moment 1) You: You leaned in.
(Moment 2) Partner: I leaned in. (quickly leans back in chair)
(Moment 3) You: You went back.

What you will see now is that we haven't just removed the holiday by encouraging you to speed up the exercise. That sort of instruction would be quite ambiguous and would lead to self-imposed agendas. Nor have we increased the number of moments. These are still three moment exercises. We have instead simply asked that the two exercises be linked, and that is what you both have done. Rather than individual exercises, this new version of the three moment exercise looks more like links on a chain. We also have not destabilised the inherent structure – these are still three moment exercises, just connected now in a moment-to-moment way.

Let's see what an extended example of this looks like. I've marked three things to help you to keep track of where we are: the moments themselves, the place where the reset was removed, which implies a new three moment exercise, and the behaviour in moment 3 that is the material for the new observation in the next moment 1. Starting from the beginning:

(Moment 1) Partner: Your eyes are watering.
(Moment 2) You: My eyes are watering.
(Moment 3) Partner: You shifted in your chair. (smiles and leans in while saying this)
    (no pause)
(Moment 1) You: You leaned in.
(Moment 2) Partner: I leaned in.
(Moment 3) You: You went back. (gritting your teeth)
    (no pause)
(Moment 1) Partner: You gritted your teeth.
(Moment 2) You: I gritted my teeth.
(Moment 3) Partner: You laughed. (puts forehead in hands and shakes head)
    (no pause)
(Moment 1) You: You're Hamlet.
(Moment 2) Partner: I'm Hamlet!
(Moment 3) You: You laughed. (smiles and stops moving)
    (no pause)
(Moment 1) Partner: You're still.
(Moment 2) You: I'm still.
(Moment 1) Partner: Your chin is shaking. (touches your hand)
Etc.

Having done this for so long, I don't know how it looks on the page but I can tell you two things from my perspective: this was a hell of an exercise and the moments in it were profound. You can already see that truthful responses alongside the observations are arising. In most other contexts, shaking one's head might not be so profound, or touching a person's hand to comfort them, but in an experience as unconstrained as this, those types of moments land home in an entirely different way. This isn't an embellished example, either, but a rather common one of what happens in this incarnation of the three moment exercise. It becomes far more visceral, personal, and the internal temperature of it goes through the roof. Let's first investigate the simple technical mechanisms that allow for this and then look deeper at how good this is for your leadership abilities. Spoiler alert: it's damn good.

What we can first glean from this example is that neither of you are working any longer on just isolated moments. You are each working moment to moment, fully alive and engaged with one another and the values of this work. Notice in the example, as well, that moment 2 was always repeated. This seems small but is profoundly important. This is not just about making a laundry list of observed behaviours but rather honouring all aspects of a simple but extremely tight structure. That one brief moment of repetition is perhaps the most important element of this exercise. It is the crucial component that facilitates much of the interpersonal depth in the exercise. If you want to confirm this for yourself, try just going a few times back and forth with only observations and no repetition, cutting out the second moment. You'll see the depth evaporate almost instantly. Repetition, even for a moment, allows you to get a depth of specificity and to have a visceral response to an observation.

Since this chapter focuses more on the topic of depth in this work, you may notice something: the first incarnation of this exercise, with the long resets in between exercises, had comparatively very little depth. The power of the experience mostly came from the observations and the intense scrutiny. Now, in this version, responses pop up quite organically, surprising both you and your partner. In this exercise, a good amount of deep, truthful responses came up rather quickly for both of you. The exercise was filled with examples of higher-level calls such as essential behaviours and even a metaphor. Notice, however, that I've said this is a fairly common example. This shows that there is now a potentially rich, deep interpersonal experience on offer from the first moment. It also shows that there is nothing mysterious about this type of deeply connected experience, considering that you and your partner attained this through simple technique.

The conclusion here is that we are building into your leadership the ability to connect deeply with another person and work entirely off of them in a dynamic, living way, not as a matter of intangible, unreplicable happenstance but as solid technique. This is why none of our exercises look the same. That is the point. The structure is the same, but no two exercises will ever look alike. The technical aim here is for you to work with the moment, in the process becoming hungry for the next moment and then the next and so on. We solved the issue of being in the moment. The challenge of working moment-to-moment is the next level this complete version of the three moment exercise addresses in a technical way. Already you might be starting to see how this ability is one of the most powerful tools a leader can possess.

Looking at the experience itself, you may notice very quickly in practice that with this modification, a potentially alarming new component to the exercise arises: this experience feels fast and it goes like a roller coaster. In reality, it isn't going any faster, but it feels that way because now we are not letting large amounts of moments escape into that long reset. Rather than isolated exercises, this becomes about engaging in a flow of authentic interpersonal experience with razor-sharp observational skills. A consequence is the now-constant, unebbing flow of the three moment exercise making it incredibly difficult to keep track of where you are in the exercise. You will discover that attempting to keep your attention on the structure and live in the values of the exercise becomes a fool's errand. It is literally impossible to do both. Is this a problem? No. This is exactly where we have been going the entire time.

To Err Is Divine

In your very first session, we spoke about investing in the reality of doing, the notion that whatever you are doing requires your full immersion. As my Meisner teacher Larry would often say, half-doing something is really not doing anything. Paying full and deep attention to your experience is how you invest fully without pretence or falsity. It may be the starting ingredient to our training, but experiencing this concept viscerally, however, can take time. If you didn't experience it in repetition, this might be the first time in this work that the full weight of that concept is brought to bear. You no longer have a choice in this version of the three moment exercise and have to pick one or the other: worry about the structure of the exercise, where your place is, as well as whose turn it is, or go fully into the experience with your partner. This is what I call 'the great either-or' of this work: there is no more grey area. Either you are in this experience or you are not.

Seemingly this fork in the path presents a challenge for you. If you just throw out the structure, you know you'll lose all the depth, so you have to keep the structure but not worry about it. Is this possible? The answer is yes. Now you can see why, in the previous session, I was so particular about our need for those holidays, the long reset that would allow you to focus on nothing but the technical structure, getting it into your bones. To make it automatic. If we did it enough times, then this automaticity has built into you some very simple components, which is the 1–2–3 nature of the exercise. If it's in your bones you will be very well served. This means that you can forget about the technical structure, trusting it is there without the need for conscious monitoring, and fully ride the experience with your partner. There's a silver lining to handling this the way we have: in the event the 1–2–3 is not rock solid, we can just take you a step back and work the exercise with the resets. When the structure is ingrained you can then progress back into the version without the resets. I hope you are seeing the beauty of utilising this approach. There are no mysteries in this work. Everything is sequential and clarity builds upon clarity.

This seems to sound good. Relax, let go, vibe with it, or something like that. At the same time, a genuine consideration and reality emerges. Fully trusting and throwing yourself into the exercise, you will discover that it is not mistake-free. There will definitely be some mix-ups. The exercise will get confused. Someone will repeat when they should have begun a new exercise and so on. You don't need to see here any examples, because that automatic 1–2–3 structure built into you both you and your partner will intuitively sense it when the exercise goes off track. Just a paragraph earlier we established that if there are too many mistakes, we have to go back a step. At the same time, the fact that the exercise can accommodate some mistakes, especially once the rhythm is in-built, implies that rather than the structure being a protective agent against any error, it seems to serve rather as a beacon to get the exercise back on track when it goes off. Say someone was repeating when they should be making a new observation. You'll both sense the mistake, and one of you will make a new observation and the exercise will be back on track. If this happens infrequently, due to the organic chaos of the experience rather than to a lack of technical soundness, then it seems not to detract from the learning potential of the exercise.

This brings up a principle in this work that quickly beckons a deeper question about the nature of your leadership. In terms of technique, are mistakes acceptable? How do we accommodate, or don't, mistakes in this work? Can they have value within training? This is a profoundly important series of questions to answer. Recall, as well, that we are not asking only about mistakes in this exercise. They might serve as examples, but because this work builds on itself, any answer to this question will be present throughout the rest of your training. The answer we choose will become a part of how you lead other people if you adopt these values into your approach. In asking what do we do with mistakes in the exercise, we are really asking how a leader trains to handle mistakes, not only in their literal training but also the tools they take outside of these sessions.

It's a serious question, and it asks that we first look at the word itself and ask, as we have done with other phrases or terms, 'What does a mistake mean according to the values of our work?' The first element we can extract is that a mistake implies a deliberate decision or action. It is hard to apply the idea of a mistake to something you had no control over. Let's take the simple example of a restaurant that you and your partner are considering going to. The reviews are all terrible, everyone says stay away, but you go anyway. Sure enough, you both get food poisoning and spend the night fighting for the bathroom. Where was the mistake? Not the food poisoning, as some might say. Consider that you never had the exact option to choose between fresh or poisoned food. The food poisoning wasn't a guarantee but a risk. The mistake was the decision to go to the restaurant in the first place. Likewise, if you had gone to a restaurant you had visited for decades with no problems and happened to get the one piece of bad fish out of hundreds you'd eaten, there's no mistake. Mistakes, it seems, generally require some conscious input and action from you. In other words, a deliberate decision.

Decision implies the second component of a mistake. If you are trapped in a building on fire, and you have no choice but to run through the flames to safety, was it a mistake to take that option? Even if you don't survive, we can't really call it a mistake, since the option was stay and be burned or run and get burned. Now let's say one option is to climb through a nearby window adjacent to the street and leap two feet down to safety with no consequences, or to run through flames so as to reach the front door. If you took the latter choice, it is much easier to consider that a mistake. This tells us that if a mistake is made, it is because there was at least one better alternative you chose not to take. Mistakes occur when you consciously infer the suboptimal of at least two outcomes to be the best one. The teaching value of a mistake is to think there was a better outcome on offer which likely would have come to fruition had your actions and decisions just been different. Whether that can be predicted with any certainty is up for debate, but that seems to be the general consensus on the educational value of a mistake. This leads us to the third, final component, which is around this concept that one outcome is better than the other. For mistakes to exist and have been made, you have to choose the wrong option or at least not choose the right one.

Our three components then boil down to this: a mistake begins with your appraisal of at least two outcomes. You make a decision and pick the wrong one. Reflecting on it, you envision that had you just chosen the other option, things would be better. It has to go this way to be a mistake. If you choose one option and it turns out to be the correct one, you haven't made a mistake, or you made what some would glibly call a 'happy mistake'. In any case, looking at our work thus far, do any of these components seem to fit with the values of this training?

Not really. For you to allow mistakes to be a part of your work implies you are consciously judging outcomes for quality and then acting in some way on those decisions. It is true that sometimes you will have two options: act on the impulse or don't, make the observation or not. To act on them is stronger technique, but that doesn't mean the outcome will necessarily be better. It is possible, for example, that a truthful response with kind intentions might provoke a negative response from your partner. This doesn't mean you made a mistake. Nor if you choose to not act on an impulse are you necessarily making a mistake. Sometimes in this work the urge to throw something might come up. I agree that while it might be truthful, it is best if we don't throw things at one another, and so denying this truthful response equally might not constitute a mistake.

This is the challenge of attempting to describe a mistake in this work. Any definitions we come to miss out on large chunks of possibilities and are hardly in line with the values of living truthfully, where what happens to you does not depend on you or your agendas but rather on the organic unpredictability of the other person and what they are going to spontaneously make you do. Leaders are often taught to be their own worst critic, to examine in excruciating detail their mistakes so as to ensure they won't happen again. If you agree that living truthfully is an important quality for a leader, then how is that habit going to help you? Short answer: it won't.

Before you worry that I am telling you to never reflect on your actions you can breathe, I am not. What we are looking at is the idea of mistakes as they apply to your leadership skills, which are directly oriented around other people and the circumstances you encounter them in. Allowing mistakes to be a part of your interpersonal leadership skills plonks you right back to that same issue we ran into from the first session. That issue is the compulsive need you have of 'doing the right thing', in other words, seeking appropriate actions. We threw that out with the core idea of 'fuck polite' being the fuel for living truthfully. If you throw out fuck polite you allow those old habits of yours – rather than the moment or your partner – to determine what is the best response. Those are the very same habits that can paralyse your leadership technique. Rather than moving towards further depths, asking yourself to identify the mistakes in your leadership technique will start to drive you in the opposite direction.

Obviously, in other areas of your endeavours, mistakes can and must exist. Decisions about policy and strategy sometimes prove the wrong course of action. Locations and investments sometimes yield a deficit in return. Plans with seemingly almost no margin of error fall apart instantly. I am sure some of these things have happened to you, and you benefited from learning from these tragedies. I am equally sure you will continue to benefit from reflecting on them. I am not saying as a leader you can never make decisions, but remember we drew a very clear line between the skills necessary to be a leader versus anything else early on. Planning, strategising, analysis – all of this is important, but it isn't solely essential to leadership. Many people at different stages in a structure or process plan, or have to analyse and make strategic decisions, but very few of those people are in in positions, or in need of the skills, of leadership.

That is the lonely position you find yourself in. No one except a leader needs to live truthfully under a given set of circumstances. This is the only set of essential skills a leader must have to ensure sustained success. Whether you get them from this approach or elsewhere doesn't matter – the skill set is what is essential. I trust that you know your vision for your field. Our interests are targeted towards making you the best leader in that field. Mistakes, then, in the context of what makes for a good leader, is what I am challenging. Mistakes depend on right or wrong, appropriate or inappropriate. When it comes to living truthfully, there can be no such thing as appropriate or inappropriate. Those are imposed judgements that fall apart in the face of the chaos that emerges between you and another human being. If those cannot be a part of the process, then it means there are no right or wrong choices. Down the road, this will be altered ever so slightly when we bring in given circumstances, but not enough to change this fundamental value: there is no such thing as a mistake in this work.

Say you and your partner are doing a three moment exercise. Your partner needs to start a new three moment exercise but continues to repeat instead. Technical structure has been broken, but these are not mistakes. Mistakes, and the judgements that determine them as mistakes, won't exist unless we call them into being. What instead has transpired between you and your partner is in actuality only a series of moments. Moments where the unexpected took front and centre. Since what happens to you in the process of living truthfully is not determined by how much you want to impose or force on the moment, then your judgements about mistakes in those moments are not relevant. The exercise was temporarily thrown off track, but did you both live truthfully? That is still our core measure of authenticity. If you did, but we prioritise the structure, the 'plan' in favour of the demands of the moment, then we have judged the quality of your work by the wrong unit of measurement. If the rules are broken in favour of a truthful impulse or observation, then you got the right value. Our alternative is to forgo truthfulness in favour of structure. Chaos is part and parcel of this work. That said, there obviously is a line. Too much chaos and we need to go a step back as the learning value evaporates. Just enough keeps you intensely plugged in to the values of this moment and becomes an incredibly potent and valuable training device.

Even if we send the concept of a mistake outside the door, we still retain our units of measurement in this work. If you think of the idea of a mistake as an either-or scenario, in that you either made the right choice or did not, we can instead replace that with the concept of a spectrum. At one end is the term 'technically weaker' and at the opposite, 'technically stronger.' Your authentic observations and responses, as well as adhering to the structure of an exercise, can exist fluidly on a spectrum. That still provides us with a metre of measurement by which you can gauge your own improvement and know what to do to better within your work. This is much healthier. Moments are imperfect, complicated, and messy things. If you attempt to impose too rigid a structure on yourself, expectations that are too stringent, or leave no room for chaos, then this is attempting to extract more structure than can be sustained by reality. Eventually your attempts collapse in on themselves. It is akin to drinking nothing but saline to get your daily water: you'll only make yourself sick after a while.

I suspect that the idea of releasing mistakes as a learning tool will be hard for most. Many leaders have qualities that go by a variety of labels: perfectionist, OCD, type A, and so on. It is hard for them to hear that the value they are training now – and that will travel with them after these sessions end – is the necessity of giving up the ability to break down reality in such simple black-and-white terms, to evaluate and either praise or chastise your leadership abilities on the premise that the mistake is a reliable unit of measurement. It is a soothing comfort to think reality can be that categorical, even if your hopes will rarely be confirmed.

Looking closely at other approaches to leadership you will find that, while the language is about being spontaneous, the way the exercises are ordered and structured, as well as what components are the target of feedback, is actually about imposing control over chaos. Learning to dominate reality through constant self-correction. At the outset there seems to be promise in this approach, but it is a fool's errand. Living truthfully for a leader is not about conquering chaos but learning how to thrive within it. You can't thrive in what you are continuously striving to dominate. For many leaders, this is one of the hardest habits to change: to learn to surrender control in favour of being fluid to the moment. To win the game by losing.

Adopting the notion of a continuum of technique will serve you very well and allows us to ask specific questions about your performance in an exercise, especially later on. Questions such as: were you sensitive to the given circumstances you encountered? Did you allow your truthful responses to be filtered by them? Did you sit on any truthful impulses even when the moment demanded them? The answers to these questions determines the strength or weakness of your technique and allows us clean margins to keep moving your abilities in a better direction. No mistakes. Just moments. As well as the ability to do it slightly better next time or to recognise when you are doing enough.

I don't expect you to give this up now but rather to discover in practice the alternative on offer. For now consider that the real-world implications of this shift in mentality bear a great deal of fruit. Leaders with a strong facility for living truthfully under a given circumstances will know how to interpret the environment into which they are going and have the ability to respond authentically to whatever they encounter in those contexts. They will not shy away from what the moment demands of them in those situations, however great, large, or seemingly impolite the response required is. Those who are less aware of their environment, less able to be truthful within it, and who do not respond authentically to the demands of the moment either out of fear, self-consciousness, or inability have weaker leadership technique. Leaders who are aware of the situation they are in and respond in accordance to the moment, will always act in a strong way. What gives them such sharp reaction times? They've stopped constantly worrying about correcting themselves. The attention-drawing nature of mistakes is a burden now removed.

What may feel like mistakes now will become moments that see the widening, rather than narrowing, of your authenticity. These are slippery concepts to come to terms with just on the page, but in practice you will discover mistakes are even more difficult to make consistent use of. For one, they have no real recourse. The moment has passed already and cannot be recreated again, so how can you ever fix your mistakes? By not repeating them again? The next time will be a new moment and may have entirely different demands. A mistake in one moment can be the solution in another. Imposing the past on the present, even if they share perceived similarities, can blind you to the different variables needing your attention. The more mistakes you perceive yourself to make the more of a growing mountain of imaginary deficits you will create for yourself. I ask this sincerely: you tell me how that is going to somehow make you more authentic in your leadership? You can't go back in time and fix the moment. It passed. You can only move forward.

What if, instead, you recognise the impulses you sit on, or the observations you are too self-conscious to make, simply as markers of needing stronger technique? It seems then the process for you to overcome these challenges becomes more simple. Mistakes will always keep you trapped in the past; while this might be valuable in certain areas of your profession, as reflection is a powerful tool, when it comes to your ability to be authentic as a leader, the centre source of your power, it will be your downfall and lead only to uncertainty and an ever-widening sphere of limitations.

I'll make my final case for why, when it comes to living truthfully under the given circumstances, that there is no such thing as appropriate or inappropriate, no right or wrong responses or observations, and no such things as mistakes. There are only moments guided by stronger and weaker technique according to a set of values. I'll do it by asking you to consider for yourself which is the optimal strategy in the following hypothetical scenario.

Two leaders are pitted against one another in competition meet for a vital negotiation. Both have equal knowledge in their field, equal resources, and so are matched in all areas. With one difference. One leader has made their authenticity dependent on correcting their leadership mistakes based on past experiences, learning how to be polished and calculating, fitting their behaviour to the criteria for what they believe are appropriate measures of interactions. They don't make a wrong step. They have learnt to be their hardest critic. They also adhere to a mindfulness doctrine: before they respond, they check in with themselves, engaged in a perpetual cycle of self-monitoring to ensure they perform optimally in the moment. When they err, the voice in their head, their inner critic, sounds the alarm and begins banging self-correcting pots and pans until they make the change. In this way, you always seem polished and measured with an inner guard dog at the ready to catch you as soon as you step out of line. This is your average cookie-cutter leader mould that many people attempt to slot themselves into. In this model, you attain freedom by making yourself your own prison guard.

Let's say that the other leader does not believe in mistakes in leadership. He or she simply puts their attention on the other person, unmired by the past and completely in tune with the circumstances in their environment. As such, they can observe others clearly and respond to them fully moment by moment, trusting that the moment will handle the necessary measures. Without the need to constantly check themselves, they have more time to respond. They are lighter, flexible, and adaptive in their behaviours. They also get the benefit of their attention never wavering from the other person, the only exception being if something more profound in the environment demands it. Their observations are clear and unhindered by politeness. Having trained themselves in the value that a response generated by an external observation is almost always fair game, they have no doubt about expressing their responses and taking initiative. Having developed this ability to have access to a wide range of authentic responses, without the need for premeditation or preparation, or needing to be calculating or concerned about outcomes, their technique enables them to respond fully to every single moment. Knowing their given circumstances beforehand (this we will get to later), they have done their homework and are prepared, and so their truthful responses are filtered organically by the demands of the moment. All this without needing to shift their attention back onto themselves and lose the other person for even a single moment in time.

You tell me who will have the advantage in this situation.

Now that we have gotten from the three moment exercise its deeper core components, it is time to begin unifying past and present, where we began and where we are now, re-encountering a familiar face along the way.

Summary

Taming the nonsensical phrases of being in the moment and avoiding the trappings of becoming stuck in your head, reframing them into a meaningful context that can make them solvable technical challenges, is only the first step in the process of making your leadership technique for living truthfully razor-sharp and honed.

Behaviour, which as we have said is the currency of living truthfully, does not exist in static moments: it unfolds in a continuous flow of specificity, a string of moments. Strong leadership technique involves the ability to interact moment-by-moment in a state of heightened engagement. Working moment-by-moment, however, demands that certain conventions be given up, namely the concept of mistakes, of which there can be none if you are putting your attention fully on another human being and responding truthfully.

In this work, there are no mistakes, only moments. This version of the three moment exercise, the complete incarnation, drops you and your partner into an unending flow of observe-and-respond, using specificity as the measure of stronger or weaker technique. The more specific your observations are to the moment, the more truthful your responses will be. In leadership terms this means that the more sensitive you are to the demands of the moment, able to see deeply into its nature, the more your responses will organically take on the quality and needs of the moment and in correct proportion.

It may be frightening to think of releasing control, especially for a leader, but in the realm of living truthfully, the paradoxical way presents the answer yet again: in giving up power, letting your actions be in total response to the situation, power returns to you in greater measure. History remembers leaders for their boldness and audacity, but if we look deeper at its core, it is celebrating that, when great moments demanded it, they did not shy away from, but rather went further into, their own authenticity. This also implies a capacity for an immense sensitivity to the demands of the moment. These are qualities we are seeking to broaden and make a core element of your leadership technique.

Tips for You and Your Coach

As the coach, this session will require you to be honest with yourself about where your priorities lie. As we've said earlier, here we come to the divide between technical structure and the chaos of the moment. From here on in this work this balance will tread on a razor-sharp margin. It is good to face it head-on in this session. One helpful image can be to think of the technical structure of exercises in this work like a necessary prescription drug. It facilitates the ability for things to work correctly, but we want to keep the dosage to the lowest possible quantity but still get the optimal benefits. This is why 1–2–3 is great for an exercise structure. It is easy to learn and easy to become automatic.

Your diligent work in the previous session, drilling that structure into the point of boredom and then some, has organically instilled it into the bodies of your clients. The fruit borne is now they don't have to worry about it and can fully ride the intensity of the experience, living richly in the values of this exercise with their partner. Technical mistakes will happen at this point in the work. The 1–2–3 rhythm will be dropped. At times students will become confused about where they are, calls will be imperfect, and so on. If the participants are getting too off track, if the form of the exercise is clearly not there most of the time and the exercise is descending into constant mush, then simply take them back to the version of the three moment exercise with the reset.

Remind them of the rhythm and order and then gradually ramp them back up to removing the holiday. While true of all exercises in this training it is especially true here that some people will progress faster than others in grasping exactly how to dive into this exercise.

If, on the other hand, chaos abounds in the exercise, 'mistakes' happen, but the students organically get the exercise back on track, then this is them living in the wonderful chaos of dealing with one another in the moment. It is worth stating this clearly here: we never, ever want to sacrifice the truthfulness of the moment for being technically appropriate. If what technique we do require is not strong, however, then the truthful responses of the moment will be diminished, as the attention of the participants will be continuously shifting back from each other and onto themselves to ensure that they are doing their part to keep the exercise going. It is hard to impose a metric, but my guess from all my experiences is that if the structure of the exercise is maintained 90% of the time or more, then all the benefits will come. Below 90% the learning value sharply declines, but again, this depends on what you see in the moment.

Once the technique is strong, they can release their concern about it and trust the structure will be there. The structure will facilitate the depth and controlled chaos of the experience while allowing clients to observe and respond truthfully with strong technique. As a coach, let the mistakes happen and only worry about it if the mistakes, or moments, begin to completely dismantle the structure of the exercise so that it does not allow students to go deeper into the experience. If this happens, simply return to where the technique is lacking, tighten it, and then send them back in at full gallop.

The only thing that is worth noting is that the intensity of this version of the exercise might overwhelm some students after shorter amounts of time than the first three moment exercise. If you notice this happening, let them do shorter runs of it, but more of them. Gradually lengthen the amount of time you keep them in the exercise. Trust me: once they get used to it, finding their feet, they will want more. As their hunger grows for this level of authenticity in a moment-by-moment fashion, so will their stamina and endurance. Good coaching, in this work as well as other approaches to leadership, is sometimes about the right feedback and instruction. Oher times it is just about patience.

Chapter 8

Chaos and (in) Leadership

A New Gallop

Our journey through both incarnations of the three moment exercise (the first one being defined by a long reset in between individual exercises while the second connected them in a moment-to-moment way) has led us to some valuable conclusions: the moment is a technically attainable value that only has as much mystery as you want to infuse it with. It is not only possible to work moment-to-moment in a state of heightened engagement, what my Meisner teacher Scott would often call a 'state of aliveness', but this facility can be attained by entirely trainable means. Overcoming the burdens often associated with hearing phrases such as 'You're not in the moment,' ultimately hollow and empty feedback, is already of immense value to a leader developing truthfulness as the foundation of all their interpersonal interactions. The same can be true of the difficult but important goal of releasing the idea of 'mistakes' from your leadership vocabulary. With all of that said, if we could successfully define the ultimate value of the three moment exercise, we would say that it offers us *specificity*. Specificity in observations, specificity in structure, and specificity in responses. We have delved deeply into the nature of observing another human being. Your eye is now razor-sharp. It is time we take that newly honed specificity and put it to good work in the next exercise. I did warn you in the last session that a familiar face was coming back.

Exercise: Switch

This new exercise is called Switch. No need to preface or explain. Let's jump straight in and then figure it out.

You and your partner are going to begin by doing the three moment exercise, the moment-to-moment version we explored in the previous session. You'll both let it unfold in its continuous, amazing flow. Let's have you both do a few to get us warmed up. All that I am going to label here are the second moment behaviours as well as the third moment transitioning behaviours that start the new three moment exercise. If any of this looks completely new, it may be a good idea to revisit the previous chapter and re-familiarise yourself with this exercise.

You: You settled in.
Partner: I settled in. (opens his arms wide)

You: You're the Don. (laughs)
Partner: You laughed.
You: I laughed. (covers mouth)
Partner: You covered your mouth. (moves chair back)
You: You went back.
Partner: I went back. (nods)
You: You nodded. (goes still)
Partner: You're still.
You: I'm still. (remains still)
Partner: You're still.
Etc.

As you can see, nothing new so far and a great exercise at that. Here's the new step that will build on it. You two will continue doing the three moment exercise. At a certain point, I as the coach will call out the word 'Switch!' Immediately you two will go straight into a you–I repetition exercise and I mean *immediately*. Don't even drop a single moment. Carry on with repetition until I call 'Switch!' and then immediately you are straight back into the three moment exercise. After a certain period of time I'll call 'Switch!' again and straight away into repetition you go. For clarity the dynamic of this experience is a back and forth alternating between the three moment exercise and repetition aided by me, your coach, facilitating the transitions.

Before we try to explain this further, let's just see what one looks like so as not to confuse the waters. Now, since we haven't seen it for a few sessions, if you look at the repetition examples and feel confused, have a flip again through Chapter 5. We are combining two elements in a unique way, but there is nothing new about the individual elements themselves. The combinations are what should feel novel, not the components.

So you and your partner start with a three moment exercise. For the purposes of this example, I'm going to label my part as 'Coach'. Also, you'll notice for both the three moment and repetition components, I have added an 'Etc.' to imply the exercise carries on after what is written. In the event an 'Etc.' isn't there, then that represents the entirety of the exercise in this example.

You: You're looking at me.
Partner: I'm looking at you. (shrugs shoulders)
You: You shrugged your shoulders. (scratches nose)
Partner: You scratched your nose.
You: I scratched my nose. (laughs)
Partner: You laughed. (blushes)
You: You're blushing.
Partner: I'm blushing. (playfully pushes partner)
You: You pushed me! (tenses face)
Partner: You're a mountain.
You: I'm a mountain. (mouth shakes)
Partner: Your mouth is shaking. (makes a fist)
You: You made a fist.
Partner: I made a fist. (goes still)
You: You're still. (they both laugh, partner nods)
Coach: Switch!
Partner: You're nodding.

You: I'm nodding.
Partner: You're nodding.
You: I'm nodding.
Etc.

Coach: Switch!
You: You raised your eyebrows.
Partner: I raised my eyebrows. (makes a complicated facial expression)
You: You made a face. (moves chair back)
Partner: You moved back.
You: I moved back.(goes still)
Partner: You're still.
Coach: Switch!
You: I'm still.
Partner: You're still.
You: I'm still.
Partner: You're still.
Etc.

This is the switch exercise in its entirety. It continuously oscillates back and forth between repetition and the three moment exercises, the transitions determined by the coach's intuitions for a good place to change. The switch exercise is special. It represents a lot of work you have done to get to this place. Not only is it an accomplishment but its execution marks certain skills in your leadership technique operating at a very high level. Let's now see if we can figure out what makes the switch exercise so special for your leadership and why it represents you moving towards a more complete technical facility for living truthfully.

The Unseen Shared Values

Whether it be in a story or training program, continuity is important. While I think it is clear how some of our values have continued to be present up to this point, other aspects of this journey are less clear. Until now, it might have seemed that we made sudden, jarring transitions without much meaning or explanation. To some we have been all over the place. First we begin the training sessions with repetition and its values and then, just as soon as you were starting to see some results in practice, we dropped it for an entirely different exercise with a polar opposite rhythm and nature, the three moment exercise. No one would think until they see switch that actually repetition and the three moment exercises are not opposites but rather complimentary. The ability to link them so cleanly has a greater application for the future of this training: on their own they are strong technical tools, but combined they form a potent force for developing a powerful means to train living truthfully for your leadership technique.

Let's look first at our long-lost familiar friend repetition. In your first encounter with it you discovered in practice that repetition isn't concerned with either the observation or where in the hierarchy it lies. Its requests are far less strict. All that really matters is that your observation meets the criteria of being a simple observation of fact. Looking back you now can identify repetition drills almost always began with a basic call, though a behavioural observation would have been fine. Given there were other values more relevant to be explored, we weren't particular about it.

Such a simplistic structure ensures that generally, though not always, the text stays consistently the same. An organic change can occur where your partner hears something different than what you intended to say, and vice versa, and this facilitates something like a 'change' in the text happening. By and large, however, these occurrences are rare. They are worth mentioning because they reveal that even in brief, momentary changes such as this the premium value in repetition is not so much the change itself but being able to catch and accommodate the change.

We tweaked repetition ever so slightly in your second encounter with it by adding point of view with the slight – but at times profound – change from 'You–You' to 'You–I'. Though subtle, when point of view demands to be a part of the moment, it often implies something profoundly significant is happening. For the most part, these moments happen less frequently. Repetition mostly stays closest to what gives it depth in the first place: the words lightly float on top of an ever-changing river of interpersonal exchanges between you and your partner. What dictates the texture and nature of how the words come out sounding has nothing to do with your personal agendas or desires and everything with the constant tennis match of observe-and-respond between the two of you. That is what makes repetition exciting and powerful: it provides a technical way to facilitate rich interpersonal exchanges with little time required to achieve results.

Going off of this last point, even now the ground you have gained has yielded a rather surprising amount of results without much time expenditure. The experience of a constant flow, unbound by the need for semantic analysis or intellectual interpretation, allows for an immense depth of interpersonal exchange. Even after just a few sessions in the previous chapters we were already talking about the concepts of deeper responses, expanding your personal range of authenticity, overcoming politeness and social conditioning when the moment demands it, as well as how to handle fears and inhibitions about leadership. Those are some rather big-picture topics for leadership to begin tackling in practice with such a seemingly simple exercise. This doesn't speak to some secret mystery buried within repetition so much as it does a misplacement of values.

For one, so many of us are convinced that language is extremely important to a leader. Words carry such a high societal value that we often mistake them as the primary value in communication. When we disable this premium, however, asking instead that you experience another human on a level beneath the words, it almost instantly brings out your authenticity as well as the areas of your personal expression that are in need of further training and development. This isn't a mystery: many of us know that the majority of communication, especially meaningful communication, is non-verbal and yet so little time is dedicated to it in conventional models of education. Or it happens much later, after lots of writing, analysis, and creative exercises. Repetition starts us right with where the majority of communication counts. The metaphor of the river does not escape us here: flowing waters run deep. Leadership is a game of understanding humans beneath the words as well as occasionally the words themselves, but the emphasis must be on behaviour rather than words. Repetition by its simplistic nature and structure facilitates a depth of experience almost unparalleled in other forms of training. It only gets deeper from here.

How does it get deeper, you might ask? The answer lies in all the work we have been doing with the three moment exercise. You may recall from the beginning of Chapter 6 that your authenticity depends on your ability to be accurate and specific in your observations. From the get-go the three moment exercise has been an entirely different beast than repetition. Just as powerful, we discovered in the previous chapter, but profound in a different way. Unlike repetition this exercise has a staccato, unchanging structure, far more rigorous than repetition. In repetition, at this stage, changes in the call happen organically if one partner hears something different, repeating that new phrase until the exercise is stopped. The exercise is rarely stopped if the change is organic, and so even with alterations the text quickly goes back to floating on top with the two of you continuing to repeat while putting your attention on one another. The specificity of the observation matters less than the interpersonal exchange since you wouldn't want to miss the moment to make the 'right' or 'best' observation.

In the three moment exercise the values are reversed. The interpersonal exchange does matter, but now specificity is what you are hungrily and aggressively after. The structure, especially in the second version of the exercise, is intended to facilitate some interpersonal depth to create a hotbed of observational opportunities. Within this, what you might call a 'mistake' is not a major problem, in fact mistakes may mean an impulse or moment breaks the rules of the exercise. This is always to be welcomed. If the exercise continuously falls apart, however, it means that the simple structure needs to be ingrained more before you will be able to extract the deeper, more potent values out of its fullest incarnation. In the moment-to-moment version, the intensity of the exchange and the power of the observations, goes through the roof. Capturing moment after moment and throwing them right back to your partner creates a heightened level of engagement in your mutual pursuits of razor-sharp specificity. Put those values into a constant flow and it is akin to having a hot spotlight suddenly turned onto you just before a high-octane roller coaster. When the ride ends, both of you walk away with incredible attunement and specificity to the moment.

That gives us two overarching values that repetition and the three moment exercise have: depth and specificity. Both now have flow to them, and so the rhythms are much more compatible. As we begin merging them, we are blending the depth of repetition with the specificity of your work in the three moment exercise. Gluing these two together begins to crank up the quality of your living truthfully considerably. I'll give you a spoiler-hint for the next two chapters: we are not merging two values so much as bringing them together to converge on an even greater one, much in the same way how a blade and handle come together to forge a sword. For now, the skill of having immensely deep, authentic interchanges with a person combined with the ability to observe their behaviour with exquisite precision gives you, as a leader, what Sun Tsu called 'supreme advantage.' Meaningful specificity is what is going to begin broadening your range of authentic responses, deepening your ability to richly intertwine with another with little to no effort.

The Storm in the Details

What you've seen just now is an example of what a switch exercise might look like. The word 'might' is incredibly appropriate here, specifically for a fine, nuanced reason we need to explore. The basic structure of switch is always going to be the same. It's a back and forth between the three moment exercise and repetition moderated by the coach. Within that, however, if you look closely you will find there are a series of moments in which there are absolutely no clear rules. Can you guess what those are? If you jumped up and excitedly said 'the transition points!' you are absolutely correct.

What makes the transitions between the exercises so important? After all I'm in charge of them, aren't I? Not exactly, as the following example illustrates. Let's look at a transition moment in a new switch exercise between you and your partner:

You: You're moving side-to-side.
Partner: I'm moving side-to-side. (raises eyebrows)
You: You raised your eyebrows. (nods)
Partner: You nodded.
Coach: Switch!

Did you notice what I've just done, perpetual pain in the ass that I am? I didn't let your partner finish their three moment exercise! That tells you the first important aspect to this: as the moderator, I can call for you to switch any time. I don't have to be polite and wait for either of you to finish an exercise. This technically places you at an interesting juncture. After all will the transition look like this:

You: You're moving side-to-side.
Partner: I'm moving side-to-side. (raises eyebrows)
You: You raised your eyebrows. (nods)
Partner: You nodded.
Coach: Switch!
You: I nodded.
Partner: You nodded.
You: I nodded.

In this example the previous observation is repeated and becomes the material for the repetition. That's one possibility. But is that the only possibility? What if something like this happens?

You: You're moving side-to-side.
Partner: I'm moving side-to-side. (raises eyebrows)
You: You raised your eyebrows. (nods)
Partner: You nodded.
Coach: Switch!
You: You're smiling.
Partner: I'm smiling.
You: You're smiling.

Rather than repeat the old observation when 'Switch' is called you made a new one that becomes your repetition call. But that's not all that could happen. Consider this possibility:

You: You're moving side-to-side.
Partner: I'm moving side-to-side. (raises eyebrows)
You: You raised your eyebrows. (nods)
Partner: You nodded.
Coach: Switch!
Partner: Your ears are twitching.
You: My ears are twitching.
Partner: Your ears are twitching.

Did you see that? Your partner just made another observation! They double-dipped the moment! How impolite of them.

As you can see the possibilities we are referring to aren't calls so much as structural grey areas brimming with potential. Every time the call to switch into repetition is made there are three possible transition points:

One. Going off of the last observation heard and repeating that.
Two. Starting repetition with a brand new observation

Three. Breaking the partner order to seize an observation up for grabs in the moment. In the scenario above it is your partner, but either one of you could do this depending on where you are in the exercise.

Of those three which is the right way to transition? What is the technically stronger or weaker choice? My winning answer: I have no idea at all. Not a clue. What's worse, you, the brave soul in the exercise, have no idea also. Despite the possibilities being immensely different, we are not the keepers to that answer. Let's explore this so we can understand why this is the case. We aren't looking so deeply at such a question just for the sake of nitpicking. We are actually teetering towards another extremely powerful and valuable principle for your leadership development.

In the switch exercise you will find the transitions are messy. They aren't clean, since any one of those three possibilities can occur, and there's no time to think about it. That can be uncomfortable, and so some participants come up with a strategy. The strategy is to pick the transition in advance. You might say to yourself that you will just be the first person to start repetition each time you transition out of the three moment exercise. The instance switch is called it won't matter where you are: you will just start the repetition. This is a clever solution and it seems pragmatic and somewhat altruistic even. After all, now your partner won't ever have to worry about dealing with the chaos of the transition. This is, at its core, an act of true kindness. The road to hell, however, is paved with many kind intentions. This one may join the lot and cause you both more grief than it helps.

When the call to switch is made what you, your partner, and everyone who does this exercise experiences is a sudden feeling of free-falling. The guard and safety rails are completely off and a void of uncertainty remains in their place. A moment of absolute anarchy emerges where the whole thing might fall apart. Not many of us like anarchy, and so the strategy here is based on an expendable-losses calculation: you are allowed, in moments of real chaos, to override the values of this training, denying the moment itself, to ensure that your concept, or agenda, goes according to plan. It feels like benevolence because your agenda is to keep the exercise going, but beneath its exterior this is a desperate move to find safety in a moment of uncertainty.

This is exactly the kind of behaviour we are training you to work against. It is also the worst habit to bring into a moment of real, pure chaos. It is this sort of pre-empting the future that causes leaders many hardships. True, you'll make the exercise easier, but so what? Look at the cost. There is zero value to you to enact this strategy. Adopt it and you only end up strengthening one of your most toxic habits. It is worth saying again: there is zero value to being fluid and flexible in fair-weather and then when a moment comes when adaptability is really needed you lock down. That's the same as clinging to the wheel during a storm instead of using it to attempt to deal with it. It is true, at the outset, there's no clear outcome from either being fluid or a control-freak, but one gives you a far greater chance of emerging on the other side.

Some people, on the other hand, will invert this safety strategy. In this scenario, you decide you will always let your partner begin the repetition and just work off of them. Though it may seem like you are truly embracing our values and letting them handle the responsibility for the transition, this is a back-foot approach that makes it an equally weak plan. It is a terrible idea because you are denying yourself the possibility of action if the moment demands it. What you have essentially decided is, in a moment of chaos, to stop listening and hope action will come from another source. Times of chaos are exactly when you need to have your eyes open and be able to act if needed.

There are three possibilities for a transition. There may be others not outlined here, but these are the most common three I have seen. Each one carries with it the possibility that it is fair game in the moment. Each one, even option three (the one where the order is broken), is acceptable provided it is what the moment demands rather than a self-generated agenda. An easy way to differentiate in practice is that a conscious agenda stays floating around in your moment, you'll feel it and it lingers, and even more strangely the audience will sense it when you act on it. What is best in the moment arises first as a visceral sensation, an impulse generated by what you are observing. Whether that is to continue the previous call, begin a new one, or interrupt the order to catch a moment, all are perfectly optional. Again, we don't want to sacrifice the demands of the moment to have appropriately perfect technique. There will be times when a transition happens cleanly, at the start of a new third moment. There will be times when it happens in the middle. And there will be times when either you or your partner walk the walk of fuck polite and hungrily make a new observation – even if it isn't 'your turn.'

Another way to think about this is to consider the balance between order and chaos that exists within leadership and how training both are of value to you. All of the exercises thus far have a fairly clear partner-order structure built into them. This facilitates training the relevant values within the exercise. Within the exercise, there actually isn't much structure at all. They are far less complicated than improvisations or games, and this is by design. We want the bare minimum of structure, the smallest dose possible. Though valuable, structure of any kind imposes artificial constraints on a moment. If you make your training too dependent on the context you learned it in, it will lose its ability to be portable. What structure we do have, however, is rigorous, and you'll discover this in practice. Have the 1–2–3 rhythm of the three moment exercise in your bones and you will have a powerful, deep experience. Be weak with the structure, however, with the exercise continuously falling apart, and you will feel the values of the exercise slip through your fingers like sand at the beach. Structure facilitates the depth of your training as a leader.

In praising structure, however, we have to be very careful not to forget its real value. This is where many approaches to leadership lose sight of the bigger goals. Structure in training is an imposition on the chaos of any given moment. It doesn't exist objectively unless we agree to bring it into existence. A small measure of imposed order is incredibly valuable because it gives you a constant and reliable lens to see chaos and to train within it. A structured approach to working within chaos is where the value is for a leader – not in getting good at the structure itself. In your field, your challenges won't come with established order but with the absence of order and the emergence of unknown variables.

This is the razor-fine line we tread when we commit to actually training leadership. Nothing is ever free. You can give concepts like authenticity lip service but teach inauthentic, harmful habits. You can also train authenticity but in such an unclear, murky way that the results cannot be replicated. That there is no instruction for how to transition between exercises built into this training is a very conscious decision. Being prescriptive about this moment would begin to rob you of the bigger values we are after. Moments are of the premium value in this work, and so even individual ones, and how we handle them, matter a great deal. If we impose a blanket instruction on how to transition from one exercise into the next, we will be forcing too much structure into the exercise. It will lose its grey-area value. The transition points in switch are entirely off the rails. They are a moment of calculated, pure chaos built into the exercise.

Examining one moment within a sea of them seems like splitting hairs. Consider, however, that individual moments in leadership are what are remembered in history. Moments that demand great things are both your blessing and curse. Understanding their nature and what happens within them is crucial for you as a leader. Do you try to force your own will onto a moment or do you work with what is happening? Whatever your decision, it will determine how the event unfolds.

Though you might not have thought of it, there has been a complementary conundrum that has been with us all along. In our previous repetition sessions, before we brought it back in switch, who began the exercise? If you go back and flip through Chapters 4 and 5 you'll notice I am quite vague about this. This is also carefully by design. For the first one or two sessions I usually select who begins the exercise and only for the first two or three partner pairs. After that I don't intervene anymore. At that point in the training, where the coach is no longer instructing who begins the repetition, something humorous happens: partners will try to agree on who starts the exercises.

'Go ahead,'
'No, no, you go.'
'No, no, I insist.'
'No, I insist!'

In any other setting, such helpfulness would be a benign and welcomed presence, but for training leadership this doesn't help much. When an exchange of this nature occurs, I almost always interject and say something infused with my attempt at mild irony, such as, 'I love how polite you two are being. Thank god there is plenty of room in this work for that!'

If I've said this, you two will probably get the message quickly. But now there's a dilemma: you both want to walk the walk of fuck polite, not choosing who begins through pleasant negotiations or insistences, but this brings up the very real problem of who begins the exercise. A strategy won't help, in that if you decide to always or never begin you'll run into the same issues you will if you attempt that in the three moment exercises. Asking me doesn't help much either:

'I don't know. More importantly, neither of you know either.'

From there you both enter a limbo where the only thing that provides the answer is that moment when the two of you put your attention on one another and something happens. From there on, the structure of repetition takes over, but that is also a single split-moment of pure chaos also built into the work.

Throughout the course of this book thus far you'll notice I give very little prescriptive feedback. It is incredibly difficult to impose any blanket rule and still honour the values of this work. When it comes to who begins repetition, the best guidance is the same for how one handles the transition points in switch: nobody knows, but you and your partner will see the answer clearly in the moment when it arrives.

Unpredictably Predictable

Moments, by their very nature, are chaotic and messy things. It is only when they align with our expectations for order that we assume stability, but things are always in flux. As such, we would be doing a technical disservice to your leadership training if we made the exercises so structured that they didn't allow for a moment of total suspension, a free fall where the only answer that keeps you in the values of this work is to figure it out mid-air.

This implies that we are departing ever more from the conventional approaches to leadership which, if you look at the implicit assumptions under their training, equate the strength of your technique with how much control you can exert over a moment. The verbiage of authenticity and spontaneity is there but sometimes people don't realise the discrepancy between what they want to train and what values within the exercises are actually being trained. In this work we cannot make the strength of your technique dependent on dominating the moment but rather developing a sensitivity to it and learning to rise to its demands. You have already begun to experience this heightened sensitivity in the three moment exercise. You sit across from your partner and now the observation just jumps out at you. You know what to call without looking for it. This is a developing sensitivity to what is profound in the moment in relation to another human being's behaviour rather than what you want to have meaning.

When your partner begins an exercise with an observation, you engage with them, putting your attention on them and letting your responses be dependent on what you observe. It is equally relevant to say, however, that at this stage you don't need to wait for them to begin the exercise: if you see it call it. What if both of you speak at the same time, since there's no clear rule for who begins? The answer is you both will feel that the chaos of the moment has interjected itself and you have no choice but to deal with it as it happens.

This is as close to a healthy approach as a leader can get. Chaos is that unpredictable force in the night that terrifies us when it arrives. In training, starting first with switch and then incrementally increasing in future exercises, you will find your experience of the chaos of the moment will become more simple. Not necessarily easier, but simple. This is the high value of talking about the transition points in switch. We don't know what will happen when they arrive. All that we know is at one point or another I, the coach, will call 'Switch!'. From there, what the moment looks like, what form it takes, its very nature – we have absolutely no idea. Even my calling 'Switch' has no real guarantee backing it. If suddenly I lose my voice, then the call won't come. Still, the chances remain fairly good it will happen. You have strong technique, but as far as the moments of chaos, it must become part of your technique to train the value that not knowing is a critical component to action, especially the actions demanded of great leaders in moments of uncertainty and crisis.

We can extrapolate this to a larger look at your aims. Developing sensitivity towards, as well as an aptitude to flourish within, chaos is one of the essential qualities of great leadership. We have to remember in discussing chaos, whether in general or in the context of your leadership training, that by its nature chaos is intangible. Impossible to pin down. As soon as you do pin it down, identifying its nature and properties with assured ease, it has been transformed into order, cleanly categorised, losing its dynamic quality in the process. The real thing is akin to attempting to inspect a snowflake on your fingertip: as soon as you feel you've identified its properties it melts into something else.

Our life experience confirms this: we have all had times when our lives were so chaotic, with an event or series of events so full of unknown variables that continued to surprise, that it was only possible to make sense of things after they had passed. One of the most profound descriptions across many forms of literature you will find is of the calm not just before but after the great storm, a sobering silence left in the wake of destruction. For chaos to remain itself, there must be an established before and a newly formed after, which contextualises it and allows us to infer and attempt to understand how it behaved. This hunger to discern causality is one of the great needs of the human condition. It is the impulse that arguably fuelled the great schools of Greek philosophy and the analytical and empirical methods of investigation that emerged from them.

The leader, especially one involved in a field or project where pioneering and entrepreneurship will be their driving tools to success, lacks the safety net of established order. Confronting chaos is essential for you. You will have to create the before and after, establishing a situation where you think you can predict the variables, and then deal with the chaos when it has been created. From there, the challenge becomes creating an accurate reflection on where order failed and chaos emerged. This is cumbersome, tedious, and oftentimes discouraging work, since our attempts to understand the world and make predictions based on our intuitions are often wrong. Leaders are still humans, and most humans cannot cope with chaos. Some people are naturally protected from stress and unpredictability by differences in their physiology, but these are exceptions and not rules. For the majority of leaders, moments of true chaos must be built into your development, and what they will look like in the future will remain entirely unpredictable until they arrive.

This is the balance between action and reflection. During the event, reflection or self-monitoring have no place. Afterwards, however, is the time to consider. Almost all great leaders have been in this position at one point or another throughout their careers. They were forced to learn how to still act, and even flourish, in the midst of chaos. This explains the deeper meaning behind the concept some hold that says you will never know someone's true character until life comes crashing down and they are forced to deal with the unknown, that moment when spontaneous uncertainty merges with the pressure of the need to act in the moment and face the torrent head-on.

At the same time, as we will discover later, this idea is still another attempt to impose order unto chaos. It means well, but is a simplistic and misguided assessment. You cannot learn someone's true character by observing what they do in a single or even a few isolated situations. For better or worse, people will always continue to surprise us. What you will certainly know more about are patterns of behaviour that emerge in the face of chaos. These patterns are most likely a mix of hardwired biology and ingrained environmental conditioning. They become more potent and reinforced over time. It is a sobering thought to consider that by the time you are deciding for yourself that you need to learn how to perform better under pressure, you will be working against decades of conditioned habits that are largely unconscious until they arise in those times of extreme pressure.

I can't in good conscience use scientific theories and then tell you I have figured it all out without actually testing any of my theories in a scientific way. What I can say is that I strongly suspect, based on my experiences, and those of my clients, that micro-dosing chaos through a structured exercise, a moment of complete free fall, for example, is extremely valuable to the training of any leader. Exposure to uncertainty doesn't tell you how to handle the future but rather trains you to engage in the present. That moment in repetition when you and your partner sit across from one another, putting your full attention on each other, or that elusive transition point in the switch exercises – these are instances when something seemingly outside the exercise suddenly manifests. It can be observed, felt, and recognised: both you and your partner are now suspended, free from the rules. The tightrope is gone. Do you fall or survive? I don't know. The only thing that can guide you are the demands of the moment itself.

For clarity, there is already plenty of chaos within the exercises themselves. Living truthfully is about impulses generated spontaneously from accurate observations. Repetition is vast, going to deep places, and the three moment exercise feels like an intense roller coaster. Both will leave your heart pounding after such an experience. On occasion, the rules break and you have to deal with it. Chaos is continually popping in and out of existence in these exercises, at times completely undermining the structure. What we want is to start increasing the dose, taking it to the next level, where you are forced to deal with a moment of extreme pressure and no guide map. That's your path as a leader. It's a crucial value we need to train and will be an increasing focus in future sessions onwards.

The simple, structured order within the exercises allows for real chaos to be experienced. Leaders must know what to do to maximise the value of established order while also being sensitive and responding within chaos. This training will continuously remind you in practice that responding within chaos is not about developing a pattern of behaviour. There is no formula for how to handle the unexpected before it happens. No matter how many times you have behaved in a certain way in the midst of chaos, you still do not know, no matter how much you insist, if you will behave that way again in the future. The arrogance of certainty has been the downfall of many great human beings, leaders and non-leaders alike.

Believing we can impose personal order on the future will ensure we will be sideswiped by the chaos of the moment, finding ourselves completely adrift. We cannot fix this. No one can. We cannot even predict its discernible form. All that can be said is that while we don't know what chaos will look like or when it will arrive, chances are strong that it will arrive, and when it does something will happen. This is why the specificity of the moment is of premium value in this training. The moment beyond this one is where all specificity fails and remains shrouded in mystery until it reveals itself. Having the ability to see it as it arises is where your strong observational abilities will greatly aid you.

Looking in depth at uncertainty and its ever-possible dominance over even the strongest of our qualities can, and often does, alarm people. It may have alarmed you. To many, what it sounds like is that accepting the possibility of chaos leaves a sort of negative space within your leadership technique, a small void forever unfulfilled. That is exactly what I am saying. Remember how I said before training began that all leaders are aspiring leaders? This is why. The illusion of finality will destroy your progress and creations faster than just about any other circumstance. Allowing for a negative space of uncertainty, of not-knowing, in your leadership skills is just as valuable as training certainty.

The best confidence you can get from any training is knowing that you can respond with authenticity in the moment and that you can do it with pure, uncensored expression. That is the benefit that comes from this training. Since behaviours repeat themselves, and conditioning grows stronger over time, this gives you a good chance that flexible technique will arise in the future when things get completely derailed and all comes crashing down. How much your training will help, how much any training will help, I do not know, and neither do you. No matter how much we wish to know. All you know is there will be a moment. That moment will demand an authentic response, and your training has given you the sharpened ability to intuit that demand. What happens from there, however, is not up to you but the moment itself. Any approach that trains a different value or expectation is setting you up for hard failure.

We cannot know the future, but we can train with real chaos alongside order and structure. In my view, this is the healthiest way to develop your leadership technique, aligning it with the reality you are attempting to succeed within.

Summary

The values that you have developed in repetition, with its immense depth of experience and opportunity for expanding truthfulness in a person, and the three moment exercise, with its razor-sharp specificity and the ability to read a human being with an uncanny clarity, are coming to a head in the switch exercise. Switch marries the depth of repetition with the specificity of the three moment exercise. Already these values are beginning to blend: you will notice that when you go into a repetition you will carry over some of that precise specificity from the three moment exercise. When you go back into the three moment exercise there will be more interpersonal depth and texture because of the repetition. As you and your partner go back and forth these values will bleed more and more into one another, setting the stage for us to take your ability for living truthfully into even deeper waters.

This richness of the human experience is a rare thing. Few people will ever touch it the way one does in this technique. For a leader to have that depth of humanity in their leadership is an utterly exciting and compelling component for those observing and encountering that person. A long time ago, when we were first exploring the values of repetition, we said the recipe was simple: if you wish to be engaging to watch, be engaged. You are now taking that principle to a whole new level. The compelling qualities it brings are only being strengthened and deepened. It is that level of skill that you will take into reading and understanding a given set of circumstances.

The essence of great leadership is the ability to live truthfully under a set of given circumstances. Thus far, this training has been devoted entirely to living truthfully. To express oneself fully and authentically is the greatest challenge for a leader. It is easy in a teaching setting, or when alone, but in the face of the pressures that come from other people and unforeseen variables, it is a daunting challenge. Many leaders have the aspirations to be truthful. In their minds they see themselves as unrestrained, full of a powerful magnetism in a difficult situation. When that situation actually arises, however, the demands of the moment are met with automatic responses, ingrained and conditioned behaviours, and habits that are not up to the challenge. Finding themselves unable to will a fully expressed authenticity when it is needed, the aspiring leader wilts.

Social conditioning, combined with the innately human trait of avoidance, contributes a great deal to this problem. Living truthfully is not the alternative, or cure, but rather a return to health for those lacking the ability to deeply express their innate authenticity. Social constraints are excellent for keeping order, but leaders must deal both with order and chaos. Unconscious habits and behaviour can be the death of good leadership. Though we are focusing solely on living truthfully now, by itself it is not enough for a leader. It needs the lens of a given set of circumstances to contextualise its relevance or else the authentic expression will not be in response to the optimal stimuli. When we finish all the steps in training the technique of living truthfully, with all of its intricate components, then there will be a readiness to handle circumstances and read as deeply into situations as you do into another human being. Cultivating authenticity comes first.

Alongside your developing your abilities to observe and respond, we introduced a new variable: chaos. Importing moments of chaos into your leadership training, where there is no clear answer or outcome, allows you to further make your technique portable, so the skills you are developing will remain transferable and adaptable to a variety of situations, especially those in which sudden, unforeseen variables and challenges emerge. As these sessions progress, we will continue to increase the dose of chaos in this work, pushing the exercises' abilities to keep their structure and for you to stay continuously light and flexible.

Tips for You and Your Coach

The value of feedback in switch comes during, and not after, the exercise. The exercise has such an immense element of self-learning that it won't need much input from you other than an initial setup. So many moments will happen that it will be very difficult to give feedback on either the quality of living truthfully, the three moment exercise, or repetition. What is most important here is ensuring clients have enough experience within the exercise to discover the values in practice. While this is true of all exercises, it is paramount here.

The best advice I can give you, then, is how I structure the experience: in general, when a pair begins, allow them a good amount of time in the three moment exercise. Then call for them to switch and allow them a good amount of time in repetition. As you continue to call for switches, gradually reduce the time before another switch is called. Continue to whittle down the time until only a few seconds is allotted for each exercise. In this way, the students might lose track of where they are, but they will begin to get the values of the exercise into their bones, the feeling that repetition and the three moment exercise are gradually beginning to merge. The premium here is not about trying to critique individual moments in either repetition or the three moment exercise but rather to ensure that the clients are getting the experience into their body. You have spent four or more sessions at this point laying the groundwork for all of these values to begin harmonizing, and this is the exercise that introduces that experience. The best thing, then, is to get out of the way and let the participants in the work feel that for themselves. This is a convergence exercise above all else.

The only other point to consider giving feedback on if it arises is if, when you call for them to switch, there is a noticeable pause, or gap. There can be a brief one, but the longer it goes, the more it implies the attention of both participants is going back on themselves to employ problem solving tactics. This is not what you want. Continue to encourage them to break out of this habit and to trust the moment. A micro pause is normal but the longer it goes, the more the students will depart from the values of the exercise and have to find their way back in. Be careful, however, of your temptation as a coach to correct this if you see it while it is happening in the exercise. This is a habit so many Meisner teachers have: they talk while the exercise is going on and attempt to guide it. Your altruistic efforts will only set your students back.

It is true that there is some evidence in behavioural studies that immediate intervention on a behaviour has more corrective power than trying to address something after it has happened, but you must consider the context here. You are not trying to 'cure' specific behaviours for the moment but rather to give the clients a general sense of what to *do* in the moment, which is to live truthfully. In the same way that participants must be careful of their own desire to minimize chaos, you as a coach in this work must be vigilant about removing your own similar desire, including, and perhaps especially, the habit of trying to guide the student while the exercise is going on. Realistically, this is really just your way of trying to reduce the chaos in the moment and direct them to the result you want instead of allowing them to discover for themselves in practice the demands of the moment. These are not guided or directed exercises. The more you make them so, the more holes you will poke in them, and their applicable value outside the coaching session will drain considerably. Remember, most of the time you will work with intuitively intelligent people, even if they don't believe it or know it. They will put the pieces together for themselves with minimal help if you allow them to.

Chapter 9

Into the Great Unknown

The Depths

Until now, our previous sessions have focused on a single exercise springboarding the learning and discussions about how your experience within it trains one or several aspects of your leadership. You and your partner did multiple rounds of the exercises, as well as examples of previous sessions' exercises for clarity and context, but each session has focused on one exercise. This was largely our structure. The only true exception was the first session in Chapter 3 where some basic actions (tying your shoes, applying make-up, counting bricks, and so on) laid out the conceptual framework of our starting points of investing in the reality of doing and public solitude, origin points that can still be seen and identified in this work. This structure has served us well. It has allowed you to be saturated in the values of each exercise through both observation and participation, which has maximised the learning potential for your leadership skills.

In this session, however, we need to change course. We are going to start with one exercise which, eventually, is going to transform into another one. This will not be an easy process. There may be growing pains, but there is no other way to take this final step and keep all the values you have worked so hard for. In this session, we are going to merge everything we have been exploring thus far. All of the values and exercises will now converge into a single one, and this singularity will transition us into the next level of your training living truthfully, that wonderfully powerful process of observing deeply and responding authentically that propels great leaders.

This exercise has no official name, but I have heard it referred to by Scott, my Meisner teacher at the Impulse Company in London, as auto-switch. It's as good a placeholder name as any, so I am going to use the same phrasing. Now, before we move forward, it is vital that you understand the essential mechanics of repetition, the three moment exercise, and the switch exercise. If you're rusty on any of those revisit the previous chapters before continuing forward. This is because giving you an example of auto-switch is fairly difficult. Don't worry – you'll very soon see why. Having said that, I will create one anyway to prompt the discussion.

Exercise: Auto-Switch

Let's have you and your partner begin. You are both going to do the switch exercise exactly the same as the previous session. You'll start in the same way we always have, with a three moment exercise that switches into repetition and continues on back-and-forth. At this point it doesn't matter who begins, and neither of you should be concerned with that either: you have both advanced to the stage of technically being able to trust that the moment itself is going to give either of you the starting observation.

This may seem like the same switch exercise as before, and it is. This is switch with no alterations. Well, except one. This time I, acting again as the coach, am not going to call switch.

'Wait,' one of you may ask, 'who then is going to call switch?'

'Nobody.' is my pain-in-the-ass, albeit sincere, reply.

'Then how will we know when to switch?'

'The answer for now is very simple: you'll know through the same mechanism that tells you what to observe. The moment itself.'

Before eyes glaze too much, I say to you both, 'Let's just try one and see how it goes.' Here's what that hypothetical example looks like. In this example, I will mark the behaviours called in the three moment exercises, but nothing else. See you if you can glean technically what is happening in auto-switch:

Partner: You leaned in.

You: I leaned in. (lifts head)

Partner: You raised your chin. (laughs and covers mouth)

You: You're a schoolgirl.

Partner: I'm a schoolgirl! (blushes)

You: You went red. (laughs)

Partner: You're laughing.

You: I'm laughing. (goes still)

Partner: You're still. (wipes eyes)

You: Your eyes are watering.

Partner: My eyes are watering.

You: Your eyes are watering.

Partner: Your eyes are watering.

You: Your eyes are watering. (sighs)

Partner: You breathed deeply.

You: I breathed deeply. (nods)

Partner: You nodded. (moves chair in)

You: You moved your chair closer.

Partner: I moved my chair closer. (touches hand)

You: You're touching my hand. (closes mouth)

Partner: Your lips are shaking.

You: My lips are shaking. (goes red)

Partner: You blushed. (partner sighs)

Partner: You sighed.

You: I sighed.

Partner: You sighed.

You: I sighed.

Partner: You sighed.

Etc.

If you could follow it, that is a fantastic exercise, and like all my examples, this is typical of how auto-switch goes, not some extreme best-case scenario. This is the level of work I see coming out of clients at this stage. You can see based on the observations alone how much spontaneous authenticity is emerging as well as how razor-sharp the observations are. This is training the technique of living truthfully, and I would argue it is taking our notion of living truthfully to an even higher level. Now your strong technique enables you to have interactions with another like this without effort or premeditation. Let's unpack why that is the case.

Sans Safety Rails

On the page, I am limited to how many jokes I can make, but my sessions tend to have a lot of humour in them. I like when my clients laugh. The work is intense, and so if there is warmth in the room there is often more courage to go into the unknown. Most of the laughter is shared, but there is often one point where I can't help myself and must giggle at my clients. That moment comes when I give the instructions for auto-switch, or I should say, the lack of instructions. There is a sudden look of paranoia and dread that floods the faces of the participants. More often than not, it is expressed in their questions. Let's look at some of the most common questions I get asked, exploring them for both literal and hidden meanings. In so doing we will begin to see clearly the depth of auto-switch as well as its value for the continued development of your leadership skills.

The first question, normally asked in semi-petrified tones, is 'How do we know when to switch?' This is not a bad question; it is actually very clean and technically sound. We can arrive at an equally good answer by rewinding through the values of both leadership and how we have trained it up until this point. Let's start with the essential and ever-present notion of investing in the reality of doing. You can find this value very much alive in both repetition and the three moment exercise; in fact, it fuels the entire success of both experiences. By fully giving into the experience between you and your partner you quickly discover that your best moments, observations, and responses are not determined by you but rather by what your partner is doing to you. That's pretty profound in itself, but it's a two-way process: when you both are imbuing this approach it becomes even more interesting. You make and vocalise observations and that gives your partner their material to respond with. Investing your attention fully in another person creates a rich organic back-and-forth flow that produces incredible results and does not depend on either of you expending effort. It sounds paradoxical, but the proof is in the results.

Let's then work off this concept of investing in the reality of doing to ask if it can answer this question: when transitioning from either exercise in auto-switch how do you know when it is the right, or appropriate, moment to transition? It's a reasonable question, but as we have learned, if you look to the notion of an appropriate moment to help you be organic and spontaneous, it becomes self-cancelling. This is the good, well-meaning student inside you looking to get the right outcome in an exercise. The only way you will get the right outcome in this work is to deal with the moments that arise, not those you wish to arise. Moments in this work, as you have seen and experienced, are emergent properties. They can take any shape or form. Looking for an appropriate moment, then, is to attempt to apply qualitative metrics that won't serve you.

The same principle can be extended to the broader concept of doing the 'right thing' in the exercise, which implies by default it is possible to do the 'wrong thing'. We already ruled out a few sessions ago that there cannot be mistakes in this work, only moments. Your technique can only be supported by the notion of weaker or stronger if it is to remain within the values of this work.

Since right and wrong, appropriate and inappropriate, have no place in this work, how, then, do you know when to transition? The question itself may be similar to the transition questions of the previous session, but now the moment in question is far vaster and much less clear. Without any one designated to moderate it can happen anytime or may not happen at all.

There's an example running parallel to our training, one most of us have experienced, that can help give some clarity in answering this question. We all converse regularly with people, but there are conversations that stand out in memory for their richness and depth, an experience that immersed us with another person where time felt non-existent. Analysing this type of experience from the outside, you would quickly notice that these conversations are often a balanced, back-and-forth exchange of behaviours. Not necessarily words, as sometimes only one person may be speaking the majority of the time, but what is constant on both sides are the behavioural interchanges. Both of you are richly engaged with one another, and your body language reflects that: nodding your head, unconsciously verbalising sounds, repeating words or phrases, leaning in, and so on. It is really quite humorous to me that we actually attempt to teach people to do these things in conversation with others in communication training, but when you are really immersed, this quality of being interested will organically take a form in your entire body. That is teaching people to mimic being interested instead of incorporating and training engagement.

Within an experience like this scenario, what is also constant is a flow between specificity and depth. When you engage with another in deep conversation you will see their body language, observe their facial behaviours, and hear their vocal intonations; sometimes you'll see in your mind the words they are saying. For as long as you are interested, you will stay attuned to these nuances. This is observational specificity, and it now places us within the values of the three moment exercise.

Let's suppose now that you notice a change, or shift, in the conversation. Say, for example, your conversation partner has been describing something that happened in their past. Rather swiftly their disposition shifts and takes on a noticeably different quality. It could be in any direction; suddenly they may seem more joyous. Or memory has taken them to a dark place. Without thinking you jump in. You might ask, 'Can you tell me more about that?' or 'Are you sure you want to talk about this?'

Both questions in their own way are a request to go deeper. You've shifted priorities. The conversation was going on the track that it was, but you sensed an opportunity to go deeper, and now you are shifting the dynamic of the conversation. There's risk in doing this – it may go somewhere you weren't expecting. It may go nowhere. But you go with your intuitions in the moment nonetheless. Into this new shift you will bring your specificity of observation, but what is most important to recognise here is this: through engagement, you have sensed, without trying to force it, a moment where more depth is needed.

That moment of sensitivity in communication is the exact same kind of moment that can journey you and your partner into repetition during auto-switch. You both start with the three moment exercise because it puts investing in the reality of the experience on steroids. Creating ultra-heightened specificity of the experience attunes you to these moments when depth is needed. The exchange goes on until organically this unique moment arises. Neither of you need to force this to happen, just as in a great conversation you don't need to force the shifts. Simply being engaged and attuned to the moment will let you know when the time is there. For lack of a better phrase, you let it happen.

This is the only way the two of you can transition between exercises and still stay within the values of this work for your leadership training. Here's an indicator: oftentimes when participants finish an exercise I'll ask them how they transitioned. The general response?

'Well . . . we were going along in the three moment exercise. Then all of a sudden we found ourselves in repetition and we both had to say, 'Okay, we've arrived.''

It may seem a roundabout answer, but it's the only one that stays within our values. We can describe the process of how it happens, but to be prescriptive about the when, or exact nature of execution, robs us of the chaos the moment offers. When they occur, the transition points will feel profound, as if something huge is happening. Because you will be bringing a sharper sense of observation into the exercise, you will be more keenly aware of when your partner does something in the moment that demands to be observed. If it is profound enough, the moment will demand it be repeated. To clarify, neither of you are looking for the profound but rather calling the obvious when you see it without the censoring fear of politeness. That is often what makes the transition points profound in themselves.

To Time We Leave It

Another question that I often hear is, 'How long do we stay in each exercise?'

It may seem like a silly question, but you'll find it's a concern that actually arises within the exercise rather than outside of it. Engaged in either the three moment exercise or repetition, a pressure might start to grow between you both. You each know a moment is coming, a rather big one, and that moment will demand a change in the entire dynamic of your interpersonal exchange. This can put considerable pressure on you, drawing your attention to the feelings it engenders and further away from your partner. This is normal, and it happens to almost every pair doing auto-switch for the first few times, so let's look at why this occurs.

Identifying the origin, or root, of this question is actually fairly easy. The question of time length comes from a sense of responsibility to the exercise itself. Neither of you want to do something wrong, and you assume that it is possible to stay in either exercise too long, or too little, for that matter. Before we look closely at the assumption itself, let's rewind this one degree further back. The question also arises from a concern for how you or your partner are going to look in the exercise. No, I am not accusing either of you of arrogance or self-absorption; rather, I'm highlighting your desire for self-defence. For many, but especially a leader, the act of being boring is one of the most primordial, ancient fears we have. Ancient? Consider this: has there ever been a time in history when losing the interest of active listeners conferred a benefit? Ancestrally, it could have been a death sentence, especially if important information needed to be communicated. Boredom represents being ostracised collectively. *You* bore *us*: that is jury by committee, and even today there are consequences when groups of people intuitively rule against you.

It may be strange to consider it this way, but communication has very much been a centrepiece of Darwinian evolution. Communication is both an essential survival and reproductive tool. It thrives at the level of kin, as well as both within and across collectives. Our behaviours have been selected to prioritise good communication skills. Ensuring our message is conveyed maximises our chances for getting what we want. Don't believe me? What's the number one fear consistently reported? Public speaking. The risks associated with botching speaking to a group outweigh fears of spiders, fire, and many graphically violent descriptions of different ways to die (researchers are a creative bunch). That is how valuable communication is to us. An ingrained fear like this does not emerge suddenly: this is generations of selective pressures on certain behaviours. The fear of how you look in front of others is the epigenetic baggage you are bringing into this work. If we're being honest about the root of this desire, then we have to be equally honest about your feeling the pressure of knowing you need to perform, in this case, by successfully transitioning into or out of repetition. Delivering shows everyone in the room that you can successfully execute the exercise.

I would argue these are most likely the same set of thought patterns that landed you into this training in the first place. The reason you have been training from the earliest sessions to put your attention fully on the other person, to let them handle the responsibility of the exercise so you can simply observe-and-respond, is in response to the very real issue of how performance pressure clouds your vision to the present moment. People say pressure sharpens them to think better. That's a myth. Anxiety may be a sharp sensation but it does the opposite to every relevant processing system except a few. It does sharpen memory but it makes memory selection unreliable. It dulls selective perception as well as interferes with conscious decisions. Unless immediate action is demanded, such as in a life-threatening situation, anxiety just does the excellent job of drawing attention to itself. If you try to employ awareness tools, thereby becoming hyper-aware of your own anxieties, then it further dampens or hinders action. You didn't choose to feel anxious, and so you can't choose to unfeel anxious. Conscious interventions are sometimes effective, but they only go so far. The likelihood is that so long as the triggering stimulus is nearby, the anxiety isn't going anywhere soon.

If you are in a flow of moments that all demand continuous action and engagement, then the only place those things will be is outside of you. Directing your attention outside of you optimises your chances for fully responding to the moment as well as minimising your anxiety. When your attention is put back on yourself to deal with the anxiety coming from pressure, your vision is only partial. It is like trying to fight a skilled opponent with your eyes only half-open, or perhaps worse, your tactile sensitivity reduced by half.

You may not wish to admit that anxiety can affect you personally, but understanding yourself, as well as the pressures you put on yourself to perform, is a large part of the battle in being able to manoeuvre out of those patterns that lock you and make you unable to respond fully in the moment. During auto-switch, if your attention begins to return to yourself and you think, 'It feels like we've been repeating for an awfully long time!' you know one thing for certain: it is entirely possible both of you are missing moments that call for a new observation and thereby transitioning into the other exercise. Or maybe you're doing fine. The answer? Put your attention back on your partner and see. What is guaranteed is that when you are having those thoughts, you are in the wrong place to solve the problem if it even exists. It is oftentimes the case that the moment you catch this wavering attention and put it back onto your partner – if a change is needed – you will see the new thing to be called or its inverse: the call that demands further repeating.

On the other side of this same coin sits the problem of boredom. Sometimes *you* may get bored in a repetition during auto-switch. Let's talk more about boredom. Boredom is, to be blunt, a bullshit feeling, but it is a wonderful one in my view. It is a bullshit feeling because we think of boredom as a latent, limp experience where nothing is happening. But have you ever found yourself bored and then checked in with yourself about how you felt? Chances are you weren't feeling great. This is because boredom is not actually an absence but rather the presence of a growing anxiety. What happens the longer you are bored? Chances are you get more fidgety. You start compulsively needing something to do. Boredom is not a drive to nothingness but rather the growing unpleasant feeling of a strong urge to break the cycle you are stuck in.

I imagine if we checked your heart rate at the height of boredom it would be fairly high. This is why boredom is wonderful to me. It often signifies an impulse or truthful response is on the way and it is normally a big fish. In repetition, people become bored when they sit on their truthful impulses but regardless, the solution is simple: if you find yourself bored in these exercises, put your attention back on your partner and respond truthfully. The more impulses you sit on, the more it will drive you insane. Eventually you will get sick of yourself not responding truthfully. Boredom indicates there is something on offer that you are not acting on, despite the moment demanding you to take that action.

When I bring these ideas up, I sometimes get a perfectly reasonable response from my clients: it's more simple than that. I am overcomplicating. The reason you get bored in the exercise is nothing is really happening. I once worked with a very talented actress in London who one day was paired in training with a partner who was just a constant bundle of energy. He gave so much expressiveness without trying that it was almost hard to figure out just what to call in each moment. His partner though, the 'gifted' actress she projected for us, was stumped. Afterwards she said she felt bored and that there wasn't really anything going on in the exercise.

'Well,' I asked, 'did you notice how he was pressing his hands together so hard there were nail indents in his skin at one point?'

She sighed. 'Yes, I guess I could have called that.'

'But you didn't think it was relevant?' I asked, trying to see if I could pinpoint what was really going on. After all, if you observe an essential behaviour like that, it is a fairly profound thing to ignore. The confusing element, however, was there was nothing wrong with her observational skills. She *had* seen the behaviour, she knew how to verbalise the observation, and yet she had deliberately ignored it. Perhaps there were obstacles not in her observations but in her responses?

Watching her work again confirmed what I had suspected in the first exercise. Her partner was putting his attention on her, allowing a fairly large range of truthful responses to emerge. For her, on the other hand, she was always profoundly measured in her responses. Her responses were, for lack of a better word, proportionately small. Too small. When I suspect a strategy is being employed, I take care not to call it out too quickly, as it might not actually exist. Sometimes truthful behaviours can occur in patterns that the coach's mind puts together to infer an agenda where there is none. Continuously, however, I would notice a small gap between her observations and repetitions. She was clearly assessing her partner and was portioning her responses according to what she saw. In other words, she was entirely on the back foot.

Now it started to become clearer to me. She had figured out a very savvy, clever way to rig the system. By seeming impulsive enough, she had found a way to hide herself. As a defence, she was adapting to me in the same way a very keen actor adapts to a director and begins to give him or her what they want. This didn't come free, though, as she was getting no benefit out of the training for herself. By absolving herself of the opportunity to put the responsibility of the exercise on her partner and respond truthfully, she now had the ability to observe her partner clinically, assessing what she did and did not like. Deciding she did not really like what he was doing, that her partner was not acting according to her taste, she became bored. Her observational skills were fine. It was her unwillingness to respond authentically that was sinking her.

The sad thing is that when confronted with someone like this, I can't call them out. There's absolutely no point. If you say to a person you suspect they were foregoing truthfulness in favour of being clever, they won't give up their hand. Either they'll deny it, and then how can you argue with that, or they will say yes, further telling you what they believe you want to hear but making no real substantial change. This might sound judgemental, but it actually isn't. Actors learn to behave like this, not because they work with wonderful directors and teachers, but because they deal with abusive or clueless idiots and learn that survival often means saying yes. She didn't need to play that game with me, but it was such a deeply ingrained habit that maybe she did not herself know how to release it.

The solution in this case was self-teaching. When we began to work on scripts and scenes, as you will do in the latter chapters of this book, she began to feel the disconnect. There was her partner, who was flowing off of what she was doing, responding authentically (while speaking Shakespeare, I might add), and she did not have the technical capability to match him. To further the point, I put her in scenes with two other people. Again, the same issue was repeated across the board. She was habitually measured, and they were responding truthfully without concern for themselves and their preferences. She could not keep up.

It is vital to both your training and leadership development to understand that nothing comes free in this work. If you are going to be open and authentic, that takes courage, and it feels uncomfortable at times. If you want to play it safe and try to fool the coach, it may work sometimes, but what's the benefit to you? A time will come outside of the training when you need to flow authentically and adapt truthfully. Sleight of hand will not save you. If you find yourself judging your partner's work in an exercise, or becoming bored, you are falling into the same trap as the actress I worked with. You are no longer in the exercise, and as a result, you're no longer engaging with the values of this work.

Here I'll extend an olive branch. It is theoretically possible that if you put your attention fully on your partner, responding truthfully to each moment, that you still might become bored. If this happens, it is arguably within the values of this work. I say theoretically, however, because after thousands of hours of doing and teaching this to numerous people across the world, I have never seen it happen. Not once. This work is provocative by nature. We share this common trait across not just other primates but mammals in general: intensely lock eyes on one another for longer than a few seconds, and the temperature of the experience rises considerably. In the animal world, such an act could signify violence, attraction, deep sadness, a warning, but the blanket label this action receives is 'extreme possibility.' Sensitivity to possibility, the ability to observe it and respond to it, is an inherent value being trained in the exercise you are engaging with. That's anything but a boring experience.

Let's narrow it further down from the animal kingdom to the human experience in this work. It may not come across as clearly through reading, but I can promise you when you fully put your attention on another being, realising they have done the same thing to you, something very quickly becomes apparent: neither of you have any idea what the other person is going to do next. Even if you have known this individual for decades, in this work they will surprise you. Your complacency will quickly flip you on your back when you realise your partner is highly attuned to the moment, social conventions of politeness now cast aside for the time being. There is a greater value here for the training as a whole: the past might predict the future, but in living truthfully the depth and range of behaviours on offer is so vast that if somebody is responding truthfully to deeply observed moments of behaviour, then you really have no idea what their responses or observations will be in the future.

How long do you stay in repetition or the three moment exercise? What do you do if you become bored? There is a fairly simple, shorthand answer to those questions: your values are in the wrong place.

Technical Clean-Up Duty

That takes care of the first two questions, those related to how to transition as well as how long to remain in each exercise. The third question I sometimes, albeit less often, but still enough, am asked is: 'When we transition, is there is a pause still?'

Pause, you may ask, what pause? In switch, the previous exercise, it so happens that whenever a transition occurs, there is a slight but noticeable pause as the participants switch gears between exercises. It is unintentional, but it is fine with me in the first few exercises, so long as it doesn't become too pronounced. That's why I give the instruction to transition without a pause. In actuality, there will be one, but if the technical skills are strong, it is only a brief one. The micro-pause in the switch exercise is more akin to switching between languages you are fairly fluent in, and so a slight moment of conscious intervention often happens with pairs in switch. That habit gets carried over sometimes in auto-switch, and this is why the question will arise.

At this point in the work, the shorthand answer most people would intuit is no, there doesn't need to be a pause when partners transition between exercises. It is largely organically disposed of in switch, as pairs become more fluent in the exercises. Rather than separate languages, repetition and the three moment exercise start to feel more like variations within the same language, and hence the pause often departs of its own accord. We have to be careful, though, in making a technical blanket generalisation. There is a deeper, more nuanced answer to this question. It is worth considering, because what we do with any one moment becomes a habit trained into your leadership technique. Even if it is just a few single isolated moments when examined in the context of a wider habit, they become worthy of investigation.

Let's ask what at this point in the training is a fairly easy question: can there be moments in any of our exercises where there is silence? Obviously, yes, because we have seen it happen. Are there examples of where silence is technically weaker in the exercises? Plenty, as whenever the attention comes back on yourself, the words evaporating with it, you aren't training any relevant values for leadership. How about the opposite, where silence is a mark of technical strength? In other words, a moment or series of moments in which words are not relevant to the experience? Consider that repetition is a deep and meaningful interaction between you and another person. Can there be a moment in deep and meaningful interactions where words are not a part of that moment? Of course. Some of our most powerful experiences with people happen in silence. Profound moments that rob the experience of words can and do happen in repetition. You'll find in practice that the more moments that go on without words, generally the more depth is leached out rather than infused into it, so there is a limit. But a moment, or two, or ten even? That's a grey area where the story can change considerably, depending on what created the silence.

This transition point in auto-switch now raises an even deeper question about the nature of what you are experiencing. Things were far easier when I, as the coach, was in charge of it, but I'm not anymore. Neither are you or your partner, as when the transition happens it is determined pre-consciously by a sensitivity to something else. To start grasping what this something else is in all its complexity, we want to ask, 'Could something happen in an auto-switch that demands a transition, either into repetition or back into the three moment exercise?' Obviously, yes, but now let's ask, 'Could that something be so profound that both partners lose words for a space of time?' What it looks like, I have no idea, but from a technical standpoint that answer must obviously also be yes.

Any conceptual notions of a pause at this point in the training have to be removed. They were relevant when you were finding your feet with these exercises, but now they train the wrong values. The concept of a pause at its core implies a prescribed flow. Repetition has a flow, but spontaneous moments can disrupt it. The same for the three moment exercise. Those disruptions can be so rich and deep that neither you nor your partner can speak. Some of those moments in auto-switch may well be signals to transition, as they imply a radical shift in the dynamic of the experience between you and your partner.

It is difficult and vague to talk about hypothetical future moments that have not arrived. What could stop your capacity for language in an exercise? What could stop it in your real-life interactions with others? In either case, the answer must be unclear. We don't know what could surprise us in such a specific way, because that's the nature of a surprise. We must also recognise that in training, the possibility for such a moment can and does exist, though it may be rare. What we are moving away from is the *concept* of a pause, which breaks up reality in a way that doesn't serve you anymore. Pauses encourage interpretation. Both pauses and mistakes are categorisations that must give way to the category of moments. If there is any consolation, the beautiful thing about all this is that you don't need to go searching for any of these moments. If something happens so profound that it causes words to be lost, trust me, you will be dealing with it even before you consciously realise it.

So is there a pause or not at the transition point, or anywhere else in these exercises? The best – and technically strongest answer – is this: I don't know. And neither do you.

The Subtle Eye of Chaos

I have been hinting that around all of these questions is a more profound concept at work, one especially relevant for the next stage in leadership development you are entering into with this training. Up until now, every exercise has depended on one of two elements: a simple structure/ rhythm and my intervention as a coach. If you look at the early incarnations of repetition or the three moment exercise, the simple structure and rhythm become quite apparent. That basic imposition was very important at the time. It allowed for depths of experience enough for you to start getting a sense of what was on offer for your leadership development in this technique. The coach's intervention was always there but it especially came into play in the first version of the three moment exercise, with its moderated pause, as well as switch, where I would give you both the cue to switch. This was equally very valuable for the early stages. It kept the exercises on track and ensured the values being trained were optimally experienced. You can draw a clean correlation up to this point: as the depth of the exercises has increased, so have the safety rails around them, the simplistic structures and my dictation of transition points in switch being the most obvious.

That safety net of both structure and heavy-handed intervention within this work has proved a worthy asset. It has kept and promoted a simplicity within the exercises that has maximised the learning experience. The simpler the exercises, the more saturation that could take place. This is seen as well in the osmosis-learning concept we discussed in the early stages of training: the phenomenon that the last couple to work does not struggle with the problems encountered by the first several pairs but instead struggles with more technically advanced issues. The osmosis effect is largely due to the simplicity of the exercises. By not needing to keep attention on the structure, you and your partner can direct attention to what the structure is designed to facilitate. The last couple to work is often the most saturated and can coast on that, employing a hunger to seek the deeper experiences and trust that the integrity of the structure of the exercise will hold and does not need much, if any, grappling with.

Context is a powerful force, and results must be replicated outside of the training. You have gained values excellent for leadership, but it has come at a price: though the skills obtained in the work are strong and extremely beneficial for your leadership technique, they are still largely dependent on factors in the classroom environment. These factors will not be present once you leave the room. You may recall in an early session I stressed the importance of not pushing participants towards a result, with specific regard to 'guiding' you to act on a truthful impulse you are sitting on. Or, on the flip side, a specific observation you may be embarrassed to call. Neither of these situations are ignored in this training but are addressed in feedback post hoc, after the exercises finish. For the purposes of introducing and defining exactly what this new phase of training that you are entering is, let's briefly revisit why it is not worth pushing you towards a result.

Directing you or anyone else in an exercise towards a result means that, while you may finally act on the forbidden impulse, or make that impolite but true observation, your feelings of accomplishment are hollow. Who owns that moment of triumph if you had to be pushed to it? Not you. You just end up feeling good about successfully taking directions rather than actually learning anything except the habit of obedience. Pushing you to a result, the coach owns the result, not you. This was the crux of the ground we covered earlier, but it becomes even more relevant now.

Sometimes I hear Meisner training compared to working out at the gym, and so it is good to have a coach push you towards greater gains. I mean, who cares how you got the muscles? The results are still yours if you just pick up the weight with proper form. This is a terrible analogy, and for as few prescriptions as I make, here is one: do not buy into this, either in relation to Meisner or any other leadership training you may hear a similar argument used in. These are not muted muscles that perform under cognitive command. What you are developing are patterns of behaviour. The more you reinforce the habit of making your successful discoveries dependent on other people, the more those other people become conditional to your ability to apply those techniques. The second you take your shiny new tools out of the learning environment and into one where the coach is not present, how much or little that coach or teacher was essential to the success of those tools may aid or hinder you greatly. To reiterate, this is true not just of Meisner but all leadership training.

My interventions as a coach may have been important and necessary in previous sessions. Imagine trying to do an exercise like auto-switch on the first day? It would be a complete mess and even if we got there you would not have all the values you had earned by cleanly breaking up the exercises and process. Now, however, we come to the turning point. Auto-switch represents the next stage in this work, which can be defined by a greater move towards ownership. Increasing your ownership demands that we take the guard rails off, removing me more from the equation, and that is what you are starting to do here. You've got the technique. Now is time to surrender the experience to something else.

By leaving the transition up to neither the coach nor the two people working, you are now submitting control of this work to the nuances of the moment. You may also recall that in the previous chapter we discussed the concept of structured chaos, which we have been introducing in incremental doses as part of the training. Auto-switch marks a dramatic increase in your dose of uncertainty. After all, no longer is your technique for observing and responding authentically dependent on the coach's intervention. That sounds great, but it's also not dependent on you or your partner's intentions. It is important to see that just about everyone, myself included, will say they want you to own your leadership technique, but training leadership values with ownership in mind is a complicated bit of business. Look at most leadership training and you'll see the coach is actually the leader, even though they continuously talk about your being the leader developing your authenticity. On some level, from a coach's perspective, this is reasonable, as it minimises chaos, controls the environment, and seems to facilitate a learning experience, even if it is the shell of one. The trade-off? If you can't own your own process as a leader, then all you have learned is that someone else can control your process. The elegance of this training is that it increases and builds self-reliability incrementally. Our next step is to further move this work towards becoming more portable, which means ownership.

One aspect of ownership in your leadership is action in the face of unknown variables. That action must come from you. When you are faced with circumstances that demand leadership actions and decisions, you cannot have a technique that has made your truthful responses dependent on the intentions or drives of anyone, be it the coach or even yourself. It is true you will initiate the action, but the variables of the moment are what you interlock with. It is the moment itself – in which you have set up the values of living truthfully by observing and responding authentically – that is now going to determine your actions. At this stage, the way we structure that is to have you and your partner in auto-switch deal with unforeseen spontaneous moments in order to transition back and forth between two complementary but also quite different exercises. To do so without forcing it, to feel as if you arrived at spontaneous action, means developing a heightened sensitivity to the moment. Eventually this becomes the foundation for how you read and analyse a given set of circumstances within a situation.

What Belief Does to Chaos

It is this aggressive push towards transparency in our work that has formed the basis for why I am so hard on other forms of business and leadership training. At the same time, I am careful of blanket accusations of malice, as this doesn't make much sense either; most people who wish to train or coach in the business sector come from well-meaning places. Many arrive with backgrounds in the arts, and so they have seen first-hand the transformative powers of the approach they teach. Their starting point for this passion is often a personal transformation. I include myself in this category – by the time I learnt about the Meisner Technique, in practice rather than academically, I had already travelled the world and made in-depth studies about the different types of performance training out there. I was also taking psychology classes at my university and beginning, albeit in an elementary way, exploring other possible means of training actors using the knowledge these fields have to offer. After an unforgettable stint in Japan at the Noh Theatre, I went to do my MA at the Royal Central School of Speech and Drama. There it was practically a new approach to performance training every week. It was only in Meisner that I first began to find the ground to synthesise and actually learn in practice about the process of first the actor and later those seeking or in positions of leadership. It challenged me and developed me. For other people in the arts, this may be another technique, or their own amalgamation of different exercises and theories, but the starting point is a sincere one: it solved our problems. There is a possibility it will solve yours.

Here, however, is where we arrive at an impasse, one that I first heard about in my psychology courses, called the illusory correlation. No practitioner of any approach, especially one that later goes on to teach others, is starting from an objective place. They believe in their work, and that gives them a certain bias to believe it works. On some level this is reasonable: would you feel confident working with someone who did not believe in what they teach? At the same time, it is that confidence that can set you up for real problems. Here's an example of the illusory correlation at work.

By now we have seen how the circumstances of a classroom impact the learning. There are other ways we take for granted this can occur. For example, try to focus in a room that is too hot or cold and you expend more mental energy on that than if you were in a temperate environment. Research shows that if there is a bad smell in the room, your stress responses will be more active. Basic components that change our physiology can impact our attention in ways that we are not aware of. Likewise, the approach of the coach can impact your appraisal of the material itself. You could be learning the best tools but if you suspect the coach is being insincere, either too harsh or too soft for your preference, then you'll be unduly harsh on the material itself.

Consider another confounder we have mentioned before: most people are generally bad at doing things in front of others the first time. It doesn't matter whether you've been performing for decades. Even skilled improvisers have a hard time some days. It could be for any number of reasons but there's a simple, predictable outcome: people manage to get better at doing things in front of the same group of people through repeat exposure. That is not a transferable skill – it is dependent entirely on the context losing its novelty. Unless you or a coach know that the first few times doing anything may be rough because of incidental conditions rather than an actual issue, then the danger of interpretation will arise. Your challenges and inability to perform in the class-room or session will be seen as some indicative of a great block or inhibition, when really it is just poor structuring or random chance. Likewise, as you go on, you generally get better but this may not be the training so much as the environment. The illusory correlation can target both learner and coach when they assume that what created the change in your behaviour had to do with the training and not competing variables.

Here's another element that can create a false sense of growth: components of your training that are self-contradictory and cause problems because of their impossibility, creating a false challenge. Fewer examples of this are better known to me than the classical approach to the Meisner Technique. As you'll recall, I yammer on and on about the nature of provocative, opinion-based observations, as well as my reasons urging you to remove them from your technique as much as possible. That's because opinionated observations create an inherently contradicting problem within the technique itself. When this happens, students grapple with problems created entirely by the training, the technique now having nothing to add to reality except a possible commentary on its own short-sightedness.

In the interest of fair criticism, it helps to let you know before I continue that I use the term 'classical approach', but really this is more facile than secure. Throughout the early to middle stages of his career, Meisner changed his approach. Likewise, given the abstract nature of these exercises, for as many teachers of this work that exist there are that many ways to teach it. The differences are not so vast, however, that some basic similarities can't be identified. I base this not only on my own exposure to this original incarnation approach but also on existing transcripts and academic research. Whether my colleagues like it or not, there are some patterns in this train-ing, and some of them create false positive challenges.

One such pattern involves observations made with the sole intention to provoke your partner. I'm not talking about provocation in the way we have been training it. I'll list some examples here in a moment so you can see what I mean. The gist of this is that you deliberately make a provoca-tive call to train you to observe the reactions of your partner. It also allegedly has the benefit of opening you, the observer, up to fuck polite, and the person being observed also becoming more emotionally open and available. Sounds great so far. The training for this in the early stages fol-lows a structure highly similar to the three moment exercise. They are so close, in fact, that we can look at two parallel examples. Let's say you are working with your partner and you notice their eyes beginning to water. You call it and they go tomato red in the face. In our training it would look something like this:

You: Your eyes are watering.
Partner: My eyes are watering.
You: Your face went red.

This is an excellent example of a three moment exercise. The second moment is cleanly captured in the third observation and it looks like not one but two essential calls of behaviour have been iden-tified. At this stage, the value of such a series of calls for leadership training should be clear, but if they are not, feel free to revisit Chapter 6 that covers the value of the hierarchy of observations in relation to both the three moment exercise and its applications to leadership skills.

In the previous example provocation is not the goal but is a direct result of clear observations. Now let's see what a different, more classical approach deliberately seeking the result of provocation using this same structure may look like. This is an actual verbatim example I wrote down from a class I guest-attended in London. I'll just use two random names, Nick and Claire, and keep you and your partner out of it.

Nick: Do you think about your mom and dad fucking?
Claire: Do I think about my mom and dad fucking.
Nick: That pissed you off.

This is a pretty standard example and I've seen and read about such versions of the exercise in Meisner training across the globe. Most teachers I have seen utilising it refer to it as provocative questioning, not the three moment exercise. As I said, this is a fairly basic, tamer example. It is not one of the more extreme ones. It's a pretty intense exercise to say the least.

On the surface, there seems to be some value in provocative questioning. It does make you feel very vulnerable to be repeatedly asked shocking, invasive questions and then to have to repeat them aloud. The argument for them also suggests that by being more open you can enter the work at a deeper level of openness. Provocations by their nature are generally pre-conscious in that they elicit a visceral response before you have time to conjure one up. There's a time-saving element within it because of this, a seemingly efficient way to get you to be open and vulnerable. I don't talk about vulnerability much. Many people have an aversion to the word, as to them it may mean weakness or being of lower status. To be clear vulnerability can mean those things but the way I use it is in terms of openness. You have learnt in practice from repetition especially that there is indeed a genuine value to be had in the vulnerability that comes from being entirely open and receptive to your partner. It makes you dynamically magnetic to watch. The idea of provocations, then, sounds like a win-win, and on paper it is.

The claims of exercises with the intention to provoke, however, quickly lose water when seen in practice. The shock of being provoked does open a person up. There is an organic response of surprise that echoes life experience. Think back to an argument between yourself and a loved one where they said something so shocking and hurtful that it completely exposed you. You'll get that same openness from an exercise partner deliberately trying to provoke. Let me ask you, however, a follow-up. Let's revisit the scenario of you just being provoked by a loved one in an argument. Yes, it opened you up. Did you stay open for very long? Of course not. As soon as we feel we are being insulted or attacked our instinctive response is for our walls to go up and defensive strategies to come out. That is an authentic, truthful human response. It is biological.

Where it gets weird in the training is when I have seen Meisner teachers go on the attack. They tell students that they are closing off and need to stay open. From where we stand, not only is this in defiance of an authentic response, but the defensive response itself comes directly from being open to your partner. To try to fight that, then, is in direct contrast to the values of the technique. You won the response through observation, it is fair game. Technically a large problem emerges as what begins to compound is a frustration of repression. As you and your partner go along insulting one another, unable to respond authentically with impulses to retreat or protect oneself, both of you are going to stew more and more. As the frustration grows, the two of you becoming incrementally more upset at the content of the words rather than the behaviours in front of you, your attention will now inevitably come back to your fuming, boiling self.

Enter some of the Meisner teachers of memory I have observed. I would witness partners eventually close themselves off to one another, sick of being insulted, and then in feedback they would be berated. For what? Not being open enough! Well, I asked myself silently, what did you expect was going to happen? In the feedback, the students would obviously become further upset due to its vitriolic nature (the classical approach to Meisner is notorious for its 'brutal honesty', and oh would that be the case). Then to add the cherry on top, as they became more upset in feedback, they would be criticised by their teachers for not having a thick skin. Be open and authentic, but you have to deny certain truthful impulses. Then be open in feedback, but closed off at the same time. Makes sense to me!

This lunacy isn't unique to an isolated one or two teachers, but part and parcel of this training. The exception is the few Meisner teachers I have worked with who see this contradiction and don't fall for it or can navigate the utility of provocations exceptionally well, like my teacher and mentor Larry. Are the rest idiots? Of course not. Some are. A few are alpha-charged psychopaths who have found the perfect opportunity to play power games. The majority, however, mean well and want the right things for their students. They see the potential this work has to help actors be raw and emotionally fully open. It sounds excellent in theory and some of those values apply also to a leader's need to be authentic and open, but they don't take the next step and actually consider if what they are teaching works in reality the way they insist it will. You cannot deliberately provoke and insult somebody and expect them to remain authentic and open. When they do open and are further hurt by insulting feedback, you also can't tell them to just get a thick skin and then expect them to be open in the next exercise.

This should hopefully show you that even in a technique as efficient as this is there are self-generated challenges and problems buried within its framework. They are false challenges created solely by irreconcilable expectations and conclusions within the work itself. If these contradictions are not ironed out, many teachers and you will feel you have grown when actually nothing has adequately addressed your individual needs due to the technique's own innate inadequacies. This is why it is helpful to look at other approaches to the same technique in our own training. No, most likely you are not going to be a professional actor. Your needs are quite different in key aspects, but in holding a lens to the shortcomings of skills that are in the neighbourhood of what you are after, it helps us understand better why, as a leader, hyper-vigilance is needed when you are learning to improve your own abilities. The Meisner technique provides a case study for the challenges that can be magnified to many approaches to leadership development. Problems within training and illusory correlations can come together to create a potent distortion that has nothing whatsoever to do with where your needs are and only lead you astray.

Meaningful Meaning

As you can see, whether it is a classical approach or a modified one like in this book, this work demands openness. It is in the heart of the work: let your responses be determined by the actions of another. There is a major demand for your willingness to flow in accordance with what is given rather than continuously fighting against the current with your insistences about how others must behave. If we are going to look at areas to be aware of within this approach, both good and bad for developing a real technique, we also have to take an in-depth look at feedback. I've already dispensed with the silly thick-skin fallacy. If I am asking you to be open, then that won't suddenly change the moment you come out of an experience at the level of authenticity on offer in these exercises. That poses a challenge, however: how do you talk to someone fresh out of a visceral experience? Now to be clear you're not going to be lying on the floor in tears or anything, but your walls will be temporarily down. Where does feedback sit within that openness when its aim is to support the growth of a leader?

Let's go back to the concept of provocation. Everything in this work you learn you will make your leadership dependent on. Whatever habits you create will be carried over. Provocative feedback is part and parcel to the majority of variations in this training. Teachers of Meisner love to be blunt and direct, to try to needle at the sensitivities of the student. It isn't my style, but if this was just a matter of conflicting approaches, it wouldn't be worth talking about. What I do see, however, is that students begin to conflate the so-called brutal honesty with plain honesty. I will work with someone with prior experience in this work, and because I don't want to expend the effort to needlessly flail them, I will be met with suspicion. That does not bode well for the client. If you make yourself dependent on provocations from others, as well as provocative feedback from your coach, how portable is your technique going to be when you go out of the room and into other situations where you don't have the provoking input of authority figures?

To make your technique dependent on specific actions, or manners of feedback, is a great way of any coach creating a returning customer. True, you are going to see incredible results in the class, guaranteed, but the second you remove the variables that got you those results by taking yourself out of the classroom environment you are going to see only watered down, weak or nonexistent technical ability. I see it all the time with actors and many approaches to actor training, not just Meisner. Because they wouldn't consider the possibility of the material, coach, or classroom environment being the source of the learning challenges, the false results they have mistaken for actual growth leave them only one possible answer when their technique dries up outside of the sessions: to consider yourself and your own abilities the problem.

Habits matter, especially ones that claim to be portable. That is why I am hyper-selective about what I include in my teaching. What worries me is that I don't meet many other teachers of this work who recognise the inherent contradictions. Meisner isn't my only area of knowledge, and I can see the same problems happening in other approaches I have skills in. It happens as well in leadership training. Teachers and coaches must be hyper-vigilant that what we teach, the feedback we give, and the way a class is structured does not create false challenges. I suspect it arises from a point of conversion: people teach the material they believed solved their own issues. Any problems that arise must be the challenge the client is grappling with in their own process rather than the material itself.

Exercise: Repetition

Ownership is the core value that I find myself more and more needing to get across to my clients as we progress in this work. Their technique must thrive independently of me once they leave the room. I am always on the lookout for ways to minimise my presence and direction in the work while not compromising the structure of the exercises that provide the learning material. Auto-switch provides that necessary next step. More than ever, you are taking greater ownership of your technique of living truthfully as a leader.

I have said that there is one final component to this session's work and that is a 'new' exercise. I will introduce it here, but it will be expanded upon more in practice in the next two sessions. It is less a new exercise and more the natural evolution and outcome of auto-switch.

Auto-switch is unique in that it is a stepping stone, a precursor to an exercise, rather than the exercise itself. The best way to talk about its final form is through asking when does one make a change in the text of auto-switch? By this, I don't mean during the three moment exercise, when changes are frequent, but rather from repetition into the three moment exercise. That change in the observation, when is it made? We have analysed this fairly in depth already, and the conclusion we came up with is that the transition is, by its nature, momentary, and therefore determined by the demands of the moments themselves. A change in auto-switch that is not premeditated just seems to happen. No one forces it to. The values of the technique are honoured, and so when the change happens it feels spontaneous and chaotic. My Meisner teacher Scott would always summarise it this way: 'A change in the text happens, and you're in the room when it does.'

Let's follow this for a moment. If you quantitatively look at the exercise, transitions take up a very small percentage of the experience. Most of the time is spent engaging in either the values repetition or the three moment exercise. That small percentage, however, is immensely important, as for a change in the observation to dominate the moment during repetition, something profound must happen. Language, after all, is not high on our list of priorities, but if the specificity observed in the moment is profound enough to warrant a change in the text, then something else also follows, which is that such a change demands to be repeated and explored. This is because if it's important enough to be called during repetition, it seems there is depth on offer. Repetition is your tool for dismantling certain inessential aspects of communication in order to explore interpersonal depth. If it's important enough to be called, then it is a moment that demands repeating. How many times an observation is repeated, if it is repeated, is still up to the moment between the two of you. To follow the line of logic from Scott's quote, then, it seems that any change in the verbalised observations demanded by the moment must warrant repetition. This means that a natural evolution of auto-switch is that the three moment exercises, filled with changes, organically go away and specific observations begin to be repeated until a new change is made.

This desire to explore depth with specificity by repeating an observation until the moment demands a change is the natural merging of the values from the three moment exercise and repetition. This hunger for both leads us out of auto-switch and into the full technique of repetition. Yes, auto-switch becomes repetition, but nothing like you've done before. This version is built with all of the accessories – the values – acquired from your hard work in early stages of repetition, the three moment exercises, switch, and auto-switch. This is a technique of repetition in which you can be razor-sharp about the behaviour of your partner, where you've got open access to a good range of authentic responses, and now you two can fluctuate between depth and specificity, mining your interpersonal changes for truthfulness. This is a different beast entirely. This is repetition, where a change in the text is now possible, supported by all the values of this work, and rather than compromising your ability to live truthfully becomes a means of training it.

Let's see an evolution of auto-switch into repetition. You and your partner start with the three moment exercise, but after the first round of it are off into repetition. For space and time here, each repeat will only be a few lines, but the repetitions can go on as long as the moment demands:

You: You're laughing.
Partner: I'm laughing. (bows head)
You: You dipped your head.
Partner: I dipped my head.
You: You dipped your head. (giggles)
Partner: You're smiling.
You: I'm smiling. (sighs)
Partner: You sighed. (puts hand on your shoulder)
You: I sighed.
Partner: You sighed.
You: Your voice is shaking.
Partner: My voice is shaking.
You: Your voice is shaking. (puts face in hands and shakes head laughing)
Partner: You're melted ice cream.

You: I'm melted ice cream?!
Partner: You're melted ice cream.
You: I'm melted ice cream. (laughs)
Partner: You giggled.
Etc.

Here we have arrived then. This is an interpersonal exchange where all the changes in the observations occur according to the demands of the moment. The text changes and then your attention is back with your partner. From there the words generally still float on top, providing an opportunity for you two to explore more depth with one another beneath them, until the moment demands a new change. We never lose that value from your very first session: in the majority of these exchanges, as with human interactions, text floats on top with the literal content of the words taking a back-seat to the more important demands of the moment. It does not matter, for example, that you partner's voice has stopped shaking and they are still repeating that is shaking (if you need a refresher on why that is, feel free to have a look through Chapter 4 where we covered the lack of need for literalness in the text of every moment). This has not become an exercise in making a laundry list of behaviours. That call, however, will springboard you both into a deep experience. Think of how profound it is for your voice to be shaking and have it be observed. When the observation is verbalised you'll repeat for however long the moment requires. Most calls will be repeated at least once, the majority more than once. That said, anything can happen. I have seen entire exercises go without a single change in the text. So long as the exercise is truthful then that is just as good as a repetition exercise filled with meaningful, determined-by-the-moment changes in the observations. All that matters is the work is truthful and, as a consequence, developing your authentic interpersonal leadership abilities.

Now that you've got a shiny new technique of repetition, our ultimate tool for training living truthfully, how about we do something crazy and turn up the intensity even more? And I mean a lot more. See you in the next session!

Summary

We began this journey with a very simplistic version of repetition. In almost all cases, there would be no change to the text, and if it did happen, it would be minor. What we gained, however, was an understanding that by dismantling language and its contents, putting words on the back-burner where they still could at times interject but more often than not would be consigned to float on the constant stream of behavioural exchanges between you and your partner, that immense depth was on offer. We merged depth with specificity when we introduced switch, bringing in the values of the three moment exercise. The specificity and sensitivity to the moment culminated when the three moment exercises you had worked on began to seep into the values of repetition.

This process instilled a value into the work: specificity and being attuned to the demands of the moment are of premium value to a leader. Furthermore, those values can be accommodated into repetition and therefore trained by technical means. Auto-switch further blurred the lines between the repetition and three moment exercise, suggesting that when two people use repetition, putting even more power in the hands of the moment, meaningful specific changes in the text are possible. Auto-switch quite naturally becomes the full technique of repetition.

Putting your attention on your partner, using the specific observational tools of the three moment exercise, allows for a depth of exchange. This depth of exchange with just one simple call goes on and on until the moment demands a change. This is often accommodated by one person suddenly seeing something profound in the moment and calling it. What is most important, however, is that the person making the call has not been out hunting for it. By simply being engaged with your partner and responding truthfully profound moments will arise. These moments do not always need to be called, but when they are, the observation that captures them is repeated until the moment demands a new change in the text.

By putting the issue of changing the text into the hands of the moment, both participants are able to fully place their attention on each other and have a deep exchange that is facilitated by the razor-sharp specificity of your now well-trained observational powers. This forms the true technique of repetition, entirely in line with the values of our work, which means that you will own your technique of living truthfully and it will be fully portable. What you have now just claimed is even more ownership over the authenticity you have been training in this work.

Tips for You and Your Coach

As each pair works in auto-switch, have them first begin with auto-switch and then in each subsequent feedback keep guiding them towards the technique of repetition. They probably won't get there fully, there might still be quite a lot of changes in the text where opportunities to go deeper are not explored, but at this stage, that is fine: what is of most value is that they begin to sense and taste in practice where this can go. Pairs at the end might just want to jump into repetition but encourage them to start with auto-switch and to feel the organic chaos where suddenly partners in the exercise seem to arrive into repetition rather than forcing it to happen.

This is the final exercise that develops the technique of repetition. There is immense value in clients feeling the organic journey from a structured exercise that still has the presence of the coach, even in an abstract way, to now where they are owning their technique of living truthfully and are now engaging with its deeper values. These values are letting one's responses be determined by their partner, and trusting the responsibilities of the text to the moment to let them know when it is time for a change in the observation being repeated.

As a coach, don't get too hung up if there are too many observations and not enough repetition or if the pair becomes stuck in repetition and moments that demand a change in the text go ignored. You will find that in your feedback you will create problems for yourself if you are too direct: if you say things like 'There were too many three moments before you went into repetition', you will inadvertently be telling them to ignore the values of the three moment exercise and go into repetition as fast as they can. As a result, watch as precious specificity is lost. Conversely, if you say 'You repeated too long and didn't allow for any changes to happen', then you will see participants become afraid of allowing themselves to have the deep experience of repetition, now worrying about the time spent in it, a completely irrelevant value if both are being true to the moment and each other.

Nudging participants towards that sweet spot of repeat-and-change, where depth and specificity are balanced, is your teaching goal. This is not an A+ formulaic exercise that only has one appearance: this is about clients finding their own technique of living truthfully and working their way into it. As the coach, then, this means that your feedback is going to be structured less around what needs to happen in the future and more around what happened in the exercise and how each individual can take their technique forward. This is where specialised sight and sensitivity to each individual person becomes paramount, because now is the time when the exercises may have a general shape and structure, but the specific nuances within them will be radically different from pair to pair and even within pairs between exercises. Everyone will be doing repetition, but their technique will look different as it takes on their individual qualities. Those small nuances, however, will form the rich material of the learning. Balance your feedback and emphasis on the technique of repetition with feedback designed to expand the range of living truthfully as each individual needs it, meeting them at the level of their personal technical needs. Keeping your eyes on general structure has been of great value to everyone. Now start to seek subtlety as well.

You are beginning the process now of making yourself as invisible as you can in the training, only appearing at the end to give feedback and support the client's journey into widening their range of authentic response and deepening their quality of observations. This is a good thing. Clients need to shake the coach off and get to the real work at hand, which is discovering for themselves what it means to live truthfully in the moment without a seeming safety net.

Chapter 10

The Knock at the Door

A Primal Impulse

The discoveries of the previous session, where gradually auto-switch evolved into the full technique of repetition, marks the beginning of a change in this work. In the earlier sessions, we spoke at length about the notion of living truthfully in a rich, moment-by-moment way. At the same time, there was always a level of imposed structure on the work: sticking to one call, the fairly inflexible structure of the three moment exercises, the times when I as the coach would call 'switch!' All of these implementations were necessary at the time to provide a framework introducing you to the values of this work. That was then. This is now. It is time that much of the imposed structure is shaken off.

Going forward, what we will still keep is the basic structure of repetition, but now we are going to trust that your technique is strong enough to keep the values we are after in balance organically, without needing to check in with yourself, or the guidance of the coach, to make sure the exercise is going well. Your intuitions will continue to sharpen as to how long an observation needs to be repeated as well as when a change in the observation is demanded. As a consequence of your progress, my attention as the coach is now gradually shifting from what 'has to be', in terms of the structure of the exercises, to what 'happens' within them. We are graduating from drills to sparring. To get there, however, we need one final step. Building on the discoveries of all previous sessions, it is time now to finish our work on the technique of training living truthfully by dealing with one final impulse, and all of the connotations and potential baggage that come with it. This impulse is so large, so massive, it gets its own exercise. Today, you will be truly swimming in the depths.

After this session, you will have the complete technique for living truthfully, which means in the next session you will begin the work of how to import that technique into a given set of circumstances. Yes, you heard me: in the next session we are on to living truthfully under a given set of circumstances, beginning the complete package for training leadership. That will be then. For now, you have your hands full.

Exercise: The Knock at the Door

This exercise is called the 'Knock at the Door'. In Meisner training, it tends to inspire a mix of fear and reverence. Reverence for its power to expose much of our preconditioned notions about human behaviour as well as the limitations we impose on ourselves when attempting to be authentic and true in the presence of another. Fear, for the same reason. The instructions around it, however, are incredibly simple: the knock at the door is a repetition exercise that begins with a knock at the door.

The format for this chapter is going to be slightly different. In previous chapters, we have seen scripted hypothetical examples of an exercise, what they may look like, as well as examples of technically stronger, or weaker, calls, etc. We have seen some, but not many, examples of when participants act, or sit on, certain impulses. While this format served us well, it will become increasingly less applicable in these next chapters, since so much more of the technique is now in the hands of both partners and there is greater spontaneity in the moment itself. Giving hypothetical examples en masse is much easier when things like mastering technical structure are the outcomes of the training session. At this point, however, your tool of repetition is now far stronger than it ever was, given you have imported the specificity of the three moment exercise fully and are using that to springboard into deeper experiences as well as accommodate changes in the observations.

What you will see in this chapter is something akin to an extended case study. I'll give an initial setup to the exercise, but from there this will read more like a transcript where two people go through this exercise for the first time. This is not intended to demonstrate how every knock at the door exercise will go. Instead, this hypothetical session will be a distillation from my thousands of hours of experience in teaching and training in this work. It will magnify the common issues and challenges that tend to arise for participants in this exercises. There will also be mock feedback, but this again would be specific to individual situations. The mock feedback, then, instead of being a strategy for you to use in your future work when you do these exercises, will give you a sense of the general territory you want to be working in to have the optimal experience in this exercise as well as the way certain challenges you encounter will be handled.

As a final note, you'll notice that I mentioned 'two people' rather than you and your partner. I will use specific names in this hypothetical class, Sam and Robert. This is because I no longer want to keep referencing you and your partner. I don't know either of you, and these hypothetical experiences may not apply at all, or I may not word feedback in this particular way for you. Having said that, though I am using two men, highly similar situations occur between two women, a man and a woman, and so on, so almost none of this is gender-specific. For your own role, imagine yourself a participant then in this session. The feedback and hypotheticals are being directed to Sam and Robert, who have volunteered to work before you do, with your deciding to hang back and make use of the osmosis effect of this training.

The setup is the same. Two chairs placed facing one another, the same as always. Sam and Robert volunteer to go first. They sit in the chairs as I fill them in.

'This exercise is called the knock at the door,' I explain, 'and here are the instructions: the knock at the door is a repetition exercise that begins with a knock at the door.'

I say no more. The surprise doesn't creep: it explodes across their faces.

'So . . . ' Sam asks, 'do you mean one of us knocks . . . one of us answers and does the exercise . . . standing?'

'I don't know,' I say, being honest, 'I have no idea what will happen in the exercise, and neither do you.'

'Right . . . ' Robert chimes in, looking for the catch.

'What we know is that most likely there will be a knock at the door. And if that happens it will be the start of a repetition exercise.'

Confusion starts to turn to dread. They both are beginning to sense I won't give any more. What neither knows yet is I don't have any more to give.

'Let's try one,' I say. That is the best strategy with this exercise. Keeping a clipped pace is important; I have learned from hard experience that too many questions asked early on make people miserable, upset, and confused. You the reader are probably wondering yourself what this is all about: imagine being the poor souls in the chairs.

'Robert,' I say, 'want to be the one out?'

Robert and I exit the classroom. We close the door. He looks at me expectantly.

'I bet you they think I'm telling you some big secret out here,' I say.

His face drops. Hope of secrets is a major motivator.

'Have you tried the new sandwich shop across the road?' I ask.

'Uh . . . yeah . . . ' Robert says, unsure of where I am going.

'Anything good?'

'Turkey and pesto?'

'Turkey and pesto, you recommend it?'

'Yes . . . '

'Great, thanks. So, I'm going to head back inside now. When I close the door just count to about a hundred and knock.'

'Just normal counting?' he asks.

'Yes, normal pace, nothing fancy, just count to one hundred and then you knock.'

'And then Sam answers the door?'

'I have no idea.' And this is entirely true. I really don't know if Sam is going to answer the door.

I can see he has more questions, but I don't let him have any more. He wants to know the future. I am the wrong person to ask. I come back into the room to find Sam where I left him, in one of the chairs. He seems cheerful, but I detect the suspicion in his eyes. I don't take the bait.

'Sam,' I ask, taking a seat with the rest of the day's participants, 'I hear an East Coast accent.'

'Yes . . . you do . . . ' he says with hesitation.

'Where on the East Coast?' I ask genially, and I am sincere: I don't know much about Sam and so I want to find out more about what his background is.

'Boston.' he says. I can hear the wariness in his voice.

'I've always wanted to go to Boston,' I say, and this is true. 'What is it like?'

As he is about to speak the knock comes. He freezes, unsure of what to do. I am still waiting for his response, and he picks up on this. He yells out, 'Come in!'

'Very good!' I say, 'I'll stop you there. Robert, do come in!'

Robert comes in and take a seat. They both look puzzled as all hell.

'A lot of interesting things happened just now,' I say, and this to me is very true. 'I want to start with you, Sam. Now, when Robert and I went out of the room, what do you think happened?'

'Honestly?'

'Honestly.'

'I think you told him *something*.' Sam says.

'Like what?'

'I don't know, but you told him to do something . . . or say something when he came in . . . you were planning something.'

'Interesting!' I turn to Robert: 'Robert, what did we talk about?'

'First, you said "I bet you they think I'm telling you some secret they don't know about." Then we talked about sandwiches, you asked me about the new place down the street. Which sandwich was my favourite.' Robert says.

'And then?'

'Oh! You told me to count to a hundred and knock.'

'That's it?'

'That's it.'

There is a bit of trickery in this on my end, but not much. I know that the moment I go outside the room with a student who is about to be in an exercise, the general consensus of the group will be they are being instructed to do something more complicated than just knocking. More teasingly than manipulating, I play to this slightly. More importantly, I don't play to the deception they are expecting. There is a valuable learning point here for the participants.

'So, when I first began the exercise I said to you both that this is a repetition exercise that begins with a knock at the door. I went outside with Robert and instantly you began to think I had been withholding information from you, that when Robert came back in you were going to have the rug pulled out from your feet in some way. Is that about accurate?'

'Yes,' Sam says.

'That, unfortunately, is normal. Most learning, and especially coaching, seems to happen by withholding information. That is the standard. Teachers will ask you to do something and then judge you for not being in their head and able to read their mind. If I had done that, if I had given you simple instructions but then said, 'But you didn't consider THIS!' and then introduced something new, it is true that I would create the illusion of a challenge and an obstacle for you to overcome as a student, but what good would it actually serve you? How does withholding information help your actual development?'

'It doesn't.'

'Exactly. So for better or worse, I mean it when I say that all I know is that this exercise is a repetition exercise that begins with a knock at the door. What happens from then on is in the hands of the future. Sorry, we don't get it both ways: we can't put so many restrictions and comforts on the future that you aren't able to train with the uncertainty that comes with repetition. Which brings me to my next question, Sam: what part of repetition is 'Come in?''

' . . . it isn't.'

'No, it isn't. But it is incredibly polite.'

Sam registers it. 'Got it.'

Careful not to give too much feedback, I let Sam know that it's his turn to go outside. Without going with him, I say to him the same thing I told Robert as he leaves: 'Count to about 100, a normal pace, and then knock.'

Sam leaves and then Robert is left sitting in the chair.

'So that thing about the sandwiches,' he asks.

'Yes?' I say.

'Did you actually want to know or were you just buying time?'

We laugh. 'Both,' I say, and again, a coach's honesty and transparency matters especially in this exercise. 'I actually wanted to know . . . but I also had a feeling Sam was going to think we were plotting. Not because of anything Sam did, but because that's what every student thinks when they are the first ones up.'

'That you're going to trick them.'

There is a knock at the door. Just as I am beginning my reply, Robert instantly gets up and goes to the door; he opens it.

'Great job! I'll stop you both there.' I say.

Both come back to the chairs. They look puzzled as all hell.

'I'll start with you, Sam,' I say. 'So you just went out, counted and then knocked?'

'Yes.' Sam replies.

'Great job. Now onto Robert: what the hell?!' I say this last bit in a joking way.

'What?' Robert asks, even more confused.

'We were sitting there, having a great conversation, and then the knock came, at which point you completely iced me!'

'Oh, was I not supposed to answer the door?'

'I'm just kidding about the icing part. But there is some technical feedback for you in this, which is I saw something really interesting happen: we were speaking, talking about things. Then the knock came. I perceived you shut off from the conversation and went into 'exercise' mode. You exited the reality of being just Robert and went into the student persona. Does that make sense?'

'Yes.' Robert says. I can see he is taking it in. Just for clarity, since this on the page, if he didn't seem to be getting it, was confused, or disagreed, I would make sure to meet him halfway since this type of feedback is deep and intricate.

'This is the problem that knock at the door poses,' I say, 'we spent the previous sessions doing all this great work on living truthfully but with the addition of a simple knock at the door everything goes out the window. The social conventions of someone knocking at the door instantly pushed you out from being your authentic self. You went from being 'Robert living truthfully' to 'Robert the good student trying to act truthfully.' Does that make sense?'

'It does,' Robert says, 'But I'm not sure what I was supposed to do differently.'

"Supposed to' is where the problems start. Our work so far has been about training in the question of 'how do I remain authentic even with the uncertainty the present moment brings?' The moment we say you 'should have done this', we are saying you should do it in the future. Since we don't know the variables of the future, that won't help you. It's why I can't tell you what you should do; I can only comment now on what happens in each individual exercise. But remember, repetition is an exercise in living truthfully. If you lose your authenticity, then you aren't doing repetition in any way that holds up the values of the exercise, and the training won't be of use to you. The only information that we have is that this is a repetition exercise that begins with a knock at the door. I can't tell you what to do *when* the knock comes because neither of us have that information.'

Robert and Sam are still confused. At this point I am comfortable with that. It is going to take time for them to understand in practice the level of ownership over their technique I am asking them to assume.

'Robert: your turn to be out.' I say.

Robert goes out. I see Sam does not look happy.

'You doing okay?' I ask.

'This is weird.'

'I agree. What's weird about it for you?'

'I just feel like you want us to do something and you're not telling us.'

'I wish I could give you both some kind of concrete answer. I've been trying to figure that out for years, and I mean it. But any kind of prescription I can give you beyond live truthfully when the knock comes is going to deny other possibilities in the future...'

The knock comes.

'. . . so there's nothing specific I can say to you beyond that.' I finish.

'Yeah, I know, it's just tricky, you know.'

'I know. Trust me. I see so many people miserable in this exercise.'

The knock comes again. Sam strikes me as looking more uncomfortable.

'The truth is,' I continue. 'I don't want to make you miserable, but there is a lot that the knock at the door brings up for people. A lot of things that need to be unpacked. And that's what is unpleasant, starting to come face to face with your own social conditioning.'

The door opens and Robert comes in, looking confused and annoyed.

'That's great!' I say, ending the exercise, and I mean it. 'Take a seat, Robert.'

Robert sits. There is still some confusion in their faces.

'So, lots to talk about,' I say, 'let's start with you, Sam.'

'Yeah,' Sam says and laughs. He knows he has been caught.

'Your strategy isn't half bad,' I say to Sam. 'Just ignore the bastard and eventually he will go away.'

Sam and Robert both laugh.

'But,' I continue, 'I don't think it actually serves you. Remember that the primary value of this work is that what happens to you does not depend on you but rather on what the other person is doing to you. For you to implement a strategy that determines the future seems to be an unwise one. It undermines the core value you've been training in but more importantly it isn't an optimal way to try to plan for the future. Rather than insisting on what will happen it is much healthier to deal with what happens as it comes. That is the only way you can guarantee you will get a handle on the wave, whatever shape it takes.'

'So I should have answered the door, then?' Sam asks.

'Let me ask you this. When you heard the knock, did you sit on an impulse to get up and answer it?'

'Yes.'

'Then there you go. That impulse came from the knock, which came from your partner, and so getting up to answer the door would be considered a technically strong act of living truthfully. BUT. Do you answer the door next time or do you not? I have no idea, and neither do you.'

'So it's okay to not answer the door?'

'Why would it not be okay?'

This question sits deep with him. 'I'm not sure,' he says.

'Think about where the question comes from. You've been conditioned to value the social etiquette of it. Someone does not just barge into your house: that would be criminal. Or at the least incredibly rude. They knock, giving you the opportunity to answer or not, which is fair. In kind, you return the gesture by, unless there is a reason not to, answering the door, which is also fair. These are values of politeness and interaction that are incredibly vital to society functioning in a healthy way, but they are not truthful responses because they deny the reality of the moment as a rule. A knock might come where you feel compelled to get up and answer the door. I don't want to pre-empt the future, but let's say a knock comes that is incredibly aggressive and sounds full of rage. Yes, you might answer the door, but you might also have the impulse to move away, or to stay put. Your instincts before thought might tell you, 'Don't answer that door.' That's the truth of the moment.

'But you have to remain sensitive to the moment that follows, just like in repetition. The knock might sound softer the next time. Or you might just say, 'Fuck it,' and go and answer it. Politeness will tell you to answer the door each time. At the same time, we don't allow for politeness, since it robs you of good technique. I think then you put yourself into an impossible situation. You didn't want to say 'fuck polite' but instead chose to do the opposite of polite, which was to deliberately not open the door. By bringing in your own agenda to stay safe in the exercise you denied the impulse that came from the knock and instead lost the truthfulness of the moment. Does that all make sense?'

'Yes,' Sam says, 'It's just a lot to take in.'

'It is. Let's bring it back to the surface a bit: do you answer the door, or do you not? I don't know. And most importantly, neither do you know until that moment gets here.'

Sam nods, taking it in.

'Robert,' I say, turning my attention. 'You did something very interesting. You knocked once, didn't get a response. So you knocked again. Then you came in. What was going on with that?'

I can see Robert is worried he is about to be scolded for doing something wrong.

'Well, I didn't get a response, nobody answered, so it didn't feel right to keep standing there.'

'So based on the feedback you got, the silence in this case, you had an impulse to go into the room.'

'Yes.'

'Even though nobody answered the door.'

'That's right.'

'That's incredibly impolite of you.'

Robert smiles. 'I guess it is.'

'Good job.'

Sam goes out. Robert and I talk about some of the ideas I covered with Sam, about how much personal baggage a knock can bring up.

'If you think about,' Robert says, 'that's going all the way back to childhood. It's one of the earliest habits you learn.'

I agree with him. 'Politeness is what weaves a healthy society together. Social conditioning is the set of agreements that helps us get through life.'

The knock comes. In response to my comment Robert nods to me and then gets up to answer the door. He no longer shifts personas but seamlessly integrates both our conversation as well as the knock. When he opens the door he says quickly, 'You knocked.'

Sam repeats.

'I'll stop you both there,' I say. Sam covers his face with his hands and shakes his head laughing. 'But at least you got two lines out!' I say, consoling them.

Sam and Robert come back to their seats. They have a mixture of bemusement and frustration on their faces but most importantly less confusion. This is a good sign to me. It shows the emotional temperature of the room is lowering, and that they are beginning to get the values in practice. They may not believe it but things are, surely and slowly, beginning to come together.

'Robert, really good work there.' I say sincerely, 'When the knock came you didn't just completely deny the reality of us having a conversation and you still went with you impulse to answer the door. That was a great example of public solitude at work. First our conversation was a part of your experience and then it no longer was, but not because you pretended it no longer existed. My question to you, however: you opened the door and rapidly said, 'You knocked.' Did you have a chance to actually look at Sam before you spoke?'

'Not really,' Robert says. 'That's what I did wrong.'

'No. That was okay, actually.'

'It is?'

'There's no rule that says you have to look at one another before starting the exercise. At the same time it does raise a good question. So much of this work is rooted in a deep interpersonal exchange. How then do you 'see' your partner in a meaningful way when the exercise begins before they are in the room? Knock at the door, after all, is a repetition exercise that begins with a knock at the door, not with a person coming into a room. This is not a flaw in the exercise but rather by design. So what tells you about your partner before you even see them?'

'The knock?' Sam asks.

'Bingo. Why?'

'Because there are a lot of ways you can knock.'

'Exactly. It could be a hard knock or a soft one. It could be one knock, it could be five in a row. All of that is what?'

'Behaviour.' Robert says.

'You got it. The knock is still behaviour. Behaviour that still comes from your partner. Just like all behaviour in this work you don't need to interpret the knock. You just respond to it. The knock, however, will tell you about what is happening with your partner and as a result can, though not always, provide the material for the first call.'

'So you verbalise your observation before you answer the door, then?' Sam asks.

'I don't know.' I say, and again, I mean it. 'I don't know if you're going to answer the door to start. If you do I don't know there will be a call. There may be something so profound it robs words. If there is an observation I don't know when it will come. The knock begins the repetition exercise but does that mean a call is made before the door is open or after, if it is ever made at all? I don't know, and more importantly, neither do you. The value here is staying open and accepting we honestly don't know until the moment arrives.'

Robert goes out. Sam and I talk.

'So, this chatting here we are doing,' Sam asks, 'are you just trying to get my mind off of the knock coming?'

'You mean if the knock comes,' I say.

'What do you mean?'

'Well, Robert has the instruction to knock. But that doesn't mean he will.'

'Did you tell him not to?'

'No. But let's face it: just because I gave him the instruction to knock does not mean he actually will.'

'He could choose not to?'

'I think that would be a non-starter to the exercise and would not do either of you a service. But let's just say that while he's in the hallway waiting Angelina Jolie walks up to him and says, "Excuse me, you look like you would be a perfect choice for the next movie I'm directing. Do you want to go and get a drink?" Even though Robert is not an actor do you really think he is going to knock with that offer on the table?'

Sam laughs. The knock comes. It is a long, continuous knock that lasts for about five or six seconds. Confused, Sam gets up, opens the door, sees Robert.

'That was a long knock,' Sam says.

'That was a long knock.' Robert repeats.

'That was a long knock.'

'That was a long knock.'

Etc.

As they continue repeating, both become aware that they are standing awkwardly in the doorway. Eventually they laugh and Sam gestures for Robert to come in. I stop them there.

'Very good,' I say, sincerely, 'lots to talk about.'

As they sit, I finish my thought from earlier, 'So, just to put a bow on that, Sam, all that we know is the person outside of the door has the instruction to knock. But we never actually know if the knock will come. It most likely will, but there is a difference between something likely happening versus believing with definite certainty this is what will happen in the future. Sam, just because Robert has gone out doesn't mean he will be the one who knocks. It might be a janitor needing to come in and change the lightbulb. Likewise, Robert, let's say I send someone else in to do the exercise at the last minute, swapping Sam out just to surprise you. The door will open and Sam won't be there. We need to be incredibly aware of expectations of the future and minimise them as best as we can so we deal with this moment and leave the future open.'

'I see,' Sam says.

'Now, Robert, to start with you. That was a very inventive sounding knock.'

'Well, we had just had that long talk about the knock.'

'I agree. Well, here is the good news for you. What you apply your leadership towards does involve a lot of creativity and planning. If you want to see a vision succeed you do need to be a creative, inventive person. But this is leadership training and all the brackets it addresses, from speeches, negotiations, presentations, so on. Leadership itself does not require you to be creative. There are a fair amount of coaching exercises that involve improvisations which are creative exercises. We'll talk about improv in the next session, but for the record, there's nothing creative about the Meisner Technique. It isn't asking you to be inventive or to come up with anything. A lot of aspects unique to your field are about being a creative individual. Leading in that field by living truthfully, however, is not about being a creative expert but an expert of the interpersonal experience. You go into a situation, open, put your attention on the other person, and let your responses come from what you observe. If you had to worry about being creative or inventive you would be putting your attention and the responsibility for the exercise onto you, not the other person. We never abandon that value in this work. So for now just count and knock. You are, however, edging in the direction of an important question: what happens when you are not the one answering the door but the one walking into the room? The bigger value there being what to do if you're the one entering into a situation rather than dealing with what enters into your domain? The answer to that is in the next session we'll give a tool to handle that circumstance. But step by step.'

Robert nods. I turn my attention to Sam.

'Sam, something very interesting happened at the knock. We were talking when that strange knock came. You answered it and your first call was an observation of the knock. That is great. A minor technical tweak might be to say, 'You knocked for a long time' so you can personalise it but that's a small note.'

'Isn't that an opinion, though?'

'It's a grey area observation, but I think in this case it would have been truthful. It relates to a comparison across a series of moments rather than the specificity of one moment, but that can happen at times. Best to keep those kind of calls to a minimum, but if the moment demands it that's what we're working with. The main note for you is the very interesting thing that happened after a few repetitions, which is you both had a moment of what seemed to me to be awkward laughter.'

'Yes,' Sam says, chuckling.

'So what was that all about?'

'Well, I think we both sort of realised that we were standing in the doorway and we weren't sure what to do next.'

'So you invited him to come in?'

'Yes.'

'Which was a very polite thing to do.'

'I see. So not what I should have done?'

'I don't know about should, but I think the politeness was technically the weaker thing on offer. It may have also been the safer thing on offer. Inviting him in seemed more like you telling him what you wanted him to do rather than acting on what you knew you needed to do.'

'Meaning?'

'I could be wrong but I suspect the politeness was in response to an impulse not acted on. We've spent the first part of this session trying to unpack some of the social baggage that comes with the knock at the door. Those things can hamper your ability to live truthfully using the tool of fuck polite. Now that you are both sensing and staying true to fuck polite, we are starting to get to the point of knock at the door, why it is there in the first place, and the moment of awkward laughter followed by the polite gesture to come in captures what didn't happen.'

'Which is?' Robert asks.

'Barring the knock, what is the main difference between the knock at the door and all the other exercises we've been doing?'

'We are out of the chairs.' Sam says.

'All the time?' I ask. 'Did I give you an instruction to leave the chairs?'

'No. But we can. Sometimes.'

'Depending on?'

'The moment.'

'Precisely. In the last session, I said that today's material would complete the technique of living truthfully. The knock at the door has one, and only one, function, which is to discover *the impulse to move*. The reason there was awkward laughter followed by politeness is because, Robert, I think you had an impulse to come into the room and Sam, you seemed to have the impulse to move away from Robert after the first couple of repeats. Am I correct?'

'Yes,' Robert says, 'it didn't feel right to keep standing there.'

'I'm actually not sure if I had the impulse to move away from him . . . something just didn't feel right.' Sam says.

'No problem,' I say, making sure both know they can tell me if I am actually on the right track or not with my intuitions., 'Then what I was sensing was solely Robert's desire to move into the room. Can Robert do that, come into the room?'

'If it's truthful,' Sam says, more as a question, making sure he also is on the right track.

'You've got it. The impulse towards movement is a deeply profound thing. My Meisner teacher Scott would tell us that when you break it down, there are really two fundamental movement impulses in the animal kingdom we are working with here: the impulse to move towards, and the impulse to move away from. That's big stuff, because it comes with it all of the associations with deliberately moving away from something based on what you get from it, or moving towards something based on the signals you pick up. It's no wonder all of the social conventions that dampen down our primal responses, like politeness and the rituals around entering someone's house, come up in this exercise to 'aid' you. We aren't used to dealing with this impulse with the safety rail off, so to speak.'

Sam nods, it is his turn to go out. While he is counting Robert and I speak.

'The impulse to move towards and the impulse to move away?' he asks.

'Well, that's even pre-mammalian programming. It is in our hardware to move towards or away. That's everything: aversion, survival, fight, flight, reproduction, compassion. All human behaviour and motivation stems from these two fundamental impulses.'

'And that's what we're working on now?'

'I don't know if I would say we are working on it in a direct sense. We are after training authenticity that now can accommodate the impulse to move. That's the complete technique of living truthfully. We want you to have easy access to all of those impulses when we add given circumstances in the next session. Within that, when the impulse to move arises, you also will be dealing with the impulse to move towards or away from. Those can be, and often are, big moments.'

The knock comes. Robert gets up to answer it. As he does he says, 'That's interesting but frightening as well for me.'

'It is for most people,' I say.

Robert opens the door. He says to Sam, 'You knocked.'

Sam immediately enters the room and says, 'I knocked.' He goes straight to the chair and sits down.

Robert says, 'You sat down.' and then immediately sits down opposite to Sam. With them now both sitting, their repetition exercise suddenly gets more relaxed and free-flowing. I let them repeat for a bit.

'I sat down.'

'You sat down.'

'I sat down.'

'You're smiling.'

'I'm smiling.'

Etc.

'Alright, good, I'll stop you two there,' I say, 'Lots to talk about.'

Sam and Robert both shake their heads. 'We didn't get it yet.' Robert says disparagingly.

'Closer,' I say, and smile, 'much closer to getting it. In fact a lot of amazing things happened here. For starters, the knock wasn't inventive. Robert got up on impulse and when he opened the door his call took on the quality of his authentic response to the knock. That's when it got really interesting, though. Sam, you didn't even look at him and went straight for the chairs. Robert, you maybe repeated once standing and then followed suit and sat down. The before-and-after effect was massive! The second you were both sitting it was like the clouds parted, and you both went, 'Thank god, familiar territory! We're back in our chairs!"

Robert and Sam both laugh.

'Now, it's very true that the impulse to move includes the impulse to sit down, get back up, never sit down in the chairs, you name it. But I do get wary of knock at the door exercises that tend to go straight into the chairs and remain there, especially if in your experience it feels like a gigantic tension release when you are in the chairs. That release is relief at not having to deal with new impulses. Now if the sitting is on impulse and working with the demands of the moment, then there's no problem, but sometimes people go straight to the chairs because it is safe, familiar territory. So, moment of truth. I'll be happy either way, you've got my word: which was it?'

Both say it almost at the same time: 'Safe territory.'

'Right,' I respond, laughing with them. 'Safe territory is great. But it's not an optimal strategy when you are training yourself to live truthfully. Expressing authenticity is not an exercise in safety. I don't mean that you should ever be in literal danger, or fearing for your safety. That's not acceptable either, and we will talk about that more in the next session. But what makes living truthfully *feel* dangerous are the possibilities of what can arise within it. If you have two people behaving authentically towards one another, deeply observing each other's behaviour, and neither are afraid to call it and respond to it truthfully, then you've got the recipe for an experience with a lot, and I mean a lot, of open territory in it. You are both physically and mentally safe, obviously, but with possibility comes a sense of danger, and it is in that specific experience of danger that you are going to expand your range of living truthfully.'

They both nod. I make sure I can sense they are following me.

'Obviously, if at any point the exercise becomes too much, you can just stop it and I won't give you a hard time for it. But if you're in that balance of observe and respond, hungry for the experiential high you get in this work, then imposing the agenda to seek safety in the chairs is like seeking safety in politeness: it will leave you missing the opportunity to express the deeper impulses won organically by letting your partner and the moment determine the need for them. You'll leave the exercises feeling more hollow rather than fulfilled.'

'I see,' Robert says.

'Me too,' Sam says.

Robert goes out. Sam is in the chair.

'Doing okay?' I ask.

'Definitely,' Sam says., 'It is starting to make more sense now.'

'It's a big shift from the last session. You're taking a lot more ownership of the work and getting used to what it means to really let the moment call on your impulses.'

'It's a bit nerve-wracking.'

'A bit?! Whenever I had to work, even after years in this technique, I would always be worried!' The knock comes. Sam answers it.

'You knocked,' he says.

'I knocked.' Robert repeats.

'You knocked.'

'I knocked.'

'You knocked.'

Robert comes into the room. For ease, I've scripted the remainder of this repetition. Just as a reminder the repeats are shortened for time, but in an actual exercise these observations could be repeated for much longer:

Sam: You came in.
Robert: I came in.
Sam: You came in.
Robert: I came in.
    (A harsh tone comes into Robert's voice suddenly)
Robert: You're still!
Sam: I'm still.
Robert: You're still.
Sam: I'm still. (raises his hands to make peace)
Robert: You're still.
Sam: You're red.
Robert: I'm red.
Sam: You're red.
    (Sam moves towards Robert)
Robert: You came closer.
Sam: I came close.
Robert: You came close. (grits his teeth)

I stop them there. 'There you go!' I say. 'Well done, have a seat!'

They sit. I can see they are shaken but that they also seem to have enjoyed that much authenticity being allowed to be expressed.

'Robert: you came in, it seemed organically, and you didn't let yourself go to the safety of the chairs. Then, as you were working with Sam, this flush of what seemed to be real anger came up.'

'I saw he was so still. I don't know why but it bothered me.'

'That's really good. My Meisner teacher Scott would always tell me you know you are doing this work well when you have a hard time remembering what you did but can articulate, moment for moment, what the other person was doing. See what happens when you don't run for safety in this work, how something deep just came up for you? You don't seem like someone who gets angry often.'

'Not really,' Robert says. 'It's forbidden territory for me, to be honest.'

'Clearly not totally forbidden. You just went there and you seem okay.'

'I feel okay. A little shaky but good.'

'The beauty is that impulses in this work are not like impulses in other contexts. They lack any emotional baggage or the context of relationships. It's not like when you get angry at a friend, loved one, colleague, what have you: there's context that is dragging a past. The anger means so much more. Here you are just asked to respond organically to the moment. Rather than a punitive situation, you'll find it feels better to act on a truthful impulse. The moment demanded an authentic response and you expressed it.'

'But I couldn't do that with my colleagues or co-workers.'

'No, but those are different given circumstances, right? In the next session we are going to begin working on how you can remain truthful at that level when suddenly there is a specific situation, or context, that demands you to be a certain way. For now, however, there are no given circumstances, only the instruction to live truthfully with another person. It is better that you train the full range of authentic expression rather than try to predict how you will always need to respond in the future and limiting your range of truthfulness. Look, there might be a situation in which you do need to express rage, when the circumstance calls for it, and so to have spent your training denying certain impulses for their 'inappropriateness' won't help you. True, it's a rare circumstance, but do you see how the principle of training authenticity is much healthier and sane, and that to orient your leadership according to the circumstances you find yourself in, rather than your insistence on controlling the future, is best?'

'Yes.' Robert says.

'I am not saying go and get more pissed off in the next exercise or make it a habit. But it is equally a problem when working with authenticity to have something be totally 'off-limits'. We need to retrain in a healthy way your relationship to that impulse, for your leadership needs. Besides, I think there was only a small amount of that impulse you let out. And the next time the moment calls for it, it will be a little easier to give yourself the permission to express that response. A bit more might come out, but it will require less effort. That means you'll have a healthier way of recognising it and expressing yourself fully. Down the road we can worry about self-filtering. For now keep going.'

I turn to Sam.

'Sam, tell me if I'm wrong: at the end there did you want to give Robert a hug?'

'Definitely,' Sam replies.

'Why?'

'He just seemed so…I don't know, miserable, when he was getting angry. I just wanted to hug him and let him know it was okay.'

'Would that have been an okay thing for you to do?'

'I don't know. Maybe I should have asked first?'

'I think the rules around co-workers and colleagues are an important thing for you. That's good. At the same time this is a different situation and set of circumstances. Here you are two people engaged in training your abilities to live truthfully. You have an agreement that you are allowed to stop an exercise if it ever gets uncomfortable, and you know that you can adopt the principle of fuck polite into your technique. Remember there are no implications or greater consequences for impulses expressed in these exercises. Example: do you feel that because Robert expressed anger at you that your relationship is now suddenly damaged or compromised?'

'Not at all.'

'Of course. Because you know intuitively that what happens in the exercise stays in the exercise. It's personal because of the authenticity, not because you are being sent a coded message that Robert is mad at you in general. So if Robert is allowed to express truthful anger, then why can't you express the kindness that comes from hugging someone or comforting them?'

'I guess it's just something you're not supposed to do.'

'Something everyone is not supposed to do, or something you've told yourself not to do?'

Sam is silent.

'I'm not saying outside of this work go and violate any rules or policies you may have. But we are in a different context now. We are working on training your authenticity so that you can be a more powerful leader. The moment in this situation is letting you know what to express. That same sensitivity, along with the way to interpret given circumstances, is entirely portable outside of this work and a strong tool for your leadership. You've given Robert the permission that he can respond truthfully even if it is something like anger, so long as his impulses come from you. You're allowed the same, aren't you?'

'I guess so.'

'If Robert is uncomfortable he'll stop the exercise. It's that simple. The same goes for you, Sam. And it makes sense that now we are dealing with the bigger and deeper impulses that knock at the door facilitates. We've always talked about deep experiences but now we are starting to properly address these issues in a more refined and nuanced way. The exercise is there to walk the walk: we don't want you to be authentic in a limited context that isn't portable. We want you to be able to express yourself honestly within a wide range of possibilities and demands. That doesn't mean act on every impulse you have – you won't be able to – even after years of this work there will always be moments where you don't respond truthfully. But we want to keep widening your range of what we call border territory, the territory of observation or expression just on the fringes of where you are comfortable going. Each time you do that you will be more comfortable with giving yourself permission and that counts for a lot in the long term'.

'Understood,' Sam says, nodding, and taking it on board.

'I'm going to get you two working again in a moment, now that you're starting to let the values of the exercise into your bones. There's a lot of depth that repetition with the possibility for movement can bring up, and I want us to spend a bit more time there. First, though, I have a homework assignment for everybody for the next session, so let me give you two a break while we go into that. I would highly recommend you all write this down and ask any questions you need to.'

Homework: The Independent Activity

I wait for the participants to get out their pens and paper. For you reading this, this will also be your assignment for your next session, so take note here. I'm keeping this assignment in the format of the rest of this chapter so that I can ask and answer the questions that normally arise when I give out this assignment.

I wait until everyone is ready with their pens and paper before giving the instructions.

'I said this was your last training session in just living truthfully before we get into the given circumstances, and that is indeed where we are sailing in the next session. So for the next class I am going to ask you to bring what in Meisner training is called an *independent activity*. The independent activity is a physical activity that can be done and accomplished alone, by yourself. And it is a literal activity: there is nothing imaginary about the physical activity itself. Now, before you ask questions, there are four components to the activity that must be met for it to be considered a successful activity.

'For your activity you are going to set a time limit. Bring in an egg timer, a stopwatch, set an alarm on your phone, whatever you deem is best. You cannot have someone else watch the time for you, but if you forget your timer you can use someone else's. The first component to your independent activity is that, whatever you choose your activity to be, it must be specific and difficult to accomplish in the time you give yourself. Not impossible, but difficult. An example of that might be if you are gluing a broken mug together, and you think you can get that comfortably done in 7 minutes, then give yourself 5 1/2, just on that cusp of impossible and possible. Specific, as well, means that there is a very clear ending to what the activity will look like when complete. Drawing a picture, for example, isn't very specific unless it's trying to replicate an already existing image perfectly. Any questions on that first component?'

'Do we have to practice figuring out the time limit before we do it?' someone asks.

'No, you don't need to practice this activity. It's actually better if this is your first time doing this. Just base the time around your best guess for a tight time limit. Now, it is up to you, but generally the more specific the time you can give yourself the better. Don't just say 'about 10 minutes', think in minutes and even half or quarter minutes. For a first independent activity a good guideline is somewhere between 4 to 8 minutes but again it's arbitrary. Just be careful of time limits longer than 10 minutes, those can start to feel generalized and lose the specificity. Can anyone tell me what this tight time limit adds?'

'Pressure.'

'Very good. The other word I am after is urgency. There is urgency and pressure in this exercise that comes from the time limit. That then brings me to your second component. Your activity must be intricate, or fiddly: it involves a great deal of tactile engagement. LEGOs or those mini puzzle blocks are excellent examples. The pieces are small and intricate, they have to go together just right or the whole thing doesn't work.'

'What about puzzles?'

'Puzzles are great. The smaller the pieces the better. Just be careful you don't pick one with so many pieces that you don't know how long it will take and can't accomplish it in a reasonable specific time. The intricacy will give you a good meter for a time limit. Clear so far?'

'So we bring in an activity and complete it?' someone asks.

'I don't know if you will complete it,' I say sincerely. 'But you will attempt to and have reasons to. Everyone clear so far?'

I can see that when the participants nod they seem to be grasping the basics but aren't sure what the actual exercise might look like. That is okay for right now, so I continue.

'Now, those are the criteria for the activity itself. You've heard some examples already. Doing a puzzle, or LEGOs. Gluing a broken mug, just please no glass since I don't want anyone to get cut. Get creative, but the important thing is that the activity itself is real and there is no element of imagination that goes into the activity itself. You are not, for example, going to pantomime any element of it. The activity itself must be entirely literal and real. This is not an improvisation. Around the activity, however, you are going to create two imaginary given circumstances, and these are going to throw fuel on your fire for accomplishing the activity.

The first circumstance is that there is a reason this activity must be done now, and not later. This reason is not autobiographical but it is meaningful to you. As an example: the torn shirt you bring in must be sewn in 6 minutes because then you've got to put it on and leave for that dream job interview that could solve the issue of you needing money to pay for your partner's surgery. Another example: the guitar has to be fully strung and tuned in 4 minutes because if you don't start recording you won't be able to send your song to your estranged sister you've been dying to reconcile with for years in time for her birthday party. Whatever it is there is an imaginary but meaningful reason it has to be done now. With me so far?'

'And this part is completely made up?'

'Maybe not completely, since the meaningful part of it is tied to your life. If you don't have a partner, or an estranged sister, then using them in your reasons may not help. But yes, you want this to be a fantasy about something that could happen, not something that has happened or is happening right now. You're not living out your past or present reality. The final component, the element that will bring this all together is this: you've established that there is a reason this has to be done now. Now you will add in that there is a meaningful consequences to not having this done in time.'

'Like a bad consequence?'

'Only in the sense that there is a reason you want to get this done now. You're under a time pressure, and so it wouldn't be great if you didn't get it done. Having said that, consequences or the activities in general don't need to have a specific emotional tone or anything, they don't need to be sad, angry, or any emotional hue. There can be activities where you are fervently doing something and the consequence to not getting it done might be you miss on that rare opportunity to bring yourself and somebody special some joy. All four of these elements, though, need to be working in harmony together. If there isn't enough intricacy then the time limit isn't as vital, if the time limit isn't close or plausible then it will be impossible from the get go and you will lose urgency. If the consequence doesn't hit in your gut deep enough then the reason for it having to be done now also won't be too strong. Everything works together. Make sense?'

'So we bring the activity and then . . .?'

'Let's cross that bridge when we get there. For now, just bring in an activity that when you do it will have those meaningful circumstances alive within you. Because this is going to be our official entry now into the given circumstances. And in the next session we are going to take this principle of the impulse to move and turn it up to a whole new level.'

Summary

The journey to living truthfully has introduced many concepts: investing in the reality of doing. Public solitude. The idea that what happens to you does not depend on you but rather on what is being done to you. The moment. Working moment by moment. Letting the chaos of the moment make its demands upon you. These are all incredibly deep, essential values for a leader to train in their technique. Now, however, we tie it all together by introducing the most essential impulse in the living truthfully canon: the impulse to move. It is an impulse so important, with so many deep implications for human behaviour and the meanings attached to it, that it has its own exercise, structured in a way that removes many of the individual social barriers that might narrow your range of living truthfully. By exposing them not through analysis or questioning but organically and in practice, you are able to identify and move beyond those barriers while still adhering to all of the values instilled in earlier sessions.

At the end of knock at the door, you will have the complete technique for living truthfully, coupled with a rich understanding of the immense range of possible expressions of your authenticity. It is this sense of possibility, combined with a powerful technique, that sets you up in a prime way to now move into your first work on the given set of circumstances.

Tips for You and Your Coach

I am going to give the feedback tips in reverse here, starting with the homework. For the homework, make sure you leave enough time for people to ask lots of questions about the activity and ensure sure they are clear on it. Don't just email the instructions before the next session; trust me, you will always end up with more technical errors that could have been fixed if you just introduced it and let people ask questions. For any result-oriented questions, like someone asking if it is required that they complete an activity in class, be honest and say you don't know if they will actually complete their task. But they have reasons to and will attempt to. From there it's in the hands of the moment.

This version of knock at the door is for me the most challenging exercise to teach. I don't struggle with it in terms of knowing what to do, but it has elements that can be difficult for any teacher to work with. As such, rather than giving you some brief tips, I need to delve much more deeply than other chapters into the nature of successful feedback for this particular exercise.

Most Meisner teachers make the knock at the door an incredibly easy exercise: they tell one person to knock, they tell the other to answer, and then the real value of the work begins when the door is open. That, however, glosses over the deeper value within the exercise, which is becoming sensitive to what the moment demands in relation to movement. To say that I know every time the door will be answered would be a false statement. In my teaching of this work in the past and in training, there were a few rare times when the door would not be answered or when the person would not knock. Those times were invaluable for the experiential lessons of how uncertainty and chaos manifest organically in the moment. To simply make a gigantic prescription and in a sense create a staged exercise to get at truthfulness would be entirely counterproductive. To get the real value of the exercise as a coach, you have to commit to make the journey with your students: maybe the door will get answered, maybe the knock will come, but for both there is a possibility that maybe it will not happen. You don't know and most importantly, they don't know.

That key value of dealing with things as they come, rather than what you insist must happen, will never come across if you make your life easier but sabotage the deeper values in this technique. Most Meisner teachers do not understand this invaluable distinction. The difference here is that the easy route will stunt the growth, portability, and ownership over the technique, but the deep journey will encourage it to flourish. Accept that though instructions are given, nobody knows if the knock will come or the door will be answered. That is in the hands of the moment.

The exercise is difficult for me because for most students there is suffering in the beginning. Most participants will feel suddenly exposed, like you are constantly tricking them or pulling the rug out from under them. They will get frustrated, begging me to just tell them what I want. This is not easy for me as I want to alleviate their pain and frustration. It is also not easy for other coaches who tend to get impatient. As a coach you have to remember it is not about the result you want to see but about working with a client on the challenges they are facing in that moment when they arise. When things like politeness or social conditioning arise, you don't need to get frustrated. You are meeting them where they are and what they need to work on, rather than insisting they arrive faster at the problems you want them to have.

This is why I highly recommend trying to make conversation with the person in the chair between the knocks. It keeps the emotional temperature as low as possible. This is not because you are coddling your clients. It is because when people get too frustrated they shut off and insist that they be the ones to control the experience, taking themselves to the opposite ends of the values of this work. The conversation can be meaningful as well: you don't have to just try to talk about weather or movies. If you see them struggling don't be afraid to ask how they are doing. If they are pissed off with you, let them talk about that and welcome it; all feelings of the participants arising from this exercise are valid. You might also get some who are open and comfortable with their frustrations in the work, recognising it as part of a learning experience. Again, you are walking with them on this path.

One brief note about any conversation or feedback in this work, however, is to be mindful not to delve into the pasts of people. Meisner teachers love to ask people about the roots of their social blocks and conditioning; you don't need to. You will see the challenges of social conditioning arise and can address those without needing to delve into the past of the person. No Meisner teacher with rare exception is a qualified therapist, and the ones who are qualified therapists will not mix therapy in with training. If participants begin to delve into stories about childhood or past events, just politely steer them back to the present moment and make sure they know you want to respect the professional coach–client relationship and not get too drawn into details about their past. They aren't relevant to dealing with the challenges of the present moment and you want to safeguard their privacy. This is true of all exercises in this work but especially here.

Feedback, likewise, should be tailored to this safeguarding. Be careful not to make students feel you are just nitpicking, which you will find is an especially easy trap to fall into with this exercise. This is why I use the pedagogic tool of recap in this exercise. I take them through my perception of the experience and ask them if I have gotten it right. If they say no, then I ask them to walk me through what they feel happened and I might adjust my feedback accordingly. Since over time I have become more skilled at this work, I don't hear that as often now so it does get easier to teach this exercise in some senses. Regardless, the purposes of recapping maintains its values: we can visit a moment of behaviour, the impulse missed, politeness, whatever is the relevant point of feedback, and clients know I am with them every step of the way, including the point of discovering the possible challenge to their growth.

Again, it is not about coddling. If people feel you are nitpicking, then they shut off. In their minds they will have figured 'the game' out that they have been suspecting you were playing all along in this exercise, which is withholding secret outcomes. There is no game, there is only what happens now in the present moment, and that is what you are guiding them to discovering for themselves. You are walking the walk as a coach, offering a portable technique, so articulating the steps you are taking with them is a valuable piece of that puzzle.

The only remaining feedback tip I can give is to make sure that the first pair working, if there will be more than one pair working, spend enough time in the exercise to get the values and to get to the point where they are actually being able to have a repetition exercise. That means they might be in the exercise three or four times longer than normal repetition; I have seen first pairs stay in knock at the door for upwards of 45 minutes or an hour even. This, of course, does not apply to the second pair since the osmosis effect of the work is that they have learned from the challenges encountered by the first pair to work. The first pair will most likely have a deep, meaningful experience in the exercise; the second pair and then on will enter the work at a deeper level of challenge by watching their colleagues go through that. If you see the first pair, however, entering burnout or shutting down, circulate them out and make sure they work again at the end of the session to reap in practice the benefits of going through this journey.

Go with your clients through the journey that is knock at the door. Be honest as a coach, always, but be patient and compassionate. This is deep water for most people, deeper than they could have known they were signing on for. Keep a sense of humour and warmth. It might sound odd that I am pointing up these virtues that are present in all sessions but in this exercise, more than ever before, they will be a tool and an ally to you. Stay present.

THE GIVEN CIRCUMSTANCES

Chapter 11

Impossibility by Design

New Horizons

The journey of developing a technique for living truthfully has been a long one. Every step and exercise was carefully constructed so as to ensure that none of the values of this work were ever compromised and that a clear, linear journey stretching all the way from its foundations to right now could be traced. It is this clarity and transparency, coupled with deep investigations into the nature of concepts such as 'the moment' as well as the learning process of a developing leader in this work, that has created your strong technique. You've come a long way from day one where counting bricks raised challenges and questions for your leadership abilities. Let's track some of these markers of progress. Now you know:

- How to invest in the reality of doing by placing your attention fully on another human being.
- How to use public solitude to handle audience pressure, which is by engaging fully with the relevant variables (up to now your partner) and getting your attention off of yourself.
- How to use fuck polite as a powerful strategy for allowing authentic observations and responses into interpersonal interactions.
- What to do if you find yourself no longer in the moment, if your attention has gone from the other person back onto yourself.
- What meaningful versus irrelevant observations are.
- How to deeply read a human being and respond authentically.
- What your own border territory feels like and how to address it.
- What to expect as helpful versus unhelpful feedback and behaviour from a coach.
- What the impulse to move versus the idea of movement is like, even though you are still in the earliest stages of this.

Those are powerhouse qualities for a leader. This is what I mean when I refer to the technical strength that you are going to import into a given set of circumstances.

Today you will be working on Meisner's independent activity. It is the complete experience for living truthfully under a given set of circumstances in an exercise. After the independent activity, we take this technique into scripted text and scenario analysis. This is not to say that in just one exercise you will suddenly have an answer for every scenario and situation you encounter. Independent activities comprise a sizeable majority of almost any Meisner training regimen. They are meant to be done not only once but many times. This is true of all the exercises in this technique, but it holds no greater relevance than here. This is because what the independent activity offers you is the chance to see first-hand, from the inside, just how dramatically your authentic responses are filtered by meaningful circumstances. What comes up in these experiences will surprise you, mostly because you will surprise yourself. It is the ultimate training ground for the sensitivity to circumstances we have been alluding to for the duration of this training.

Through engaging in this exercise you will first-hand begin to viscerally understand the mechanisms by which scenario and environment will alter your own authenticity. You'll discover that it is possible to be truthful even when the constraints of a given set of circumstances are introduced. This exercise has the additional immense benefit of honing your sensitivity to subtle variables in your environment that can cause things to change on a dime. We have been talking the talk for a long time about this concept of living truthfully under a given set of circumstances. Now it is time to put it into practice and begin training your sensitivity to circumstances.

Authenticity is a challenge for anyone in this work at any level. Our own personal boundaries, what my Meisner teacher Scott calls border territory, will come up from the first exercise and remain there until the final session. There is no exercise in this entire technique that will bring you closer to your border territory than the independent activity. This is not happenstance but is built into the very design of the exercise. It takes you to the fringe of the behaviours you are, and are not, comfortable expressing authentically. You will find this is because so many moments within the independent activity are charged and packed to the brim. This doesn't mean that it asks you to be 'big' in terms of your expressions. The demands of the moment might ask for a large expression of behaviour or a subtle one, or a deep response, but what it does mean is every moment when the exercise is done properly is filled with meaning. Consequently every moment will provide a challenge to your authenticity that is richly soaked up by your technique and awareness. We are not cresting on the shallow waves of our work: we are taking the boat we have built and sailing into the deepest waters out there.

The Meaningful Ingredient

In cooking, salt is often likened to a magnifying glass. The right concentration of salt in any dish serves to magnify its other components, showing how masterful ingredients and flavours are working in harmony. Used in the right amounts, salt showcases everything on offer in a good dish and gives us the opportunity to experience it much more vividly. We also have a magnifying glass of sorts for the values within this work. The salt in the independent activity, the thing that brings out everything of value in the exercise and puts on full display your technique of living truthfully, is pressure. Not just any pressure either but a very specific type. Before we talk about why pressure is so valuable, let's investigate exactly the kind of pressure I am referring to and see if understanding it in relation to our training gets us closer to its value.

Not all pressure is created equal. It is very easy for people to put themselves into a general state of agitation that feels like pressure. I could send you up in front of the group and ask you to 'act' stressed or anxious. You might even find after a while you genuinely begin to feel those states. There's a problem with this approach, however. In being so non-specific, you create a type of anxiety that on some level you know is fabricated and false. It may have the surface flavour of 'real' but in fact is extremely fascicle and inauthentic. A better question to ask might be whether it is possible to create an authentic pressure for you, the kind that squeezes you and floods you with urgency. What we are looking for in the pressure that is valuable to your training is individual specificity or, as my Meisner teacher Larry Silverberg refers to it, extremely meaningful. If we can find organic ways to access it, we also want to ask can we utilise it while still keeping within our values that what happens to you does not depend on you but rather your partner and now the circumstances outside of you?

These questions show that the pressure in the independent activity comes from a real and very meaningful place alongside working with your partner. You'll recall in the previous chapter I assigned some homework for this session. This is because the independent activity is of little value to you if created on the spot. You want to give yourself time to delve deeply into the components of the exercise beforehand. This already reveals an aspect that will become much more important as we progress: the independent activity is not an improvisation exercise. In this session we'll talk more about improvisation for leadership, but for now what is important to flag up is that time spent in reflection on the activity is of real value. We like surprises in this work, and thinking deeply has never been part and parcel to this training. This is one exception where your consideration will go the distance. There are plenty of variables that will surprise you along the way.

Here's a recap of the four criteria you are asked to meet regarding your activity. Some components regarding the activity will be covered here, but if you are still unsure about the basics, feel free to look at the final section of the previous chapter just prior to the Summary section for some more detailed examples.

- the activity must be intricate or fiddly and must have a very specific outcome for when it is done
- it must be possible to just barely complete within the time limit you set for yourself
- there is an extremely meaningful reason it must be done now and not later
- there is an extremely meaningful consequence to it succeeding or failing

The independent activity is filled with meaningful pressure unique to you. When an activity is going well, that meaningful pressure feels extremely real. There are some components of realness to aid this pressure. The time limit and tactile demands of the activity alone are going to infuse it with enough intense reality that, from the moment your timer begins, you are going to need to stay sharp to get your activity done. That is, of course, if you have set your time limit carefully: just barely enough to get it done. Not too little so that you know it is impossible or too much to be leisurely. Just enough that if you hustle and everything goes perfectly, you'll get it done in time. Likewise, when an activity is going well the circumstances – in effect the scenario – you've created around the activity are going to flood the exercise with meaningful pressure. When the circumstances are really powerful, it will feel like tossing gasoline onto a burning propane tank.

I keep using phrases like 'when the activity goes well'. What do I mean by that? Just as with all our work, the right metric to be applied is technical strength. When all four of the components are strong, then the exercise and the experience within it will be strong. The technical strength or weakness in an activity will be measured by the amount of meaningful pressure it puts on you to complete your activity. If you have a difficult-to-complete activity that must be done for meaningful reasons in a very limited time span, with a powerful consequence attached to either success or failure, then you have an activity going very well. It is important for me to state, however, that you do not need to worry about getting this 'perfectly' on the first go-round. Or any go-round. Independent activities are meant to be done often, not just one time. They are the complete meal of the Meisner training and so figuring out these components in practice is part of the training.

Through multiple experiences in this exercise you begin to discover sources of meaning for yourself and how to generate pressure to use them for your leadership training.

This brings us to the value of pressure within this work. Meaningful pressure brings out an array of truthful responses, some of which you might find extreme or uncomfortable. Your border territory. In the previous session you may recall that I said more and more these exercises will take on individual hues. Border territory and extreme personal meaning is the defining variable of why this happens. You will all be doing the same exercise, but your border territory is going to almost always be entirely different from anyone else you might work with. As a result the truthful impulses you act, and do not act on, will be unique not only to you but your experience in the moment with your partner.

Inner Fire

What much of all this means is something you are about to discover in practice. Before we begin, however, I am introducing something new, something that is going to ignite this exercise and turn the temperature up even further. It is a variation on Meisner's technique of preparation, and it is also what you will all be working with today. The one note I am going to make is that this version of preparation is highly modified from the version used with actors, so if you go and study this work in workshops for actors, which still has great benefit in my view, you might find preparation to be slightly or radically different than the version we are working with today. As far as which is more right than the other, this is obviously the kind I think is best for non-actors with other goals. If you are interested in preparation beyond this book, then take as many approaches as you can and keep what works for you but especially look into the work of Larry Silverberg, who was my Meisner teacher and is unparalleled in his work on the values of meaning and fusing your authenticity with your technique.

Much of this approach to preparation comes from what I learned at the Impulse Company, including some of the verbiage. In the high-level training offered there, preparation has one function: to put a fire into you before you walk into a room. By 'fire', we mean a heightened state of awareness, for you to be full of a sensation that has energetic and dynamic aliveness. You already know what this energy feels like if before you walked into a presentation, negotiation, speech, or any other event where you had to 'deliver' and be observed, and you have felt downright awful. The overwhelming anxiety and all of the physical sensations that accompany it has the same level of intensity that we are after in preparation.

Before you get concerned, let me clarify something: the goal is not to make you feel awful or like a nervous wreck. Rather we want to work with a very real variable. Though so many approaches to mindfulness and relaxation are about reducing anxiety, the anxiety never goes away. Even after decades, speakers and actors find themselves still getting anxious before going in front of others. It is a potent energy that is designed to sound the alarm bells and protect you. Anxiety with all its implications does not seem to serve you very well. Aaron Beck, the founder of cognitive therapy, once said it doesn't really help anyone at all. Still, it is a huge reserve of energy. Rather than a self-tormenting cycle of panicked thoughts and tight stomachs, preparation is the means by which you take that energy and come into a room full of something alive and energetic, using it as a force that serves rather than hinders you.

The starting criteria for preparation is that it is for the person outside of the room and not the one inside. That already gives you a sense of the exercise: in the independent activity, one person begins outside of the room and the other inside of it. Sound familiar? If you're thinking the knock at the door you are correct, as the independent activity incorporates the knock at the door. The person inside is doing their activity while the person outside waits an amount of time and then knocks. Instead of just counting, however, the person outside the door is now doing a preparation, the specifics of which will be covered shortly. Everyone in these sessions has two turns: once doing their activity, and then another later on working on preparation. It is very important here that you not base your expectations for the independent activity session on what happened in the knock at the door exercise in the previous chapter. The basic premise is the same: there will be a knock at the door and that begins a repetition exercise. The presence of a preparation and an activity with given circumstances, however, is going to put the exercise into a completely different dimension.

You don't need to do a preparation if you are the one doing the activity. The circumstances, if they are meaningful and you have given them enough consideration, will be generating the same high-octane energy as a preparation. Consider that all of the charged work you have seen people do in repetitions, or three moment exercises, has been without any preparation whatsoever. The power that comes from putting your attention on your partner and letting them take you on the journey has so far been enough. Preparation only serves to bring the person knocking into the room, in the deeper and so capitalized sense of the word Ready.

That criteria leads to the most important point I can make about preparation: preparation does not determine what is going to happen once you go into the room. Its job is just to get you through the door, full and alive. Once you get into the room, put your attention immediately on something else and start working off of that. I use the phrase 'something else' because today especially might incorporate other elements of relevance than just your partner. If, for example, you walk into the room, see your partner is attempting to mix a baking recipe, and there is spilled flour and broken eggs everywhere, depending on the moment, that might command just as much attention.

Regardless, whatever happens to the preparation then is entirely up to the moment. The preparation might continue to inform your responses. It might die immediately, or it might wax or wane. It is all entirely up to the moment. Preparation is not about trying to put yourself into a certain mode for success, it is just about generating a level of kinetic fuel that gets you into the room and ready to live truthfully under a given set of circumstances.

Exercise: Preparation

Before we put all this into practice, let's cover specifically the kinds of preparation on offer to you. There are two types of preparation: physical and non-physical. Neither is better than the other, but the one that gets you the most charged is the optimal one. If you are trying to work with a preparation and the kind you are trying doesn't seem to help, then change course and try something new. These are tools to serve you, and so the specifics of which one will have the most impact on you will depend entirely on your personal preferences and temperament

Physical preparations are just as they sound: they are purely physical in nature. Run up and down the hallway. Do some push-ups. Or jumping jacks. Go right up until the point of exhaustion, when you are pushed to the edge of your personal physical limit. The great ballet dancer Nureyev would work out until he was exhausted before a performance so that, he would say, have 'nothing to hold onto.' Physical preparations are excellent. They always work and are rooted in reality and so skirt the risk entirely of your attention becoming trapped on yourself. Whenever you are in doubt about a preparation, do a physical one, you will always reap the benefits from it.

Although physical preparations are excellent and can lead to deep and surprising places, rich territory lies in the non-physical ones. Unlike with the hierarchy of calls, where the ones at the top are the rarest, the hierarchy of preparations is ranked in order of how effective and powerful they tend to be, starting at the bottom with:

memory
imagination
fantasy
spin

Memory is the first and it is considered by some, myself included, to be the weakest of them all. Memories serve largely functional purposes, adding meaning and credibility to ourselves in the present. Likewise, memories are always present and so seem to provide easily accessible material. The risk people run with memory is in trying to recapture the emotional content of it. Just because that funeral of your loved one broke your heart and left you sobbing in grief for years does not mean the memory of it will do that when you try to use it to generate a high-level of dynamic energy. Sometimes we heal and the pain lessens dramatically. Likewise, joyful memories can sour when circumstances change. Memory, due to its time-bound nature of being in the past, can trap you into attempting to recreate what is now no longer natural to your mind. This could inspire a level of guilt or shame, leaving you thinking, 'Well, I felt that way back then, why don't I feel that way now? What is wrong with me?' Nothing is wrong with you if this happens. It is the nature of memory that it changes as we do.

To make the best use of a memory, the secret ingredient is detail. When you pick the memory you want to use for a preparation, don't focus on how you felt. Try to re-experience it sensorily in as much detail as possible. If, for example, your memory happened at a restaurant, imagine the feel of the linens. The grooves of wood on the chairs. Is the chair warm or cold? What does the fabric of the seat under you feel like? Hear the clinking of the glasses, see the condensation and rolling drops down the crystal as the ice begins to melt. What do you smell like in the memory? A particular fragrance, maybe, or have you got an attack of body odour?

Engage with your memory as sensorily as possible. Lose yourself in trying to remember the details and experiencing them. If the memory is good material, it will begin to fill you with that aliveness, and you will know it is a strong preparation. Again, remember not to judge the emotional nature of the preparation by your expectations of the past. If the memory is a joyous one and your preparation leaves you in pain, then don't begin to judge it. If the memory is a dark one but you feel joyous and filled with light, then that is also fair game. You are not reaching for the appropriate but rather engaging with something and letting whatever comes up be fair game. The stronger the engagement and meaning, the more full you will become from it.

Imagination is the next step up in the non-physical preparation hierarchy It is preferable to memory because the possibilities within it are not constrained by any one reality or sequence of events. For people who have active imaginations, the imagination preparation can be an excellent one, and the preparation is just that: you engage in a completely fictitious, imaginative scenario. You are the wizard or detective in your favourite novel, re-enacting a scene from the book or film, or using your imagination to do something in a purely imaginative world. Again, engagement with as many specific details as possible maximises the potential of the preparation to take hold. Give yourself a scenario of sorts. Try to sensorily connect with as many of the small nuances and elements as you can. For very visual people, imagination can create a powerful preparation.

Many of us, however, engaging with the non-physical preparations, tend to find optimal success in the next level up from imagination. Markedly more potent than either imagination or memory is fantasy. What makes fantasy so unique and viscerally compelling? Fantasy, by nature, fuses the world we live in with the possibilities we envision for our brightest, best, and richest futures. Our fantasies are powerful in that they tend to engage all of our senses quite naturally. It is quite easy to feel, when in the throes of a fantasy, the texture of something, how it will taste on your tongue, the scents, sights, and sounds of the experience. Since fantasy appeals to our desires it tends to engage us quite powerfully.

When I say that fantasy appeals to our desires, I do not specifically mean fantasies where something you want occurs. The opposite is equally true: fantasising about something happening that you wish to avoid also appeals to our primal desire to avoid catastrophe and pain. Plausibility is key here to the fantasy's success, taking a very real element of your life and infusing it with something fictional that, if it happened, would be extremely powerful and meaningful. Gaining that plausibility comes from using as many parts of your reality as you can incorporate. Take, for example, the fantasy of seeing someone important. Let's say, from what could be a variety of meaningful reasons, you no longer have contact with them. Already we've got some powerful material. It could be a loved one you lost, a close business associate or best friend you fell out with, a once trusted source now turned enemy. The possibilities are well-nigh endless, but choose in this case a person who deeply means something to you.

Consider now what would you do if you were given this one chance to see them again, to be close to where you could hear the sound of their voice or even touch them. Such an encounter could have so many implications: joyful, dark, painful, or otherwise. Is there, say, a favourite place you two might go? In your fantasy, go there together. Say the things you did not say before. Relive old details and experience new ones so there is a constant blending of memory and imagination. You'll find that, as consistently good and reliable as physical preparations are, a well-done fantasy preparation takes things to an entirely new level of depth and dynamic energy. It gets you worked up like few things will.

It is important with all non-physical preparations, but especially with fantasies, to stay open. Don't go seeking emotional content from a non-physical preparation. This is only going to leave you trying to force things, winding up ultimately unsatisfied. Look instead for meaning. In the places where you feel that sense in your core that you are somewhere important, stay and explore. Meaning is what gives you the best preparations, but where meaning takes you and how it makes you feel is often a surprise to us. This is good. Sometimes when introducing preparations, clients get worried. They won't want to try to pump themselves up and end up feeling angry or sad. This is the wrong metric to be concerned about. For now, don't worry about coming in if you feel sad. You aren't training for a specific meeting or pitch. You are exploring what it means to get in touch with your points of meaning and use that to generate a heightened state of aliveness. We've spent the whole training encouraging you not to be result-oriented by showing that there are far better and more efficient options than trying to dominate and exert control over a situation. Your preparations are the same. If they take you somewhere that surprises you, even better. Don't worry about the outcome; focus on developing the process that can generate such a powerful outcome.

The final type of mental preparation, and arguably even more powerful than fantasy, is what my Meisner teacher Scott would call 'spin.' Spin is best defined in this way: spin is a very specific type of cognitive process where you consciously engage with an unresolved issue in your life. Don't worry, this isn't a Freudian exploration of your deepest pains. There are often unresolved things happening in the present that we can engage with. An example might be That One phone call you've been needing to make but have been putting off, or That One conversation that needs to be had but you keep avoiding it. Or is there something going on, say in the world, that gets to you but you are powerless to solve by yourself? Engage with it. Imagine how it will go, get into all the details and move towards the things it brings up for you. The more churned up you get about it the better.

Spin is particularly powerful because of all the non-physical preparations it is the one that is most easily accessible on offer. We sometimes have to think and explore for meaningful memories, as our relationship to certain memories can change. Imagination demands invention and some inventions come up as less powerful than we thought they might. Fantasy asks for openness and a willingness to be seduced by its possibilities, and some days we are not that open. There is rarely a day, however, where there is not some one specific thing you don't want to deal with and may have been putting off. Getting into that is often quick, and usually the meaning is fresh, since there are immediate reasons you put it off but still let it get to you. Exploring our areas of avoidance often yields rich veins of deep meaning. Spin is a potent and efficient form of preparation and it is why it sits at the top of the preparation hierarchy.

In the same way that physical preparations have a clearer marker of when they are at full-burn, non-physical ones give an indicator as well. As you engage with the preparation, when you are at the point of being almost overwhelmed – or have even crossed over into being overwhelmed by the preparation – that is when you release it into the knock. In either case, physical or non-physical, the point of when you feel you couldn't go farther with your preparation is the moment to knock. Generally this translates into roughly two to five minutes, though it can definitely be longer or shorter depending on the individual and the preparation they are working with.

Exercise: Independent Activity

The important value here is to stay open. Don't make any assumptions about what is going to happen. We don't know that the knock will come, even if you partner has the instruction to knock. We don't know that the door will be opened. And we don't know that the activity is going to be completed. We know that when the circumstances are working, you have very compelling reasons to complete your activity, but that doesn't mean it will be completed. This reality will increase the pressure within the exercise.

For this session, I'm going to build off the previous session by using an extended case example. More and more as these exercises progress, it becomes increasingly difficult to use the abstract 'you and your partner', and so some names and faces help make the feedback and example more concrete. Unlike the previous chapter, which was entirely a scripted scenario, these examples will be balanced by broader discussions like in the earlier chapters. For now, however, let's see how Tony and Laura do. As before, imagine yourself a participant in this group session and that today you have chosen to see a few examples before you work.

Tony is the first to ask to do his activity. Laura has also brought an activity but for now she will be working on preparation. Likewise, later on Tony will do a preparation also when he is outside the door for somebody else. Tony asks if he needs to tell me and the group anything about his activity before he begins. I tell him no, that he can just start. He opens up his plastic bag and from the box we see he is doing a LEGOs set. The room is also set up slightly differently for the independent activity. There is a table with a chair for the person doing the activity. There is no second chair.

'Do I start when the pieces are out or include pulling them out of the box in my time limit?' Tony asks. His question is one many people have with activities which is when does the activity actually start? Some things, for example, come pre-wrapped, do you include the time it takes to get them out into the activity's time limit? The answer is to look at the circumstances you've created. In Tony's case I don't know his circumstances but if, for example, in the scenario he has created the LEGOs pieces belong to someone he knows and were already out of the box then his set up will include taking them out of the box and making sure they are all out before starting his time limit. If, on the other hand, in Tony's circumstances he has just come home with this LEGOs set, or it has been sitting in the box, and suddenly he needs to complete them right now for whatever reason he has created, then that will be included in the time. Tony tells me then he will include opening the box in the time limit he has allotted himself.

Once Laura goes out, I let him know he can begin. As soon as I say begin he sets the timer and is off with a vicious speed. He hastily tears open the box and pulls the bag out. His hands are shaking, and without realising it he is muttering under his breath, 'Come on, come on'. Already there is physical evidence that the activity is working fairly well. His body is taking on the meaning in his circumstances. The urgency and pressure from the time limit are working well.

He works with a fury, assembling pieces as best he can, and gets about three minutes in when there is a loud, banging knock. Tony does not get up to answer it. He says nothing. The knock comes again. 'Go away!' he yells. The door flies open and Laura comes in. I can see her face is red and her hands are clenched. Clearly her preparation is alive and well.

'You told me to go away,' she says.

'I told you to go away.'

'You told me to go away!'

They continue repeating for a few moments. Tony finds it harder to concentrate now with the repetition and he drops a piece on the floor. 'Fuck!' he screams before he knows it and tries to find it. Laura stands with her arms crossed, looking at him.

'You said fuck.'

'I said fuck.'

'You said fuck.'

'I said fuck.'

Tony finds the piece and goes back to the activity, but he suddenly goes silent. Laura stands there.

'You're quiet.' she says.

There is no response. I can see she doesn't know what to do.

'You aren't saying anything.' she says.

He still doesn't repeat. The timer goes off and Tony lets out a huge sigh. He has not finished his LEGOs set. He then looks at me.

'What?' I say.

'Well, isn't the exercise over?' he asks, still clearly upset.

At this point I do end the exercise since there is plenty of good material to go into about what happened and the technical strengths and weaknesses present within this experience. Here we can together analyse the components of the exercise that would be addressed in feedback.

The Four Criteria

Since independent activities are usually quite heated events it is good to have a brief cool-down period, especially for the person who has been working on the activity, although powerful preparations can certainly leave someone feeling shaken. The best place to start is by evaluating the four components of the exercise and talking about whether or not they worked. It is also now my opportunity to ask and give feedback on the exercise in a more structural way before getting into the deeper topics.

First, the physical elements of the activity. Let me ask you, the reader, do you think the activity physically intricate? He chose to do a LEGOs set. Consider that LEGOs demand a very specific construction to be considered successful and the pieces from Tony's set are small enough that he really had to engage with being precise. There's another piece of evidence that can help us answer this. Remember that when Tony dropped a piece it took him some time to look for it. Tony's behaviour tells us the piece was both small and essential. I don't know about you but I would answer yes, there was certainly a strong level of intricacy in the exercise as well as a clearly defined outcome for when the activity would be complete.

Now we go onto the second criterion: do you think this was difficult to complete in the time he gave himself? There might be some evidence but we may have to ask Tony for input on this. Let's say I ask Tony in feedback how long he allotted and he tells me five minutes. I ask him if on reflection this was a strong time or can that Lego's set not be accomplished in five minutes even under the best circumstances? The timer went off and he still had a ways to go. He thinks about it. Eventually he says no, it is not possible. Had he given himself another minute and a half it would have tightened the plausibility of its completion up considerably.

This gives us some valuable information. We could say that because he failed to finish it, it was difficult to complete in the time he gave himself. There is a difference, however, between difficult and impossible. If I tried to run a mile in one minute it certainly would be difficult in the time I gave myself, considering that impossible things are generally difficult. Difficult is where we want the activity to be, not impossible to accomplish in the allotted time limit. By asking Tony for his input, since he was the one inside of the experience, we are able to gather that this aspect could have been improved with more time. Overall, our analysis of these two components is that this was a strong activity choice and with a little more time allotted would have been even more effective.

We are only, however, halfway through determining whether this was a successful activity or not. Now onto the criteria for the circumstances. Here, however, we have to be very careful. We have gone this entire training program without needing a single personal detail about one another and have done just fine. At the same time, evaluating someone's given circumstances for an activity seems challenging without any information from them. Let's see if we can find a balance between information and what we can glean from the exercise we've just seen.

Let's explore our third requirement for the exercise: did it seem to you like there was a reason it had to be done now and not later? It seems like we could answer this from the reason itself. To get that, however, we would either have to speculate or invade Tony's privacy to ask about the reason itself. Is there a better option in front of us that can help us determine an answer without vague guesses or crossing boundaries? What about Tony's behaviour? Consider first the blatant urgency of his actions. Shaking hands, unconscious mutterings to himself, not answering the door at first and then choosing to remain silent so he could focus on the activity. The uncontrolled swearing outburst. Rather than descending too deeply into our own opinions about the reason itself, we can treat his behaviours as evidence. Do these behaviours suggest evidence of something needing to be done right now and not even ten minutes later? Personally I would say it is clearly a yes. The answer lies in his behaviours.

Basing our assessments of an activity's technical strength on an individual's behaviours gives us a clean metric by which to measure according to our values. You don't want the quality of your work to be judged by basic opinions like 'enjoyed it', 'didn't like it,' or 'not how I would have done it.' Rather the key to helping individuals become better at given circumstances is by asking what the circumstances did, or did not to, to your behaviour. Tony was not fabricating or creating these involuntary behaviours. They were arising in response to his circumstances organically. In other words, his truthful responses were being filtered by them without conscious input. We'll come back to that later, but for now the relevant point of focus is that huge amounts of personal details don't need to be divulged in training. In your training you can use immensely personal circumstances and keep them private. All that matters is if they impact your behaviour – that is the evidence we can use to judge the strength of the circumstances on.

Now we come to the last element essential for the success of circumstances around an independent activity: to you, did it seem like there was an extremely meaningful consequence to Tony not completing the activity? Let's again base our answer on his behaviours. From the first moment, his hands were shaking. There was also his outburst on dropping the LEGOs piece. Perhaps even more interesting is his behaviour after the dropping it. If the activity wasn't so important, he could have just said, 'It doesn't matter, I'll get it close to right.' Clearly the scenario he constructed demanded precision, that set had to be completed with all pieces intact. Remember the frantic way he searched for it? The searching especially, the dire need to find the missing piece, strongly indicates the pressure of a consequence. We don't need to know what the consequence was, but whatever it was, it seemed well alive within him, filtering his behaviours in a quite obvious way.

Our conclusion: from behaviour and some simple questions alone we can infer that this, though not a perfect independent activity, was an extremely strong one and a superb first entry into Tony's training his ability to live truthfully under a given set of circumstances.

Alternate Possibilities

Since the circumstances were clearly alive and working within Tony, I don't need to ask him about any details of his circumstances. They were going strong, and so there is no point. He doesn't need technical input on it. This is not always the case with activities, especially the first time around. What if there seemed to be less urgency or not as much pressure to get it done manifesting through his behaviours? In this case, I might ask him for a one or two sentence summary of his circumstances and try to coach more meaning into the circumstances. In this alternate hypothetical scenario, here's what a scripted example of that might look like:

> 'Tony, it seemed to me like there wasn't a lot of pressure to get it done, you were pretty relaxed in the exercise.'

'Well, I needed to concentrate.' Tony replies.

'Sure, but it seems that if the reason to get it done was that extreme your body would have taken on more qualities of those circumstances. Was it a big deal if you completed it?'

'Not really, to be honest.'

'You don't have to tell me all the details, but if you're comfortable with it, just give me a one or two sentence description of what's happening and why you need to get this done.'

'This is a present for my son. He loves LEGOs and I want this to be waiting for him when his birthday party starts in five minutes.'

'Wouldn't he want to build them himself?'

'He's too young. He likes it when I build them for him.'

'Is it a big deal if it gets done?'

'Not a big deal . . . I mean we could just do it together later.'

'I like the part about him loving LEGOs. I wonder if we could build on that and add some more meaning into the circumstances which would increase the pressure elements of the exercise for you. His health also matters a great deal to you.'

'He's my world.'

'Tell me, then, if this works or doesn't. What if your son had been sick for some time in the hospital, and you didn't know at one point if he was going to make it. Maybe he went into a coma or at least was on the verge. Before he got sick, maybe you bought this LEGOs set and told him you were going to build it for him, but you never got around to it. What if today you got the call: he finally woke up again, pulled through, and he's coming home today. The first thing you want him to see when coming back into your house is that LEGOs set done. That will communicate that while he was sick and away you were thinking about him. Do you think that might give it a bit more urgency and meaning?'

Notice that I don't ask if his son was ever sick or if he has a history of health problems. I don't need to. A sick child is meaningful enough. Also, the scenario has the potential to be as joyful as it is painful and everything in between. If it takes, it is full of possibility. As I work with students on hypothetical examples, I ask them for input. A scenario like this may be dramatic, but that doesn't mean it might actually move somebody. Sickness might not be meaningful, but injury is, or something entirely different like obtaining custody. I may be on the wrong track entirely, and what Tony really wants to explore is a set of circumstances where his son gets his dreams fulfilled and he plays a role in that. We explore for what touches the participant, increasing the meaning for them so when they do their activity they know, in their core, 'this needs to be done now or I'll miss *this one chance* and I won't get a second chance.'

This level of meaning in the circumstances is what we are after. You can't pin down circumstances by their emotional content. Humans are complex, messy creatures and meaning is what brings out that authentic expression, not trying to paint circumstances with broad brushstrokes. For Tony, his activity was a good one. His body took on the pressures and qualities of the moment, the time limit, and the meaning. Emotionally and mentally, he is perfectly fine, but the experience did shake him up a bit. Generally, once I've ask about the components of the activity and we've assessed it together, the emotional temperature of the room has gone down considerably and we can now talk to the deeper, personalised feedback needed for each of them.

Safety in Danger

In feedback, I begin with Laura. Her preparation was clearly a strong one. She came in full of rage and fire. I only ask her if it was physical or non-physical; again, there's no need to press for more details since what she was doing worked. Instead we walk through what the experience was like, especially coming in without the door being answered. She tells me her non-physical preparation filled her with a powerful form of hurt anger. She knocked and nobody answered. She knocked again and heard the call for her to 'Go away!' and then she came in. We confirm together that is all excellent work on truthful impulses. During the exercise, however, I noticed that at one point when Tony was deliberately ignoring her, she fell silent, unsure as to what to do.

'Tell me, Laura, when he stopped talking, was there a response that came up for you that you didn't act on?'

She tells me there was: his silence hurt and infuriated her. She wanted to sweep all of those LEGOs off the table.

'But,' Laura quickly adds, 'I can't do that, so I figured I'd just help out and be quiet.'

'Why can't you do that?' I ask. 'Why can't you sweep the LEGOs?'

'He'll get mad.'

'I don't know but it's definitely a possibility. Say he does, though, why is that a problem?'

'Well, I don't want to hurt him.'

'Even though he did insensitive things that called up a perfectly valid response?'

'I guess.'

'I think you had earned the moment fairly. You have a right to express your own rage. He's doing it in the exercise, so why can't you? You don't need to take care of him, he can handle himself. That doesn't mean you don't act on an impulse to be compassionate or kind, but that's not what came up in the moment, is it?'

'No.'

'This exercise brings out huge demands from the moment sometimes. I agree, it's dangerous to go and sweep the pieces. Not in a literal sense. You two aren't going to physically hurt one another, but it's a huge thing, and he might get furious, or cry, or laugh, or whatever the moment demands for him to do. But you don't need to take care of him. You've put your attention on him and have a right to express the authentic impulse that comes up in the moment from that. Even if it is incredibly impolite.'

Laura's challenge that she's encountered is not a unique one. Large, impolite impulses tend to come up in the independent activity. Acting on them is a challenge to anyone's authenticity. What's important to note here is the nature of the feedback itself and how my goal is to avoid being prescriptive. It is very important to me that Laura does not hear that in the next exercise I expect her to meddle with someone's activity, because then that *will* run the risk of becoming physically dangerous. The reason is simple: there is a key difference between the impulse to provoke and the idea to provoke. If Laura provokes on impulse by destroying Tony's activity, she is doing it because she has had her attention constantly on Tony and so the impulse is a truthful one. Within that, however, other impulses could have arisen. Laura could have seen Tony struggling and felt the impulse to help. That would have been equally valid, there are no points given here for intentionally stirring the pot. If that is the one that arises, and Laura acts on it, it will have been for the right reasons.

Let's look at the opposite possibility, which is the idea to provoke. Not always, but occasionally, I will see some actors bringing in an agenda to mess with things regardless of the moment. Normally when I see that I stop the exercise immediately. You have to look at it from a commonsense perspective: the activity, when the elements are working strongly, puts a great deal of meaningful pressure on a person. If you are the one outside the door, you have no idea what you are walking into, but most likely it is going to be something where the emotional temperature is running very high. What keeps an independent activity safe, then, is always keeping your attention on your partner and honouring that 50–50 balance of observe and respond. It's the same value that keeps repetition a safe and powerful experience.

An extended version of that plays out like this:

> You observe your partner. Then you respond. Then you observe again. And you respond based on what you see in that moment. And so on.

We have talked before about when the balance tips too far in favour of observing. The exercise loses its aliveness and authenticity because too many impulses are being sat on. That makes for a lacklustre experience but doesn't raise safety flags. The exercise becomes physically dangerous when the balance tips too far in favour of responding, which in extended form looks like this:

> You observe your partner. Then you respond. And you respond again. And you respond again. And so on.

It is the lack of observation, of seeing what you are doing to your partner, that is going to set you up for problems. To walk into an independent activity with an agenda is a very bad strategy. To see someone in the throes of extreme meaning and say, 'I'm going to go and mess with that,' is not only a complete deflation of the exercise, since now you've replaced living truthfully with carrying out an agenda, but it is plain stupid. If someone is in the middle of an extremely meaningful situation and you decide to constantly needle them, it puts you on a trajectory towards a not-so-good result. In the exercise when this happens it sets it up for an eruption that is not going to be productive in the least.

The impulse to provoke is different. It is true that if Laura swipes Tony's independent activity off the table, he might fly into a fit of pure rage (he also might not – there is a huge range of possibility, one of which being he might just try to pick up the pieces since the clock is still ticking), but the exercise won't escalate into violence because in the process of observing-and-responding both are going to recognise that neither are trying to deliberately provoke or enrage one another and so the exercise will continue to evolve. If both participants are comfortable with it, there might be some very light shoving but things never go beyond that point.

This is one of the benefits of the training that arises in the independent activity. You might be reading the above example and say, 'Wait, this is a leadership class, I'm not going to have to shove someone ever, why are you letting it go that far?' The answer is I obviously agree that most likely you are never going to have to face a situation where the moment demands you shove somebody and it doesn't transition into self-defence. At that point, self-defence is not a question of leadership but survival. Realistically, however, that doesn't mean you will never be in a situation where the impulse to be violent never arises. You might find yourself in a heated argument that continues to escalate. If you have taught yourself that certain impulses are never allowed, you are setting yourself up for the very real and dangerous possibility that they might erupt. This is true whether or not you have a temper or consider yourself Zen incarnate: you are human. Everyone has a button that pushes them, and everyone has a breaking point.

When certain truthful responses are continually repressed, they tend to build up, taking on a quasi-demonic stigma. This is what it means to 'see red': if you never allow yourself to express rage, when you finally do, it is going to be an eruption so out of proportion to the situation that you are going to be the key agent in things escalating through the roof. By letting Tony and Laura both open the lid on their rage when the moment demands it, a grey area begins to emerge. Suddenly the impulse is no longer such a thing-to-be-feared but just another part of your range of authentic expression. If you find yourself in an argument with someone who is screaming and red-in-the-face, and you have a healthy and comfortable relationship to your rage, you won't be overwhelmed by the very real and human impulse to be violent. Instead you'll be able to recognise it and channel it into something else, such as moving away from that person rather than towards them.

I try not to give hypotheticals for the future like this very often, because I don't know the future, but this one serves as a good example: there is a value to continuing to widen your ability to be comfortable with who you are. If your rage, pain, intimacy, or any other impulse terrifies you, then this is a safe environment where those can come up, when appropriate to the moment, and can be expressed and recognised. It is not so much cathartic therapy as unpacking certain stigmas around behaviours that could end up causing you greater problems as a leader if you find yourself in a situation where they suddenly spill over and explode and you have no practical training for how to reel them in or go with a different expression of that impulse. That is when impulse overrides circumstances and your ability to respond. Better you deal with them here then be surprised by them.

This takes us to a bigger picture approach when it comes to leadership training. It can be very tempting to train yourself only for the scenarios you think will happen. In your mind, the temptation is to believe you never are going to be in a situation where:

you get angry, sometimes to the point of dealing with the impulse to be violent
you feel deep pain or hurt
you are so joyous it would be impolite to express it
you experience overwhelming betrayal due to the actions or indifference of others
there is intimacy between you and another person

Those kinds of moments above: never going to happen. That's not appropriate for the work force. I agree in theory that those impulses are not generally appropriate. I also agree that doesn't mean you are never going to be in a situation in which they arise. People do get angry. They struggle with impulses of attraction. They hear things that catch them off guard and wound them. Despite your best efforts sometimes the petty actions of others do get to you, and they cut deeply. It seems that attempting to predict all the variables for the future is a suboptimal strategy since, arguably, that might be what causes many of your problems in the first place.

The revealed heart of this returns to the same issue you have worked with since day one: there is a value to planning for the future. At the same time, there are some variables you cannot plan and control in advance. Let's say you have set boundaries for how you must behave in all situations. This leaves you wide open to another person who doesn't have those same boundaries and, within what is reasonable for those circumstances, can play a little dangerously. I learned this in acting auditions: actors are always coming in polite, smiling, and enthusiastic. They shake hands with their auditioners, thank them for seeing them, and so on, because they have been taught that good manners are the best behaviours for an audition, and as such, are the only ones allowed.

I have spoken to many casting directors, however, and more than once myself have sat on an audition panel where the job doesn't go to the goodie-good but rather the actor who comes in with a 'don't care, don't want it' attitude. You would think this makes them have less appeal, but the opposite is true: they are more free and flexible, and their decisions have a feel of play to them. They are far more interesting to watch because they haven't censored themselves so much that you can't even discern their individual personality anymore. You can see this mirrored in other fields where generally disagreeable people are paid far more than agreeable people.

The 'don't care, don't want it' strategy doesn't always work, but it does far more often than you would want to believe. In my field, a major part of it is not even due to the person defying the conventions. These rebels only look novel because others create the opportunity for them to shine by limiting their behaviours so much in the first place. As a result, the rare few who don't have the same inhibitions about what is and is not allowed come into the situation with a range of ability that is naturally far more vast. Simply by being around everyone else following the rules gives them the opportunity to break them in a smart way, and that instantly differentiates them. It makes them more exciting.

What this example shows us is two emerging models of how to approach yourself as a leader: first, define the future according to everything that will and won't happen. Once done, squeeze down your range of authenticity to fit into your own self-created box of limitations. Model two is have an immense and wide range of authentic expressions you are comfortable with. Having developed that, put your attention on the moment and the relevant elements within it and let that determine what response arises as well as which don't. You'll be able to express all of the same behaviours of the first model and then many more when the future suddenly doesn't meet your expectations but demands that you respond to a spontaneous change. In the first model, the more common one, you'll be bowled over every time the future throws a wrench into how things 'should' go. Reality constantly defies our insistences on the future, more often than most of us want to accept.

Strategies of Safety

The independent activity is the place where you take all of that strong technique developed in previous sessions and use it to expand your range of authentic expressions and impulses in a rich and powerful way. The demands of the moment in this work are not always big, but they are almost always extremely meaningful. That is a powerful and wonderful place for you to develop the power of authentic observations and responses within a set of given circumstances that great leaders are known for.

This brings us back to Tony and my deeper feedback for him. Initially we simply asked if he met the criteria for the exercise, but ticking boxes alone isn't enough for feedback. Especially since there were a set of behaviours within the exercise that, should Tony continue to allow them into his technique, would pose major problems for him and lead to exceptionally bad habits in his leadership technique.

The set of behaviours I am referring to relate to when Tony developed and employed a strategy to deal with the impossibilities of juggling both finishing his activity and dealing with Laura: he decided to ignore her. First he told her to go away, which does not fit very well with any call in repetition. Then he stopped repeating altogether. Tony's strategy may have worked in a superficial way but it only did so because he imposed a fairly superfluous agenda on the exercise, which was to deny both Laura and the moment, pretending they were not important. For Tony, this robbed him of the opportunity to go to some incredible places in the exercise, one of which would have been discovering where the pressure of the activity, combined with engaging with Laura, would take him. They would most likely be places of extremely powerful pressure he is not used to experiencing. Exploring these deeper ranges is valuable. This is about widening, not narrowing, the range of possibilities within your technique.

For Tony to not compromise the values of the training and get something of value out of the exercise, he has to deal with both Laura and the activity. That does not mean the impulse to be silent will never arise, or there comes a moment where silence is demanded more than words, but Tony brought in the idea to be quiet so as to get the activity done. This isn't engaging with the situation but running from it. Meisner often said that the independent activity was designed to put you into a puzzle box with no solution and watch you twist in it. The problem of being under time pressure and having to deal with an unknown variable is part and parcel of this experience, not a strange anomaly of this one example.

Tony's fear, of course, was not unfounded, and so we have to be careful in framing this as a negative. He employed the strategy because completing the activity was so extremely meaningful, and not completing it would result in a major consequence. His time limit wasn't perfect, but it was good enough, and his activity was incredibly challenging to complete while stressed. The elements were strong, but seeking safety in a strategy hampered rather than aided the experience.

This brings us to a key point about the exercise we said earlier would be touched on more in depth. Consider a moment we haven't discussed much yet: what happened when Tony did not finish the activity. He simply looked at me and told me the exercise was over. But is that really true? After all, within the four criteria for the independent activity, there is no instruction that the activity must be completed, nor that the exercise finishes when the timer runs out. The circumstances and time limit are designed so that you are going to throw yourself into doing it and you might get it done on a razor's edge. One additional valuable aspect many use in creating a consequence is to not give yourself the option of a second chance: if the consequence happens, that's it. There's no going back, or take-backs. You cannot escape it. That tends to fuel the exercise a great deal. We don't know if Tony used this tool, but his behaviour tells us it may have been a powerful factor.

While we know you will have plenty of reasons for completing the activity, even with all of them working within you, there is still no explicit instruction that the activity must be completed. This is also deliberate: I want to allow you to have the possibility of both real success and real failure always within your reach in the exercise. I have seen many independent activities completed but just as many not. Failure is not only possible in the independent activity, it is a wonderful one in that it takes you to some incredibly rich and deep areas. Succeeding under pressure is just as powerful as failing under it. Both will bring you into contact with immensely powerful responses from the moment. This is why even though the set time limit might only be 5 minutes, for example, an independent activity can go on for 15 or 20 minutes, or even longer. Tony was correct that the activity was finished when the time limit went off. Had he stayed in the experience, however, the exercise would have been far from over, as the repetition between him and Laura, as well as the weight of his failure, would have continued the experience.

For Tony, the feedback is simple but on point: you have to deal with all elements of reality. If you decide to start choosing what to pay attention to or ignore you are now no longer listening to the moment and situation but rather trying to force it to be what you want it to be. That attitude is going to set you up for problems in your leadership. True, you might not finish the activity, but that's just as real and valid as if you finish it. The repetition component of the exercise would continue and the depth and openness created by both possibilities is massive.

The Unacceptable Offer

The power of the independent activity to create meaningful, real circumstances is what sets it apart from other models of training involving scenario work. This includes improvisation, which is one of the most popular tools in leadership and business training. I have said before that the independent activity is absolutely not an improvisation exercise and must never be treated as one. Improvisation is an excellent tool for training certain qualities that might at first seem like leadership, such as problem solving skills, planning, or group synergy if it is an improvisation involving more than two people. This, however, reveals its inner nature: at its core, improvisation is about creativity, in particular a type of living creative writing, planning, and on-your-feet-thinking. This makes it excellent for certain skills but incredibly poor for teaching you how to fully surrender to an experience.

Despite what some people might say, improvisation is not complementary to living truthfully. They do not play well together. The reason for this is simple: you cannot think about a scenario and be in it at the same time. The mechanism for attention must fluctuate back from the people in the scenario onto yourself as you decide whether or not to accept offers, make offers, play an objective, change tactics, or whatever else the elements of the improvisation have laid out for you. Good improvisation is doing this efficiently and quickly. We established in the first few chapters you cannot both be inside of an experience and outside of it at the same time. You can exit rapidly back and forth, but this is an incredibly bad general habit to develop for leadership. Despite its claims, improvisation doesn't facilitate you allowing your responses to be fully determined outside of you, but rather puts its emphasis on listening to others and your surroundings and then thinking on your feet to generate ways to forward the exercise.

In living truthfully, 99 or 100% of the time your attention is on the other person, unless something in the moment demands for it to be off of them. This percentage is far lower in improvisation. This is why improvisation might be a good tool for training other aspects of your needs involving creativity, but as far as living truthfully goes, it is inefficient. Living truthfully is not a creative process. There is no element of invention at work, since what happens to you is determined by the other person and the moment, and we keep the observations as concise, clean, and simple as possible.

Blending the values of invention and spontaneity for the purpose of training, improvisation leads to murky results at best. My Meisner teacher Scott summarized it best: 'Improv will not make you better at repetition, but repetition will make you better at improv.' Meisner himself called his repetitions 'improvisations' at times but if you look at the descriptions, feedback he gave, as well as how he structured them, they don't look anything like conventional improvisations. My own teaching experiences with professional improvisers confirm this.

Improvisation games might be fun, enjoyable, and certainly they are challenging, but you will not get the depth of authenticity training from an improvisation that an independent activity offers. In improvisation you can get moments of authenticity as deep and rich, but you have to work for them, and replication is incredibly difficult and unclear. In the independent activity, that depth is on offer from moment one. I think if leaders in training wish to take improvisation to improve leadership skills, they must be very clear with themselves about what they want from the improvisation since improvisation is not a simple, clear method of training. For any area related to living truthfully, such as speaking, presentations, interviews, negotiations, and so on, you will find in practice this training is far more technically clear and efficient.

One question I do receive when covering improvisation is regarding the circumstances in this work. There are fictional circumstances in the activity, but is this the same as improvisation? On a basic front no, since you are not creating the circumstances on the spot and have brought them in pre-written. There are some approaches to improvisation that base their work off a scripted scenario, whether a full script or paragraph, so there is some overlap here. Where the difference comes is in the testing of your circumstances. If the circumstances are meaningful enough, the moment you begin they grip you and immediately begin filtering your observations and responses. If they don't, if you don't feel much or they dry up, then that becomes the targeted material for feedback where we attempt to strengthen the circumstances. What is never asked of you, however, is during the exercise to take the attention off your partner or the activity to try to remind yourself of why the situation is powerful, or to juice it for more or forward 'the plot' somehow. There is no element of self-generated invention. That cannot be said for any form of improvisation I have ever come across, even nonverbal ones. Despite their claims about pure spontaneity, the values themselves reveal their hand. The overlap is mild, but the goals and outcomes are profoundly different and incompatible with one another. The results reflect these differences.

Where Dragons Wait

You have spent your time developing the technical means to facilitate truthful, authentic experiences. Having done that, you will find the independent activity is the big league where you get to play at a very high level. It is the culmination of all of your work and is a pure expression for living truthfully under a given set of circumstances. This does not mean that all circumstances you encounter outside of training will have equal intensity or pressure. Some will be more subtle, and the next few sessions cover that. I can assure you, however, that the more comfortable you get with living truthfully under extreme degrees of pressure, even ones where failure is inevitable, the more you will be able to do it and thrive in your own field without folding. When pressed to the fire, a leader who not only survives but shines is a rare but powerful entity.

Given that, do more than one independent activity. At the Impulse Company, several months alone was devoted to activities and an equally sizeable portion at the True Acting Institute. Activities is where the real rewards are. They will always be profoundly different each time. New partners, new circumstances, new activities – all of this will serve to continually expand your own range of authentic responses as well as connect you even further to the meaning that fuels your fire. Failures in activities and creating circumstances are equally as good and important as successes.

However many sessions you have, my hope is that you can do as many activities as possible. You have put all this work in. This is the arena where you reap many fruits and go to the border territory of your ability to be authentic every time. The beauty of it? Each time you go back to your border territory it will be just a little further out. From here on there will still be challenges, but the range of your authenticity will only continue to expand. That is an excellent quality for a leader to develop.

Summary

The independent activity is the apex of training in the Meisner Technique and so is the apex of training for your leadership skills. It is the complete expression of living truthfully under a given set of circumstances. By engaging in a difficult-to-complete activity with a time limit, and extremely meaningful circumstances creating urgency, you will find yourself under a degree of pressure unlike any other you have experienced in a training session. In working under these conditions, still able to observe and respond truthfully, you will discover a range of authenticity far greater than you knew you were capable of. Preparation, designed only for the person outside the room, is like throwing more gasoline on the fire. When your partner enters in the throes of a successful preparation they will be such a powerhouse of aliveness that it will be a mistake to ignore them. Engaging with both partner and activity creates a layered, sometimes impossible, scenario that makes completing the activity just that much harder. It is in this immense pressure cooker that you experience and train, in a deep, visceral way, what it means to live truthfully under a given set of circumstances.

Tips for You and Your Coach

Teaching the independent activity will require all of your senses to be alive as a coach. Rather than looking for the appropriate, stay deeply connected to what is. If both the activity and the preparation are good, there won't be much you need to say. If they are weak, then there is a technical metric by which you can help the client get better. The type of feedback needed for the independent activity is simple, yet deep. It is why I recommend giving a cool-down time after the exercise where you analyse and talk about technical criteria of the activity before getting into the nuances of what happened to the individuals in the exercise. People can be quite raw and open coming out of the exercise; give them a chance to get their bearings so they won't be overwhelmed with feedback. They will still be open and receptive, albeit feeling more safe and able to take on board what you have to say.

Every coach has their own personal boundaries for what is acceptable within an exercise, and it is helpful for you to think about what yours are. Personally, I am fine with things such as touching, hugging, kissing, or even some light shoving when things get emotionally heated as they are all superb expressions of high-level authenticity and take people deep into unexpected territory. It is helpful to make up your mind, especially regarding the latter, when conflict and aggression take on physical expression. I never let things escalate to where people are actually hurt and have learned through trial and error how to spot when this might happen. It is important to understand that I am not talking about some giant fight that erupts. When the exercise maintain its 50–50 balance, I have never seen that happen. It only occurs when one or both partners stopped observing and just started responding. That, unfortunately, I have seen, albeit only a handful of times, and it was not a reflection of good technique.

Of more concern to me are incidentals. People in the heat of the moment can accidentally slip, or bump into things, and this is where it is helpful to be perceptive and make sure clients are safe so they can throw themselves into the experience. Likewise, if a participant lets me know they prefer not to be touched, that is more than fine. Let your students determine their own boundaries; it doesn't mean they have to be applied to everyone in the room. To go into the metaphorically 'dangerous excitement' that is this work, people need to feel safe. You only love a roller coaster because you know the danger is confined to what you are comfortable with. It is the exact same principle in the independent activity.

As you develop your perceptions as a coach with this work, if an exercise ever feels off, dangerous, or just not right in a safety sense, listen to your instincts and stop it immediately. The safety of your students is paramount in this work. Activities are rich, intensely authentic experiences, and your instincts are the guide to keeping them on track. It is the same with when choosing to end the exercise. You end it based on your instinct that everything of value in that exercise has been experienced.

Invariably you will see participants sit on truthful impulses in the exercise, and that is the material for your deeper feedback. It is also good to notice when they are half-sitting on the impulse, or expressing it in dosed amounts. An example of this is wagging fingers. Sometimes, when things escalate to a confrontational zone, I will see participants wagging a finger at each other. I call them on this, since wagging a finger is coded behaviour: it is threatening to be impulsive rather than just being impulsive. Keep encouraging your students to go for the authentic, real thing, rather than just implying to their partners that they can if they are just pushed far enough.

If I am doing my job to help you, then what you will see now is that these latter exercises such as auto-switch, repetition, knock at the door, and the independent activity are less about technical structure. This is because the technical structure has been built in from day one and is largely automatic at this point. Both participants and coach will intuitively feel when the exercises lose technical steam, but that was not always the case. The technique is a learned skill and will only need tuning up from time to time. Now, what you are seeing is that feedback and focus looks at the next stage, which is talking about what happened. This makes feedback individualised and impossible to standardise beyond some blanket concepts. In the same way that participants are going deeper into their own journey using their intuitions as a guide, so too will you find as a coach that your intuitions will serve you better than any advice I can give on the page. The same guiding principle for a good observation applies here: you'll know it when you see it.

Chapter 12

A Broken Back Shows the Way

Reality Reintroduced

The journey into the independent activity was your first exposure to the training of living truthfully under a given set of circumstances. The discoveries within it are often profound, pushing you to the very edges of your authentic range and making you hyper-attuned to the demands of the moment. It sharpens up both your observational abilities as well as a sensitivity to your responses within a situation like few other exercises can. Independent activities serve as an excellent introduction to what it means to be functioning under the extreme pressure of the moment, attempting to deal with all the variables arising within an extremely meaningful scenario. Introduction, however, is the key word here, as now we can go further, importing your strong technique into scenarios with less flexibility. Yes, we are now moving into scripted scene-work

To introduce the material today, consider that the independent activity is unique to any other exercise in this training in that it has not one but two essential components. The first component is the experiential one where you enter and live truthfully under a given set of circumstances. In some cases, you will be doing an activity, and so the meaning around your circumstances will filter your observations and responses. In other exercises, you will do a preparation, finding that your ability to live truthfully can be informed both by the preparation as well as the situation you find yourself entering into when you come into the room. In either case, the independent activity forces you to deal with what comes up in the moment as well as your partner. That, however, brings up an interesting question: for the person doing the activity, where did the given circumstances come from?

This reveals the second component that makes the independent activity different from any other exercise in this work. It is the only one training device the Meisner Technique involving an element of creativity, that of a writer. Using points of your life that are extremely meaningful, you create a set of fictional circumstances that will be lived in. After creating them, you go and test them for their strength and potency.

This is, as with all our work, by design. There's a real benefit to being the author of your circumstances. The independent activity thrives on pressure created from your attempting to function within extremely meaningful circumstances. Oftentimes you know best what is important to you, and so it is easier to begin training with a scenario created by you rather than one from an author. As we saw in the previous chapter, the writing component of independent activities differs from that of improvisational exercises, where you are constantly fluctuating between the roles of writer and executor, or in other words the creator and experiencer of the moment. The independent activity is far more clear-cut: in selecting an activity you write the circumstances for, then in the exercise put your creative muscles aside and go and live truthfully under your created circumstances, testing them for their potency and meaning.

Now that you have begun to become familiar with the given circumstances in a deep, experiential way, it is time to import those developed abilities of sensitivity and clarity into scenarios not of your creation, those written by other people. This will create the groundwork for your beginning to be accustomed to observing and responding authentically within situations where you don't have an element of control, and the variables are unfolding in real-time. The more you do this with a variety of scripted scenarios, the more adaptable these skills become to out-of-training contexts. In today's material, you will also begin to intuit the core elements of a scenario which is a vital next step towards analysing a situation in such a way that your leadership skills might thrive within it. Using excerpts from well-written plays, we can begin this process.

When the Actor in You Speaks

In just a few pages you and your partner are going to begin working on scenes. When approaching a piece of written material, and importing the values of this training into it, several questions arise. Believe it or not, these will be questions similar to those an actor might ask when approaching a text. What do we do about characters, for example? We are trying to live truthfully, so by trying to 'act' the scenes in a more truthful way, will we get closer to understanding what is going on within the circumstances? Should you try to identify experiences from their lives and see if it matches with ones from yours? How about stage directions? Would a bit of blocking be helpful, so we can really get into the circumstances? Maybe some costumes or clothing? We aren't trying to create a staged performance, but we are attempting to create conditions under which scripted scenarios can aid your leadership development and stay true to the values of this work.

Consider, however, that outside of training you won't have control over many scenarios, so we have to be careful about what habits we choose to condition here. Which of these elements within a script, then, is essential for you to consider when beginning to build a bridge? This bridge is between your technique for living truthfully under your own given circumstances in the independent activity and circumstances that you have not created. Which of these elements will aid in the development of your capacity for bringing your authentic skillset into unpredictable situations with unknown variables?

The simple answer? Nothing. Nothing to every one of those questions above. None of those elements – character, blocking, props, etc. – will help you in starting to hear the elements of a situation in an objective and relevant way. Trying to be performative, to enter the situation by dramaturgical means, is only going to drive you further into your own head by directing you to put more attention on yourself to understand and interpret. The more you do that, the more you are going to lose the essential set of values in our work, all of which thus far have to do with *the other person*. We need a way for you to pick up a piece of text and not immediately get sucked into the temptation of bringing in agendas or objectives, all of which come from *you*.

Exercise: Breaking the Back of a Text

The exercise that solves the problem of how to hear the key components of a situation without the pitfalls of interpretation is called breaking the back of a text. It is named this way for two reasons. The first reason comes from its design, which is that this is an exercise for fresh, or first, readings of text and so embodies the idea of breaking new ground. Although as you will see it can be used at any stage in the process, its primary function is for the first encounter of a piece of material, which will be that way for you with the scenes you work on today unless you are already familiar with them.

The second reason is more telling: it relates to the performative habits both actors and non-actors bring to a scene when they start work on it, attempting to represent the lives on the page in an artificial, literary, and abstract way with their own analysis and creative designs. There is analysis in this work, but analysis before seeing a situation clearly is what I am referring to. Those are the habits you have worked to weed out of your leadership abilities. When encountering text, however, they tend to come flooding right back in. Something drastic needs to be done to break those tendencies for good. Rather than beating you down into submission, the text is the better thing to be broken at first read.

To summarise the key points thus far: this is a reading of a scene aloud between you and your partner, sitting across from each other just as you would in a repetition exercise. It will be the first time either of you have read these scenes (barring of course if you know them already, in which case we would just select a different scene). In training sessions, neither of you would receive these scenes in advance. As such, no preparation is required.

You'll read these scenes aloud using the breaking the back exercise. The metaphorical back of a text is broken by virtue of a few guidelines:

First, when being given your scene, don't read ahead. Just take the piece of paper and resist the temptation to start reading it.

Second, during the reading, you want the majority of your attention to be on your partner, with very little on the page. To accomplish this, only pick up a couple of words of your lines at a time. It is fine if the sentences are broken, have no cohesion, no meaning whatsoever. Don't worry about grammar, pacing, etc. As you get more comfortable with breaking the back you might be able to pick up a few more words, but the real value is in just getting a couple of words, putting your attention on your partner, speaking them, then going back for a few more, putting your attention on your partner again, speaking them, and so on. Do not speak anything while your eyes are still on the page.

Third, hold the page high so the words are easily accessible, with your partner's face in sight of your page.

Fourth, put the index finger of your free hand (one hand holds the page so this would be the other hand), on the place where you are. This avoids the issue of losing your spot, trying to find it, getting your lines again, all the while losing precious moments that could be with your partner.

Fifth, ignore any stage directions. This includes pauses, gestures, intonations, movements, etc. This is a first reading. Your only concern is with the words and the person sitting across from you.

Sixth, speak your words flat, without inflection. Notice I did not say monotone. Being mono-tone is still an imposed inflection. In the beginning it might sound and feel monotone but really it is more robotic: you are pressing out any ability to let emotion, interpretation, or inflection come into the lines.

Seventh, and most crucially: stay with your partner. Don't look at your page while they are speaking. Keep your attention on them. How will you know when it is your turn to speak? When your partner stops talking. Yes, this slows the reading down considerably. As a consequence that places the premium on being with each other rather than stuck in the page.

If you follow these guidelines you'll find that your reading in this way will remove any possibility to be performative. Breaking the back gives you even ground to start on when encountering a scenario. It also allows you from the first moment to begin with the right values, with your attention on your partner and the words being a part of that experience. You are going to read and let the words float on top of being connected with your partner. Sound familiar? It's no coincidence that my Meisner teacher Scott often called this exercise 'a repetition exercise with a piece of paper in your hand.'

Here are three examples of scenes I use in sessions that focus on the breaking the back exercise. These are juicy, rich scenes. They are, respectively, for two women, two men, and one man and one woman. That having been said, the genders matter less for a first reading. If you want to read all three, go for it, there's nothing lost in the value of these exercises. Participants like to have options, however, and this is why I break things up accordingly in this way. One final note is not to worry about how well you fit the roles or not. When I pick these scenes, I tend not to worry about matching participants to their scene, in other words, casting. The value of this work is on the ability to observe deeply and hear clearly. These are scenes with potent, powerfully charged language. That is of more value than casting for a hypothetical production we aren't putting on in the first place.

So, you and your partner have three scenes to pick from. Again, don't read them first before deciding. Just pick a scene and a character for each of you. Get into position following the guidelines just presented. Keep your pages high and in sight of each other. Take only a few words at a time. Make eye contact and say your words flat. Stay with each other.

Two Women

Top Girls by Caryl Churchill
Excerpt from Act 3

Marlene: I came up this morning and spent the day in Ipswich. I went to see mother.
Joyce: Did she recognise you?
Marlene: Are you trying to be funny?
Joyce: No, she does wander.
Marlene: She wasn't wandering at all, she was very lucid thank you.
Joyce: You were very lucky then.
Marlene: Fucking awful life she's had.
Joyce: Don't tell me.
Marlene: Fucking waste.
Joyce: Don't talk to me.
Marlene: Why shouldn't I talk? Why shouldn't I talk to you?/Isn't she my mother too?
Joyce: Look, you've left, you've gone away,/we can do without you.
Marlene: I left home, so what, I left home. People do leave home/ it is normal.
Joyce: We understand that, we can do without you.

Marlene: We weren't happy. Were you happy?

Joyce: Don't come back.

Marlene: So it's just your mother is it, your child, you never wanted me round,/you were jealous of me because I was the

Joyce: Here we go.

Marlene: little one and I was clever.

Joyce: I'm not clever enough for all this psychology/ if that's what it is.

Marlene: Why can't I visit my own family/ without all this?

Joyce: Aah. Just don't go on about Mum's life when you haven't been to see her for how many years./I go and see her every week.

Marlene: It's up to me. Then don't go and see her every week.

Joyce: Somebody has to.

Marlene: No they don't./Why do they?

Joyce: How would I feel if I didn't go?

Marlene: A lot better.

Joyce: I hope you feel better.

Marlene: It's up to me.

Joyce: You couldn't get out of here fast enough.

Marlene: Of course I couldn't get out of here fast enough. What was I going to do? Marry a dairy-man who'd come home pissed?/Don't you fucking this fucking that fucking bitch

Joyce: Christ.

Marlene: fucking tell me what to fucking do fucking

Joyce: I don't know how you could leave your own child.

Marlene: You were quick enough to take her.

Joyce: What does that mean?

Marlene: You were quick enough to take her.

Joyce: Or what? Have her put in a home? Have some stranger/ take her would you rather?

Marlene: You couldn't have one so you took mine.

Joyce: I didn't know that then.

Marlene: Like hell, /married three years.

Joyce: I didn't know that. Plenty of people/ take that long.

Marlene: Well it turned out lucky for you, didn't it?

End

Notes: in the scene there are overlaps symbolised by the '/'. While we would work this in fairly early if staging, don't worry about the overlaps in the first read. Just do the exercise as if there were none considering these would be built in after a first read.

Two Men

Uncle Vanya by Anton Chekhov, translated by Michael Frayn
Excerpt from Act IV, Scene 1

Vanya: Leave me alone!

Astrov: With the greatest of pleasure – I should have been on my way a long time ago. But let me say it again – I am not leaving until you give me back what you've taken from me.

Vanya: I haven't taken anything from you.

Astrov: I'm serious, now. Don't waste my time. I'm late enough as it is.

Vanya: I haven't taken anything.

    They both sit down.

Astrov: No? All right, I'll give you a little longer, and then I'm sorry, but I shall have to use force. We'll tie you up and search you. Seriously.

Vanya: If you like. *(Pause.)* To be such a fool, though – to shoot twice and miss both times! That's something I shall never forgive myself!

Astrov: If you wanted to put a bullet in something you might have done better to try your own head.

Vanya (shrugs): It's a funny thing. I'm guilty of attempted murder, but no one's arresting me, no one's charging me. So they must think I'm insane. *(Gives a bitter laugh.)* I'm insane, but not people who adopt the mask of a professor, of some learned sage, to conceal their total lack of talent, and their dullness, and their utter callousness. They're not insane. Nor are people who marry old men and then publicly deceive them. I saw you, I saw you with your arms round her!

Astrov: Yes, sir, I had my arms round her, sir, and pooh to you. *(He thumbs his nose.)*

Vanya (looking at the door): No, but it's an insane world, if you people are still part of it.

Astrov: And that's another stupid remark.

Vanya: So what? I'm insane, I'm not responsible for my actions – I have the right to make stupid remarks.

Astrov: The joke's worn thin. You're not insane, you're just someone who's got a bit odd. You're a buffoon. There was a time when I had the same idea – that being odd must be sick, must be abnormal. But I've come round to the view now that oddity is the normal condition of mankind. You're entirely normal.

Vanya (covers his face with his hands): I'm so ashamed! If you knew how ashamed I felt! There's no pain in the world to compare with these pangs of shame. *(In anguish.)* Unendurable! *(Bends his head low over the table.)* What can I do? What can I do?

Astrov: Nothing.

End

One Woman, One Man

Macbeth by William Shakespeare
Excerpt from Act 1, Scene 7

MACBETH
How now! what news?

LADY MACBETH
He has almost supp'd: why have you left the chamber?

MACBETH
Hath he ask'd for me?

LADY MACBETH
Know you not he has?

MACBETH
We will proceed no further in this business:
He hath honour'd me of late; and I have bought

Golden opinions from all sorts of people,
Which would be worn now in their newest gloss,
Not cast aside so soon.

LADY MACBETH
Was the hope drunk
Wherein you dress'd yourself? hath it slept since?
And wakes it now, to look so green and pale
At what it did so freely? From this time
Such I account thy love. Art thou afeard
To be the same in thine own act and valour
As thou art in desire? Wouldst thou have that
Which thou esteem'st the ornament of life,
And live a coward in thine own esteem,
Letting 'I dare not' wait upon 'I would,'
Like the poor cat i' the adage?

MACBETH
Prithee, peace:
I dare do all that may become a man;
Who dares do more is none.

LADY MACBETH
What beast was't, then,
That made you break this enterprise to me?
When you durst do it, then you were a man;
And, to be more than what you were, you would
Be so much more the man. Nor time nor place
Did then adhere, and yet you would make both:
They have made themselves, and that their fitness now
Does unmake you. I have given suck, and know
How tender 'tis to love the babe that milks me:
I would, while it was smiling in my face,
Have pluck'd my nipple from his boneless gums,
And dash'd the brains out, had I so sworn as you
Have done to this.

MACBETH
If we should fail?

LADY MACBETH
We fail!
But screw your courage to the sticking-place,
And we'll not fail. When Duncan is asleep—
Whereto the rather shall his day's hard journey
Soundly invite him—his two chamberlains
Will I with wine and wassail so convince
That memory, the warder of the brain,

Shall be a fume, and the receipt of reason
A limbeck only: when in swinish sleep
Their drenched natures lie as in a death,
What cannot you and I perform upon
The unguarded Duncan? what not put upon
His spongy officers, who shall bear the guilt
Of our great quell?

MACBETH
Bring forth men-children only;
For thy undaunted mettle should compose
Nothing but males. Will it not be received,
When we have mark'd with blood those sleepy two
Of his own chamber and used their very daggers,
That they have done't?

LADY MACBETH
Who dares receive it other,
As we shall make our griefs and clamour roar
Upon his death?

MACBETH
I am settled, and bend up
Each corporal agent to this terrible feat.
Away, and mock the time with fairest show:
False face must hide what the false heart doth know.

End

Notes: Though the language in Shakespeare is denser than contemporary scenes, don't let this worry you. Break the back as you normally would without trying to have the text make sense. Sometimes you'll find the lines are much more clear if your read them this way without trying to string them together for meaning. I include this example to show that even when working with incredibly dense content this approach works just as well.

Flattened Aliveness

Now that you've broken the back of at least one scene, let's talk a bit about the things people tend to experience while doing it. While your first encounter might be different, generally these are the experiences common to the first time in this exercise.

The first thing to note is that in the beginning, breaking the back feels weird for most people. It feels constrained, intentionally repressed, awkward, lacking in any real flow or vibrancy. It is called a repetition exercise with a piece of paper in your hand, but it feels almost impossible to conflate that with your dynamic experiences in repetition. Other participants, however, have an entirely different experience. For them, the words sound crystal clear, and they immediately gain a sense of what is going on in the scene. Both of these are perfectly normal first encounters, so what's going on? Let's explore this more deeply and search for answers that might reconcile these seemingly contradictory experiences of this strange exercise.

To begin this discussion, let's talk about what repeat exposures in this exercise get you. Part of the disadvantage of reading this in book format, rather than seeing it in a session, is that you only get exposure to three scenes in this chapter. While you can work with all of them generally in a real session, depending on the size of the group, you'll normally see five or six readings, possibly more, from other participants working on different scenes. One important side note before we continue: at the end of this chapter I will give examples of plays with lots of excellent material for two people in the event you want to take this exercise further than what this chapter offers you in terms of material. You'll notice that I stress two people scenes only. It is entirely possible to break the back of a scene with three or four people, but we never do it. It is also possible to do repetition between three people, but we never do that either. Why? Whether between two or a thousand, the same thing ends up happening in a repetition between two people.

Consider a conversation you had recently with a larger number of people, let's say four for the sake of the example. Not all four of you are speaking equally to the group the same time. It would be absolute chaos. The natural flow of a conversation between you and multiple people is you put your attention on one person, then another, and so on, and if at times you speak to everyone in the group simultaneously, then your attention is on the group as a single unit. This is why even in slightly larger groups there is an unspoken value of everyone being heard, and when someone is in a small group but goes unheard or is repeatedly not allowed to speak the general universal feelings are those of hurt and minimisation. Specific attention is largely constrained to focus on one singular target at a time, whether it is an individual or a collective, so training with one person on an in-depth exchange between two people still has all the values of training with multiple people. That's why we always work with two people. The values you develop with another person will transfer over to how you work with 50 at a time if need be and logistically are far simpler to train.

Going back to our initial starting point of repeat exposure, looking at the experience itself tells us this exercise orients itself around your attention being on the interpersonal dynamic. Inside the exercise, you might think because of how you are speaking in such fragmented ways that all that is coming out of your mouth is word mush. To make it even more strange, you might be able to understand what your partner is saying clearly but not what you are saying. Conversely you might hear the language perfectly, getting a deep, rich understanding of the nuances and specifics within the scene. Or you might only get pieces of it, but you start to get a visceral sense of the situation and context. Coming out of the exercise, you might think that your audience will be deeply bored, with none of it having made any sense. I can confirm that almost always the opposite is true: we in the audience understand the scene incredibly clearly. The writing and more importantly the situation and relationships are well defined and received. That hints to something very interesting about how starting with no interpretation and reading aloud clearly can give us so much information about a situation and the elements within it.

Things in the exercise can feel weird the first few times because they go against the natural grain. We aren't used to, especially when reading text, chopping it up into bite-sized chunks to the detriment of all meaning within it. Consider, however, that repetition used to feel against the grain but paradoxically that initial feeling of doing something so abstract created a powerful conduit for training something deeply relevant. The same is true of breaking the back of a text. Many of us are conditioned that text must be honored, but what does that mean? Oftentimes it means when you are given a pre-written speech (actors deal with scenes but I imagine you'll deal more with blocks of text – nonetheless the values still apply), almost instantly you go into analysis mode.

You'll begin dissecting the words, planning moments, timing breaths, and creatively coming up with ways to incorporate gestures into the speech as well as determining the gestures themselves. This is because the writing is *important*, and you feel you need to rise to its level of importance.

Except where's the value in that? Rather than discovering the text, you've decided to immediately begin employing your own faculties and powers of analysis. What if the speech needs no analysis? I'm not saying it never does, but there's a distinct difference between reciting copy from a technical manual and reading Churchill. More broadly, consider where your priorities have gone. The second you get a speech, immediately decades of schooling and conditioning fire up the habit to go straight to what you will do with the speech. How's that in line with the values of authentic leadership? The relevant variable is always outside of you, whether it is another person, a body of people, and now, a situation. Scene or speech, the values are still the same: what is outside of you will determine what happens to you.

This doesn't mean that you can never plan within a speech, presentation, or scene, but the question of relevance we are exploring is where do you begin? Do you begin with the least relevant priority or the most? In chopping up the words, sometimes stripping them of meaning while other times not, you break the habit of imposing your own choices as well as your desire to immediately begin analysing. That goes counter to conventional wisdom and possibly years of practice. Instead, here you are starting with your priorities in the right order: immediately the words are connected to the experience outside of you. They are a vital part of it, but now they are starting where they will end: always tied to, and flowing off of, what is happening around you. As a result, when you speak the words, they will take on the quality of the moment you find yourself in. Already we are starting to get closer to how this is in line with the values of repetition.

Repeat exposure will continue to illuminate this more clearly. Whatever your experience the first time around is, it is fine, you are just getting your feet wet with this exercise. The second time around, with a new scene, if you had a hard time understanding the first scene, you now might find yourself catching more without trying to. You'll begin to richly hear what is coming out of the scene and the elements within the situation. You'll begin to get a clear eye for intuitively detecting given circumstances. After doing this with four or five scenes, you are going to find you'll pick up more words without trying and that the real value on offer is not the rich writing, although that is profound, but the effect your partner is having on you as they speak those lines to you. More and more you are going to begin observing them and finding that text either floats on top of the interactions between you two or can hit you quite suddenly by itself, becoming the primary object of meaning in any given moment. Sounding more familiar? As I said earlier, it's no coincidence that breaking the back of the scene is often called a repetition exercise with a piece of paper in your hand.

As your comfort grows in the exercise, allowing the nuances of the moment and your partner into the experience, you can relax your flattening of the text. This does not mean to suddenly inflect and put on accents, but it means that now, as you are more sensitive to the dynamics of the moment between you and your partner, your voice can also take on the quality of the moment if it demands it. This might just feel like reading in your 'natural' voice, but really you're allowing yourself to enter the situation even more fully without needing to impose anything on it. The value here is that the more you continue to do this exercise, the more you will find you are living truthfully while allowing a foreign set of given circumstances (ones not written by you, unlike in the independent activity) to have an impact in the moment if the moment calls for it.

This is an immensely powerful next step as you begin to import your ability to live truthfully in situations further and further removed from your control. By hearing the given circumstances so clearly, you are going to find your ability to observe and respond authentically translates into a variety of external circumstances and situations. This is the healthy version of scenario training unlike the ones that trip so many leaders up. Rather than preparing you for specific situations and continuously trying to predict all of the variables and determine the appropriate response for each one, you begin to associate your ability to observe and respond authentically with a variety of scenarios, thereby developing a general technique for living truthfully that becomes accessible across situations, contexts, and circumstances.

After the first couple of reads with different scenes, when you are feeling comfortable with the exercise, what is recommended is to do a short round of repetition with your partner before you enter the scene. The coach will hand you each your scene. Since you aren't reading ahead, you can just do a round of repetition to plug in to one another. When the coach cues you, you can exit from repetition and immediately begin reading, letting the effects of the repetition bleed over into the words. This aids in the process of importing your ability to live truthfully into a set of given circumstances that are not your own with more specificity and visceral reality.

Words, Words, Words

In addition to developing this ability to hear circumstances clearly, breaking the back of any piece of text gives you a way to prepare for presentations or speeches that involve pre-written materials. Whether you write them or not doesn't matter. If you're writing it, then you've already trained a valuable habit through the independent activity where you write the content, put the writer's hat aside, and then live truthfully under that given set of circumstances. Even if you are writing your own material, you'll follow the same process of breaking its back so you can begin to import your ability to live truthfully into the text. If you have a partner you can practice with that means you two might do a round of repetition, and from there you'll break the back with them simply listening and work off of them. If you are on your own, you can pick a point on the wall and speak the words to that. It doesn't have the same vitality as working with your partner, but the beauty of the mark on the wall is that it still can be a good place to import some of the values of openness when memorising. In both cases, you are putting your attention on something external and letting the words be a part of that experience.

This cleanly segues into the question of memorisation. Say you've broken the back of a text and now must commit it to memory. How does one memorise a piece of text in a way that keeps the values of this work alive? This exercise is your answer. Breaking the back is an excellent way to memorise material because, as you go on, you will pick up more words every time. The page will always be accessible, but for longer and longer periods of time your attention will remain on the primary point of value which is not on the page but *out there*, off of yourself and onto something else, whether it is someone or a specific point.

One further benefit to using this approach for memorisation I've seen in practice is that it is one of the best aids for anyone who struggles with dyslexia. Dyslexia can be one of the greatest challenges for a leader when they encounter any written medium. The pressures to keep up with what to the outside world feels like a 'normal pace' can be immense and causes great distress. Breaking the back is a wonderful equaliser for people with dyslexia for both absorption as well as memorisation. Slowing down, taking your time, and retrieving small amounts of text in a technically clean way has helped many dyslexic learners I've both seen and taught in this work. To my knowledge it was never designed as a learning aid for this particular challenge some people grapple with, but it seems to address it extremely well.

Memorising using breaking the back raises a broader issue that can be addressed more in-depth now. People are often sceptical of this training being applicable to a situation where you do not have a partner present, such as an solo speech or something delivered, but here is the point where you begin to realise that, even if you are the only one on a stage or at the front of the room, you are not alone. If there is an audience you are speaking to, you have your point of focus to observe and respond from. The knock at the door ingrained the habit that you don't need to see your point of focus to respond to the energy it is putting across. If there is a camera in the room, and you've got a mark on the wall, you've got the same thing to work off of. That said, if you're being filmed, ask if you can have someone stand in front of the mark so you can have a face to work off of; if you can, great, but if not, the mark is just fine also.

Breaking the back brings us to a fine nuance of the way we have handled this work: you haven't made your success as a leader dependent on another person. You've made it dependent on getting your attention off of yourself. You can do that with a person, an audience, a camera, or just a spot on the wall. The values translate into many situations without your needing to adjust anything. You'll still go into a set of circumstances open, determine what you need to put your attention onto, do so, and respond truthfully from there. The circumstances will filter your observations and responses as needed. It is a simple value, but it has not been an easy one to obtain. Your hard work and training continues to pay off here with a heightened sensitivity to one of the most valuable skills you can take from a training program: the ability to discern the most relevant points of attention across situations and to have the technical capacity to respond to them authentically.

Now that you have begun the process of ironing out all extraneous details in a set of circumstances, it is time for us to bring in a method of analysing them that continues to honor the values we have worked on this entire journey. In every session, you are moving closer towards complete ownership and portability of this work into your leadership technique.

Summary

The values of the independent activity brought you to the point of being able to fully live truthfully under an extremely meaningful given set of circumstances. The circumstances of the activity are written by you, and as such are the easiest to enter into, given their personal nature. Now we begin the next step of the work, which is importing the ability to live truthfully into a given set of circumstances you are not familiar with. This is accomplished by you working with your partner on a scripted scene using an exercise known as breaking the back of a text. Breaking the back is likened to being a repetition exercise with a piece of paper in one's hand: the words are largely secondary, the primary value being on your experience with your partner. In this way, you will be able to hear clearly the elements of scenario and its context without bias or interpretation. This serves as a valuable precursor to beginning to analyse a situation in a way that lets you cleanly understand its unique circumstances. Those circumstances will organically filter your responses of living truthfully.

Breaking the back is also an extremely effective way of memorising in that it takes the attention off of yourself and allows you to constantly tie pre-written words, even content written by yourself, to external variables, moving your starting point with text to beginning with the premium value: that which is outside of you.

Tips for You and Your Coach

Breaking the back of a text is a relatively simple exercise with simple values. In the beginning especially it is going to be robotic, not sounding like normal speech, and that is the point. You and your clients will discover that, seemingly paradoxically, by removing the very human compulsions of being performative, acting 'natural,' as well as knee-jerk interpretation and analysis, the readers will much more deeply begin to hear the elements at play within a scenario. Encouraging them to slow down, take their time, and to follow all the guidelines will yield the best results. If you find some participants try to act the script regardless, encourage them to flatten the text out even more. For extreme cases, asking someone to speak it like a robot is a good starting place. Over time, you can lessen the robotic inflection to let the voice naturally come back into it as the habit to 'do something' with the words lessens.

The only other note is to continually encourage students to keep their attention on one another even when not speaking. Starting with repetition into the read will help. You are not looking for fireworks in the reading. You are looking for meaning to slowly begin emerging organically and to retrain the ears of your clients to hear a situation objectively and without interpretation. After working on two or three scenes, they will start to discover the values more and more in practice, where it counts.

Other plays with excellent two person scenes:

One man, one woman:
Angels in America by Tony Kushner
Reasons to Be Pretty by Neil LaBute
The Shape of Things by Neil LaBute
A Streetcar Named Desire by Tennessee Williams
Things I Know to Be True by Andrew Bovell
Two women:
The Children's Hour by Lillian Hellman
Closer by Patrick Marber
Dancing at Lughnasa by Brian Friel
Iron by Rona Munro
Top Girls by Caryl Churchill
Two men:
American Buffalo by David Mamet
Glengarry Glen Ross by David Mamet
A Number by Sam Shepard
The Normal Heart by Larry Kramer
True West by Sam Shepard

Chapter 13

Life Examined

New Eyes

I think by this point it's no understatement to recognise you've come a long way. As we near the end of the formal training, most people might be tempted to say 'You're not the same person you were on day one.' This, I hope you can see, is nonsense. You're still the same person and have retained the authentic core of your chaotic, engaging self. That has been the entire point at the heart of our work. No persona, no pretending: you are enough. The reason you feel different now is you are working with a set of acquired skills that have expanded your range of both observations and responses.

Looking back, the work you have done through the training exercises the Meisner Technique offers for leadership development is extensive. Consider that we began this whole journey with a seemingly simple concept: the best markers of authenticity begin in investing in the reality of doing, of giving yourself fully and completely to a task, regardless of whether it is a material activity or an interpersonal exchange. Simple, however, is not always easy. The rabbit hole led us into the tools of public solitude and fuck polite, which allowed us to break down the components of leadership into a concise phrase imported directly from the Meisner Technique: living truthfully under a given set of circumstances.

Investigating and training living truthfully took us through the journey of observe-and-respond, tackling issues such as the unit of the moment, working moment to moment, all the while delving deeply into the vast range of authentic expressions constantly on offer. The knock at the door uncovered the challenge of movement, as well as the ingrained social obstacles that come with it. All of this culminated in the independent activity, where the explosive pressure that the given set of circumstances puts on you pushes your abilities to listen clearly and deeply to the elements of a situation without interpreting from the get-go to the fringe. This was only further fuelled by either fiery preparations or extremely meaningful circumstances.

With the burner raging at a ten on the intensity scale, we turned it down considerably in the previous chapter, where you began the process of importing your ability to live truthfully into a given set of circumstances not created by yourself. This continues the practical aspect of making this technique flexible and portable, moving you ever towards owning a general ability to use it across contexts. This was accomplished by introducing you to some of the juiciest scenes from theatre scripts and then just as quickly flattening them to a chopped up robotic reading through an exercise called breaking the back of a text. While it may have seemed sadistic to put such wonderful writing through that, what repeat readings using this exercise reveal is that the words are not flattened for the sake of it but to reduce pre-emptive analysis and interpretation, instead connecting the language to variables outside of you—in this case your partner. By allowing the words to float on top of a personal interchange between each other, the exercise begins to take on the values of repetition. This is why my Meisner teacher Scott often likened it to 'a repetition exercise with a piece of paper in your hand.'

Looking back, the journey has been vast. That said, we are not out of the woods just yet. While the practical exercises on offer are coming to an end, the richest fruits of the work arrive here. In these last steps, you will be introduced to an approach to exploring scenarios and the dynamics within them that facilitates the values of this work. We are, of course, talking about analysis.

As you may imagine, any approach to analysis compatible with this work is a tall order. Analysis happens entirely in the head. Breaking the back taught us it is possible to be somewhat objective, but the more you begin to break up reality, searching for the meaningful variables, the more of a challenge it will be to keep your lens of interpretation out of the equation. Up until now, we have shied away from interpretation of any kind. You have spent this whole journey discovering in practice why bringing in an agenda is going to rob you of the riches of the experience. Higher cognitive processes have been the enemy of the more humanistic, at times primal, experiences this training has to offer.

If things stayed that way, however, it would place you at an extreme disadvantage. You can't expect every situation to have the same levels of meaning that independent activities offer, nor do you want to walk in entirely blind. There are situations, after all, in which you will have to enter to get something you need. Our journey, then, leads us to asking if there is any form of analysis you can use that gives you the best of both worlds: the ability to interpret deeply while still being able to let the given circumstances of that situation filter your truthful responses in the rich, organic way you have trained for without catching you off guard.

Answering this brings us to some clearer conclusions: this work places interpersonal power as the object of premium value. Situations are often composed not only of immaterial variables but also the input of human beings. Humans, as you have probably inferred from the training, are incredibly dynamic, with intricate psychology. You know from training that it is impossible to be in the head of another human being; at the same time, a method of analysis that can predict and allow you to test information about the possible psychology of a person in a specific situation would prove a deep advantage to you, especially if that information can be utilised to, just as in an independent activity, filter your observations of, as well as responses to, their behaviour. Even better is a form of analysis that can also incorporate the sensitivity you have developed to environmental variables both large and subtle.

In this session, we are going to look at a method of analysis that meets all of these needs and criteria. For the first part of the session, we will apply it to written scenes. Written scenes are excellent to analyse because all of the relevant information is on the page. They lack the true uncertainty of reality, but you will never be able to analyse in a way that tells you the future. Rather, a healthy, reasonable aim is to apply a method of analysis to many static situations, in this case, scripted scenes, that eventually will turn into a general form of interpretation that can aid you in future scenarios as they unfold in the present.

Making that latter component more concrete, in the second half of this chapter we will look at how this analysis can be used as a pre-emptive strategy, not to plan out the future but to give yourself a better advantage for understanding the possible circumstances you are entering into and to discern the relevant variables within them.

The benefit of learning to apply a form of analysis to other people runs deep. First, it gives you clarity about the situation from their point of view. Delusion, and its offspring desperation, often arises when there is a discrepancy between our own expectations and conclusions regarding why others behave in certain ways. Being able to analyse another person clinically will aid in your being consistent with yourself, which in the long term protects you from somebody picking up on a motivation you might not be aware of and using it to put you at a disadvantage.

Exercise: Text Analysis

This is one approach to text analysis found within the Meisner Technique. It comes primarily from my teacher Scott Williams and his work at the Impulse Company. There are equally powerful ways to analyse a scenario; in my view, fewer things even compare with Larry Silverberg's approach to analysis. The reason I am focusing here on Scott's approach is because Larry's is far more attuned to actors and utilises an entirely different process of working. Both are profoundly valuable, so if you find yourself wanting to have additional tools for interpersonal analysis, then I recommend Larry's approach to text work. You might find yourself having to parse some actor variables from what you learn, and for this reason I am using the Impulse approach.

Step one of any analysis is to break the back of the scene before working. Once you have flattened any desires to input your own agendas and have set your values in the right place, in such a way that you can live truthfully while speaking the words, you can begin the detective work that is text analysis. Text analysis for our purposes is not designed to make you an actor or a better one, though it is used for this, of course. Analysing a scene gives you concrete interpretive methods for discerning both overt and subtle qualities of given circumstances and learning how to thrive within them. It also lets you dispense with irrelevant variables, including speculations. We are moving ever farther towards bringing your technique closer in line with reality and its many nuanced variables.

Here's a scene I've written for this chapter. Go ahead now and with your partner break the back of the scene. If you need a refresher on any of the components, feel free to look through the previous chapter, especially at the criteria that are very clearly laid out in the exercise section. You'll be working on either Ray or Kate. To remind you, don't worry about casting, a gender, and so on. Just choose either role you want to analyse. Nor do you need to be concerned about the interruptions and overlaps signified by a '/' symbol as you break the back of this scene. Just read the text in sequence. Here's the scene:

Start.
Ray enters. Kate is waiting. There is a pink box on the counter.

Kate: Hey.
Ray: (*startled*) Oh.
Kate: Oh.
Ray: Sorry. Didn't know you'd be up.
Kate: Didn't know you'd be out.
Ray: Well, I told you, Jerry needed—
Kate: At 7.
Ray: What?
Kate: At 7. Your meeting went on for eight hours?
Ray is silent.
Kate: So. How is he?

Ray: Who?

Kate: Jerry.

Ray: Right, good, good. He thinks he can get away for a weekend next month.

Kate: That's nice.

Ray: I was thinking…

Kate: Thinking?

Ray: Well, we could go with him.

Kate: *(shaking her head.)* Jesus.

Ray: I know you're busy right now but come on/

Kate: Busy.

Ray: it could do us, yes busy. It could do us a little good. Some sun. Warm sands.

Kate: You want to go to the beach?

Ray: Why, you don't?

Kate: Ray. It's November. Fucking November.

Ray: I know it is/

Kate: What sun is there going/

Ray: I just thought/

Kate: to be? What warm sand?

Ray: Okay. Sorry.

Kate: If you're really sorry you can tell me what's going on.

Ray: I did tell you/

Kate: What's really/

Ray: already.

Kate: *actually* going on, bullshit. Bullshit, Ray. And you know it.

Ray: I don't know what your problem is but you need to sort yourself out.

Kate: My problem.

Ray: Yes.

Kate: Sleep.

Ray: Sleep?

Kate: That's my problem.

Ray: No one asked you to wait for me.

Kate: I asked myself.

Ray: Why?

Kate: Curiosity. To find out where my deviant husband

Ray Deviant./

Kate: goes when he thinks/

Ray: Big word, Kate. Big word

Kate: I'm asleep. Or slips out of bed and says he's just going for a walk around the yard. A three hour walk around the yard. Big fucking yard we've got these days, isn't it?

Ray: I like to be with my thoughts. Alone.

Kate: And those drives you go for? On these 'lonely' nights?

Ray: People drive, Kate. Sometimes they do.

Kate: And sometimes they lie. And you've been doing it more than a few times.

Ray: I don't need this right now. I really don't. You've got no-

Ray looks down, sees the pink paper box.

Ray: What's this?

Kate: Cheesecake.

Ray: From where?

Kate: Sullivan's.

Ray goes instantly quiet.

Kate: Jerry brought it by earlier. He said he hopes your cold gets better and you'll be missed at dinner.

Ray: (deep breath) Kate-

Kate: Ray.

Her tone stops him. Ray goes silent.

Kate: Don't you care about it, anymore?

Ray: What?

Kate: Being whole.

Ray: Whole?

Kate: Yes. When people do sinful things it hurts them. Breaks them up into fragments. Every time you make yourself dirty it kills us a little more. Kills me.

Ray: I don't know what you're talking about.

Kate: I've been having this dream at night.

Ray opens a drawer. Looks around in it.

Ray: I'm calling Dr. Stephens.

Kate: A dream where I come home from service. I'm/

Ray: She always got you back on track./

Kate: younger, and instead of the house being empty there's a man waiting for me. And he has these hands that hurt me, he grips my bare shoulders and my body, the bones just turn to powder. He touches my skin and it slides off and becomes water. I'm drowning in a chalk sea. The last thing I see before I go under is him leaning in. You. You leaning in with that fucking grin you get, your spit is hot. And those nights when I have that dream and I wake up and you're gone…sometimes I feel so relieved, like you were just the thing in the nightmare and I'm back in the old apartment again. Alone. Clean.

Ray: Something is wrong with your meds. Again. *(slams drawer shut)* Fuck. Where is that card?

Kate: They don't have one strong enough to keep pushing it down. Remember when we were building that shelter?

Ray: Yeah. I do.

Kate: You and me. Together. Felt so good.

Ray: …it did.

Kate: God used to put his Hands on me, Ray. Did he ever do that to you?

Ray: Come on, I still go to church.

Kate: That's not what I asked. Did you *ever* feel it, feel something?

Ray: Sometimes. Maybe. I don't know.

Kate: I see. Whatever it is you're doing, whoever you're fucking or if you're, I don't know, Ray. Or wait. Maybe I do. Maybe you've had a little trip?

Ray: Stop.

Kate: A small stumble. Putting something into your arm again?

Ray: Stop.

Kate: The wagon's always too high for you, isn't it?

Ray. STOP.

Kate: Why should I stop? You've been shutting me out for months now. So who's got to stop, Ray, who?

Ray: I shut you out? Really? Because you've been a real ten in the intimacy department lately.

Kate: (thrown off at first) You're really going to turn this on me?

Ray: No, but you, you get to share some responsibility too.

Kate: For what? What wasn't enough?

Ray: The whole thing. Everything. I don't know, Christ—

Kate: Don't you fucking dare bring up that name, not fucking right now.

Ray: I didn't mean/

Kate: Close your mouth before you say another word of poison. I'm giving you a last lifeline, Ray. It's not just for you, it's for me. I can't lose my community. Don't disgrace me like this.

Ray: Kate.

Kate: Please, let's try and fix it ourselves. Like you promised we always would. Before whatever this is gets out and I can't show my face anymore. Talk to me, please. What have you been doing, when you think no one is watching?

Ray: Some things can't be fixed, Kate.

Kate: Then tell me. Just talk to me and then I'll know. That's all I want right now. Just to have some clue of where I am again, and how to find my way back. Talk.

End.

Once you've finished the exercise it is now time to analyse. Whether you are working on Ray or Kate, the way to analyse this text is the same. You are both going to begin with analysing your character. Both you and your partner have broken the back of the scene, so you've heard clearly some or all of the elements within the situation. The next step is to analyse it in a way that allows you to enter under the given circumstances and respond truthfully to one another. The key to this? Point of view. You have trained this whole time to be fully inside of an experience. Rather than asking you to 'create a character', the premium is on discovering the elements of a person's point of view from within your own experience in the scene. In the independent activity, you didn't need to consider this, as it was your own point of view you were working from. Consider how much point of view filters your impulses. A scenario extremely meaningful to you determines your behaviour in profound ways. This next step is how you bridge an experience of deep meaning with the life of another.

I prefer the word 'detective' in relation to this form of analysis because it implies not a final conclusion but investigation. That's the best model for analysis of any situation. Getting it right on the first go and then never worrying about it again is the wrong metric. Instead, you want to use your skills of analysis to arrive at the most likely conclusions and then test them. To get the material for testing, you want to ask and answer three questions about your character. These really aren't questions best answered in your mind, so I've provided a section for you to write your answers to these questions. As you'll soon see, there's no value in trying to keep track of these variables in your head. Go and grab a pen, as there might be a lot of information to keep track of. I'm going to do the analysis as well, and once you are done, we'll compare what we came up with.

Here are your three questions with a bit of clarifying information.

One. What is the knowledge of the character in this scene?

The value here, just as in repetition, is to avoid speculation. Only list the facts the character knows, even if dramaturgically (in the greater world of the story) they are not true. For example, if a character knows their significant other is lying to them but we know from other scenes this is not true, still write down that, in that scene, the knowledge of the character is that their partner is lying to them. For clarity, you are only analysing this scene and do not need to research the rest of the play for our purposes, so write down as much knowledge as you can find in simple, bullet-like sentences. Stay simple and list all knowledge. If you come across something you think is knowledge but you are not sure, just leave it out. Generally, most likely you'll wind up with about 15–30 pieces of knowledge, but this can vary greatly depending on what scene you are analysing.

Two. What is the character literally doing in the scene?

The word 'literally' is on point, in that all we are talking about here are essential physical actions. Though this seems fairly simple, you'll have to carefully look over the text to find out what physical actions are really vital. Take the example of stage directions. Sometimes stage directions are crucial to the circumstances. One person strikes another in anger, for example. With rare exception, that is going to profoundly impact the circumstances. At other times, however, the stage directions are the scene as the writer sees it playing out in their mind. Someone might say something with a direction of 'mildly irritated' attached to that line, or shaking their head in frustration. Now, mildly irritated or a head shake could be essential to the circumstances but more likely than not this is the writer attempting to help actors get it right. The beautiful thing? You're not an actor, and even if you were, these are more helpful suggestions rather than essential demands and so have no place in your analysis. You'll have to use your own powers of discernment to glean what is really necessary to the circumstances and what is more of a staging suggestion or an acting tip.

Just as with the first question, simplicity will be your friend in this. If a character is making a mojito for example you don't need to write, 'opens the fridge, takes out the rum, closes the fridge, places the bottle on the counter, opens the ice chest, massages the mint' – you get the idea. Instead, the best thing to write is that he or she is 'making a mojito.'

At the end of this question you'll have a list of answers, probably significantly fewer than the first question. I'll give you a helpful hint, however: there are almost always, including this scene, a minimum of two essential actions. Can you guess what they are? Don't read ahead. As you go back through the scene, try to look for two obvious essential actions that will be present in almost every scenario or interaction you ever analyse. If you overthink it, you'll miss them.

Before we get to the third question, let's look at what you will most likely have after answering these questions. What you will find from answering questions one and two is that you have is a fairly detailed list of facts about the situation your character is in from their point of view. This supporting evidence is what you will use to deduce an answer to the third key question.

Three. What is the need of the character in the scene?

The word need has been very carefully chosen. What you're not seeing are words like 'goals' or 'objectives'. Why? They're obviously important. True, but they aren't the deepest thing on offer. Consider your own leadership needs in relation to this question. Your personal goals arise from something within you. They are formed, along with the behaviours and strategies to execute them, because they are propelled by a deeper yearning. The thing that gives it away is that goals are uniquely time-oriented. We might have immediate or even long-term goals, but both of them arise from something more constant at our core. That deeper, more primal force that drives your goals is a need. Needs are intricately tied to meaning, something you have experienced first-hand that can be of extreme value for a leader. You have explored your own personal veins of extreme meaning in the independent activities, and now you are going to begin hunting for how to recognise evidence of needs in other individuals. Having an understanding of the deeper core elements that motivate an individual gives you a powerful window into their existence as well as the behaviours that arise from them.

In this form of analysis, you will use the gathered information to try to boil down what the need of the character is in the scene. Needs are difficult to put into words, they are extremely nuanced and often filled with complexities. A helpful simplification tool many people, myself included, use is wording a need as a metaphor. However you phrase it, what is most important is not that you word it cleverly but that you do so in a visceral way that has an impact on you.

Let's take a look at that scene. Referencing the text, and the suggestions for how to approach these questions, write your text analysis for either Ray or Kate. I've left you a good amount of space, but if you need more feel free to continue on a separate page. When you're finished, turn the page to see mine. We won't make it a contest, but use my notes to compare, seeing which is more clean and makes more sense to you.

Kate

What is Kate's knowledge in the scene?

_____

_____

_____

_____

_____

_____

_____

_____

_____

_____

_____

_____

_____

_____

_____

_____

_____

What is Kate literally doing in this scene?

_____

_____

_____

_____

_____

_____

_____

_____

_____

_____

_____

_____

_____

_____

_____

What is Kate's need in this scene?

_____

_____

Ray

What is Ray's knowledge in the scene?

_____

_____

_____

_____

_____

_____

_____

_____

_____

_____

_____

What is Ray literally doing in this scene?

_____

_____

_____

_____

_____

_____

_____

_____

_____

_____

_____

What is Ray's need in this scene?

_____

_____

_____

Side by Side

Now that you have completed a text analysis for either of your characters, I'm going to list mine here as well. Like I said, don't compare these necessarily for quality but rather for simple accuracy. For clarity, though I've written this scene, when it comes to analysis, believe it or not, that doesn't give me any leg up or advantage. This is because if I want to properly analyse this scene I still need to discover if the needs of these two individuals are true. Writers often change their perspectives on characters, so again my analysis is certainly not how yours 'must be,' but is rather my exploration of two humans in a situation with fresh eyes. Read both analyses, starting with the character you didn't analyse. This will give you a more relaxed eye to look at the process before getting to your own character. For both, look at my evidence and ask if based on that evidence I have enough to support the needs I've arrived at. I'll start with Ray.

What is Ray's knowledge in the scene?
His name is Ray.
He is married to Kate.
They live together.

He has been out.
He knows Jerry.
He told Kate he was going to meet Jerry.
It's November.
He slips out of bed when he thinks Kate is asleep.
He tells her he is going for a walk around the yard.
He goes for drives.
He knows what Sullivan's is.
He told Jerry he could not come to dinner because of a cold.
He knows Dr. Stephens and has her number.
Dr. Stephens always got Kate back on track.
Kate takes medication.
Kate goes to church services.
Kate attended church when she was younger.
Kate believes in sin.
They built a shelter together.
He still goes to church.
Kate's doses have been off in the past.
He used to take drugs through a needle in the arm.
They (Kate and Ray) sleep in the same bed.
They have made love before.

What is Ray literally doing in this scene?
Ray is talking to Kate about being out with Jerry, taking a vacation, being alone, that there is something wrong with her medications, calling Dr. Stephens, and that she has been lacking in the intimacy department and shares responsibility for the current situation. He is listening to Kate talk about him lying to her and Jerry, his disappearances, him destroying her with his sin, her nightmare, her relationship to God, being disgraced by his lying, and his past drug abuse. He is looking for Dr. Stephens' card.

What is Ray's need in this scene?
Ray's need is to not have this conversation.

Let's take this number by number. In the first question, looking for his knowledge, I found a fair amount of information that would have required speculation on my end. The obvious example being we know that Ray is doing something without Kate's knowledge but really there is no clear evidence to support a more specific conclusion. We also know there is something to do with a meeting and Jerry, confirmed when we find out Jerry brought by a get-well cheesecake and unintentionally exposed Ray's double lie. The relevant thing to note is the evidence that supports there was an actual meeting. What the meeting is, and what Ray's relationship to Jerry is, is unclear. They might be work colleagues, friends, brothers, a combination, or something entirely different. It is not clear, so I don't speculate about elements that may be important but are unclear. I simply don't have the relevant information and must accept that, working with what I have rather than what I suspect to be there.

Another bit of possible knowledge: Jerry says that he is going on vacation, somewhere with beaches and Ray thinks it is a great idea for them to join him. Sounds like fairly reasonable knowledge to include in our analysis. Or does it? Let's start with that vacation. Ray implies that

Jerry said this during the meeting. Any details about the meeting would be a lie, given that Ray never attended, but that doesn't mean Jerry could not have said this in another interaction. By itself Ray's connecting it to the meeting might not be enough to cast doubt on the validity of this information as knowledge, but now other elements have to be considered: a beach vacation in December. Ray tries to placate Kate with images of sun and warm sands, and when she calls the obvious his stumped reaction implies he hasn't even thought about this himself. A rival hypothesis emerges. It could be he is attempting to deflect Kate's suspicions by distracting her with the prospect of a vacation that he is fabricating on the spot. If the secret is important enough, this is entirely plausible. The most relevant piece of information for me? At the end, the conclusion is unclear. There's enough grey area for me to doubt how true either option is that I can omit anything about the vacation as knowledge.

As a counterbalance, we can examine something said much later, in relation to Kate's medications that, on first glance, might appear as speculation. At one point Ray begins to rummage through a drawer looking for Dr. Stephens' card. There's clearly some knowledge there. How about when he says Dr. Stephens was always able to straighten Kate out in the past. Knowledge or not? We may not know exactly what the before-and-after of this alleged straightening out looked like, but we do know that Kate has had dosage problems with her medication. Whatever the medication is, it has a direct impact on her behavior. A phrase like that may sound speculative, but two important pieces of information exist to be considered. The first is that the type of language Kate is using in the second half of the scene has triggered something in Ray. He detects a clear shift from what is a norm in her interactions with him. His immediate association? Call her doctor, rather than anyone else, and urgently. In addition, we can't rule out the second piece of information, which is the possibility of self-serving motives coming into play. For some time Ray has been hiding a major secret that he clearly doesn't want Kate to discover. We can't be sure but the possibility of her being medicated enough to dull her behavior to his advantage could be incredibly important to Ray. Either possibility supports the idea that Dr. Stephens can straighten Kate out enough. A final additional component must be considered: when looking for the card, there is urgency in his behavior. This also lends also some weight to how important contacting Dr. Stephens is. Given Ray's physical behaviors and the context they are manifesting in, to me there is enough evidence to support his knowledge that Dr. Stephens is a problem solver when it comes to Kate's behavior.

This is what I mean by looking at the strength of the evidence. As you are starting to see here, context is everything. It is true that with further information, certain grey-area comments we intuit may be important could change into being either definitively knowledge or definitively speculations, but maybe not. Without additional information, taking the bait of your temptation to predict and determine unknown variables in the future will only work against you. In analysing anyone, real or fictional, you don't need to deliberate about any pieces of information that may need guesswork—you can simply omit them and no harm will be done to the strength of your analysis. In fact, the analysis becomes strengthened by any speculations left out, since we are only working with 'what is' rather than making immensely interpretive and creative leaps. We are doing our best to simply stay with what Ray knows to be true.

On to the second question, you'll notice I said there are always two pieces of essential action with extremely rare exceptions. These actions are talking and listening. It sounds blatantly simple, but these are vital elements of communication the scene hinges on. If Ray isn't talking, or Kate isn't listening, then nothing in this exchange would be possible. With immensely rare exception, talking and listening, and being specific about the content of each action, are two very valuable pieces of information about actions essential to a set of circumstances.

You'll also notice I didn't include many other possibilities not essential to the circumstances. We know he is talking and listening but how? Maybe they are both sitting at their table, Ray leaning slightly back with one hand still on the table. Or maybe Kate is standing while Ray is sitting. Perhaps they speak their lines in muted tones or shout them. There could be beats, or pauses, throughout, and so on. These are all staging decisions. None of these elements were essential to Ray's actions in the situation. It doesn't matter how we stage it so long as they are in the same room. All that matters in this case is that he is speaking, and listening, to Kate. The same can be also said of the action of looking through the drawer—it doesn't matter how we interpret him doing it, but that we have observed and captured a behavior essential to the circumstances of this situation.

Coming to my answer for the need, you may have the most questions about my answer and why I chose it. Here's why I think we can have a comparative discussion: when analysing behaviour, there are endless possibilities until you begin to analyse from the facts of the situation. Since we are after the need of the character, we don't need to worry about facts of the play so much as the facts of their point of view. Just as with the other questions, there are many possible answers for a need, but the majority of them fall prey to speculation. The facts can point us in some clear directions, and the likelihood is that, even if we will word it differently, you and I will arrive at a similar proposal for a need we will test in the next steps. Here are the facts I worked from to arrive at Ray's need.

Let's start with some relevant basics. We know that Ray lives with Kate. They sleep in the same bed, they live together, they go to church together, and have a past of some appearance of mutual emotional investment in the relationship. We can glean this last fact from Kate's memories of building a shelter together as a golden period in their relationship. We can't be sure if Ray's agreement is sincere or not but there's less evidence to support it as a sarcastic or deflective comment. We also know that they both as well valued at one point mutually agreed on communication. Something, however, has changed. Ray is hiding something from Kate, he knows this, and the likelihood is that he has been lying to her for some time. The lying is very important, especially in context of their relationship. Whatever is happening, it is equally vitally important to maintain it as well as its secrecy from Kate. There's been no indicator he has tried or even considered ending their marriage, and there's no indication he intends to end whatever it is he is doing alone, so for the time being he is living in the belief that he can juggle both. In addition, again from Ray's perspective, Kate's problems with her medications have resurfaced. This has happened before and has become common enough that he can recognise the indicators. The unusual language she uses is profoundly visceral, from her sexual nightmare of disintegrating and drowning to at times biblical ways of speaking about wholeness and cleanliness. There is also the very real possibility that their intimate life is suffering, Ray's comment cuts but it isn't met with surprise or confusion. We wouldn't be making a leap to conclude there are deep, serious problems in their relationship.

At the same time, looking at the situation outside of Ray's perspective we can see he is deeply in denial about his capabilities within this situation. The possibility of cleanly living a double life is a house of cards many people fall victim to. Ray is no exception. Look at the number of deflections he uses even before he knows she has caught him, as well as the relative ease he does it with. She asks where has he been and immediately he gets her to the vacation idea. It is also nearly 3:00 a.m. If you'll look at Ray's information, you'll notice that the time specifically wasn't included in Ray's knowledge precisely because we don't know if he lost track of time or not. In a more clear-headed moment, Ray would know that being out so late to talk to someone about an upcoming vacation would be a vapid and bizarre justification. Rather than recognising it, instead he uses his excuse to further his deception. When later she presses him he changes the conversation once again, turning to problems with her medication, even striking at their intimate life and implying she has a high level of ownership in their relationship problems. What we find is that there is more than enough evidence from the situation to suggest this is a man desperately trying to be light on his feet. Why? Because now he recognises Kate knows the truth about him having a secret life and discovers she has for some time. We also have enough evidence from Ray's behavior to indicate that there might be problems with Kate's dosage, but the scale is unclear. Consider, after all, that even if she is having severe problems with her medication she still recognises the pattern of Ray's behavior.

The challenge of a secret life is one many people have had to struggle with. We have to be careful, however, of the kneejerk desire to be immediately judgmental about this and write Ray off as a betrayer to his marriage. If we do this, then we impose our desires to control the unknown onto an ambiguous situation. As a result, this could cloud your conclusion for a need, arguably the most vital element in this type of analysis. The reality is he never reveals what he is hiding. Reflecting for a moment on some of the extremely meaningful possibilities for why a person may have a private life might give us a sense of both Ray's denial and the suffering he is going, and putting Kate, through.

We can first examine perhaps the most supported possibility, which is an addiction relapse. Consider that for decades and decades the societal stigmas against mental disorders, diseases we know now involve vast areas of the body, including the central nervous system, the hypothalamus, synapses, inhibited memory systems, the microbiome, and pain sensors. Whether it has been depression, anxiety disorders, dissociative disorders, or compulsive disorders, every disease that attacks cognition and well-being is a biological disease. For many generations, however, such afflictions were seen as a lack of character. The shame that comes from society stigmatizing compounds the challenges that a person suffering with mental disorders encounters when trying to seek help. The same challenges still rage today for people with compulsive disorders, still commonly thought to be defects of character rather than having their roots in biology. We know Ray has battled and, to Kate's knowledge, overcome such a demon. Whatever our individual views on this, we cannot ignore the profound existential guilt generated from addiction relapses and how that can dramatically inform a person's deeper needs.

Or perhaps Ray's need for secrecy is something entirely different. Maybe he is involved in illegal work of sorts. Kate implies there may be an affair. It is possible, but also intricately open-ended. It may be conventional, or perhaps Ray is hiding something about his sexuality he is too frightened to tell Kate about because of her views. In all of these examples from the perspective of the individual in those circumstances, the temptation can be to deny what you are really going through, especially if there is a fear of social punishment attached. We know that both Kate and Ray are involved in religion, Kate much more so. There may be an element of communal retribution at play, whether it is abandonment, severing ties, or seeing one or both of them as less-than. There's some evidence that Ray is not as strong in his faith but would he wish such disgrace on Kate who clearly is? He doesn't bat an eye at her use of the word 'disgrace', or tell her she is overexaggerating. Clearly these are not things he wishes to consider, and how much, or little, he weighs these consequences to Kate is unknown. Whatever Ray is doing, the great pretending for him is that there won't be consequences if he just hides things well enough. The less Kate knows the better.

We all have our opinions about withholding a secret life from our partner. It is a charged, loaded topic. What we have to be careful of when it comes to analysing the point of view of another is imposing those views on their reality. That clouds us from recognising the inner workings of the person we are dealing with. For whatever reason, Ray is has been hiding something major from Kate. Ray is deeply in denial about it spilling over or her finding out. Sticking with the ambiguity of the situation reveals how disastrous his inner life must be and allows us to understand why, to preserve his own survival, he has to stop talking about the truth at any chance he can get. Kate is smart. She is tortured, but he knows she sees him. This is not just brushing it off: this is deeply connected to his need to have some stability in his reality and to keep things as they are. Worded for simplicity: he needs, desperately, to not have this conversation right now.

Now that we've spent enough time in Ray's point of view, let's look at things from the other side of the table. I have a feeling we are going to arrive at some conclusions that will help us get a clear sense of the circumstances, not just of Kate, but of their dynamic.

What is Kate's knowledge in the scene?
Her name is Kate.
She is married to Ray.
They live together.
It is around 3 am.
Ray is out.
Ray lied about going to a meeting with Jerry at 7.
Ray lied to Jerry and said he could not attend the meeting because of a cold.
Jerry dropped off a get-better cheesecake from Sullivan's.
It is November.
Ray slips out of bed when he thinks she is asleep.
Ray lies about going for walks in their yard and is gone for hours.
Ray goes for long drives.
When people do sinful things it makes them impure.
Ray's sins are killing her.
She is a patient of Dr. Stephens.
Dr. Stephens prescribes her medication.
She has had trouble with dosages in the past and has had to adjust them.
She goes to church services.
She has been going since she was younger.
She dreams that her bones turn to powder and her skin turns to water when Ray touches her. Ray is grinning and his spit is hot.
When she wakes up alone sometimes she feels relief.
They sleep in the same bed.
She and Ray built a shelter together.
God used to put His Hands on her.
Ray struggled with addiction to a drug that is injected in his arm.
They have been intimate before.
She belongs to a community.
She used to live in an apartment.

What is Kate literally doing in the scene?
Kate is talking to Ray about his lying to her about Jerry, his drives, walks, sneaking out of bed, lying to Jerry, what his sins are doing to them, her nightmare, and how she will be disgraced if what he is doing gets out to their community. She is listening to Ray talk about the meeting with Jerry, taking a vacation, calling her doctor to get her medication adjusted, her lacking in the intimacy department, and how some things cannot be fixed.

What is Kate's need in the scene?
Kate's need is to live clean again.

Just as with Ray, let's take this question by question.

Answering question one in this case is more challenging than answering it for Ray. There are a lot of visceral declarative statements in here, and discerning what is knowledge versus something spoken in the heat of the moment is not easy. Kate's lines are filled with heavily visual images and she is aggressively forward in confronting Ray. At the same time, we have to consider a few things. Hyperbole often masks true intention, and in extremely meaningful situations people say things that often feel true in the moment but on later reflection turn out not to be accurate. Clearly this situation has immense meaning to Kate, so we want to parse what seems to be true knowledge from either the emotional temperature of the situation or the impact of her medication, if any.

Let's take, for example, her comment that the wagon of recovery is always too high for Ray. This certainly could be actual knowledge she is declaring to Ray: maybe she has always known he would never make it and that relapse was just a matter of time. At the same time, however, we have to look at another possibility: the addiction comment comes up quite late in their conversation, after she has been repeatedly fishing for a confession. Her wording is clipped, as if her question about relapse could be more rhetorical that sincere. She also knows it is a subject that brings him incredible pain. We don't have to take this at face value: consider Ray has a quick deflection for everything up until that point. When she hits that button about his addiction, however, all he can do is repeatedly use one word: 'Stop'. If you were in an argument, in deep agony yourself, and you wanted to really cut someone, what better thing to use as ammunition than utilising another's most profound inner struggle? We aren't judging Kate for this. People in circumstances of great pain say the most awful things. It could be knowledge that Ray was always doomed to relapse, but that there is a competing alternate theory makes me question if this is really her knowledge or if she instead wants to deeply hurt Ray. We don't have to make a decision either way—since it is speculative, we can omit it as her knowledge.

But how about that dream she describes? The discretion of the analyst is important, but for me, that seems deeply different than some of her other comments. It is so incredibly specific that I find myself working harder to justify that this cannot be knowledge. What are my alternative explanations? Problems with her medication? Possibly, but I'm not sold. Her behavior does not indicate psychosis or delusion, and behavioral problems due to an incorrect dose don't usually turn people into the best creative improvisers. Spur of the moment? Nowhere else in the text does she say anything that supports her having the ability to come up with something so vivid. She may be able to, but stacked against other possible momentary comments like 'the wagon is always too high for you' I'm less inclined to give that much credence. Some long-calculated image she conjured up to shock Ray? There's zero evidence in the scene to support that. With such specific images and details, gleaning for the likeliest possibility I am going with the decision that this is her knowledge.

Regardless of the components of Kate's lines, the key knowledge that presents itself is Kate's knowledge towards Ray's secret life. She is clearly past the point of wondering if something might be wrong—she knows he is up to something. We also know that she and Ray used to communicate far better, from her use of the phrase, 'Like we used to.' Whatever Ray is doing is problematic enough to hide from Kate, meaning it must be some serious sin that places her against the values of her community and faith. The consequences for living with sin don't just extend to an afterlife but torture the conscience of someone who genuinely believes they are an accomplice to a moral transgression. Look at her behaviour and what she is doing—she says it, and it has some truth to this: this might literally be killing her.

I think question two is fairly obvious in this answer, so I will move on, the reason being the same metrics apply to her behaviour in this question as Ray. There are many things she could be doing but the actions essential to these circumstances are simply talking and listening.

This lets us get into the meat of her need. To help you see how I got to this answer, let's start with the concept of hope. Kate seems to me like she still has the faintest glimmer of hope for her future. She is sharp and at times says cruel things, but towards the end implores Ray to communicate with her so that they can work together to solve this problem. She also expresses her pain to Ray that the situation is killing them and that there are consequences for her relationship to her community, implying she still has much to lose. But the most obvious evidence that some hope survives? She is still there. She hasn't left yet. The memories of togetherness and team work still have some meaning. This to me suggests that on some level there are still the dying embers of hope that somehow something salvageable can come out of this for her without it all crashing down. Embers, however, are the key image here. She knows this is a sinking ship, and on some level she feels complicit in the nightmare she is living in. The evidence? She has known for months that Ray was doing something, and she never confronted him until now. This brings with it huge components of shame, guilt, and self-blame. Also, in her description of her dream she says, 'Clean. Again.' implying she was on the right life trajectory at one point and is not now.

At this point we have to ask, what's her alternative, her out, if Ray doesn't cooperate? I don't think she has one. Things have gone too far, she is in too deep. Any way out ends in tragedy. Either she loses her community or she lives in sin. Her conscience will not allow her to stay in the situation. She is too self-aware to keep pretending. As a result, the dynamic she is in is impossible, it cannot be sustained. Once we recognise this we can get closer to the need by asking, what would the reverse of this situation be for Kate? She would know she would be living in the truth again, her reality would be consistent with her values. She wouldn't be stained by Ray's sins. Maybe Ray would be in the picture or not, we can't say for sure, but if he was he would be on a moral road again as well. All that pain tainting one's soul washed off. She once was clean. She needs to live clean again. A life no longer spent suffering in the shadows but in the light of knowing you are on the right path.

Here's the good news about this form of analysis. I don't have to agree with either of these people's views to investigate them. Nor am I analysing myself, so my judgements are secondary. I personally share almost none of Kate's religious views, but I can still explore her perspective and understand it to know what is driving her behaviours, from her words to her actions. My mission in this analysis is to get a clear understanding of the dynamics of a scenario and the needs of a person within it, rather than starting with how I want people in these situations to behave. I chose this scene specifically because it has two radically different world views and so is bound to push a button for you, forcing you to leave your opinions at the door if you wish to analyse them clearly and reliably.

What this form of analysis reveals for leadership is that there is an immense value in not judging people by our own standards but to enter their reality on a deeper level. This allows us to better understand what makes them tick and what fuels their behaviours. One of the many benefits of analysing play texts is that plays are often filled with world views sometimes radically different than ours. For example, very few of us share the world view of David Mamet's titular murderous character in *Edmund*, but analysing him gives us a powerful window into a set of human experiences vastly different than our own. When it comes to analysis, leaders are collectors of world views. They listen, observe carefully, and use simple methods to glean relevant information. This doesn't mean you don't have your own world views, but when it comes to your leadership, imposing your views and opinions over a situation can cloud you from entering it with clarity. Clarity plugs you into the given circumstances and allows you to live truthfully from there. Opinions are a form of speculation that only obscures.

Exercise: Testing the Analysis

So you've done your analysis, and you've arrived at your character's need. I said earlier not to worry if you arrived at a wildly different need than I did. Why? Because neither need is a final conclusion. Whether we converged or differed, both of our needs would need to be tested, and that is what you are going to do now.

To test your need, you and your partner are going to read the scene you've just analysed aloud. The reading now is a less strict version of breaking the back. You are not imposing a tone on it but are also not inflecting or adding on. What you are after is testing the need of the character. Rather than trying to force your conclusion to fit the reality of these circumstances, you're going to search for whether your need is true or not. To do this, put your attention on your partner, read the scene with them again, and see if it is true based on the feelings that arise inside of you throughout and at the end. You are not looking for the intellectual answer but the visceral experience that tells you from within whether or not you were close. In a normal session, at the end we would have a check-in and see from your experience if you were close or if during the read another need presented itself as you went on. Since I am not here, go ahead and read this scene aloud with your partner. Don't force anything, and at the end, see from the inside if you were accurate. Stay with each other.

The Microcosm

Let's say you read the scene, and at the end you conclude the need you deduced is true. Does that mean it is the end of your testing? Not at all. Each time you read the scene it will be a retesting of that need. That keeps the process open-ended. For our purposes, this will be the last time you read the scene, but the key value is always on testing. That will aid you when attempting to discern the needs of actual people, to understand what is driving their behaviours and allow that knowledge to filter your responses. Not all needs are accurate, however. If you discover the need is not true, then it is back to the drawing board based on the evidence you have.

In either case, what this exercise is instilling in you is the idea of how to analyse another human being based on what seems to be small, possibly irrelevant, details. Small details, however, add up to a meaningful body of information, and this alone will tell you something about the psychological reality of another human being. We often hear about the value of understanding another person's perspective, but this is often only for the purposes of spreading empathy or compassion. As far as leadership goes, there has to be a wider outcome of application than simply a justification for being kind to somebody. Since interpersonal power is the greatest value to your leadership journey, then this analysis gives you sharp clarity on the mechanics of situations and the people within them.

We have explored the concept that the best leaders have a seemingly uncanny ability to understand our plights and successes in their entirety, connecting to us with effortless ease and making us feel truly seen. They accomplish this through their ability to internally enter our world view and understand our needs, observing and responding to our behaviour and intuitively testing their knowledge of the situation as the interaction progresses. This is being spoken to at a layer that is at the essence of our conscious experience. Goals and objectives are ephemeral. They change over time, but the thing underneath that powers them is deep and constant. Our existential needs anchor us to our choice of jobs, relationships, regrets. They provide the material for the hope that paves our future. If you can accurately pin the need of another human being, you now have a major component of your given circumstances. Taking that on board and living truthfully, your responses will be filtered by the needs of the people in the circumstances and so will come across as attuned, understanding, and deeply engaged. Your internal experience will converge with its outward manifestation. In the real sense of the word, you will appear to be authentic.

Exercise: Interpersonal Analysis

Analysing the future is tricky. This whole body of training has focused not on predicting the future but on responding to the variables of the now. At the same time, recall that in an independent activity, you create a set of circumstances that have the highest chance of taking hold of you during the exercise. Looking at likelihood has been a reasonable companion to you. Rather than attempting to force your agenda onto an organic moment, you have planned for the variables most likely to succeed. Whether they do or don't is still up to the moment itself. At the same time, it tells us there is some possible return on offer in working with future outcomes.

To be clear, I just want to remind you here that the variables we are talking about are those directly essential to leadership, which are the interpersonal components of observing and responding within a given set of circumstances. That doesn't include strategies specific to your field of leadership. Those are essential to the success of your visions, but when we talk about the challenges of analysing the future, we are really trying to find a way for you to work with the variables outside of your control. That includes the behaviour of others, the dynamics of a shared situation, the unpredictability of interactions and circumstances, and so on. There is no approach that can predict these in a definitive way. Oftentimes you think you know exactly how something is going to unfold and then find yourself brutally surprised and overwhelmed. The next time anyone suggests a strategy that 'works every time', just remember the times in your life you were sideswiped by under-appraising the dynamic role chaos brings to any situation.

The best outcome for an analysis of the future follows the thinking not necessarily of the Meisner Technique but the lessons some approaches to the martial arts offer. Self-defence training is not about dominating the future but rather maximising your chances. By your working with the relevant variables and developing your sensitivity to them, you increase your chances for optimal results. Paralleling them with your training, a good analysis allows you to enter any interaction and situation sharp, with some semblance of knowledge but ready for unforeseen variables to surprise you. That is the chaos of the moment you have trained in and are now adept to flow from.

Taking the next step to further your scenario analysis abilities involves using the same approach to analysis as just presented, albeit with some minor modifications. Our aim now is to use this process of analysis not to predict the future but to lay out the territory for the given circumstances you will be entering into. As with a character, the point of analysis begins with a single individual of relevance to the situation you are going into. You don't need to do this type of analysis for everyone in the scenario, given you might not know who will be present, but if you have some concrete names, then analyse the most relevant people in that situation. That could be one or several.

In the case of analysing another person, it is a very simple process of applying this method of analysis. I won't include blank lines here because this is now part of your process, but just as before on a piece of paper write down your analysis. Pick a single individual and use their name in your analysis. If you want to analyse multiple people that is fine; you'll do a separate analysis for each individual. I'm now going to give an example of a hypothetical analysis for a future interaction. I'm going to analyse Robert. I've chosen him for my analysis because, in my circumstances, he is an executive at a company, and I need him to approve his company's spearheading a project I would like to see move forward. In this scenario, I've never met Robert, and so I want to have a sense of the territory I am going into with this meeting. To get this, I'm going to need the answers to several questions:

- What is Robert's knowledge in this situation?
- What is Robert going to be literally doing in this situation?
- What is Robert's need in this situation?

Like before, let's take this analysis question by question. For the first one, this immediately shows me something: I know very little about Robert. He's a decision-maker at a company and he's the guy who can make my project happen. So what? That tells me nothing specific about this individual. In some rare cases, that may be all I have to go on, but more often than not, information can be found out about people, especially those in higher positions of power. On to the Great Internet I go. I look for his biography, any talks he has given in print or media, any testimonials that may exist, and I consult any sources I know with direct experience interacting with him, as well as his résumé, if I can find it. What I need, just as with Ray and Kate, is the knowledge of that individual, including what I deem to be true about their perspective. Let's say I arrive at these pieces of information:

His name is Robert.
He is an executive at [company name here].
He is 56 years old.
He is single.
He has agreed to meet about my project.
Recently his company has gone through financial hardship, as a competitor has emerged and is taking revenue.
He is exploring new material.
He is from Pennsylvania.
He went to Harvard Business School.
He has been with this company for 20 years.
He has brokered four collaborative partnerships between his company and others.
He worked as a grocery bagger to help pay for college.
He is on the board of organisations x, y, z.
He supports charities [names here].
Hard work is the backbone of society.
Successful negotiating is about winning without the other person realising it.

You might be wondering what's up with those last two pieces of knowledge. Let's say that through research I found these two quotes. People use a lot of colourful phrasing or speculations in presentations and interviews, but these two phrases seem to line up with his background. These may not be objective truths about the world, but they fall in line with facts he knows to be true about the world. If later I discover this information is not as sound as I originally thought, then I can discard it as irrelevant to my analysis of this person.

As you can see, you don't need to become a biographer. You may end up with a list of five items or 50 if there is a lot of print or media about them. What is of more value to you than just facts is seeking the knowledge of that individual. These can be simple facts, but also truisms about their experience of reality. Generally, anywhere from 15 to 30 pieces of knowledge are a reliable amount, though this can vary.

This brings you to the second question: what is Robert going to be literally doing in the situation? This isn't as easy to answer as it is in an analysis of a play text or real situation that has already happened, given it is about an event in the future. Rather than attempting to fabricate an answer, we want to be clear about what is most likely going to happen in this situation. While you don't know the specifics of what will happen, just as in our training, what you can know is the basic territory of what you are going to be walking into. Will you two be alone in the room? Will the conversation be recorded or filmed? Will someone be present via a conference call? These are all basic physical facts about the situation that may be on offer. At the very least, there will always be two available to you. Let's say in a very short email Robert agrees to meet me on a coffee break near his office. We can get some pieces of information prepared to answer our second question:

He is having coffee alone with me.
He is listening to me talk about my project and how it fits with his company.
He is talking to me about his company's model, my budgeting expectations, my experience in the field, and the needs of his company.

Now this last one is interesting. How do we know what Robert is going to be talking about? We can't gauge what exactly will be said, but we can infer that some elements may be present. Consider the information that his company recently has taken a loss due to a competing service and that they are searching for new projects. He has a history of creating collaborations, so I may have an advantage in that he will be more open to new ideas and revisions to his business model. That's not the only way this can go, unfortunately. My project might be outside of his budget. I am also new to him, and so in a time of financial instability bringing new voices is risk or reward. These may not be brought up in conversation, but the likelihood is they will be is a factor.

I can't know the future, but I can glean the likely specifics of the situation. It is very possible the conversation will go a different way. There might be more people present than expected. This isn't a problem—it is a value we have been working with since the independent activity onwards. The circumstances can take any shape or appearance, reminding us not to set expectations but to work within possibilities and be flexible when the moment changes things on a dime. There may not be a conversation at all. Or the likely possibilities I have identified will unfold and filter my observations and responses accordingly. Either way, I am technically prepared to handle it.

Now that I've got some key information, I want to figure out who is the guy I'm talking to. What gets Robert out of bed in the morning, what drives him to seek new strategies in the face of major change rather than cling to old ones? Meeting with me is clearly part of that process. What is Robert's need in this situation?

To help us make a case, we've got some information from the first two questions. Clearly Robert excels in this position of leadership. He's held a stable business model for 20 years and now is adapting rather than handing the reins to someone else. We know that he is a man who values hard work: he uses the example of working as a grocery bagger to help pay for his tuition. He also graduated from Harvard Business School. Clearly Robert has standards for himself when it comes to work. That said, however, there's another element we have to consider. He isn't the kind of leader to simply work away in the shadows and behind the scenes. Robert likes to be involved in the public eye. He serves on the boards of other organisations and is involved in charities. He might be doing this for a variety of reasons, and so since we don't know his exact motivations, we can't include that into our distilled a need. We do know, however, that anonymity is not important to him in these areas, as he has not made any clear efforts to hide or downplay his involvement with social groups.

What we come up with, then, is a man who has high standards of work ethics and is actively involved in public social enterprises. This is someone to whom public image is very important. Let's add into this a third element: the company he has been a part of for 20 years has come into financial troubles recently. It is possible that he is facing some scrutiny for not being able to predict and handle this, but we can't be clear about that. It is equally as possible that this was inevitable and he is being seen as the perfect person to weather the storm. The key common denominator in either possibility? Extremely meaningful pressure. From Robert's past behaviours we can understand that this is a moment of challenge for him to rise to. The gains his company has made are a reflection of his own high standards. Doing right by his own company is doing right for the things that get him out of bed in the morning. Recognition is also important. He needs to come out of this on top in a way that is not only clear to him but others.

Given that there are two primary elements at work, overcoming the great challenge and for all to see, I peg a need: Robert's need is to be the great hero of his story.

Many of us live our life according to narrative. We are always the lucky one, or never seem to have any luck at all. Not all of our lives actually conform to such patterned rules, but certainly in many aspects we see ourselves more as characters than as people behaving under the laws of unpredictable causality. For some their story, as well as the accompanying persona constructed for the public, depends on the world acknowledging it. Its reception is paramount. We don't need to judge them for this. Many of us fall into similar patterns, and extensively good deeds can come from our need to be the hero of our story.

You might word it differently, but what is essential now is that if you were the one meeting with Robert, you have a need you can test. When you go into the meeting, you put your attention on Robert and, living truthfully, seek to test your theory. Rather than being an analytical conclusion, hunting for a need is a visceral, experiential process. You learned this in testing the needs of either Ray or Kate, but now you are extending searching for the need beyond your own experience and intuiting it from an interaction. Along the way, information might arise that confirms a different need, and so this will be equally valuable information for you, but if you begin to sense that this is the truth, you will have a strong ground from which to authentically observe and respond.

Within even this, you can import some strategic structure. You don't want to speak to Robert as a child, or worse, reveal you think you might know some deep psychological need of his. Rarely are we ever aware of our own needs, and this puts us at a disadvantage at times. Instead, you are working to see if you are on to something with your theory that Robert does need to be the hero of his own story. As you work with him, you will notice his essential behaviours when you introduce new ideas, phrases, or concepts. Being connected, your language, tone, and mannerisms will organically take on the qualities of the moment with this need present. If you find yourself anxious, don't worry—this is fuel in the same way you've worked with in preparations. You aren't trying to be All Zen but rather are actively engaged. If you have been correct about your analysis, the end result is Robert will feel validated and spoken to in a personal, meaningful way, and that places you in a very strong position. All this will have been achieved without the need for complicated strategy, bizarre faux-Machiavellian tactics, or trying to shove your own agenda onto the nuances of the moment.

This form of analysis can be done for a variety of situations: meetings, negotiations, speeches, presentations, and interviews. In all cases, it provides a valuable framework in which to place the research you would do about another person and their professional history. Testing and being accurate at assessing the deeper needs of people at work in a situation provides you access to their personal feelings and motivations in an organic way. In this way, you can let that information filter your ability to live truthfully and adjust as you need to.

That Wide Unknown

People are never just 'getting work done'. Even if they are performing perfunctory tasks, there is still a need at work. Understanding this need gives you critical insights about the given circumstances that person exists within daily. Smart leadership analysis cannot predict the outcome of the future but can give you enough knowledge of the relevant variables to optimise your chances of success. It is easy to work hard at overanalysing. Harder but of far more value is working smart at analysing the relevant variables. This gives you just enough information to springboard your abilities to live truthfully under the specific given set of circumstances you are entering into. The deeper value ends up being the same as preparation: what happens once you are through the door is up to the moment, but now you have done enough research, having a strong technical facility for handling what the moment throws at you. In other words, you can observe with clarity a set of given circumstances and know how to live truthfully under them. That skill will be more valuable to your leadership than all the gesture-planning, breathing, mirroring, and improv exercises you can ever hope to do.

Summary

The ability to analyse a situation and the relevant variables within it are essential to the continued success of any technique that claims to train and develop leadership skills. This is not an easy challenge to surmount. The more organic and authentic the leadership is and the higher the content of spontaneity, the greater the challenge becomes to analyse the relevant variables within a situation and find a way to import the values of authentic leadership. The challenge is to filter the variables through a lens of analysis and have what comes out on the other end still be just as authentic. Given the value the Meisner Technique places on the interpersonal, starting with the human connection and letting authenticity flow from that as a primary source, the situation analysis that is most relevant focuses largely on world view. By developing an understanding of a person's world view in a situation, from the rudimentary available knowledge all the way to their primal needs, you will have a way of allowing your interactions to be filtered by that information.

First you do the analysis with scenes from plays, living inside of your analysis of a scripted person and developing a grasp of the visceral experience of testing a need. The next step is to make an actual person the target of your analysis and to let your interpretation of their need be the testing material for your interactions with them. In both cases, the given circumstances organically filter and support your ability to live truthfully, rather than taking away from it. An analysis built on understanding and testing, rather than predicting and insisting, will always give you the balance between knowledge and adaptability, keeping you flexible, keen, and able to work with anything thrown at you.

Tips for You and Your Coach

When people hear the word 'analysis' they generally think of a more cerebral process and that the end result of analysis is a fixed understanding. While this is true in most cases, for our purposes analysis must lead to a visceral experience, to a type of open-ended understanding that comes from entering another's point of view. The validity of the analysis is not confirmed by intellectualising but rather experiencing: if a participant's experience within the work confirms the need of a character, then they are on the right track. What is important in the scene-work is that they know this is not about performing—you are not suddenly asking them to 'deliver' the need but rather to stay with the experiential nature of the training and see if they can discover the need of the character from the inside.

Generally this type of exploration is powerful. One successful testing of a need is normally enough to solidify what it means to be in contact with the primal needs of another person. If you see your clients trying to perform or act, remind them that, even though they are testing a need, their behaviours in the scene-work are still largely determined by the other person. They are seeking the experience of living truthfully under a given set of circumstances, not performing believably under a given set of circumstances. You'll find it won't matter if they are actors or not: some clients cannot shake the habit to be performative. In this case it can be helpful to ask them to go back to a breaking-the-back style read, where they will impose a flatter tone on the lines. The needs don't come across clearly in this sort of situation, but they will still reveal enough of themselves to give them something to work with. What is important here is not to restrict both students unless needed: one can still observe and respond while letting their voice take on the qualities of the moment while the other keeps a flatter tone. This will still bring out the needs for both more clearly than if each student focuses on keeping the tone flat. Your discretion will be vital in helping navigate the waters between staying true to each other in a read and testing the needs within the situation.

Needs are often best worded as metaphors, but not always. What is important is that the client understands the difference between a need and an objective or goal. Sometimes it can be helpful to start with the objective and then ask what is fuelling that. If, for example, in a scene we say that the character's objective is to close a deal, the need can be what closing that deal means to them, for example, 'being the big dog on the block,' or something along those lines. As long as the client connects with the qualitative difference between a need and an objective it matters less how the need is worded.

The final note here is on the last portion of analysis, of applying it to another person. What is critical to understand here is that when your clients test for the needs of others, they are not working to make them happen or assuming they are true. This is a process of inquisition and testing using the ability to live truthfully with heightened intuitions. In training, I don't use any demonstrated exercises for this part since the whole point is on developing the ability to apply it in one's own personal context. This is best taught over more than one session, where a client has the opportunity to explore testing another person's need in reality and checking in with the coach on how it worked or did not. Since a large degree of success in leadership is dependent on the inter-personal dimension, using analysis of others in a meaningful way that parallels with the values of this training is critical. Analysis is not designed to predict the future but rather give clients more relevant information about the circumstances they are entering. This is information that is not fixed but can be tested and refined.

The temptation is to use any of this work as a means to solve the future before it arrives, rather than seeing it as a level of trained flexibility and adaptability to unknowns. Always encourage your clients to stay open.

Chapter 14

New Ground: Additional Exercises for Living Truthfully within a Given Set of Circumstances

Fine-Tuning

While the formal training has concluded, there is an array of exercises and principles based on the training that can target more specific application needs. This brings up something valuable about the Meisner Technique: while it is rigid in its adherence to the concepts that underpin it, within the concepts there is a degree of flexibility. Exercises can be used in a variety of ways and variations on those exercises can address certain needs. This chapter focuses on several ways that further exercises and tools in the technique can be used to target specific leadership challenges and situations. We will go back and forth between specific exercises and recommendations for application to certain types of situations, as well as some concepts that can support you further.

Completing the Hierarchy

Ever since Chapter 5, we have been working with the idea of a hierarchy of observations. The hierarchy is a way to prioritise the relevant points of observation when it comes to leadership and interpersonal interactions. They allow you to get a sense of how to break up reality meaningfully and to categorise it in a relevant way. Certain elements of the hierarchy, such as essential behaviours, are superb, since they are frequently on offer. Other observations, such as metaphors, are exceedingly rare, and so for their rarity and specificity to the moment earn a higher rank in the hierarchy. All observations within the hierarchy, however, are examples of good technique. The ranking relates more to stronger or weaker tools than a 'good' or 'bad' observation; all is based on the needs of the moment.

Towards the end of our examination of the hierarchy, I implied there was an additional observation even more powerful than metaphor. The reason it is not introduced early on is that this is a tool that solves problems not for a weak technique but rather a strong one. To put it bluntly: this is an observation for when you need to call your own bullshit.

As you gain proficiency in this work, having done multiple rounds of repetition and especially independent activities, a curious phenomenon emerges. In the beginning, it is quite obvious to the coach and observers when you sit on a truthful impulse, either to observe or respond. There is a notable moment of processing that diverts you towards another option. It interrupts the flow and, though subtle, can easily be felt by the audience. As you get better in this work, you learn that there's no value in inhibiting any observation or most responses. As your technique grows, eventually a reversal begins to happen: you sense when an impulse arises that is border territory but you've also learned that other impulses may be on offer. Safer ones. In effect you choose to act on the impulse you are more comfortable with, knowing that neither coach nor audience will be able to pick it up anymore. Your truthfulness becomes the best camouflage for impulses not acted on.

This happens entirely within your conscious experience in the exercises, and unfortunately all the way from novice to master Meisner teachers won't be able to reliably spot this at this stage. This isn't manipulation but a desire to seek safety in the impulses you have experiences with. The problem for you? Continue to do this and you'll feel a growing disconnect between yourself and the technique. You'll know that there are impulses you're not acting on but because no one can call them any more you'll start to rationalise it. Maybe it's not as big a deal. Maybe it's okay to hide from that one impulse, especially if the rest of the time you're being truthful. Whatever your reason this isn't consequence free: eventually the cognitive dissonance will start to make itself known and you'll begin to convince yourself something in general must be wrong. Either you've stopped growing in the technique, it's no longer for you, or it once worked but it doesn't really anymore.

In all of these reasons there is an element of truth. You have stopped growing in the technique, and it doesn't work anymore. Unfortunately this is because at the higher level you now work you've pushed the perceptual abilities of the coach and audience to their limit. It doesn't mean they'll never spot an impulse you didn't act on, but you'll secretly know more often than not the one you're receiving feedback on isn't 'the right one', the big fish you keep hiding from. You'll notice I'm not describing what this impulse looks like because it is highly personal. For someone it might be hugging in the moment. That seems fairly benign to those of us who have no problem with it, but that's the point. Each one of us will find in practice there is individual border territory we don't allow ourselves to go towards. If you're just impulsive enough, you discover, you can still train the values the majority of the time even if you are not true to yourself, as well as the needs of the moment, a few of those times.

We need a solution that enables you to reclaim your technique when you are working at a stronger level, and a solution that doesn't involve judgement. Some days you won't sit on impulses. Other days you will. Sometimes there will be patterns – the impulse to kiss, for example, or to express rage, might be the one you constantly pivot from. Whatever the impulse is, berating yourself won't help. Your inner critic will be screaming at what you 'should have' done. Should have is in the past, however, and we cannot correct past moments according to the standards of the present. Sitting on an impulse is sometimes inevitable. The evidence? Because it happens. That doesn't mean there can't be a technical middle-ground to help you in these situations.

This call comes from my work with Larry Silverberg, and to me it is the most powerful call in the hierarchy. This is because it helps maintain strong technique even on days when you might be tempted to not fully give yourself over to the experience, a temptation which deprives you of the growth and learning that makes you hungry for this work in the first place. It is called the *missed moment call*.

The missed moment call is not technically perfect; in fact, by some standards, it is downright sloppy. You might recall an earlier discussion about the balance between pristine technique and denying the chaos of the moment with too much emphasis on technique. We want to keep that line honored and though it may seem paradoxical, few things do it better at the highest level than this rare call.

Let's say you and your partner are doing a repetition exercise, either by itself, a knock at the door, or an independent activity. The key common denominator is the full technique of repetition. A series of moments arrive where you and your partner have been involved in a tender, gentle exchange. On impulse your partner gets up and moves away from you. This hurts. At the same time you, for whatever reason, feel guilty about expressing hurt. An impulse arises and you deny it. Let's track that series of moments with some calls here:

You: You're looking at me.
Partner: I'm looking at you.
You: You're- (partner gets up and moves away) You got up.
Partner: I got up.
(Here you have an impulse to express your hurt but deny it, instead going with the previous call)
You: You got up.
Partner: I got up.
Etc.

You can probably see why, in real time, there is a very low probability that moment will be caught by the coach. You two are working at a high level and likely in the next moment or two an impulse will arise that you express truthfully. That moment you inhibit, however, won't just go away. You'll feel it throughout the exercise. In feedback, since no one is talking about it, it becomes bigger and more problematic than it needs to be. That's the reality we're working with, so in the event you didn't express the impulse, what if you name the thing you sat on? Let's see what happens if you employ a missed moment call to come to your aid:

You: You're looking at me.
Partner: I'm looking at you.
You: You're- (partner gets up and moves away) You got up.
Partner: I got up.
(Here you have an impulse to express your hurt but deny it, instead going with the previous call)
You: You got up.
Partner: I got up.
You: I wanted to scream at you.
Partner: You wanted to scream at me.
You: I wanted to scream at you.
Partner: Your face is red.

Notice here one key thing before we address the elephant in the room: a missed moment call does not derail the entire exercise. True, it changes the entire dynamic, but that would happen regardless of the observation if it was true to the observation. What it doesn't do is dismantle the whole exercise. Nor is the person articulating their missed moment now compelled to act it out, in this example to scream at their partner. They are just voicing what didn't happen in the moment. Your partner repeats and you both go on until a new observation demands to be called. In this case the essential behaviour of redness in the face. The exercise goes on unhindered.

Now, let's talk about the elephant in the room: by our standards we've set, this is a very, very weak observation. Not only are you denying the other person but the attention is coming back onto yourself fully and your observation reflects that. I agree, it is not technically ideal. In an ideal world you would never sit on your impulses and always have perfect technique. Or if you did sit on them, they wouldn't continue to harangue you long after the moment had passed. Such a world, and the technique within it, would both be pristine. But this is not the reality you have to work with; we have to honour and work for excellent technique but in turn not only allow but invite the messiness of moments to come up at times. When these moments arise they break the rules of technique, including calls that may not seem technically strong by one metric but are superior because they encapsulate the truth of the moment between you both.

Sitting on an impulse does not feel good. That is true on day one or day one million, it never feels better to deny a truthful observation or response. It feels so unpleasant, in fact, that the missed impulse often rattles around in your conscious experience, calling volumes of attention to what you didn't do and removing your attention by increasing degrees from your partner. Those are moments lost. You'll lose many more moments dealing with an impulse bothering you than just naming it and getting on with the exercise. It is a practical tool that solves a very real practical problem that arises after doing this work for a while. It also begins to close the gap that you'll keep creating between your authentic experiences and your work in this technique. It's not clean but it's practical: if you sit on an impulse, with it distracting you for not having acted on it, just name it. It may also give you some good mileage towards finally expressing it when it does arrive in the moment the next time.

The one primary concern people sometimes have with the missed moment call is that it may give people permission to sit on impulses rather than act on them. Why express the big thing when you could just name it and that's just as good? The simple answer is that's not really how this process works. Strong technique means you are used to expressing your authentic observations and responses. This is a tool for an impulse that arises after you've acquired that technical strength and for a multitude of reasons you are still not acting on it. The visceral experience of using it won't feel like taking an escape route so much as relief. It's out, it no longer torments you. This is why this call is not used early in the training as you are still learning the difference between an impulse that comes from you versus another person, as well as what it feels like to deny a truthful impulse. Missed moment calls are for when the coach cannot spot the impulse you aren't acting on any longer but you still know it is there. If you tried to introduce it early you would find a level of redundancy introduced: you would be articulating the impulse we all know you sat on. Better to save this for higher level work where it will shine.

So, the next time you are doing an exercise and sit on an impulse, go ahead and name it. You'll be helping everyone but most importantly you'll be keeping ownership over your technique. That completes your hierarchy of observations which now takes the form shown in Figure 14.1.

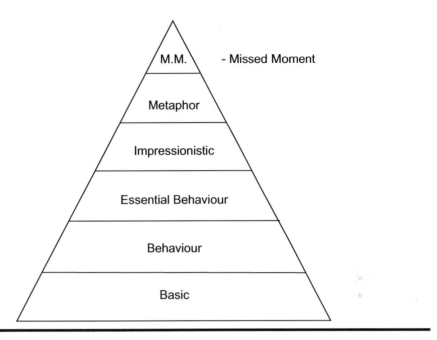

Figure 14.1   Hierarchy of Observations.

Speeches and Presentations

On the surface, speeches and presentations, particularly those done by oneself and not as part of a group, seem to present a unique challenge for the Meisner Technique. After all, it is just you and nobody else up there, so how can you observe and respond? For those seeking complex answers, you might be disappointed, as it is quite simple: if you have an audience, you are not alone. Large bodies of people who come together still put off a collective energy that can be felt. This is what you have to observe and respond authentically to. In your presentation you can still feed off of this energy and work with it while delivering your material, especially if you are able to make eye contact with your audience. Remember, whether it is the general group, or certain individuals within it, your attention can still only be directed to one single point at a time. Whatever that point is can be observed and since observations brings up something in the same token it can be responded to. As far as your technique goes there is no difference between a speech delivered to hundreds or a conversation between two people. The values are entirely portable.

For any of these following exercises I recommend always doing them with someone else in the room. Let them be witnessed if you can. Also, if you are working with pre-scripted material, it is good to have someone on script for you if you are not sure about the words yet. You'll find these exercises are best done with the words solidly ingrained, but everyone drops a line here or there. Having someone on script that you can simply call out 'line' to saves you the trouble of losing the truthfulness in what you are doing by exiting the exercise, getting the words, and then going back into it. It is far more efficient and effective with all of these exercises to have them be witnessed.

The Activity

I have advised against the self-monitoring approach to speeches that constantly asks questions such as:

'How is my breathing?'
'How are my hands?'
'Am I making too many gestures, am I not making enough?'
'How's my delivery?'

and so on. Since I keep picking on gestures, I have to clarify that training in this technique certainly does not mean you cannot build gestures and actions into your routine. You can wear a director's hat, decide on what to do where, and then put on your living truthfully cap and just make those directions a part of your given circumstances. The given circumstances are not confined to those of a situation but to your personal circumstances. They are far more pliable and flexible than just being bound to a script or a scenario. Physical actions then can easily become a part of your given circumstances.

Before gestures are chosen and actions determined, it can be helpful to connect your words to something physically engaging. This is not done to create a scene but rather to connect the experience of speaking a scripted set of words with tactile sensations. This will begin to give you permission to be physically engaged and, as we know from the independent activity, it is entirely possible to be physically engaged in something and living truthfully. If you go all the way back to the first session, we were on to it even then with a phrase called 'investing in the reality of doing.'

Since investing in the reality of doing is the foundation on which this work is built, and since activities have been so helpful in the past, then let's incorporate an activity. The setup is this: in the same way you chose an entirely real activity for the independent activity, you will do the same here, a simple, solo activity. Only this time there won't be a time limit, a consequence, and so on. This is your opportunity to fully invest in the reality of doing without filtering the experience through an extremely meaningful given set of circumstances. The activity does not necessarily need to be fiddly but it has to be physically engaging. An example might be that while before peeling an apple would have not been a good choice for an activity, primarily for its lack of intricacy, it becomes a strong choice here. The same with doing your nails, or some make-up.

Begin your activity. After about 30 seconds, once you are into it, start speaking your scripted words. The important thing here is to let the activity determine how the words come out. Don't use any pre-planned gestures or vocal intonations. Simply do your activity and let the words be a part of that experience. You might find surprising things come up for you, such as laughter, or if you hit a frustrating part in the activity, frustration becomes a part of the words. Whatever happens is good. The important thing is you are not colouring the words or imposing anything untruthful onto them that comes from your intentions to 'do something' with them.

The experience is quite similar to repetition: here your words are like the canoe and the activity is the current on which they float. This is an excellent base to begin your work from as at the end you will have had the experience of the words taking on the quality of the moments in the activity.

Ingraining into your speech this level of openness creates a wonderfully organic place to present or speak from. It doesn't tell you how the speech will sound in the future, but it does tune your ear to if the words are sounding truthful or not. It also lays the groundwork for your discovering in an organic way the best places to plan any gestures or actions, or if you decide to leave it up to the moment. In either case, this tactile sensitivity is a powerful asset to weave throughout the words.

Partner Activity

Using the same guidelines from the previous exercise, you will be using an activity here, only this time it will be an activity that you do on your partner, meaning it involves direct physical contact. Adding a component of human collaboration into the mix heightens the tactile awareness and engagement even more. Examples of the partner activity includes face painting, doing make-up or nails, a henna design, etc. In all of these cases notice that there is a specific finish to the activity.

Activities such as throwing a ball back and forth might be engaging and connected, but the ending is not as clear, and so the pathways to get to the destination and develop tactile awareness are unclear as well. That said, sometimes you won't know if any activity is a good choice or not until you try it, and this is part of the learning process. What is important is to let the words be a part of the activity, not the other way around. Wait until you are about 30 seconds into the activity before beginning to speak. Don't let your desire to inflect or intonate interrupt the natural rhythm between you and your partner. The words are just a part of this experience. The experience drives them, not the other way around.

Partner activities are excellent in that you get the benefits of the solo activity with an extra added layer of human contact. Even though there is value in this I personally don't recommend doing activities together that involve verbal communication. Things like puzzles, or games, might be physically engaging, but the need at times for communication within the activity might take you away from the function of the exercise. With rare exception, the activity is top-down, meaning your partner receives the activity but is not an active communicator in the process. In my experience this helps keep the waters clearer. That said, experiment, discover for yourself what works in practice.

Partner activities carry high rewards. The only potential downside, aside from some messy nails or a bad make-up job, is that the coach cannot be the partner, so a third person is needed. Given that by now you will be used to working with at least one other person than the coach, this should not be a problem, but it is one more logistical thing to consider, whereas the solo activity can be done even without anyone else present.

Recorded Speeches

Whether it is scripted or impromptu, speeches that are recorded for media seem to pose another challenge for the Meisner Technique. While you may have an audience you can directly observe and respond to in a live speech or presentation, when it comes to recording you might only have a mark on the wall or cue cards to look at. There are two components to this that the Meisner Technique can address, with some basic prescriptive concepts to help you along.

First, it is important to remember that if there is a crew filming, you are still not alone. While crew members are focused on elements of you, such as lighting, make-up, etc, there is still an audience present giving you attention. In this case, the same principles as a speech apply: even if you cannot look at the people in the room, you can feel them. Second, if you are alone and recording by yourself, then the mark on the wall becomes your point of focus. The answer here is more philosophical than anything else, but it still applies: just because the mark on the wall you are looking at is currently a mark on the wall does not mean it will always be there. This still gives you the mindset of staying with your mark moment by moment. It won't be as visceral as working off another person, but it still gives you something transitory to plug into.

Tactile Aids

Solo activities are a great way to prepare for the type of situation described above. Instead of looking at another person, you can do activities by yourself and make a point on the wall the object of your attention. Depending on the angle of the camera, as well, there is a tool that some professional film actors will use if the shot is above the shoulders. The tool sounds simplistic but is often very powerful for engaging you physically in the moment. Bring in something small that you can have in your hands, such as a coffee mug, bracelet (beads work well), an orange, something with a unique physical texture. As you speak to the camera explore the texture with your hands. This keeps you physically present and engaged in the moment. The camera won't pick up on what your hands are doing since it is a close-up shot, but the nuances in texture it creates comes across beautifully.

If the shot is wider, you can apply the same principle without something in your hands, keeping rooted within the tactile sensations of the moment while you speak. Feelings of cold, pressure, or other conscious sensations all become points you can direct your attention to. I recommend this last step only for when you are completely alone, since the attention is technically on you and this is less compatible with our training values. If there are other people in the room, or something in your hands, then you have something more compelling to root you in the moment. This is, however, a practical tool for a very specific situation where you find yourself unable to look at anyone, feel anyone's presence, engage with something tactile, and are finding your conscious awareness is becoming generally dispersed rather than honed and specific. There are many different things that can be done to engage you sensorily while on camera, but these are good starting points.

Structured Improvised Scenarios

Structured scenarios are different than independent activities. In the structured scenario, either you or the coach choose a lifelike scenario, and you improvise within it. While I am not a fan of working with structured scenarios, since they are a model of improvisation, many people in the business world feel they are helpful. There is a difference between analysis of a situation, which we covered in the previous chapter, and attempting to pre-plan the future. Improvisation, with its murky lack of clarity amongst results and variables, easily falls into the latter category. Still, if you would like to use structured scenarios, such as mock interviews, negotiations, and so on, there are some ways you can incorporate Meisner exercises to help aid in your work. I would like to point out for clarity that the aid in my experience has always been one-directional: repetition continually makes people better at improvising. I have never once worked with an improviser, either professionally or trained for years, who was better at living truthfully than any other student when they began. Repetition will make you better at improvisation, but improvisation will not make you better at repetition. For those who wish to use improvisational models, however, repetition will enhance the quality of your work in the improvisation.

Improv + Repetition

The repetition can be done either seated or standing, and both have their own benefits. Seated repetition allows you to focus entirely on the variables of your partner. Beginning a repetition standing, however, allows you to deal with your partner and other variables within the environment, such as space and movement. Both come with unique advantages, and so I recommend doing both in improvisations. Repetition in this way is entirely flexible. You can start seated with the understanding that you and your partner stay seated the entire time. You can begin seated, and if the impulse arises, get up and move. Likewise, you can start standing and remain that way, or you can at times sit if the impulse is there. It is entirely flexible and can be modified in this way as you or the coach see fit.

The basic structure I recommend is to begin first with repetition and then at a certain point go into the improvisation. This can be determined by setting a timer, going with the moment's demand for a change in the text, or most easily by your coach saying a quick word like 'Go' or 'Begin' after a period of time. In my view, any of the three is just as good, so personally I recommend having someone to prompt you, as it minimizes the risk of the attention getting stuck on you with thinking, 'When are we going to go? Is it time yet, is it?'

From there, some options present themselves. You can go from repetition into the improvisation and let the improvisation run its course, checking in at the end about how it might have helped or did not help. Alternately, at times your coach can direct you from the improvisation back into repetition and back into the improvisation. Structurally, that might look like beginning with repetition, going into the improvisation when your coach calls 'go', carrying on for a bit with the scenario, and then when you hear 'go' again, going back into the repetition to sharpen up your observations and responses, and so on. This is similar to the switch exercise, but instead of between the three moment exercise and repetition, it is between the improvisation and repetition. This allows for a continuous top-up of living truthfully throughout your improvisation.

Does this help you? I've been candid about my view that improvisation is a weaker model for training leadership skills, even though it certainly has its strengths in other areas. I don't know why you would spend time trying to use repetition to elevate a tool that is suboptimal. I would rather we find scripted scenes and work from there, since it removes the creative writing element and allows you to focus on living truthfully. I am aware that there is an argument that since life is somewhat improvisatory, then improvisation is good training, but to me this argument is self-cancelling. The spontaneous nature of reality inside of an improvisation class hardly mirrors the thousands of variables you encounter outside of the class. The artificial constructs of improvisation detach its values from being portable into other situations. In attempting to mimic life, it ends up having to narrow it using structure.

This is why I continually emphasise the bare minimum of structure. There is nothing in life like repetition, but its abstract nature makes it more portable in my view, not less. Scenario training is like working with a warped and mangled view of the real thing. Because we are not training for scenarios but rather individual skills, repetition makes you more adaptable, not less. Still, it is not my experience, it is yours. If you believe that improvisation has helped you and is valuable, repetition can aid in making your improvisations sharper and more truthful.

Preparation and Activities

Additional incorporations of preparations and activities can be utilised. Remember that preparations are not target-specific, meaning it is not as helpful to try to do a preparation that is ideally suited for a situation because you don't know what kind of a situation you are walking into. If just before a meeting you do a preparation that leaves you buoyant and energetic, and the person you are negotiating with has had a wretched day, your happiness might piss them off further. This can happen, of course, with any kind of a preparation, but that further illustrates the concept: as a leader, you are not walking into a scripted scene like an actor would. Many approaches to leadership, however, treat you that way. 'Psyche yourself up' or 'go in at your best'. Remember that your actions don't exist in a void, and even what seems like benign preparation advice can work against you, especially if you find yourself trying to keep 'making it happen' in the situation as it goes further south.

For clarity, there are ways to do targeted preparations in the Meisner Technique, and for actors, few people have a more masterful approach to this than my teacher Larry Silverberg. You would not believe the magic he gets out of people in scene work. It is for that reason that I have intentionally left that approach out of this work. Actors may not know what happens next, but so much is predetermined in their line of work that the level of uncertainty for them is on a different scale than it is for you. They've got a script, you don't.

Great acting is often judged in the subtle, humanistic, nuanced responses to the moment. This the scale that actors are working with. It would be a foolish move to conflate the preparation needed for scene and text work with the kinds needed for entering real-world scenarios with largely unknown variables. We use scene and text work as a bridge in this technique, but it is not the end point. If you are playing with improvised scenarios or speech rehearsal and want to use a preparation, go for it, but I caution strongly against trying to use it for a targeted outcome. This might work in your training but has a high chance of biting you hard if you take that value into other situations. In general, however, whether it is a negotiation, interview, or presentation, the energy and dynamics of the situation itself are enough to get you charged up. Preparation is not a cure for the anxieties of presentation. That nervous energy you feel is your preparation. Rather than going away from it, which will only increase it, or trying to reduce it (thereby reinforcing to your body that there is a threat that must be avoided), embrace it and utilise it. Your given circumstances will give you a preparation. Rather than judging it, go with it and use it to live truthfully.

All that having been said, preparations can be done before going into a situation. During structured scenario training, you can go out of the room to do them or try them inside. It is a flexible tool in that sense. Activities as well can be incorporated, with one partner in the improvisation doing an activity while the other does a preparation, thereby orienting the scenario around the structure of an independent activity. Don't be surprised, however, if you find the improvisation lacks much of the urgency or life the independent activity contains, so instead of trying to recreate that intensity, focus on what you partner is doing in that moment and let the nuances of their behaviour and the moment still bring out the authentic responses in you.

To me this is more bells and whistles than relevant training, but different people succeed with different processes, so my advice is when using activities and preparations in your structured improvisations, remember that the inherent value is still the same: what happens to you does not depend on you, or on any intention you bring into the improvisation with you. It all depends entirely on what the other person is doing to you and, by proxy, what they are going to make you do. The moment and the other human being in the room determine your response, not the agenda you think you are bringing in. As we have said before, the given circumstances filter your responses; within those givens are the importance of your goals and needs being met. But never let your needs or goals distract you from the clarity you get when you put your attention on the other person, or people, and go with them moment by moment through the process. That is much more likely to get you what you want. Whether your points or arguments are brilliant are secondary to this.

Refining the Given Circumstances

Long-Form Scene Work

In terms of incorporation, this is possibly the one I prefer the most, as I find it utilises in the best way the values of the Meisner Technique as well as specific devices within the exercises to train them. Scene work is as it sounds: incorporating elements of the technique into a scene with the lines memorized. Working with scripts for our purposes is not designed to make you into an actor. Scene work makes you a better leader for the same reason it makes an actor better at their job: it allows you to delve more deeply into the principles the technique trains with actual language and dramatic action, rather than the more abstract qualities found in repetition and activities.

In terms of scene work, the elements I like to use for leadership work are as follows:

- First, I select a scene that involves two characters, both of whom have a rich range of truthful responses available to them. Sometimes these characters are involved in some field related to leadership or business, but to me this is a secondary consideration. What you are utilising to gain an advantage in the field of business or leadership is living truthfully under a given set of circumstances, and so I look for scenes with profound given circumstances that demand an immense range of truthful responses from you. I try to keep with contemporary writers; authors such as Shakespeare, Chekhov, or more abstract ones like Beckett or Ionesco are a golden opportunity for actors to explore their technique. The hurdles of stylized language or vague circumstances, while not impossible, are challenges of less value to non-actors. The small exception to this is in breaking the back of the scene exercises where you discover that even dense language can be heard clearly and the variables of a situation understood without much effort if your values are in the right place.
- Second, I begin with the approach we have covered in the latter part of this book: you and your partner will break the back of the scene.
- Third, you'll do a text analysis which we'll test.
- Fourth, I'll ask you to memorize your lines cold. Don't worry about the punctuation, inflections or sentence structure. Just memorise the words. Once you've done that we can iron out any other inflections with some partner activity work, similar to what was described earlier.
- Fifth, for flexibility, we might do a seated repetition exercise or standing and go straight from it into the scene.
- Sixth, we incorporate an activity for both people in the scene. Depending on what we discover in the analysis, the activity might be something tactile, like making a cup of tea, or it might be interpersonal, such as investing the same level of attention into your partner as you do into your activity. The circumstances will give us the clues we need to come to that conclusion.
- Seventh, for characters who enter, you'll do a preparation.
- Eighth, as you do a more staged version of the scene, as your coach I'll feed into you given circumstances you may not be taking on board fully or might not be aware of. I do this to get you deeper into the point of view of that character, to feel their needs viscerally and to experience the organic balance of the demands of the moment with what your partner is demanding of you. This also helps you develop an eye and ear for relevant circumstances in extremely meaningful situations and learn how to seek them out in your interactions outside of training.

At the end of this process, you may find a few things: you may discover that your ability to analyse a situation you are going into improves, as does your understanding of how to discover the needs of others. You might also find that now a bridge has been created between some of the abstract language constraints of repetition and the real-world dialogue of these scenes. Long-form scene work takes time, and it is not essential, but it is excellent at improving your abilities to live truthfully under a given set of circumstances.

Summary

I've not included a 'Tips for You and Your Coach', as these ideas are intertwined throughout this chapter. What is worth noting for both coaches and participants, however, is that there is both a high and low degree of flexibility within this technique. The high flexibility comes in the pliability of the exercises themselves. Activities, repetitions, and preparations can be utilised in a variety of ways and complemented with other exercises, including improvisation. The priority, however, must never be on the novel ways to change up the exercises for the sake of it. If a session or class gets boring or loses the powerful forward energy characteristic of this technique, then my guess is something in the technique is not being emphasised. The reason for this is simple: there is nothing flashy, complicated, or 'big' about the exercises themselves. They are always simple and abstract in nature. Repetition was never intended to be interesting or exciting in itself. It is a conduit that allows for human interactions of a heightened nature to emerge and that is what is interesting or exciting. After doing and teaching literally thousands of hours of repetition, I can guarantee that the exercises never get more interesting. The interactions within them, however, what arises organically between two people in the moment, has never ceased to amaze, surprise, or intrigue me.

The question is one of values, and this is where there is immensely low flexibility in this work. Think of how much care and attention we have paid this entire journey to ensuring and protecting the concepts in this work and to making sure that the exercises were in line with the deeper values. This is because it is very hard to train relevant authenticity and very easy to screw it up. This is the cautionary note I can give about modifying or changing the exercises. If you wish to do it, then do it so that it further illuminates and deepens the concepts within the technique that support your leadership growth. Be always aware, however, that if those concepts are lost, the exercises might get more interesting or dramatically exciting, but they will lose the values (I am also confident in saying that exercises that have the values of observe and respond alive within them will be anything but uninteresting) that make the work so profound for leadership in the first place.

Meisner is at best about complicated simplicity. There is minimal structure, but it is incredibly thought out and carefully placed. This is to ensure that the complexities in the work don't arise from the exercises or their structure but rather from grappling within the very real and human values that arise within them. That is what makes this technique ideal for leadership: at its core, it is about not getting better at exercises, or fitting into a prescriptive mould, but rather engaging with the essential human experience characteristic to all great leaders across time.

We began this journey with a discussion about Bruce Lee, it is only fitting we end with a phrase my JKD instructor Clive uses that summarises this work perfectly:

'Simple. But not easy.'

Chapter 15

Afterword: The Essential Hunger

My first Meisner class with Scott Williams, in a tiny room in the upstairs second floor of the Actors Centre in London, changed my life. At the time, I was struggling to find my voice on my master's degree and was living in a noisy ten-bedroom hostel as I was desperately searching for a single room (I had been accepted into my program of study about ten days before it was due to start which gave me less than two weeks to upend my life in the States and move across the pond). Between the course load, barely sleeping at night, and feeling in general like a fish out of water, I was a mess. I needed to find some kind of outlet that would give me the training I was needing. Drama school was a different approach than I was used to, and it wasn't cutting it for me.

Having wanted to study Meisner for years, I signed up for a weekends class with Scott Williams, who ran the Impulse Company in London. At the time, I had no idea about the Impulse Company or who Scott was. I just needed a lifeline to ground me, an answer. One class with Scott Williams, I am unashamed to say, changed my life. So much of the weight I was dragging around – the pressures I had put on myself, the worries, the doubts, the fears – vanished and as an actor I felt more free and competent than I ever had. While Scott is an incredible teacher, it was really the work itself that was the answer to a headcase actor like me. My need led me to the right path. At the end of the class, Scott used a phrase that has always stayed with me: stay curious.

From there on I was hooked. I joined the Impulse Company a few months later, attended as many of Scott's classes as I could, some weeks doing as much as over 20 hours of training while also going to school full time. I racked up over a thousand hours of training with Scott, and while I never taught for the Impulse Company, I began to run my own Meisner classes in London. At a certain point, I felt I needed more experience in the classical approach to Meisner, and I went for a summer to study for a another few hundred hours with Larry Silverberg, one of the leading experts on the Meisner Technique, with over a dozen published books. Larry blew my mind open about the technique and its possibilities. I have never seen acting so powerful as in his classes, and the raw joy of being directed by him felt like acting with jet-propelled rockets attached to your feet. Larry is a powerful, ferocious genius, and I was always treated with profound honesty and compassion.

Through working with both Scott and Larry I was able to synthesise my own approach to teaching this work. That is what great masters do for us when we work with them in depth: they give us the materials to make our own path. While illness prevented me from studying with Scott and Larry further, I would love for nothing more than to work with them again one day. There is something so good about returning to the source of your roots. It is like drinking the cleanest water filled with the essence of meaning. I wax poetic, but I stand by it.

The majority of the exercises in this book come from Scott Williams's approach to the Meisner Technique that I learned over the course of my time with him. Scott is a radical in this field, similar to another practitioner and well-known dramatist, David Mamet. Both studied with Meisner and went off and did their own thing with the work, Mamet creating his Practical Aesthetics technique and Scott continuing to call his work the Meisner Technique, albeit with a new makeover and tune-ups. Controversial as he is, in my view what Scott did is the greatest gift one can give of this technique: perhaps without realising it, he changed and modified so much of the work that he broke it open for everyone, making it accessible to be applied to so many fields of inquiry. In his classes I met anthropologists, physicists, web designers, psychologists, the list goes on – all who found crossover value to their own fields. Scott took a profound and classical approach to acting and broadened it to the world's benefit. That is why I think my understanding of Scott's approach to the work, rather than the classical model, is the most applicable to leadership and business training.

In my work with actors, I teach both approaches, Scott's and Larry's. I use Scott's work as the foundation and then build in what I learnt from Larry, ending with his powerhouse work on a technique called personalisation. Through my work with synthesising the wisdom I learned from each into my own approach, a desire began to grow: I wanted to use this technique to give something to other fields and professions outside of acting. I saw the good it was doing for non-actors, and I wanted to write a book that introduced to the conversation of the world the power that the Meisner Technique, be it a classical or radical approach, can offer to improving it. My passion for researching leadership and finding out more about the qualities of great leaders led me to synthesise again. This book is the result of my doing my best to stay curious.

Describing the exercises in this book is not easy. They are living expressions of moments between people, and as soon as you write them down and say, 'There! Do that!' you've placed an unnatural corral on the chaos of the moment. Prescription becomes order, losing the richness of the moment. As I was writing this book, I spoke to a good friend and colleague about this challenge. He asked me if I was going to make a DVD to include in the book of examples of the exercises. That would make incredibly clear and easy to understand what was so hard to write in chapters. I thought it was a perfect way to solve the problems and drove home feeling satisfied. I almost went with it. Almost.

There is a temptation to go and watch videos of these exercises. Don't. You'll only be seeing people living truthfully in the moments between each other. The same couple in a future exercise might look entirely different. Structures vary so much between Meisner teachers that even just looking for the basic structure and calls won't help you much either. Even if you see the structure that I like to teach, how the calls are worded are still entirely subjective to that moment. There might be a basic form, but trying to apply generalisations to specifics will only cloud and weigh down your technique.

The better way to stay curious in this work is to go off of the basic principles in these chapters and make them your goals. Play around with the few training examples and create your own. See intuitively if they fit with what you understand your aims and goals to be alongside the values of this work. Living truthfully might have a technical shell in this work, but at the end of the day it is an intuitive experience. It is your own authenticity, and if repetition or independent activities or text analyses are the conduits that express and widen it, then great, this training has served you. But if you try things in this book and they don't feel intuitively authentic, then also follow your intuitions and seek answers elsewhere. As Bruce Lee wisely wrote, 'Research your own experience; absorb what is useful, reject what is useless and add what is essentially your own.'

In writing this book, my first proper one, I have several hopes. I hope I have honoured the values of this work, even though I have at times strayed from the traditions of how it is done. I hope I have honoured the two masters I learned so much from, even if at times I went in a different direction.

Most of all, however, I hope that I have inspired in you, a leader with a vision, the hunger to stay curious.

Index

Note: Page numbers in *italic* indicate a figure on the corresponding page.